Y0-DVY-019

REVIEW 11

REVIEW

Volume 11   1989

Edited by

James O. Hoge
*Virginia Polytechnic Institute
and State University*

James L. W. West III
The Pennsylvania State University

University Press of Virginia

Charlottesville

THE UNIVERSITY PRESS OF VIRGINIA
Copyright © 1989 by the Rector and Visitors
of the University of Virginia

This journal is a member of (CELJ) the Conference of Editors of Learned Journals

First published 1989

ISSN 1090-3233
ISBN 0-8139-1252-0

Printed in the United States of America

The editorial assistants for volume 11 of REVIEW are LaVerne Maginnis and Robert M. Myers, both of The Pennsylvania State University, and Katherine Graham of Virginia Polytechnic Institute and State University.

Funding for *Review* is provided by the generous gifts of Mr. and Mrs. Henry J. Dekker and Mr. and Mrs. Adger S. Johnson to the Virginia Tech Foundation, and by a grant from the College of the Liberal Arts, The Pennsylvania State University.

Contents

Black Figures, Signs, Voices 1
  by David Lionel Smith
    Review of Henry Louis Gates, Jr., *Figures in Black: Words, Signs, and the "Racial" Self;* Houston A. Baker, Jr., *Modernism and the Harlem Renaissance;* John F. Callahan, *In the African-American Grain: The Pursuit of Voice in Twentieth-Century Black Fiction;* Hazel V. Carby, *Reconstructing Womanhood: The Emergence of the Afro-American Woman Novelist*

The *Canterbury Tales* for a New Age 37
  by Martin Stevens
    Review of Lee Patterson, *Negotiating the Past: The Historical Understanding of Medieval Literature;* Beverly Boyd, ed., *The Prioress's Tale;* Robert M. Jordan, *Chaucer's Poetics and the Modern Reader;* Carl Lindahl, *Earnest Games: Folkloric Patterns in the* Canterbury Tales; Leonard Michael Koff, *Chaucer and the Art of Storytelling;* Laura Kendrick, *Chaucerian Play: Comedy and Control in the* Canterbury Tales

Houses and Their Heads 71
  by John Sutherland
    Review of Ruth Dudley Edwards, *Victor Gollancz, A Biography;* J. W. Lambert and Michael Ratcliffe, *The Bodley Head, 1887–1987*

The Vanishing Lives and Language of Victorian Poets   81
  by John Stasny
    Review of James Richardson, *Vanishing Lives: Style and Self in Tennyson, D. G. Rossetti, Swinburne, and Yeats;* David G. Riede, *Matthew Arnold and the Betrayal of Language*

Conrad as Nihilistic Conservative   93
  by Elizabeth B. Tenenbaum
    Review of Anthony Winner, *Culture and Irony: Studies in Joseph Conrad's Major Novels*

Taking Comedy Seriously   103
  by Thomas M. Leitch
    Review of James Harvey, *Romantic Comedy in Hollywood from Lubitsch to Sturges;* Harry Levin, *Playboys and Killjoys: An Essay on the Theory and Practice of Comedy;* Nancy Pogel, *Woody Allen;* Scott Cutler Shershow, *Laughing Matters: The Paradox of Comedy;* Richard Keller Simon, *The Labyrinth of the Comic: Theory and Practice from Fielding to Freud;* Gerald Weales, *Canned Goods as Caviar: American Film Comedies of the 1930s*

Sex and Consequence   133
  by James Grantham Turner
    Review of Alice Browne, *The Eighteenth Century Feminist Mind;* G. S. Rousseau and Roy Porter, eds., *Sexual Underworlds of the Enlightenment;* Peter Wagner, *Eros Revived: Erotica of the Enlightenment in England and America*

Clarity and Opacity in Elizabeth Bishop   179
  by Thomas Gardner
    Review of Robert Dale Parker, *The Unbeliever: The Poetry of Elizabeth Bishop;* Thomas J. Travisano, *Elizabeth Bishop: Her Artistic Development*

Contents ix

When England Became Victorian 189
  by Stanley Weintraub
    Review of Richard L. Stein, *Victoria's Year: English Literature and Culture, 1837–1838;* Marlene A. Eilers, *Queen Victoria's Descendants*

How (and how not) to Explore the Burneys: 197
Questions of Decorum
  by Betty Rizzo
    Review of D. D. Devlin, *The Novels and Journals of Fanny Burney;* Slava Klima, Garry Bowers, and Kerry S. Grant, eds., *Memoirs of Dr. Charles Burney, 1726–1769, Edited from Autograph Fragments*

Redefining Norris and Recovering the Primary Story 219
  by Joseph R. McElrath, Jr.
    Review of Barbara Hochman, *The Art of Frank Norris, Storyteller*

Worry, Wogs, and War 233
  by Kinley E. Roby
    Review of Cecil D. Eby, *The Road to Armageddon: The Martial Spirit in English Popular Literature, 1870–1914;* D. C. R. A. Goonetilleke, *Images of the Raj: Southeast Asia in the Literature of Empire;* Wendy R. Katz, *Rider Haggard and the Fiction of Empire: A Critical Study of British Imperial Fiction*

Plantagenet England on Display 247
  by Jean F. Preston
    Review of Jonathan and Paul Binski, eds., *Age of Chivalry: Art in Plantagenet England, 1200–1400*

Author, Intention, Text   255
  by Guy Cardwell
    Review of *Union Catalog of Clemens Letters*, ed. Paul
    Machlis; Mark Twain, *Early Tales and Sketches, Vol. 1,
    1851–1864*, eds. Edgar Marquess Branch and Robert
    H. Hirst, with the assistance of Harriet Elinor Smith;
    Mark Twain, *Early Tales and Sketches, Vol. 2, 1864–1865*,
    eds. Edgar Marquess Branch and Robert H. Hirst, with
    the assistance of Harriet Elinor Smith; Mark Twain,
    Adventures of Huckleberry Finn: Tom Sawyer's Comrade,
    eds. Walter Blair and Victor Fischer; *Mark Twain's Letters, Vol. 1: 1853–1866*, eds. Edgar Marquess Branch,
    Michael B. Frank, and Kenneth M. Sanderson; associate eds. Harriet Elinor Smith, Lin Salamo, and Richard
    Bucci

Milton's Gaze   289
  by Mary Thomas Crane
    Review of Joseph Wittreich, *Feminist Milton*

Revising Anglo-American Feminism   301
  by Linda M. Shires
    Review of Toril Moi, *Sexual/Textual Politics;* Deirdre
    David, *Intellectual Women and Victorian Patriarchy: Harriet Martineau, Elizabeth Barrett Browning, George Eliot;*
    Patricia Yaeger, *Honey-Mad Women: Emancipatory Strategies in Women's Writing;* Leonore Davidoff and
    Catherine Hall, *Family Fortunes: Men and Women of the
    English Middle Class, 1780–1850*

What Do We Do with F. O. Matthiessen?   319
  by David S. Reynolds
    Review of William E. Cain, *F. O. Matthiessen and the
    Politics of Criticism*

Contributors   325

Editorial Board

Felicia Bonaparte
City College, CUNY

Anthony J. Colaianne
*Virginia Polytechnic
Institute and State University*

Paul Connolly
Yeshiva University

A. S. G. Edwards
University of Victoria

Ian Jack
Cambridge University

James R. Kincaid
*University of Southern
California*

Cecil Y. Lang
University of Virginia

James B. Meriwether
*University of South
Carolina*

Hershel Parker
University of Delaware

George Stade
Columbia University

Peter L. Shillingsburg
*Mississippi State
University*

G. Thomas Tanselle
*John Simon Guggenheim
Memorial Foundation*

Stanley Weintraub
*The Pennsylvania State
University*

Black Figures, Signs, Voices

David Lionel Smith

    Henry Louis Gates, Jr. *Figures in Black: Words, Signs, and the "Racial" Self.* New York: Oxford University Press, 1987. xxxii, 312 pp.

    Houston A. Baker, Jr. *Modernism and the Harlem Renaissance.* Chicago: University of Chicago Press, 1987. xviii, 122 pp.

    John F. Callahan. *In the African-American Grain: The Pursuit of Voice in Twentieth-Century Black Fiction.* Urbana: University of Illinois Press, 1988. 280 pp.

    Hazel V. Carby. *Reconstructing Womanhood: The Emergence of the Afro-American Woman Novelist.* New York: Oxford University Press, 1987. 224 pp.

In recent years Afro-American literature has gained increasing respectability as an area for serious scholarly study, and even as Afro-Americanists have made strong claims for their field as a distinctive area of inquiry, the scholarship in Afro-American literary studies has become increasingly dependent upon recent developments in Euro-American critical theory. At the same time, Afro-Americanist scholarship has come to share the prevalent quirks of contemporary criticism: in particular, a preoccupation with synecdoches as "master tropes" of critical discourse; an impulse to graft personalizing or autobiographical gestures into the critical text; and an obsession with positing revisionist accounts of literary history. This essay will examine in detail four important recent books on Afro-American literature. These books reflect some of the tendencies I have noted, and they provide a fair sample of the range of work presently being published in the field.

In the 1980s Henry Louis Gates, Jr., a self-consciously paradoxical figure, has been the most celebrated and most reviled, the most influential and the most controversial critic of Afro-American writing. The reasons for his paradoxical status derive both from his work and from the circumstances of his extraordinary celebrity. Indeed, Professor Gates is so closely associated with the apparent boom in black literary studies that it is difficult to say whether the boom made him or he made the boom. Furthermore, his own public rhetoric has been a coy mixture of avant-gardism and traditionalism, arrogance and modesty, high theory and low humor. He has made the African-American tradition of "signifying" his own critical signature ("Signifyin(g)") and left audiences and readers to wonder what all this sound and fury signifies.

It is ironic, yet also perversely appropriate, that this critic, who has mounted such blistering polemics against the use of nonliterary standards to judge literary works, should find the reception of his own critical work so bound up with questions of his public standing and reputation within the profession. Obviously, his texts *per se* can be read and assessed like any other texts, without regard to their author. But the importance of this work—for better or worse, the most influential criticism of black literature in this decade—cannot be understood in isolation from the almost mythic figure of Henry Louis Gates and his relationship to the specific historical development of black literary studies.

Professor Gates had fame thrust upon him early in his career when he became one of the first recipients of the MacArthur Foundation Prize Fellowship. A Yale assistant professor still in his twenties, he became overnight one of the most prominent literary critics in the United States, though he had published no book and his articles were just beginning to appear. Furthermore, much of his early work was defined explicitly as an attack on the Black Aesthetic Movement and the critics associated with it. Gates's description of a summer conference at Yale in 1977 aptly fits his own early work: it was "an attempt to take the 'maumauing' out of the black literary criticism that defined the 'Black Aesthetic Movement' of the sixties and transform it into a valid field of intellectual inquiry once again" (p. 44). Not surprisingly, many black critics took offense at the barbs of this young upstart and regarded his MacArthur and succeeding awards as rewards from the white establishment for Gates's assaults on the dominant black intellectual tradition, not as acknowledgments of his brilliant work. From the outset, then, Gates was regarded with resentment and suspicion by many black critics.

In ensuing years Gates became the editor of many important projects relating to Afro-American studies. He had written much of *Afro-American Literature: The Reconstruction of Instruction* (1979), the papers from the Yale Conference, published by the Modern Language Association. In 1983 his essay, "The Signifying Monkey," appeared in *Critical Inquiry,* announcing itself as a radical new departure in black literary studies. He "discovered" and edited Harriet Wilson's *Our Nig* (1859), apparently the first novel published by a black American woman. Random House published his new edition in 1983. He edited *Black Literature and Literary Theory* (1984) for Methuen, which has become the most familiar contemporary document on black literature and theory, and he subsequently edited two special issues of *Critical Inquiry,* which were later published as the book *"Race," Writing and Difference* (1986). Earlier this year Oxford issued a thirty-volume series of Nineteenth-Century Black Women Writers under his general editorship, and Norton has announced that Gates will be the general editor of a forthcoming Norton Anthology of Black Literature. Now he is editing a special issue of *PMLA.*

This would be a remarkable string of accomplishments in an entire career. To achieve so much within less than ten years is certainly unprecedented. (Nor have I listed all of his important achievements during this period.) Still, nagging doubts remained. So much hype surrounded Gates's work. His essays often indulged in hyperbole and sometimes made dubious historical and theoretical claims. Furthermore, he showed a notable talent for recycling his own work. "The Signifying Monkey" reappeared in *Black Literature and Literary Theory* (as well as in *Figures in Black*), and his forthcoming book bears the same title. The introduction to *Black Literature* reappeared in the journal *Black American Literature Forum.* And, of course, the *Critical In-*

quiry issues became a book. Meanwhile, Gates had a habit of listing his "works in progress" for contributors' notes with a confusing prolixity. Throughout this period of Gates's intense editorial activity, Oxford constantly advertised *Figures in Black* as "forthcoming." Given all Gates's publicity and the tantalizing claims made in his essays and lectures, the publication of this book was a much-awaited event. The hoopla made the actual substance of Gates's scholarship hard to judge. So much seemed to be done with mirrors.

One other factor of suspicion must be noted. The experience of blacks in academia has in many respects been depressingly similar to the experience of blacks in American society. From the time of Frederick Douglass there has always been some "spokesman for the race," though black people have never held an election to choose one. For better or worse, these spokesmen have always been chosen by whites. In academia this has meant the acknowledgment of one black scholar as the official authority on all things black. Since so many white institutions have given Gates editorial oversight of projects on black literature, it is hardly surprising that many black scholars came to regard him suspiciously as the new black overseer. His own personal merits, however great they may be, are really not the issue. The long tradition of race relations incites suspicion. Hence, Gates's critical work does not approach its audience in a vacuum. Attitudes pro and con have long been established.

All this considered, *Figures in Black* appears on first sight a disappointment. First of all, Oxford has not served Gates well in producing the book. The dust jacket is bland and unattractive, and the book is not well bound. (The first gathering began to fall out of mine as soon as I opened it.) The rough surface of the paper diffuses light very unevenly, making this book hard on the eyes. But worst of all, this volume (like Hazel Carby's Oxford book, which we shall come to) abounds with signs of inattentive editing. Typographical errors are excessive; names of famous scholars are misspelled (Cornel West as "Cornell" [p. xxix]; Nathan Huggins as "Ruggins" [p. 200]). The sections of the introduction are numbered I, II, III, V, VI, omitting IV. Such glaring errors undermine the reader's confidence in the editorial attention to matters of substance. As for the book's contents, however, one is immediately disappointed to learn that virtually all of these chapters have appeared previously. The work which we have awaited to confirm Gates's scholarly eminence seems to be the work which we have been reading all along.

In actuality, this turns out to be not quite true. Though these are Gates's familiar essays, they have in many cases been substantially revised and emended. Some of them, such as "Songs of a Racial Self: On Sterling A. Brown" and "The Signifying Monkey" have been greatly improved by revision and elaboration. Others, however, such as "Literary Theory and the Black Tradition" (originally published in *The Reconstruction of Instruction* as "Preface to Blackness: Text and Pretext") seem even more confused and troubling than their original versions. Still others, especially "Dis and Dat: Dialect and the Descent" and "The Same Difference: Reading Jean Toomer, 1923–1983" reconfirm one's sense that Gates is the most fecund and brilliant critic of Afro-American literature now before us. All things considered, these essays reinforce rather than mollify one's sense of Gates as a figure of unresolved paradoxes.

The difficulty of describing the argument of *Figures in Black* is not just that it comprises work written for disparate occasions across an entire decade. There is, in fact, no single method uniting these essays, and, furthermore, Gates gives several different accounts of his critical mission. Sometimes he declares in very affirmative terms his commitment "not to shy away from literary theory, but rather to translate it into the black idiom, renaming principles of criticism where appropriate, but especially naming indigenous black principles of criticism and applying these to explicate our own texts" (p. xxi). Here, he sounds like Houston Baker and many of the other cultural nationalist critics whom he so frequently attacks. A few pages later, he declares: "The methodological diversity and the critical bricolage of the essays collected here are not meant to argue for a program or a platform but rather to contribute to the study of both Afro-American literature and contemporary criticism the assembled examples of one critic's attempts to address a 'two-toned' audience: those whose concern is black literature and those whose concern is the study of the institution of literature today" (p. xxx). One might view this stance as a kind of Emersonian contempt for "foolish consistency" which reemerges as Whitman's impulse to "contain multitudes." But negatively, it can also be read as a calculated evasion.

Though *Figures in Black* does not pursue a single argument or methodology, it does have dominant concerns and tendencies which we can specify. As an historian, Gates elaborates a particular account of the tradition of racial writing, stressing the linkage between white ethnochauvinism and black writing which responds to it. As a theoritician he argues against essentialism, especially against viewing "'Blackness' as an entity, rather than as a metaphor or sign" (p. 39). He argues for theory, especially for a semiotically based version of post-structuralist theory, as the proper tool for understanding literary relationships. Concomitantly, he argues against "the confusion of realms," which addresses literary relations in non-literary terms. (Implicitly, and very indirectly, this also entails an attack on Marxism.) Finally, as a practical critic, he advocates "Signifyin(g)" as a critical stance. Signifyin(g), in this context, is a style, an attitude, and a formal relationship (of signifier to signified-upon) rather than a methodology. Hence, it is eclectic, drawing upon whatever established methodologies suit its purposes.

Professor Gates notes in his introduction that his undergraduate major was history. Though one ought not impute causal import to this fact, it is nonetheless interesting in view of his commitment to ground his criticism in the context of long historical traditions and his penchant for broad historical generalizations. He sees the dominant patterns in black writing as responses to the ethnochauvinist claims made by Europeans "at least since Purchas published his *Pilgrimage* in 1611" (p. 15). In his reading of history, "mastery of the arts and letters was Enlightenment Europe's sign of that solid line of division between human being and thing" (p. 25). Accordingly, blacks have approached writing as a demonstration of their own humanity, which Gates regards as "a posture that belabors the social and documentary status of black art" (p. 3). Black writing, in his view, has never fully recovered from its discursive origins. For example, "the confusion of realms, of art with propaganda, plagued the Harlem Renaissance" (p. 29).

In Gates's account this misguided tradition plunged to its *reductio ad absurdum* with the Black Arts Movement of the 1960s and 70s: "Race as the controlling mechanism in critical theory reached its zenith of influence and mystification when LeRoi Jones metamorphosed himself into Imamu Baraka and his daishiki-clad, Swahili-named 'habari gani' disciples [*sic*] 'discovered' they were black. With few exceptions, black critics employed blackness-as-theme to forward one argument or another for the amelioration of the Afro-American's social dilemma" (p. 31). The critics of that movement, represented by Stephen Henderson, Houston Baker, and Addison Gayle, he dubs "race and superstructure critics." By contrast, he defines his own critical project as a corrective intervention. "Black people have been theory resistant," he argues (p. 27). But now it is time to bring literary theory to bear on black writing. "A literary text is a linguistic event; its explication must be an activity of close textual analysis" (p. 41).

The original version of this essay concludes with a list of objectives, which Gates repeats here: "We urgently need to direct our attention to the nature of black figurative language, to the nature of black narrative forms, to the history and theory of Afro-American literary criticism, to the fundamental relation of form and content, and to the arbitrary relationships between the sign and its referent. Finally, we must begin to understand the nature of intertextuality, that is, the nonthematic manner by which texts—poems and novels—respond to other texts" (p. 41). This revised version, however, appends a new assault on the Black Aesthetic critics as well as his formulation of "signifyin(g)" as a critical strategy. We will return to signifyin(g) momentarily. The immediate issue, however, is Gates's account of intellectual history and how he uses it.

Despite Gates's broad range of historical references and frequent rhetorical gestures of off-hand erudition ("at least since . . . ," etc.), his discussion is remarkably ahistorical. He often claims that particular texts initiate a tradition over which they exert "prescriptive" force, but he never provides evidence, either through critical elaboration or scholarly citation, of actual relationships, except at the level of ostensible similarity or logical plausibility. He asserts, for example, that "Thomas Jefferson's remarks on Phillis Wheatley's poetry, as well as on Ignatius Sancho's posthumously published *Letters* (1782), exerted a prescriptive influence over the criticism of the writing of blacks for the next 150 years" (p. 5). This may be true, but Gates certainly offers no persuasive evidence of its truth. The demonstration of textual similarities is not equivalent to proving or explaining actual influence.

An even more troubling example occurs in the third chapter, his essay on chapter one of Frederick Douglass's *Narrative*. He asserts: "The slave narrative, I suggest, is a countergenre, a mediation between the novel of sentiment and the picaresque, oscillating somewhere between the two in a bipolar moment, set in motion by the mode of the confession. (Indeed, as we shall see, the slave narrative spawned its formal negation, the plantation novel" (p. 81). This is a startling, original, exhilaratingly suggestive claim. Unfortunately, despite his interesting analogy, commenting that "both the picaro and the slave, as outsiders, comment on, if not parody, collective social institutions" (p. 82), he does not persuasively demonstrate the existence of an actual link between these traditions. Similarly, his argument "that the plantation novel was the antithesis or negation of the slave narrative becomes apparent when we consider its conventions" (p. 82) evades the real issue of establishing historical influence. Two genres can have similar conventions for many reasons other than direct influence. For instance, they may have a common generic ancestor.

Furthermore, Gates notes that "within two years of the publication in 1852 of *Uncle Tom's Cabin,* at least fourteen plantation novels appeared" (p. 82). This accords with the conventional scholarly wisdom and with much contemporary testimony that Southern novelists wished to "refute" Stowe's portrait of the South. Yet this contradicts Gates's original claim. *Uncle Tom's Cabin* is not a slave narrative. Gates admits as much two chapters later, observing that "Stowe did indeed invent the Negro novel" and that "it seems to have spawned almost immediately a rash of anti- and proslavery novels" (p. 134). It might be possible to argue for *Uncle Tom's Cabin* as a slave narrative because of its borrowings from Josiah Henson's autobiography, but Gates does not make such an argument. If he intends to demonstrate the logic of intertextuality, he ought to say so explicitly and not confuse the discussion by citing publication histories and other social facts. What is one to make of such a garbled historical account?

Other factors, too, make Gates's historiography troubling. For example, he often conflates different periods, different cultures, different continents. Throughout this volume he conflates African and African-American cultures under the heading of "the black tradition." But to take a more immediate example, he uses European and American sources interchangeably. In attempting to establish the popularity of slave narratives in the United States, he cites data mostly from Britain. Further, he tells us that at least ten slave narratives were among that elite five percent of books which sold over five hundred copies between 1835 and 1863. But without additional data, such as the percentage of total books published constituted by slave narratives during that twenty-eight years (a long and eventful period), we cannot infer anything from his figures. He notes that many of the narratives were published first in England. But this is no evidence of popularity. American books were often published first in England, because British copyright laws were much more advantageous. Though there is ample evidence that slave narratives were popular in both England and America, Gates does not cite any of it effectively. In any case, the popularity of the genre in England, which had abolished slavery, does not necessarily have the same entailments as its popularity in the United States, which had not. Apparent similarities, as anthropology has taught us, are often false comparisons.

On the other hand, Gates also fails in some cases to make relevant comparisons which clearly need to be made. For instance, one of his constant complaints is that black literature has been judged by standards "not primarily literary." This is unquestionably true. But it is also true of most literature. How much of nineteenth-century American literary criticism could we honestly describe as predicated upon concerns "primarily literary" in the distinctively New Critical sense which Gates attaches to that phrase? Or to speak of the history of criticism, the author castigates Afro-American critics for being "theory resistant" as if they were somehow alone in their traditional preoccupation with thematic issues. But there is something profoundly ahistorical about an account which imputes the character of critics' work not to their education or to their milieu or to their personal preoccupations but simply to their race. Gates argues in various ways that the thinking of black writers has always been bound by racial discourse. Yet he is inexcusably inattentive to the ways in which they are also implicated in the various other discursive tendencies which constitute Euro-American culture.

Perhaps most troubling of all, however, is Gates's neglect of published scholarship relevant to the issues he discusses. To return to a previous example, the question of how certain genres of American writing develop into other genres has been addressed by a variety of scholars, including some of the most eminent in the field. Sacvan Bercovich comes immediately to mind, and Richard Slotkin's work on Indian captivity narratives and other popular genres would be especially pertinent to Gates's historical inquiry. And a good deal of recent feminist scholarship by Jane Tompkins and others is concerned with the relationships between genres, with special emphasis on the sentimental novel of the mid-nineteenth century. The failure to cite such work raises questions about the standards of scholarship which Gates wishes to espouse. This is a question to which we shall return shortly.

Though much of Professor Gates's critical argument rests upon his particular reading of literary and cultural history, he makes his strongest claims as a theorist. He defines the theory of "signifyin(g)" at several points in the volume. For example: "*Figures in Black* considers the several ways in which a discrete black text interacts with and against its critical context. I use the word *context* throughout this book to refer to the textual world that a black text echoes, mirrors, repeats, revises, or responds to in various formal ways. This process of intertextual relation I call Signifyin(g), the trope of revision, or repetition and difference, which I take from the Afro-American idiom" (p. xxxi). Or, in slightly different terms: "Signifyin(g) is a uniquely black rhetorical concept, entirely textual or linguistic, by which a second statement or figure repeats, or tropes, or reverses the first. Its use as a figure for intertextuality allows us to understand literary revision without resource [*sic*] to thematic, biographical, or Oedipal slayings at the crossroads" (p. 49).

Gates claims that this strategy originates with the vernacular practices represented by the Signifying Monkey tales and that "the figure of the Signifying Monkey, in turn, is the profane counterpart of Esu-Elegbara, the Yoruba sacred trickster" (p. 48). In the New World Esu is frequently known as Legba or Papa Labas; and he is a counterpart to Hermes, from whose name we derive "hermeneutics." Hence, Esu becomes "our metaphor for the act of interpretation itself" (p. 237). The black critic, by this argument, is a signifier. Indeed, "learning to signify is often part of our adolescent education" (p. 236). By implication, then, critical sophistication is a standard entailment of Afro-American acculturation. Black critics are one up on white critics. The opening lines of "The Blackness of Blackness" make this clear in Gates's characteristic, off-handed manner: "Since Ferdinand de Saussure at least, signification has become a critical aspect of much contemporary theory. It is curious to me that this neologism in the Western tradition cuts across a term in the black vernacular tradition that is approximately two centuries old" (p. 235). In other words, white critics have finally stumbled into black people's briarpatch. Clearly, Gates's Signifyin(g) is a signifying strategy.

The appeal of such an argument for black critics, especially younger ones, should be immediately apparent. Unfortunately, the validity of the argument is questionable. That signifying is a common feature of African-American culture is indisputable, and the relation of the African to the American traditions has been well established by a large body of scholarship, which Gates amply cites. But his central claim, that vernacular signifying provides a useful model for professional critics, is not adequately established by his arguments. In the vernacular signifying is a style, an attitude, a set of subversive and oppositional strategies.

As a metaphor, Gates argues, the monkey "is not only a master of technique, . . . he *is* technique, or style, or the literariness of literary language. . . . In this sense, one does not signify something; rather, one signifies in some way" (p. 239). Gates demonstrates persuasively that signifying is a style, but he does not demonstrate that it is substantially interpretive. We know from the vernacular and from his examples that signifying is an effective mode of self-assertion. But is it, and can it be, a reliable mode of understanding? Gates takes for granted that it can, but he never makes a persuasive case.

Indeed, though it is obvious that signifying can provide a compelling model of personal style for the individual critic, we must ask ourselves whether it is an adequate or desirable model for serious critical activity. In the vernacular signifying is an oppositional strategy, sometimes playful and sometimes vindictive, intent upon one-upmanship. One signifies at someone else's expense. Signifying is quintessentially devious, deceptive, self-aggrandizing, insinuating, provocative, and evasive. The trickster obeys no rules but his own. For example, Gates cites the example of the monkey falsely informing the lion that the elephant had insulted the lion. The lion attacks the elephant and is trounced. The monkey has signified upon the lion. Unlike the "master tropes" (metaphor, metonymy, synecdoche, irony), Gates argues, signifying is "the slave's trope" (p. 236). But viewed differently, signifying is the trope which requires a victim.

Professor Gates identifies explicit instances of signifying within texts, such as Janie's devastating confrontation with her husband, Joe, in *Their Eyes Were Watching God*. He also argues persuasively that signifying relationships exist in the intertextual revisions of one text by another, such as Ralph Ellison's responses in *Invisible Man* to Richard Wright's *Native Son*. In particular instances, signifying is clearly a valuable critical concept. But this does not mean that it is adequate as a model for critical discourse. When I speak of "critical discourse," I mean in the sense defined by Thomas Kuhn and Foucault: that a discourse is a commonly accepted set of rules and standards, including rules of evidence, definitions of truth, and acceptable forms of argument. Participants in the discourse are accountable to the standards of the discourse and of the discursive community because they are engaged in a collective effort to develop knowledge within a certain set of terms. If we think of criticism in this way, how can Signifyin(g) avoid the self-indulgent and idiosyncratic excesses of signifying?

The question of accountability is especially vexing. Gates reminds us that in order to escape Lion's wrath, "today / Monkey does his signifying / A-way-up out of the way" (p. 239). Such evasiveness seems antithetical to criticism as the cooperative functioning of an intellectual community. Furthermore, the notion that signifying is the slave's trope does not necessarily mean that signifying is directed against the masters in the cause of liberation. Most often, signifying occurs among slaves. In this sense, it is wholly in the tradition that Gates's most barbed and sustained signifying is directed against the Black Aesthetic critics.

He sees the signifying intertextuality of black literature in a similar sense: "Black writers read and critique other black texts as an act of rhetorical self-definition" (p. 242). Yet we know with equal certainty that black writers also respond to *white* texts. Though Gates occasionally acknowledges this, as in his comments on Ishmael Reed's parody of the detective novel genre in *Mumbo Jumbo*, he shows much more interest in black-on-black signifying. Thus, he regards *Mumbo Jumbo* primarily as "a pastiche of the Afro-American narrative tradition itself" (p. 240). This is an odd way to view a book about which the author has declared: "My main job I felt was to humble Judeo-Christian culture" (*Shrovetide*, p. 159).

Signifyin(g) as a critical perspective can effectively illuminate the revisionist relationships between texts. It offers us no guidance, however, in recognizing and analyzing the originality of a text or the terms and strategies by which a text defines its own individual concerns. This is surprising, since Gates asserts that his intention is "to defamiliarize the texts of the black tradition . . . so that I may more readily see the formal workings of those texts" (p. xxi). Though he can write very astutely about formal matters when he chooses to, his theory of Signifyin(g) is defined explicitly in terms of intertextual relations, not intratextual structures, and most of his critical attention is turned to the treatment of racial identity and ideas about race and writing in various texts and traditions. This reflects the tension in his work which I noted earlier: while he presents himself rhetorically as a literary formalist, he proceeds most often as an historian of ideas. And indeed, Signifyin(g) works most compellingly as a tool of ideological struggle, not as a mode of close literary analysis.

Though Gates claims that Signifyin(g) derives from "the black tradition," his critical deployment of it echoes heavily the poststructuralist theories of his former colleagues at Yale: especially Harold Bloom and Paul de Man. As we have seen, he casually notes the coincidence by claiming that European criticism has finally arrived at where the black vernacular had always been. This, however, is too breezy an explanation. Indeed, Gates depends so heavily upon certain key concepts made familiar by other major theorists ("revision" from Bloom, "intertextuality" from de Man, "difference" and "repetition" from Derrida) that we must wonder what the black tradition has contributed to his Signifyin(g) except the term and its style. Furthermore, his very cursory mention of these critics (de Man's name does not even appear in the index) seems worse than inadequate, considering the heavy conceptual debt which even his vocabulary owes to their work.

This is especially unsettling in view of the second footnote to his sixth chapter—in my opinion, his most brilliant essay. This note cites George Steiner's *After Babel* and remarks: "This note was accidentally omitted from the first published version of this essay, as was proper citation of Dr. Steiner's argument" (p. 288). One can easily understand how a footnote could be accidentally omitted. But the passage in question is the central theoretical statement of the essay, which even includes language quoted directly from Steiner's book. Gates's application of Steiner's theory to the problem of dialect in Afro-American writing is inspired; and this new version of the essay is revised and expanded, giving Steiner full credit in the text itself. The original version of

Black Figures, Signs, Voices 15

the essay, however, does not mention Steiner at all. How can an essay fail to mention the source of its central idea?

To raise this question is not to insinuate that Gates has been guilty of scholarly dishonesty. But the issue of acknowledging theoretical debts, placed alongside the issue of scholarly thoroughness discussed above, raises again this question: what standards of scholarly accountability does Signifyin(g) entail? Too often, these essays appear indifferent to scholarly precedent, slipshod in their historical reasoning, and casual in their methodology. Contradictory claims abound. For instance, the Introduction begins with a set of perceptive ruminations on the problem of what Edward Said has called "travelling theory." Gates argues: "To imitate these theories of criticism drawn from the Western literary tradition, or to attempt to apply them as if they were universal procedures similar, say, to surgical techniques, would be both naive and self-subversive, because theories of criticism arise from a remarkably small group of specific texts" (p. xv). Yet the appropriation of established theories is a fundamental strategy of Signifyin(g). He explains, rather ambiguously, that "I have tried to work through contemporary theories of literature not to apply them to black texts, but to transform these by translating them into a new rhetorical realm" (p. xx). Later still, he comments that "the methodological diversity and the critical bricolage of the essays collected here are not meant to argue for a program or a platform but rather . . . a record or an account of one critic's confrontation with the role of theory in the study of a noncanonical literature" (p. xxx). He both questions and endorses the borrowing of theories. He offers a manifesto for black critics (pp. xxi–xxii), and yet claims not to present a program. He defines goals as iconoclastic as the transformation of existing theories and as modest as simply recounting "one critic's" ruminations. With so many claims and disclaimers, republications of old work and promises of new work (two books "forthcoming"), it is exceedingly difficult to make confident assessments or criticisms of the critic.

But this, too, is part of signifying. This is a coy and playful book. For example, Gates reminds us that "Esu always limps because his legs are of different lengths: one is anchored in the realm of the gods, and the other rests in this human world" (p. 237). To see the self-reference in this god of interpretation, we need only remember that the critic himself walks with a cane. More transparently, he quotes the blues man Skip James in his introduction: "After I got that much from those [other guitar players], then I just used my own self: Skip. I don't pattern after anyone or either copycat" (p. xxx). Skip, of course, is Gates's own nickname. The trickster appears in many forms. Gates is Esu, Esu is the Signifying Monkey, the Signifying Monkey is black creativity.

Gates's favorite trope throughout this study is synecdoche. In various contexts, the part comes to represent the whole. Racist discourse represents Western Culture, three critics and one poet represent the Black Arts Movement, signifying represents the black tradition. If this strategy of reliance on tropes enables valuable insights, it entails even more costly blindnesses. Nonetheless, it seems appropriate to invoke one further synecdoche here. An apt synecdoche for the Signifying Monkey is his mocking grin. It is doubtless an apt figure for what Signifyin(g) signifies.

Signifying aside, *Figures in Black* raises a crucial question which it does not attempt to resolve: the question of "blackness." Very astutely, Gates argues that "Blackness is not a material object, an absolute, or an event, but a trope; it does not have an 'essence' as such but is defined by a network of relations that form a particular aesthetic unity" (p. 40). This is a splendid starting point for a theoretical statement on the status of "blackness," but regrettably, Gates never develops this idea. He doubtless addresses it in a forthcoming volume; but meanwhile, how are we to understand what he means by "the black tradition"? What is a "black text"? Do we define a text by its internal characteristics or by the ancestry of its author? If the former, do we include works by white writers, such as Joel Chandler Harris's Uncle Remus tales? If the latter, do we include works which contain no identifiable black characters, such as James Baldwin's *Giovanni's Room*? Does "the black tradition" include all "black texts," or only those which meet Gates's definition of "literary"? The Black Aesthetic Critics, given their explicit political agenda, could justify dismissing such questions as trivial. But how can an essay called "Literary Theory and the Black Tradition" which accuses black people of being "theory resistant" (p. 27) fail to address such basic points of theoretical definition? No aspect of *Figures in Black* is more disappointing than its failure to address seriously such fundamental questions.

The importance of such questions becomes clearer when one considers that Gates's insistence upon viewing black texts as "systems of signs" does not mandate the isolation of "blackness" as a point of definition. Quite the contrary, one can easily imagine the grouping of texts into traditional categories of genre, period, and style, without regard to "race." It might even be argued that the intertextual context of works cannot be fully understood so long as the works are segregated into restrictive canons based on race or gender. At the very least we might want to think more broadly in terms of *American* literature. Indeed, it might also be argued that to define literature in terms of sociological categories such as "black" reflects a "confusion of realms." I do not wish here to argue any of these points, but I am suggesting that these are points which an adequate theory of racial writing must address. It is not sufficient simply to replicate our commonplaces of social definition, thereby begging the theoretical question.

At his best, Gates can blend historical argument, theoretical insights, and close readings with a facility which seems inspired. This occurs in "Dis and Dat: Dialect and the Descent," which is the best essay on the aesthetics of dialect in Afro-American writing that I have ever encountered. It is also, arguably, the best short discussion of the Harlem Renaissance. This essay is concerned with the linguistic gestures which give cultural weight to Afro-American poetry. It culminates with a brilliant discussion of the word "down" in the spirituals. Gates eschews the easy demolitions of straw men and other self-indulgent postures which sometimes mar his work, and instead, he turns his full attention to examining how Afro-American experience yields structures of language and feeling in the masking idiom of dialect. Regarding the spirituals, he concludes: "In these images, dialect is at its most effective, and the poet not only has accepted his or her role as the point of consciousness of the language but has pushed that language to express that which is untranslatable" (p. 195). In striving to understand what is best in this cultural tradition, Gates reveals his own best qualities of understanding. This essay ought to be required reading for every student of American culture.

Interestingly, Gates is always at his best in this book when he discusses James Weldon Johnson. That underrated man of letters was arguably the most astute Afro-American critic of the first half of this century. Even when he disagrees with Johnson, Gates engages Johnson's views with an attentiveness and precision which make both men shine. These discussions whet one's desire to know more about that extraordinary novelist, composer, critic, poet, and politician. If only Gates would consider writing such a book. In Johnson he has clearly found a topic worthy of his own formidable talents.

Indeed, though he has gained his fame as an editor and theorist, Gates has made his most original and substantial contributions as a literary historian. Admittedly, I have criticized his historiography at length. And the point remains that his theoretically oriented historical arguments are often dubious. When he narrows his sights, however, and writes about the career of Jean Toomer or the biographies of Frederick Douglass, his work is judicious and illuminating. He is at his weakest, on the other hand, when he turns polemical and sassy, as in his comments on the Black Arts Movement. Even then, he is acutely perceptive in identifying how polemical stances distort the work of other critics. The irony is that Gates does not acknowledge the corresponding liability in his own work. Unfortunately, Signifyin(g) is a risky business. Though his initial investment in it has paid off handsomely, it may already have passed the point of diminishing returns.

The publication of a book by Houston A. Baker, Jr., is always an important event in Afro-American literary studies. Throughout the 1970s Baker was the preeminent critic of Afro-American writing, and the recent celebrity of Henry Louis Gates has not substantively diminished his stature. Nonetheless, certain peculiarities have always characterized his work. For example, he has always been primarily an essayist. Though he has published several influential collections of essays, he has never published a sustained, full-length work of scholarship. Also, each of his books has been informed by a different set of theoretical orientations, such as speech act theory in *The Journey Back* and poststructuralism in *Blues, Ideology, and Afro-American Literature*. The title of his current book, *Modernism and the Harlem Renaissance*, suggests a work of historical scholarship. But in fact, at one hundred seven pages, this is hardly a full-length study, and it is divided into eleven short essays on various topics. Only about a third of the book discusses what we commonly define as the Harlem Renaissance; and true to form, Baker has left behind the deconstructive and Althusserian readings of his previous book. No familiar theoretical label fits the methodology of this volume. Indeed, Baker's prediction that "my following discussion . . . will seem, at least, nontraditional" (p. xiv) is an extreme understatement.

Modernism and the Harlem Renaissance is a very odd and bewildering book. It is painful to have to write disapprovingly of work by a scholar who has contributed so much exciting and original criticism to the discipline, yet it is even more painful to encounter a book so idiosyncratic, disorganized, and ill-conceived. It seems more like the notes for a book than a finished product. The problem is not its length—though one must doubt that this topic could be adequately addressed in a hundred pages—but rather its dubious arguments and its failure to integrate effectively the disparate elements which it comprises: historical arguments, theoretical claims, visual documents, literary analyses, and autobiographical reflections.

Admittedly, this book is not intended to be a conventional work of scholarship. Scholarship, in fact, comes under attack early on. It is rather an extended meditation on a complex historical problem by a noted scholar. To use Baker's own terms, it is a "cultural performance," grounded in the context of "family history." This book is dedicated to the author's father, who died in 1983, and Baker declares in his preface that he regards his father "as a metonym for [Afro-American] history" (p. xiv). The book ends with a page of photographs from the Baker family album. Confronted by a work framed in such poignantly personal terms, the critic feels churlish to utter any criticism at all. Nonetheless, a work which makes overt historical and critical claims enters the realm of scholarly discourse, regardless of its genre or personal import.

Modernism and the Harlem Renaissance begins by taking issue with the scholarly tradition which has viewed the Harlem Renaissance as a failure because its writers did not achieve works which resembled the classic texts of modernism. The challenge for Baker is not to measure these writers in terms of white modernist norms but rather to define "modern Afro-American sound." To identify the characteristic strategies of Afro-American expression, he formulates the concept of "the mastery of form and the deformation of mastery." Like Gates's Signifyin(g), this concept describes the way in which Afro-American creative utterances appropriate and revise existing forms or statements. Unlike Gates, however, Baker explicitly rejects formalist aesthetics, insisting instead that his concern is with a social understanding of cultural performance. Hence, he advocates a focus on "areas of expressive production" rather than on individual artists (p. 8). Most of the book, subsequently, is a reassessment of various Afro-American writers and texts in terms of their "sound" and their enactment of mastery of form and deformation of mastery.

Baker particularly focuses on Booker T. Washington's *Up from Slavery*, and his discussion of Washington provides a useful illustration of his method. According to Baker, the violently racist culture of turn-of-the-century America required that any Afro-American spokesman must wear the minstrel mask in order to have a public voice at all. Minstrelsy was the dominant mode by which whites, the masters, described and demeaned black people. Hence, Washington's use of various darky jokes, which Baker calls "*sounds* of the minstrel mask" (p. 29) reveals his mastery of this form. But Washington's real intent was to lull his white audience in order to serve his own purposes: specifically, to win support for Tuskegee Institute. This devious use by the slave of the master's forms is the deformation of mastery, and Washington's virtuosity with such strategies distinguishes him, according to Baker, as "the quintessential herald of modernism in black expressive culture" (p. 37).

Baker expands upon this point: "I am interested in the strategy to precisely the extent that it ensures cognitive exploration and affective transformations leading to the growth and *survival* of a nation. Washington is 'modern' in my view, then, because he earnestly projected the flourishing of a southern, black Eden at Tuskegee . . ." (p. 37). Baker's reappraisal of Washington is an apt manifestation of his commitment to recover and celebrate the masterful performances in our "family history." It also indicates his own movement away from the dominant theoretical tendencies of the academy and toward re-embracing the black cultural nationalist commitments which characterized his own earlier work. On the other hand, this argument simultaneously exposes the weaknesses of Baker's new method. Though his reading of Washington's rhetorical strategies is cogent, he draws further inferences which rhetorical analysis alone cannot justify.

Baker conflates literary, historical, biographical, and political realms, but the rules of evidence in these realms are not identical. Thus, Baker's persuasive reading of Washington's rhetoric does not substantiate his claim that "Washington had a regional . . . authority in matters black and southern" (p. 38). We need to consider a different kind of evidence in order to assess the extent of Washington's knowledge and the quality of his judgment. Similarly, Baker accurately paraphrases Washington in saying that "his avowed goal was to train the Afro-American masses in a way that would ensure their inestimable value to a white world—that would, in a word, enable them to survive" (p. 38). But such assertions in the texts of a notoriously duplicitous "spokesman" do not justify the biographical inference that such "nation building" was Washington's dominant motive or the political inference that his good intentions were necessarily the same as valid agendas.

One also may agree with Baker's reading of Washington's rhetoric and yet question his endorsement of Washington's behavior. Even in the realm of his texts we find a variety of guises. Though we may applaud his Brer Rabbit routine in the Atlanta Exposition Address, Washington was not always so benign. Even a cursory reading of *The Booker T. Washington Papers* shows that he moved ruthlessly against his black critics, and he exerted dictatorial control over much of the black press. A brief letter to Emmett Jay Scott in 1903 illustrates the latter point. "In case the Boston crowd persist in advocating the holding of another Afro-American Council, I should like you, so far as you can exercise influence to exert it in the direction of causing the colored Press pay absolutely no attention to this understaking [*sic*] (BTW Papers 7, p. 225). This is not the place to enter an argument about the strange, authoritarian personality of Booker T. Washington. My point is simply that the problem is far more complicated than Baker admits; and which texts we consider will determine how we conceive the scope of the problem.

Actually, Baker even further complicates the matter near the end of the book, when he declares: "Washington—like my father—never believed for an instant that white men and women were anything other than temporarily empowered exploiters who could be masterfully spoken out of money—money that might, in turn, be used to build a free, black nation on the ruins of a slavery the exploiters had maliciously instituted and malevolently maintained" (p. 102). It is not clear what, if any, evidence Baker has for this claim about Washington; and a great deal of evidence, most obviously Washington's adulation of Samuel Chapman Armstrong, indicates that Washington did not regard all whites in such terms. Furthermore, by equating his father with Washington, Baker rhetorically poses a dilemma for any potential critic of his assertion. Yet even if Baker were correct in his claims, a declaration in this form would be an unscholarly gesture.

But to raise the issue of scholarship brings us back to the beginning of Baker's argument. In his preface he asserts: "Much of what passes for self-consciously 'scholarly' effort on the part of black men and women in the United States is often production self-consciously oriented to win approval from those who have a monopoly on definitions of SCHOLARSHIP. 'Careerism' is one sign for the black scholar's inclination to preserve the critical vocabulary *and* the assumptions of a dominating culture in his or her analyses of his or her own 'dominated' culture" (p. xvii). On one level, this book is Baker's attempt to define a new kind of scholarship which does not reinforce racist hegemony. Yet this passage insinuates that existing "definitions of scholarship" are inherently encoded with the assumptions of racist hegemony. If this claim is valid, which seems unlikely, Baker provides neither evidence nor argument to support it. What his own "model of discursive analysis" lacks, at the same time, is standards of verification and other basic mechanisms for judging the validity of any given argument.

This absence seems not altogether coincidental, given Baker's emphasis on performance as a guiding metaphor for cultural production, "sound" as the criterion of authenticity, and celebration as the appropriate mode of response. The objective which he proposes is not the "objective analysis" of traditional scholarship but rather a redemptive and self-vindicating activity of appreciative reclamation, which he calls "renaissancism." As he puts it: "The family *must* explore its own geographies by transcending an old economics where the familiar signs are LITERATURE, ART, and particularly and most expressly FAILURE. Renaissancism's contemporary fate is our responsibility, demanding a hard and ofttimes painful journey back to ancestral wisdom in order to achieve a traditional (family) goal. That goal is the discovery of our *successful* voices as the always already blues script—as the salvific changing same—in which a new world's future will be sounded" (p. 106).

This helps to answer the question of what all this has to do with the Harlem Renaissance. For Baker the Harlem Renaissance is not a period or a movement but rather a metonym (or perhaps a synecdoche, depending on how one views the relationship of these two phenomena) of black expressive culture in its perpetual movement from the slave past toward the realization of a self-affirming black nation: what he calls "family modernity." It is a book about "renaissancism," not about the 1920s. Rejecting scholarship as we know it, Baker here advocates a new form of intellectual engagement. Viewed in these terms, this is not a failed book about the Harlem Renaissance but rather a radical new kind of performative utterance.

Yet despite its idiosyncracies, *Modernism and the Harlem Renais-*

sance is not unique. It has much in common with the work of Henry Louis Gates. Its central concerns are very similar to those addressed by Gates in his "Dis and Dat: Dialect and the Descent." Baker's discussion of "sound" is similar to Gates's discussion of dialect, just as "mastery of form and deformation of mastery" is rather close to "Signifyin(g)." The main difference in the application of the latter concepts is that Gates primarily concentrates on relations among black texts, while Baker emphasizes the rebellion of black writers (or speakers) against the white tradition. And more broadly, Gates insists upon the autonomy of literature, while Baker sees literature in relationship to social and political relations.

As a cultural performance, *Modernism and the Harlem Renaissance* is a fascinating document. Whether this kind of writing is preferable to conventional scholarship or even more politically useful is another question. In any case, this book is a self-consciously idiosyncratic, profoundly personal gesture. It is not a model for emulation nor a contribution to knowledge but rather a scholar's exhortation to other scholars that they abandon the worship of false idols and return to the one true faith.

Of the four books being reviewed here, John Callahan's *In the African-American Grain: The Pursuit of Voice in Twentieth-Century Black Fiction* is the most conventional in its methodology. That is, it self-consciously eschews any explicit allegiances to recent tendencies in literary theory. It is essentially a series of essays, offering thematically linked close readings of *Cane, Their Eyes Were Watching God, Invisible Man, The Autobiography of Miss Jane Pittman,* and *Meridian*. These are preceded by a chapter which considers two short story collections from the turn of the century, one by a white and the other by a black writer: Joel Chandler Harris's *Uncle Remus: His Songs and Sayings* and Charles Chesnutt's *The Conjure Woman*. Despite its deliberately traditionalist bias, however, Callahan's book has several traits in common with these others which mark it as a book of our own time.

Most obviously, Callahan joins the recent trend toward selecting a mode from Afro-American culture—"call-and-response" in his case—and using it as both a synecdoche of the culture and a heuristic device for interpreting Afro-American texts. Second, this book is revisionary in its historical reading of Afro-American culture. Even the title reflects this intent. Callahan announces in an author's note that at the urging of Alice Walker he uses the term "African-American" rather than "the safe and somewhat vague term, Afro-American" in order to call explicit attention to "both African descent and the African contribution to American culture." Finally, like Gates and Baker, he offers an autobiographical account as a grounding and justification for his critical practices.

Callahan is profoundly influenced by the work of Ralph Ellison, especially by the essays in *Shadow and Act,* and his choice of "call-and-response" as a guiding trope reflects this influence. He explains:

Committed to a 'literature of necessity' by virtue of their *and the nation's* distinct predicament, African-American writers seize the opportunity to regard their reading audience as both characters and citizens. This particular fiction enables black writers to imagine white Americans becoming more open to African-American personality and experience as readers than most were as citizens. In the end this repeated act of fictionalizing is a liberating patriotic act, for it allows the writer to call on the reader to become simultaneously an individual and, indivisibly, a member of the potential national community. American identity becomes a fluid estate: not only are blacks true Americans but 'the true American,' as Ralph Ellison notes, 'is also somehow black.' [p. 19]

This view regards African-American fiction as inherently political, not in the terms of protest literature but rather as an enactment of democratic possibility. The high idealism of this conception typifies Ellison's version of liberal humanism and provides the best formulation of democratic pluralism that a liberal humanist perspective is likely to achieve. As Callahan aptly sums up: "Against the grain of a society where both orality and literacy are menaced, African-American writers use the oral tradition to project values of community and citizenship" (p. 20).

As a heuristic model, "call-and-response" works splendidly to highlight and examine instances of cooperative exchange within texts or between the text and its public. It works less well with other tendencies; and, furthermore, Callahan seems reluctant to explore the failures or even explicit rejections of communication which characterize some texts. Like any synecdoche, call-and-response is only a part of what it represents, and invoking the whole from the part proves exceedingly difficult. But often, the part, and not the whole, really is the point of interest.

Despite his obvious interest in an interracial rather than an intraracial national discourse, Callahan discusses only individual African-American novels, not pairs or groups of novels by both blacks and whites. By following the tradition of discussing black literature in isolation from white writing, Callahan misses the opportunity to explore call-and-response to the full extent of its potential. He can show how black texts call to a generalized American audience, but cannot effectively demonstrate the interplay between black and white texts within our literary tradition. The one exception is his chapter on Harris and Chesnutt. Callahan argues, regarding black folklore, that "once Harris pressed the tales into service on the Jim Crow side of the reopened civil war, black writers, led by Charles Chesnutt, undertook rescue missions in their rebellion against white supremacy" (pp. 28–29).

Callahan's comparison of these two writers is illuminating. He notes, for instance, the important difference between the narrative frames used by Harris and Chesnutt. The former created Uncle Remus, who tells his stories to a young white boy: a situation which recapitulates Harris's own childhood relationship to George Terrell, the former slave who first introduced him to black folklore. But Harris's experience was atypical, because "in [black] folk culture adults told tales to adults with slave children gradually initiated into the storytelling ceremony" (p. 30). Accordingly, Harris's entire understanding of the meaning of cultural context of folk tales was distorted. By contrast, Chesnutt's Uncle Julius shares his stories with an adult white couple in a complicated, interactive relationship: "Unlike Remus and the little white boy, John and Uncle Julius are each performer and audience; they engage in a variation of call-and-response." Furthermore, by creating both John and his wife, Annie, as Julius's audience, "Chesnutt enacts the fiction of a pluralistic American reading public" (p. 40).

Callahan's treatment of these writers is compelling, and it makes excellent use of the insights provided in Robert Hemenway's seminal essay on Harris, published as an introduction to the Penguin edition of the Uncle Remus tales. Just as Hemenway's essay suggested that Harris would be a rich subject for a psychobiographical study, Callahan's discussion demonstrates that the comparative approach has untapped potential for producing complex new understandings of our culture. Callahan is perhaps too harsh in his treatment of Harris as merely a nostalgic white supremacist. Indeed, many Americans hold visions of democracy far less egalitarian than Callahan's very liberal formulation, and such competing definitions need to be taken into account. Nonetheless, Callahan's assessment of Chesnutt as the superior artist and as a paradigmatic figure among African-American fiction writers is quite persuasive.

In the remaining chapters Callahan is at his best with the writers toward whom he has always shown, in his previous work, the strongest personal affinity: Ralph Ellison, Ernest Gaines, and Alice Walker. His chapters on Toomer and Hurston seem to me less satisfying by comparison. Each of these chapters presents a close reading of a single novel, though in some instances relevant pairings with novels by white authors would have been possible, had Callahan chosen to maintain the pattern of his Harris/Chesnutt chapter. Toomer's *Cane* and Waldo Frank's *Holiday* were paired from their inception, as these two friends toured the South together with the intention of writing books out of the experience. *The Autobiography of Miss Jane Pittman* (1971) would make a fascinating comparison with William Styron's *The Confessions of Nat Turner* (1969). And what might Callahan have done with Faulkner's *Light in August* (1932) and Hurston's *Their Eyes Were Watching God* (1937), two books which both begin with a woman walking down a dusty road, one seeking a man and the other having left a man behind? To raise these questions is not to suggest that the author should have written a different book but rather to indicate the possibilities raised by his own design. It may be, however, that Callahan's implicit theoretical commitment to New Critical close reading makes such possibilities hard for him to pursue. We shall return momentarily to this point.

Despite excellent interpretations of particular moments in *Cane* and *Their Eyes Were Watching God,* Callahan's application of call-and-response seems less persuasive with these books than with the others. One reason may be that both of these books evince a profound ambivalence regarding questions of community. We know from various sources, including Nellie McKay's biography and Henry Louis Gates's excellent essay in *Figures in Black* that Toomer anguished over the question of his racial identity and eventually decided to reject any identification as a "Negro." Though he had not reached that point in *Cane,* the sense of uncertainty is nonetheless palpable. Frustration and the failure of communication are powerful motifs in *Cane.* Callahan does not deny these tendencies, and he discusses the problems of frustration and failure perceptively. Still, the figure of call-and-response does not seem entirely appropriate to explain the tangled themes of *Cane.*

Similarly, *Their Eyes* offers complications which raise serious questions about the applicability of call-and-response. Professor Callahan offers a persuasive challenge to Robert Steptoe's criticism of Hurston for having denied Janie a direct first-person narration. Callahan insists that rather than accept "the fashionable value of authorial control she substitutes a rhetoric of intimacy developed from the collaborative habit of call-and-response." This view allows him to conclude regarding the shape of the narrative that "because of her intimate yet impersonal form, Hurston invites her readers to respond as listeners and participants in the work of storytelling" (p. 118). This account seems exactly right as a description of the novel's communal aspect.

Nevertheless, Janie relishes and maintains her marginality. Though she loves certain interactions of community, she also wants to set the terms of her engagement with the community, including in the final instance, the option of communicating her story to them only through an intermediary. This stance of self-conscious marginality is a recurrent pattern in Hurston's work, and it corresponds to her own role as a folklorist and fiction writer, forever entering and mediating between communities—the folk and the modern, the illiterate and the literate, the black and the white—but never surrendering autonomy in exchange for full membership in any community. The figure of call-and-response does not hide this willful independence, but it is also not ideally suited to illuminate the ambiguities inherent in this essentially modern attitude toward community.

This ambiguity is not deeply embedded in *Invisible Man* but rather is explicitly the problem which scene after scene of the novel explores. And since call-and-response is Ellison's own figure in the novel, it works splendidly as a heuristic model. Callahan develops subtle modulations of the concept as he examines the dialectic between the narrator and his various audiences and the discontinuities between the narrator's rhetorical intentions and the effects his rhetoric produces. At the end of the chapter Callahan concludes that the author is in conversation with his own work, just as the work is in conversation with its audience. By modulating call-and-response into conversation, Callahan brings his discussion into an area currently being explored by Richard Rorty and other contemporary pragmatist philosophers. This move, however, is both stimulating and troubling. While Rorty's work would seem to underscore Callahan's arguments about conversation within a community, it also raises serious questions about whether such conversation can mediate between disparate communities, binding them into a single, large, liberal pluralist democracy.

Indeed, Callahan notes this problem himself. Discussing the stadium scene of *Invisible Man*, he notes the dangers of "the speaker's temptation to derive his identity from his audience." How, Callahan implicitly asks, can an individual maintain his personal integrity when "his coherence as a human being depends on service and on confirmation by those served"? (p. 167) This is also the novel's question, and as posed, this conflict between individuality and community is a binary trap which endlessly replicates itself, never achieving real resolution. This tendency is mirrored in the novel's structure and is perhaps the greatest flaw of that superb book. The problem, however, is not so much the author's shortcoming as it is a fundamental limitation of liberal discourse. The preoccupation with integrity and identity conceals from us the importance of *transformation*. The form of mediation which breaks the trap of binary opposition is not an intercourse between static poles but rather a dialectic which transforms those originals and produces a new synthesis. In the process, something is gained but something is also lost. By definition, change requires some sacrifice of "identity," and the quest to recover identity (or authenticity) is a nostalgic gesture bound always to fail. It is no wonder that Ellison's protagonist ends up in "hibernation."

In the folk context call-and-response is the activity of a community reaffirming its own communal identity. In these literary texts which Callahan examines, call-and-response is the expression of distinct individuals seeking but also defying and challenging community. The pluralist dream of an egalitarian democracy comprising disparate communities or individuals seems in either case both admirable and futile. But whether it is achievable or not, it is a dream which most of us Americans in some sense share. Certainly, John Callahan has done a fine job with *In the African-American Grain* of revealing how these novels explore the possibilities and implications of democratic pluralism.

Hazel Carby's *Reconstructing Womanhood: The Emergence of the Afro-American Woman Novelist* differs in several fundamental ways from the other works reviewed here. Her book is primarily a work of intellectual history and more a work of "critique" in the Marxist sense of that word than of "criticism" in the familiar literary sense. She does not distinguish between "literary" and "non-literary" concerns, nor does she rely on establishing some synecdoche as a "master trope." Instead, she argues for a new way of understanding intellectual history, both by foregrounding previously neglected figures and by advocating a fresh methodological approach. And most conspicuously, her methodology really does bring a new frame of reference to Afro-American literary studies, because it is based on the work of Stuart Hall and the cultural studies program which he developed at the University of Birmingham—a body of work little known in this country except in Marxist circles.

In a pair of long footnotes, Carby describes her own theoretical debts. She comments: "I am particularly drawing on that aspect of cultural studies which has analyzed issues of race and the study of black culture." Here, she cites the work of Stuart Hall and several other British Marxists. She further explains: "My position is that cultural studies is not disciplinary, nor does it seek to be a discipline even in the sense that American studies, Afro-American studies, or women's studies are interdisciplinary; rather it is a critical position which interrogates the assumptions of and principles of critical practice of all three modes of inquiry" (pp. 178–79). This critical stance enables Carby to raise questions about the definitions, procedures, and ideological assumptions used to construct knowledge in a given area. To repeat the terms I used previously, this stance makes Carby's approach to cultural studies a mode of *critique*, not of criticism. Such a perspective is an exciting innovation in Afro-American studies, a field which has too long relied on threadbare hand-me-downs of theory which could only produce the most conventional of results.

In lieu of the autobiographical narrative which has become virtually obligatory among contemporary critics, Carby begins by describing a well-known historical episode: the Columbian Exposition of 1893. Focusing on the minimal and insultingly selective inclusion of Afro-Americans in this "White City" which was explicitly advertised as a symbol of American progress, Carby argues that "The Columbian Exposition embodied the definitive failure of the hopes of emancipation and reconstruction and inaugurated an age that was to be dominated by 'the problem of the colorline'" (p. 5). Carby does not offer her reinterpretation of the "White City" as a master trope for Afro-American history. Rather, it serves to locate and embody historically the problematic which she proposes to examine.

Characteristically, she describes her project in explicit contrast to the dominant modes of inquiry: "This book is not a conventional literary history, nor is it limited to drawing on feminist or black feminist literary theories, but it is a cultural history and critique of the forms in which black women intellectuals made political as well as literary interventions in the social formations in which they lived" (p. 7). The book is concerned with the origins of black women's fiction in the nineteenth century, with particular emphasis on situating each author's work within the specific discursive formations of the given historical moment.

Carby breaks down that larger statement of purpose into four basic areas of concern. First, the book examines how "black women had to confront the dominant domestic ideologies and literary conventions of womanhood which excluded them from the definition 'woman.'" The book traces the dominant ideologies of womanhood and how black women adapted those ideologies to reflect their own situations. Second, *Reconstructing Womanhood* "questions those strands of contemporary feminist historiography and literary criticism which seek to establish the existence of an American sisterhood between black and white women." This poses a sharp challenge to contemporary feminist scholarship and especially to those tendencies within feminism which endeavor to describe white and black women as equal victims of patriarchy. Carby asserts: "Considering the history of the failure of any significant political alliances between black and white women in the nineteenth century, I challenge the impulse in the contemporary women's movement to discover a lost sisterhood and to reestablish feminist solidarity." Her intention is not to undermine the objective of "feminist solidarity," but she insists that "only by confronting this history of difference can we hope to understand the boundaries that separate white feminists from all women of color" (p. 6).

Carby's third objective is even more broadly ambitious. Traditional scholarship has viewed the turn of the century as an age of great men: Booker T. Washington and W. E. B. Du Bois. She proposes to revise our understanding of that period by calling attention to the writing of black women such as Frances Harper, Pauline Hopkins, Anna Cooper, and Ida B. Wells. And finally, as the book's title indicates, she proposes to examine the emergence of black women as novelists, situating them both in relationship to their historical antecedents and their contemporary contexts. This list of objectives is exciting because of its scope, its originality, and its audacity. Yet given the poor state of scholarship on most of the areas Carby targets, it also seems like much more

Black Figures, Signs, Voices

than can be adequately addressed in a book of well under two hundred pages.

Throughout the book Carby is at her best in challenging the views of other critics. This becomes apparent with her discussion of recent black feminist criticism in chapter 1. She traces this tradition from the publication of Barbara Smith's essay "Toward a Black Feminist Criticism" in 1977 and subsequently analyzes works by Deborah McDowell and Barbara Christian, noting the important contributions of each to the development of this critical discourse while also assessing their weaknesses. Smith's essay was a pioneering manifesto at a time when black feminist criticism was just beginning to take shape. It erred, however, according to Carby, in its inadequate account of the relation between fiction and reality and its equation of a black feminist perspective with the biological facts of being black and female (pp. 7–10). She credits McDowell with offering a useful critique of Smith's essay, especially in terms of her attention to methodological questions, but she asserts that McDowell defines feminism too broadly (pp. 11–13). Christian's work, she concludes, "represents a significant strand of black feminist criticism that has concentrated on the explication of stereotypes at the expense of engaging in the theoretical and historical questions raised by the construction of a tradition of black women [*sic*] writing" (p. 14).

Carby's own position offers a sharp contrast to the work of previous black feminist critics. She asserts: "What I want to advocate is that black feminist criticism be regarded critically as a problem, not a solution, as a sign that should be interrogated, a locus of contradictions. Black feminist criticism has its source and its primary motivation in academic legitimation, placement within a framework of bourgeois humanistic discourse" (p. 15). Her inquiry, in other words, is a study of specific, historically located struggles over language and signs. Hence, even concepts like racism, sexism, and rape have to be defined within a specific historical context and not regarded as transhistorical, essentialist categories. Her approach is to examine how black women use writing to define their own identity within specific contexts and not to assume that these women belong to some "tradition" which maintains the same intentions, strategies, and definitions throughout the course of history.

In each of her discussions, Carby summarizes and analyzes the pertinent historical and literary scholarship. Indeed, her assessments of the scholarship provide some of the most compelling and lucid moments in this book. Her discussion of the cult of true womanhood (pp. 24–27), comparing black and white women during the antebellum years, is splendid. In subsequent chapters, her concise and accurate summaries of arguments by John Blassingame, Nina Baym, and August Meier are all similarly excellent. Throughout, Carby displays an admirable talent for challenging conventional wisdom without dismissing or misrepresenting those scholars with whom she disagrees.

Her best chapters, in my view, are chapter 4 on Frances Harper and *Iola Leroy* and chapter 5 on Anna Cooper and Ida B. Wells. Her two chapters on Pauline Hopkins, however, are also important for their sustained treatment of a figure who had, until recently, been virtually forgotten; and the final chapter, though overly brief, offers provocative treatments of Jessie Fauset and Nella Larsen. At one point, Carby declares that "the novels of black women should be read not as passive representations of history but as active influence within history" (p. 95). She reads the essays of Cooper and Wells in the same manner. To conceive writing in this way gives us a different context within which to assess this writing. Such works, for Carby, are not just aesthetic artifacts, self-expressions, or reflections of the epoch. As she notes of *Iola Leroy,* Harper intended to hand her readership a political weapon (p. 94). If this is the case, then it becomes the job of the critic to consider what materials are available for the fashioning of such literary weapons and also how effective they turn out to be.

On this latter question, Carby is sometimes puzzlingly quiet. Her argument that *Iola Leroy* should be viewed as a "handbook" for black intellectual activism and self-help is persuasive, but she does not offer an adequate assessment of the ideas which the book proposes. We cannot doubt Harper's good intentions, but how useful was her emphasis on temperance? Similarly, was Anna Cooper's Euro-centrism and advocacy of Christian missionary work a likely blueprint for the social advancement of the black masses? Given the sharpness with which Carby addresses political issues in other contexts (as, for example, in her comments on Jessie Fauset), her decision to stress the political intentions of these writers rather than to analyze their political ideas seems peculiar.

The conclusion of this book is too abrupt. Indeed, it can barely be said to have a conclusion. It just stops, never pulling together the various thematic strands which run through the book. And the truncated final chapter is conspicuously out of proportion with the previous chapters. Like Gates's *Figures in Black*, this book contains an excessive number of typographical errors. (In an especially unfortunate one, the pro-slavery ideologue Thomas Dew appears as "Thomas Drew" [p. 27].) But despite these minor problems, *Reconstructing Womanhood* is an exciting work. It maintains a high level of scholarly integrity and introduces methodologies new to Afro-American literary studies which can be productively appropriated by other scholars. And it presents fresh, provocative readings of many important texts. Hazel Carby has written a challenging and original book which does not rely on idiosyncratic excess and rhetorical tricks to assert its distinctiveness. *Reconstructing Womanhood* is likely to be indispensable reading in this field for a long time to come.

John Callahan's title *In the African-American Grain* self-consciously invokes the title of William Carlos Williams's seminal volume of essays, *In the American Grain*. But it also brings to mind another antecedent: one which moves in a different direction. In the seventh section of his "Theses on the Philosophy of History," Walter Benjamin reflects upon the parade called "civilization." He concludes: "There is no document of civilization which is not at the same time a document of barbarism. And just as such a document is not free of barbarism, barbarism taints also the manner in which it was transmitted from one owner to another. A historical materialist therefore dissociates himself from it as far as possible. He regards it as his task to brush history against the grain" (*Illuminations*, pp. 256–57). Speaking from the standpoint of the Marxist tradition, Benjamin reminds us of the profound difference between working with the grain and working against it. It is the difference between smoothing the grain in its natural course and raising the grain for closer scrutiny.

What would it mean to brush African-American writing against the grain? Following Benjamin, it would mean to inquire regarding the social conditions under which the works were produced and transmitted. It would also mean seeking out their "taint" of "barbarism," which presumably means their complicity in the dominant culture, the complicity which allows them to be transmitted and tolerated at all. If we assume, as all four of these books do, that works of Afro-American literature are characteristically—at least on some level—gestures of self-assertion and self-affirmation, then we must also recognize that to feel the need for self-assertion and self-affirmation implies an acceptance, though perhaps not an endorsement, of the fact of subordination. This may be as subtle as an acceptance of the group identity—"blackness" or any cognate name—first mandated by the oppressor as a synecdoche for the master/slave relationship. Such an acceptance constitutes a taint, an infectious sliver, which regenerates the tongue of the oppressor in the mouth of the oppressed.

The grain of our past is already established. But if we go with the grain, we can only hope to polish the surfaces which we already know. Perhaps the highest challenge of the critic is to work against the grain so tenaciously that we destroy this familiar veneer, exposing submerged strata and unrecognized patterns, embodying aspects of identity which conventional definitions and affirmations have long concealed. Our task may be not to affirm but to discover who we are.

The *Canterbury Tales* for a New Age

Martin Stevens

    Lee Patterson. *Negotiating the Past: The Historical Understanding of Medieval Literature.* Madison: University of Wisconsin Press, 1987. xiii, 239 pp.

    Beverly Boyd, ed. *The Prioress's Tale.* A Variorum Edition of the Works of Geoffrey Chaucer, Vol. II, Part 20. Norman: University of Oklahoma Press, 1987. xxviii, 195 pp.

    Robert M. Jordan. *Chaucer's Poetics and the Modern Reader.* Berkeley: University of California Press, 1987. viii, 182 pp.

    Carl Lindahl. *Earnest Games: Folkloric Patterns in the* Canterbury Tales. Bloomington: Indiana University Press, 1987. xi, 197 pp.

    Leonard Michael Koff. *Chaucer and the Art of Storytelling.* Berkeley: University of California Press, 1988. x, 298 pp.

    Laura Kendrick. *Chaucerian Play: Comedy and Control in the* Canterbury Tales. Berkeley: University of California Press, 1988. xi, 215 pp.

Now that modern criticism of the *Canterbury Tales* is settling into the second century of its existence, it is perhaps a worthwhile endeavor to take a closer look at some selected scholarly production of two years to discover what sorts of projects and issues occupy the attention of Chaucerians. It would, of course, be foolhardy to characterize the books chosen for this review as representative of present-day activity or to suggest that the approaches found here are likely to be trend-setting. The human sciences, and surely foremost among them the study of literature, have undergone and are undergoing such permutations that it is no longer possible to speak of one or two dominant schools of interpretation as was possible in a simpler time, the post-War era, when the choice for a model among Chaucer scholars was straightforward: either one followed the New Criticism with a program of interpretation often not openly declared (intention, after all, was regarded a fallacy) or one became a Robertsonian, an approach that in contrast was overdetermined. Some few, who failed to interest themselves in theoretical positions, and who were attracted at once to the verbal icon and to the icon of Christian art, may even on occasion have crossed the boundary.

What is therefore most immediately obvious about the books in this review is their variety of approach. In part, it will soon become clear, this variety has its origin in the kinds of studies I have selected to examine. One focuses on the history of scholarship and evaluates theoretical positions. Another presents a definitive edition. Still another establishes a new descriptive poetics. The remaning books fall into the general classification of criticism, each addressing the *Canterbury Tales* in particular. Apart from the fact that all the books are concerned more or less with Chaucer and his poetry, the six books—even the one in which contemporary theory is quite justifiably absent—are similar in insisting on the importance of *how* we read Chaucer. The emphasis is clearly on the assumptions and the tools we have available to understand Chaucerian poetics. Each book, therefore, as an act of interpretation (and that includes the edition), aims to persuade its reader to adopt a methodology with which to perceive more successfully the meaning of the text. If any one characteristic stands out as common among the new methodologies—and here I do exclude the edition—it is that readings are no longer meant to enlighten as self-standing acts of interpretation; rather, they are to be seen as paradigmatic or exemplary. The pairing of Canterbury pilgrims, especially those seen as opposites, forms a favorite subject, for these figures afford the means to test the efficacy of the approach that has isolated them. Most important perhaps as a summary observation is the fact that these books are not intent, as their *raison d'être*, on making substantive discoveries. Rather, they justify themselves as new ways to perceive. My review begins with the broadly historical, the editorial, and the theoretical. It ends with an examination of three specific interpretive approaches.

Patterson's *Negotiating the Past,* as its title indicates, is not exclusively devoted either to Chaucer studies or to the *Canterbury Tales.* Yet, in some respects, at least its first chapter and perhaps also its second rank among the most important writings on Chaucer scholarship in recent years. The book itself is basically concerned with historicism and medieval studies. Divided into three parts—"Historicism and Its Discontents," "Inventing Originality," and "Medieval Historicism"—it offers six chapters (three previously published) which focus on the historical context within which we read Chaucer, the texts of *Piers Plowman,* and a variety of medieval romances. The meaning of the title phrase "negotiating the past" is perhaps best explained in Professor Patterson's own words:

The difference between past and present must be both absolute and yet, if history is to be written at all, negotiable; the present is the custodian of the past, and yet its obsessive interest and unwitting reenactments allow the slave to become the master; the poetic text is created by history and yet continually proclaims a transhistorical value—a paradox that also governs the relation of subjectivity to the material world from which it derives, and so on. [p. xiii]

Patterson sees the need for diachronic study; he asks in the face of the synchronic, "totalizing vision of an entrapping world" of the New Historicism and of Foucault's view of the "carceral society," for a transhistorical understanding of the individual's place in history (p. 65). At the same time, he rejects the positivist's enclosure of history as a moment in the past presumably recreated with scientific objectivity. Historical study is misperceived in either case, and the individual disappears in both: the time-denying model of the New Historicist and the time-obsessed model of the positivist. What emerges from this study is a perceptive analysis of historical method and its underlying theory. The contribution of the book is stronger in its power of analysis than synthesis. The essays that demonstrate the transhistorical negotiation of history that Patterson wants to encourage are not significantly new or different in approach from what the most solid of contemporary scholarship, including Patterson's own essays, has been doing all along. At best, especially in the lively discussion of the Alliterative *Morte D'Arthur,* he shows how a fine-tuned diachronic understanding of the process of history can make the historicism of literary works come alive.

But my interest in this review must focus especially on Chapter 1, "Historical Criticism and the Development of Chaucer Studies." Here Patterson lays the foundation for his general look at the historiography of medieval literary scholarship. Chapter 1 presents a wide-angled critical review of the genealogy of Anglo-American medieval studies (with little emphasis on the "Anglo"—one of the few shortcomings of the chapter). As critical historiography of medieval studies and what it means to be a medievalist or Chaucerian in American scholarly circles, it is simply splendid. It compares in method, approach, and acuity of historiographical insight with a similarly fine opening chapter, O. B. Hardison's magisterial "Darwin, Mutations, and the Origin of Medieval Drama," in *Christian Rite and Christian Drama in the Middle Ages* (Baltimore: Johns Hopkins University Press, 1965). Patterson focuses attention in this chapter on the two coordinate movements already mentioned that dominated Chaucer studies for over a quarter of a century after World War II: the New Criticism, especially as exemplified by Donaldson and Muscatine, and the Exegetes, led by Robertson. But to place those movements into a larger historical perspective, he goes back, much as Hardison did, to the nineteenth-century foundations in the field. He believes, rightly I think, that all historical study is political, even that which claims to be objective and scientific. The notion that medievalists are a special grouping in the profession is to some extent the result of a self-inspired isolation based on the notion that their "historical criticism" is somehow purer, because more external and documentary, than the scholarship of other fields. As Patterson points out, for the medievalist, "the phrase 'historical criticism' is a code word for a densely annotated and narrowly argued reading of an often aggressively moralistic cast" (p. 3). Medievalists like to see themselves as above the fray, as unpolitical (recall the fierce resistance of many to political relevance in the sixties). Patterson shows that this delusory asceticism is traceable largely to the positivism that reigned over scholarship in the nineteenth century. The recovery of the medieval vernacular text was very much a political enterprise. It divided into two intellectual camps. The first, led by the likes of Bishop Percy, Wordsworth, Carlyle, and the "Young Englander" movement, was "universalist, institutional, and deeply conservative" (p. 9). Its object was to look to the feudal past as a model for social organization. The second, especially in the popular writings of Ruskin and Morris, though also concerned with the celebration of primitive origins, was pluralist and individualist. Its orientation was liberal-progressive, and it influenced such pioneer scholars as J. M. Kemble and F. J. Furnivall, who saw "medieval literature . . . as the expression of a human nature valuably different from our own . . . because it was unconstrained by narrow and dehumanizing institutions" such as the Church (p. 14). It is this mode of "transhistorical humanism" that formed the Chaucer of Whig historiography.

All of this led to a bifurcation in the second generation of scholarship which curiously looked to both nineteenth-century camps for its inspiration. From the universalists, it borrowed the emphasis on recovering the historical context. From the Whigs, it looked to establish a Chaucer who spoke as an individual genius to all time. The first of these perspectives—and sometimes the same scholar worked in both modes—focused largely on external documentation, and it yielded evidence based on minutiae and on genetic explanation. Its principal medium was the source study, which was so influential that it found literary origins not only in written sources but also in specific occasions and historical persons. John M. Manly's effort to find real-life counterparts for the Canterbury pilgrims is perhaps the best-known example of this scholarly bias. Interestingly, the prevailing realism and naturalism of the early twentieth century was a concomitant to source study, and the two combined to present the literary text as a mirror (sometimes distorted) of historical fact. But it all was done in the interest of emulating the methodology of the sciences.

The other mode curiously devalued the scholarship of the

universalist approach and produced highly subjective appreciations which typically obviated "the need for interpretation" (p. 18). R. K. Root's *The Poetry of Chaucer* (1906) was the first book written in this vein, but others like those of Kittredge (which is perhaps least representative of Patterson's classification), Patch, Tatlock, Lawrence, and Malone offered the same general orientation. The two approaches seen juxtaposed paradoxically produced a scholarship that canceled itself out. The disregard by the Whig approach of the recovered contextualism leads Patterson to characterize American Chaucer criticism prior to World War II as a historicism which "decrees that the more that is known about a text the less it can be said to mean" (p. 18).

The post-World War II period produced the two schools which all Chaucerians must still take into account. The first of these was that of the New Critics, who, in their liberal, humanist bias (now more likely seen as elitist and, therefore, conservative) rewrote "the traditional conception of the Whig Chaucer." In the hands of E. T. Donaldson, the New Critical Chaucer eschewed historicism and highlighted the ever-present author as proprietor who adroitly hid from the reader behind curtains of irony (witness "Chaucer the Pilgrim"). The intent was to highlight character (thus continuing by indirection the bias of such roadside drama critics as Kittredge and Lumiansky) and to demonstrate that the program of *Canterbury Tales* was the emancipation of the individual, an ahistorical theme that was the basis as well of the most powerful New Critical study of its time, Charles Muscatine's *Chaucer and the French Tradition*.

It is clear that Patterson very much admires Muscatine's particular kind of humanistic literary history which focuses on stylistics. One wishes, however, that he had expanded more fully on his own theoretical approach, which throughout the book is left less well articulated than one would expect. His appreciation for the Muscatine model is relegated to a footnote (p. 25, n.38), when either at the end of this chapter or the next, which reviews Marxist and New Historical approaches (both of which he finds inadequate as models), he owed the reader a constructive summary and surely a normative guideline that would explain just how his own transhistoricism differs from or improves upon

Muscatine's. It isn't quite enough to ask the reader to form his own answer to that question by extrapolating it from the four substantive essays that follow the historiographical and theoretical chapters of overview. In his fight against "absolute historicism," a force he seems to see equally in operation at the universalist beginnings of medieval studies and at the present time in the New Historicist approach (which hasn't really touched medieval studies, as Patterson himself observes), one comes to wonder—and I say this not at all in derision, because I admire the way Patterson practices historical scholarship—whether he himself is a closet Whig. Certainly his view that "we inevitably enter into elaborate and endless negotiations" with the past (p. 72), a process from which we can glean the transhistorical essence of humanistic values, is a way of looking at history as a source for enlightenment and at some unarticulated level of self-improvement. And that is indeed the essence of Whiggism. Perhaps in these days when the dominant theoretical arguments assume an all-encompassing power in the dialectic of history or in the institutions of a "carceral society," it is not fashionable to make such an admission.

But while Muscatine's form of New Criticism receives at very least a qualified approbation from Patterson, there is no doubt where he stands on the other dominant post-War school, the Exegetes. In part, of course, the Exegetes are the easiest "school" to gloss; that is so because they spelled out their program so articulately. Neither Donaldson nor Muscatine ever really expatiated on the theoretical grounds which formed their criticism, but *The Preface to Chaucer* is predominantly a theoretical work. This makes Robertson an easy target. The particular kind of historicism which Robertson advocates is anti-humanistic, conservative, and institutional. Its method, like that of the New Historicism, is formalistic in the sense that form dictates content and meaning. In its rigorous objection to Romanticism, which it sees as co-extensive with modernism, the exegetical school of the Robertsonians declares itself as opposed at once to objective historicism and subjective criticism. Patterson sees the exegetic method of Ernst Gombrich and the iconography of Emile Mâle, with its emphasis on religious devotion, as the source of the

American school of exegetical studies. With the emphasis on the hegemonic authority of a clerical culture and its totalizing ideology, the Robertsonian school contributed, in Patterson's view (and in mine), to the isolation of medieval studies in America. By claiming that the medieval period was self-enclosed and entirely dominated by the overarching spiritual values of the Church, the Exegetes thrived on the "otherness" of their adopted culture, and, as a result, with their emphasis on codes (e.g., Latin, iconography, and Augustinian commentary), they enlarged upon the separation from the rest of the canon of English departments that had already been put into practice in the study of medieval literature. It occurs to me that the Exegetes created a professional *Lebensart* that was a mirror image of their conception of medieval culture. Professionally they lived what they preached.

Patterson recognizes the debt that the exegetical school owed to German cultural historians like Auerbach, Spitzer, Curtius, and Panofsky. The whole story of that debt still awaits telling, as does the debt of American medieval studies to English scholars like Stenton, Smalley, Tolkien, Lewis, Woolf, and Whitelock. One wonders, furthermore, what influence European politics, especially the rise of national socialism, might have had even quite indirectly on medieval studies. Was the flight of Auerbach from Nazi Germany, his exile in Turkey, and his eventual presence at the Advanced Institute at Princeton influential in the flourishing if not the formation of the exegetical school? He certainly played a large role in bringing awareness to typological interpretation. And did the Nazi emphasis on Germanic culture encourage a largely unspoken resistance to the folklore studies that created the cult of the hero? Do we, in this oblique way, perhaps owe the Christian *Beowulf* to Hitler? These are larger questions that Patterson clearly couldn't address in an essay-length study devoted to Chaucer scholarship. It is, however, a tribute to the stimulation of his book that this type of speculation is encouraged by the sweep and power of intellect that it manifests.

An essay such as this is perhaps not the place to consider recent publications in textual editing and commentary, since work of that sort requires special attention to data which can overwhelm the more general reader. But one can hardly disregard what may turn out to be the most important venture in Chaucer scholarship during the present generation. I therefore feel compelled to make some observations about the mammoth project launched by the University of Oklahoma, under the general editorship of Paul G. Ruggiers, *A Variorum Edition of the Works of Geoffrey Chaucer*. To date that edition has yielded six published volumes: *The Canterbury Tales: A Facsimile and Transcription of the Hengwrt Manuscript, with Variants from the Ellesmere Manuscript,* Paul G. Ruggiers, ed., Vol. I; *The Miller's Tale,* Thomas W. Ross, ed., Vol. II, Part 3; *The Nun's Priest's Tale,* Derek Pearsall, ed., Vol. II, Part 9; *The Physician's Tale,* Helen Storm Corsa, ed. Vol. II, Part 17; *The Prioress's Tale,* Beverly Boyd, ed., Vol. II, Part 20; and *The Minor Poems, Part One,* George B. Pace and Alfred David, eds., Vol. V. When completed, the Variorum will consist of eight volumes, most of which will appear in multiple parts. The projected edition of the complete *Canterbury Tales,* which will appear as Volume II, will consist of twenty-five hard-bound fascicles, one for each of the tales and one for the General Prologue. This review considers the most recently published fascicle, the edition of *The Prioress's Tale* by Beverly Boyd, as a way of examining the project at large.

Perhaps the most controversial aspect of this edition is the fact that it actually contains a newly edited text. As Donald C. Baker, one of the founding editors, makes clear in his general introduction to the *Canterbury Tales* volume, "a variorum text, as the term is generally understood, is primarily a text which will bear the weight of the notes *variorum*" (p. xvii). As used in this context, *variorum* is an adjective (gen., pl., masc. of Latin *varius*) extrapolated from the phrase *editio cum notis variorum.* The important element in a variorum edition is not the text but the notes and commentary, and frequently, as Baker points out, a variorum edition will forego entirely the re-editing of the work and key its commentary to the most authoritative edition already in print. It is noteworthy that until the University of Oklahoma launched this project, no variorum edition of Chaucer existed, a fact that itself is curious since Shakespeare and Milton, the two other chief canonical poets in English literature, did attract such editions in times that were entirely hospitable to scholarly undertakings of this nature. The reason for the absence of an earlier Chaucer variorum is not difficult to infer: the Chaucer manuscripts present such a difficult array of editorial problems that an authoritative text, even including the editions by Manly and Rickert and by Robinson, which have often been so regarded, does not exist to this day. It is perhaps ironic that the Oklahoma project should emerge precisely at a time when the sort of categorical objective historical scholarship that has always been associated with variorum editions has come under serious questioning. This is, of course, not to say that variorum editions necessarily conflict in theory and execution with the reigning dogmas of our time, but there is little question that such editions, with their concern for providing a scientifically derived editorial apparatus and their objective commentary which highlights the canonical place and genealogy of the work as literature, are out of keeping with some of the major present-day critical and theoretical emphases. I welcome the fact that forty-two of the leading Chaucer experts have agreed to contribute major scholarly efforts toward this project. In the aggregate, this edition will keep alive and perhaps even foreground a great tradition of literary scholarship, which surely will serve all ages and all emphases. Indeed, one hopes that the edition, once completed, will be updated periodically, so that the newer approaches will gain the same attention as their predecessors.

    The second controversial point about this project is the choice of the Hengwrt manuscript as a base text for the entire edition. The reason for this decision is clearly enunciated: the Hengwrt as a text "is as near as it is possible to get to what Chaucer must have written" (Baker, Vol. I, p. xviii). The intricate work of Manly and Rickert, which is still authoritative in its "Corpus of Variants," even though its editorial methodology has been brought into serious question by George S. Kane in a landmark essay, has demonstrated that Hengwrt required fewer emendations than any other text. For the sake of a line-by-line commentary, that is a very important critical point on which to base a variorum text, and consequently Volume I produced a facsimile of high quality with facing-page transcription that also includes all textual variants from the other authoritative manuscript, the Ellesmere, in side notes. The need for a new transcription was manifest since neither Manly-Rickert nor Robinson, the two most widely hailed full scholarly editions of the twentieth century, rendered a clearly identified copy-text. Robinson's edition, moreover, which serves as the base for the new *Riverside Chaucer,* has a cosmeticized text which regularizes the meter and the grammar. And even in its latest incarnation, this text has been shown to lack editorial independence since in fact it did not use the Ellesmere manuscript as its sole copy text but relied rather on the old Skeat edition for most of its emendations and its glossary (see Ramsey). The decision by the Oklahoma editors, therefore, to publish a facsimile with transcription of one of the two most authoritative manuscripts of the *Canterbury Tales* has most assuredly been vindicated. It is now possible for any Chaucer scholar quickly to ascertain how in all particulars the two manuscripts differ, and that feature alone is of enormous service to all serious readers.

But what of the choice of Hengwrt over Ellesmere? This is an issue that goes beyond the limits of an essay such as this, and, in any case, it raises so many complex questions that it clearly cannot be resolved here, if anywhere. It does, however, elicit some questions that deserve recognition. One must ask, for example, whether it is theoretically justified to choose a text as preferable because the accidentals and the variants are the part that seem to reflect most accurately the text that the author left us. The Chaucerian text is particularly difficult to establish, in part, as John Fisher has recently shown with exemplary clarity, because we have no idea of the shape of the foul papers on which its principal manuscripts are based. The fact is that the Ellesmere is also a highly authoritative and demonstrably early manuscript, which may or may not have been based on the same exemplar as Hengwrt. But what is preferable about the Ellesmere by virtually universal consent (the major dissident is Norman Blake) is its much more coherent order and its virtual completeness (if one accepts the widely held view that there was not to be a return journey). It is worth noting that the total number of errors in the Ellesmere as compared with the Hengwrt is very small indeed, and the emendations that would have been required had the

Ellesmere been chosen as the base text would not have significantly burdened or altered its apparatus. If the Ellesmere had indeed been made the base text, the facsimile text presented in the *Variorum Edition* as Volume I would have produced as a reference text that version which the vast majority of Chaucer scholars prefer. It would also have presented the tales in an order that is surely preferable to the garbled version presented by the Hengwrt manuscript (e.g., the Wife of Bath following the Cook, the Manciple in the middle of the text, the absence of the Cannon's Yeoman, the Melibeus as next to last before the Parson). One is led to wonder, all the editorial justifications notwithstanding, why in light of these larger considerations the editors chose the Hengwrt over the Ellesmere.

Beverly Boyd's edition of the *Prioress's Tale* can serve as a good example of the accomplishments and usefulness of the *Variorum Chaucer*. In its contents, it follows the established order laid down for all volumes. A large section is devoted to "Critical Commentary," which in turn is divided into a discussion of "Sources and Analogues," "Date," and a "Survey of Criticism." A second major section is devoted to "Textual Commentary." The final major section of the book is an edition of the text proper, which, in this instance, reproduces the Hengwrt text of the Prioress's Tale with emendation from Ellesmere only when Hengwrt is damaged and with light modern punctuation as well as capitalization. Collations with significant variant readings from other manuscripts and copious line-by-line annotations appear as footnotes to the text. Annotations provide a wide variety of comment on the meanings of difficult words, glosses from printed editions (which the Variorum includes among its "Corpus of Variants"), explanations of variants, interpretations of passages, liturgical allusions, iconographical symbolism, typology, spelling conventions (the annotation on *Jesu* in line 1789 is a model), historical contexts, and many other topics. One has the sense that these annotations are surely exhaustive and should therefore be of enormous help to any future scholar working on the Prioress's Tale.

Professor Boyd, whose personal qualities of grace, humility, and compassion register strikingly in the preface, remains almost entirely hidden from the reader in the text of the Critical Com-

The *Canterbury Tales* for a New Age

mentary, the part of the book that casual readers are most likely to peruse. I think this absence is a shame. It gives the commentary a sheen of objectivity that veils the critical judgment of a well-informed, thoughtful scholar. This is, of course, one of the traditions of the variorum species, but Boyd herself, in a moment of deliberate self-revelation, is aware "that there may in fact be two ways to do the impossible" (p. 62) when she praises Derek Pearsall, editor of the Variorum Nun's Priest's Tale fascicle, who notably does speak animatedly at times in the first person while still rendering the assignment of covering the waterfront of scholarship and criticism. If one is, therefore, willing to accept the survey of commentary, despite its veil of anonymity, as indeed a personal and expert account of what kinds of studies have been undertaken and what issues have mattered, one gains an interesting perspective on how Chaucer has been read over the years.

Since the discussion of "Sources and Analogues" and of "Date" is essentially noncontroversial, I will pass over those two sections to say a word about the "Survey of Criticism," the third and largest of the three chronologically treated sections under "Critical Commentary." One recognizes quickly in this survey how dominant Romantic realism has been in the criticism of this tale—and one suspects of Chaucer in general. Wordsworth, who we learn translated the tale in 1801, powerfully influenced most later commentators, with his observation of the teller's "fierce bigotry" as background for her "tender-hearted sympathies." This dual nature has served critics in all manner of ways to psychoanalyze Madame Eglentine, to give her status as a real person, who in the eyes of one of her most famous commentators, George L. Kittredge, saw her psyche in terms of "thwarted motherhood." That issue—the dual personality which inevitably conjoins the tale to the teller and hence to the portrait in the General Prologue—and the post-War concentration on its anti-Semitism, which is admirably summarized by Boyd (though I regret that she didn't include Albert Friedman's seminal article in her overview), constitute the basic critical concerns in the nearly two hundred years of modern criticism. In terms prepared by the Patterson essay, it seems clear, for this tale at least, that humanist, mostly ahistorical considerations have dominated, that Romantic sentimentalism is an easy ally of realist critics, and that the Exegetes have taken up very little of the critical space afforded to the Prioress.

The *Variorum Edition of the Works of Chaucer* is a major contribution to Chaucer scholarship, one that will unquestionably occupy a prominent place on our shelves. I am grateful to Boyd and the other editors, especially to Paul Ruggiers who created the project and pushed it forward, for making the text of the *Canterbury Tales* and the record of modern scholarship so easily accessible. It will be interesting to see in what ways its style will change over the years, and how both the treatment of the subject and the content of the criticism will make their belated entry into the postmodern era.

If new editorial projects reflecting old editorial concepts seem somewhat out of harmony with the times, theory and its applications surely fit the prevailing temperament. Robert M. Jordan is the first to give us a new theoretic base for the reading of Chaucer in a book-length study. Using the formulations of structuralism and Russian formalism, especially the work of Saussure, Jacobson, Genette, and Todorov, Jordan sets out to write a postmodernist guide to Chaucerian poetics.

The first chapter, entitled "Poetics and Rhetoric," provides the theoretical groundwork. Jordan argues from the outset against the application of a "realist poetics" such as guided the Jamesian concept of fiction and much of modernist Chaucerian literary criticism. The dogma of realism insists that the text of a poetic work is nonreflexive, it provides an "illusion of textlessness" (p. 17), and it insists on the organic unity defined by the equation of the sign with the thing that it represents. Thus the literary text imitates a segment of reality; it has no life of its own since it is governed by the shape of the world for which it is representational. In "The Art of Fiction" James sees "a living thing," a continuity between the text and the reality it represents, an organic fusion. Jordan says that Chaucer's fictions may give the illusion "that a fictional character possesses personal autonomy" (p. 18), but, in fact, they are the creation of a "rhetorical" or

The *Canterbury Tales* for a New Age 51

"pluralistic poetics," in which language is seen as a "medium distinct from its referent" (p. 12), one that creates its own realities. His nonorganic view "foregrounds the activity of writing" (p. 16), and it leads to the conclusion that, for example, Chaucer's pilgrims are not rounded characters or even types of real persons but rather voices which have been inscribed by Chaucer into the text. Jordan sees a distinct similarity between late medieval nominalism and present-day formalism in their insistence on the primacy and the ambiguity of language and in the "pluralism" that both systems of thought have fostered.

The next four chapters in the book focus on the major dream poems (the *Troilus* is curiously omitted entirely from Jordan's consideration in this book). In the *House of Fame* he sees what is essentially Chaucer's *ars poetica,* and as such it shares in subject matter, approach, and attitude with the techniques and viewpoints of modernist fiction (he uses such figures as Joyce, Nabokov, Borges, Beckett, Barth, and Calvino as examples). The central issue is not plot and character but the games we play with language. Contrary to the argument of many critics, there is no single thematic point or controlling theme in the *House of Fame.* Jordan holds that the poem, for example, is not about the conjunction of Fame and Love and Fortune. The "tidings" that it reviews are not fixed accounts that report a reality or an "ineffable idea"; they are written accounts in which everything is subordinated to "surface effects" (p. 45). The poem moreover does not provide us with a singleness of purpose, a logical progression: it is impossible to find agreement about the meaning of the narrative continuity from the story of Aeneas and Dido, to the flight of the Eagle, to the House of Fame. "Chaucer's poem . . . states as one of its themes and illustrates throughout by its own example that there is no singular truth" (p. 49). The Man of "gret auctorite" is an invention of sport. The poet is there, centrally, as a controlling presence; he is, however, a player of solipsistic games rather than an oracular authority. The interest for the reader should be on the sheer prolixity of the poem, on the rhetorical games, on all the surface effects by which the absent author ironically demonstrates his presence.

In the *Book of the Duchess,* Chaucer's earliest dream vision,

Jordan discovers an "unspoken poetics." The poem in his view is principally "about poetry." And while it is also an elegy and a poem of consolation, it cannot be read dramatically, and it must not be read to highlight the "unified consciousness" (p. 65) of the narrator or the Black Knight. In fact, the controlling compositional idea of the poem is expository, not narrative or lyrical. With its stylized expression of grief, it demonstrates critically the function of *amplificatio,* the micro-rhetoric that governed medieval lyric poetry. But Jordan's main interest lies more nearly with what he calls a "macro-rhetoric"—the way in which the parts of the poems cohere in a nonorganic reading.

Here unfortunately, as elsewhere in the book, a sensible and helpful approach to Chaucer's poetics remains a curiously empty shell. It shows us a method of reading the poem without ever entering its deepest levels of meaning. We get very little particular insight into the inorganic coherence of the three main parts (the dreamer's experience, the Ovidian story of Ceys and Alcyone, and the dream about the Black Knight). Nor are we guided to see what is surely at once an attack on and a defense of rhetoric, a point that, I believe, can be clarified with an examination of the similarity of language used to bewail the loss of love and the loss of life, an opposition that would yield especially well to deconstruction. The method here employed, moreover, does not allow for a consideration of the poem's outer purpose: how, for example, does the poem accord as a self-referential text about poetry and a poem to console Gaunt for the loss of his Duchess? These are critical questions of enormous importance. They deserved exploration in a chapter that tackles a good many basic issues that have never before been stated with such clarity and insight. This chapter and those on the *Parliament* and the Prologue to the *Legend of Good Women* are perhaps best regarded as a theoretical frame within which a new nondramatic or nonnarrational mode of interpretation can be developed.

It is, of course, finally in the *Canterbury Tales* that Jordan's poetic theory finds its richest ground for application. With its apparent mimetic frame, it has misled generations of scholars to highlight its alleged dramatic and narrational mode, and Jordan's "rhetorical poetics" are no doubt mined to best advantage here. Indeed, according to Jordan, Chaucer presents us in his last work with a new "essay" in poetics. Here the "narrative Chaucer is self-reflexively shaping the ever-shifting relationship between the presentational voice and represented content" (p. 120). Jordan proceeds to a discussion of the "representational voices" through a compositional analysis of three paradigm texts within the *Canterbury Tales:* the General Prologue, the Prologue and Tale of the Pardoner, and the Nun's Priest's Tale. The whole is designed to demolish the realist fixation on the persona and on "reified characters" and to show how the style and the voicing of the text change even where the reader might be hypnotized into finding an illusory representational depth. In the figure of the Monk, for example, we look in vain for a consistently characterized pilgrim-narrator; it is difficult to pin down a single narrative voice as one moves from "moral disapproval" to "sensuous appreciation" (p. 125). The whole of the General Prologue is crafted by an "unstable presentational voice" which varies in style and compositional pattern in a way that establishes the mode of the entire poem.

Jordan chooses to focus on the Pardoner because he is conceived as the most realistic of all the pilgrims in his act of storytelling. And yet, time and again, voices intrude in his fiction, such as the one that introduces the sermon on morality in the Prologue, which are not at all ascribable to the narrating persona. "The Pardoner is not fully 'alive,' the text is" (p. 136). By contrast, the Nun's Priest is a very indistinct narrating persona. The tale is Chaucer's, not the Nun's Priest's, and what we find in it is the same as in the Pardoner's Prologue and Tale, a mixture of presentational modes. The rhetorical variety of the tale, which brings to the reader "the discourse worlds of courtly romance, dream theory, physiological catalogue, narrative exemplum, beast fable, classical tale, philosophical disputation, and antifeminist lore" (p. 138), deemphasizes dramatic illusion and highlights the "brilliance of surface" (p. 147). Jordan concludes from these examinations that "the only subject is the absent poet" (p. 148).

The last chapter of the book focuses on endings, which Jordan sees as a patchwork of disunified styles. The Manciple's Tale is the "ultimate self-conscious fiction" (p. 152) since its basic concern as a narrative is with the function of language. Even here we find a variety of discourses and voices embedded in the narrative, and, once more, Chaucer is more interested in the act of simulating discourse than he is in presenting psychologically plausible speakers. But ultimately the concern of the Manciple's Tale is "the truth value of language consciousness" (p. 162). It resolves the issue by paradoxically advocating silence in a "torrent of language" (p. 162). The Parson's Tale, as the second ending, is stylistically completely different from the Manciple's because it is totally nonpoetic and nonliterary. Jordan regards it as a digression, since it is attributable to no known speaker in the *Canterbury Tales*. By positing an ending to the pilgrimage in the "celestial Jerusalem," the tale gives us a conclusion that is entirely alien to the fictive frame created in the General Prologue. It presents a rhetorical ending which gives greater emphasis to compositional surfaces than to verisimilitude. The Retraction is, of course, Chaucer's own leave-taking, though it is put in the framework of the "litel tretys," presumably the Parson's Tale to which it is attached. For Jordan it is altogether fitting that it, too, contains a compositional disunity, since we observe in it a shift from the Parson as speaker to Chaucer himself.

Jordan's book is clearly just a beginning. It gives us, as we enter a new century of Chaucer criticism, a well-defined base on which to examine Chaucer's major poetry as works of literary discourse. While much of what Jordan says is perhaps not new to the most recent vintage of Chaucer scholars (see, for example, Marshall Leicester's fine essay on the General Prologue or the brilliant last chapter in Jesse Gellrich's *The Idea of the Book*), his is the first truly theoretical book on Chaucer to have appeared in the postmodern era. It will no doubt be extremely influential.

Interestingly, the three interpretive books on the *Canterbury Tales* with which I have chosen to end this review essay have very little to do with the historical, editorial, and theoretical approaches reviewed thus far. Not one, for example, would agree with Jordan that the key to a new understanding of Chaucer is to recognize the text first and foremost as literary artifice. Two of the critics, in fact, give weight to the *Canterbury Tales* as an oral performance (Lindahl and Koff), and all three put a premium on the interaction of storytellers. The latter emphasis leads almost inevitably to a consideration of a dramatic if not mimetic text. Yet each of the three looks upon the work from a different angle: Carl Lindahl is a folklorist who claims familiarity with literary criticism and social history (though his artless admission in these times that he practices "informed new criticism" will surely raise eyebrows); Leonard Koff expresses allegiance to hermeneutics and seems to draw inspiration from a number of reader-oriented theorists, though his method most resembles that of Wolfgang Iser's "implied reader"; and Laura Kendrick draws on psychoanalysis and developmental psychology to explain the nature of play and game in Chaucer. The approaches, then, are varied, confirming even more strongly than we may have realized hitherto that virtually every new book on Chaucer brings with it an individualized rationale and plan of reading.

According to Lindahl in *Earnest Games* we have failed to recognize sufficiently the evidence not only that Chaucer's text was addressed to an oral audience, rather than to the silent reader (as we normally assume in our time), but that the work reflects the mode of a folk performance. Evidence for this proposition, according to Lindahl, lies in the frequent allusions to listening. Yet such evidence strikes me as unreliable. The instances in which Chaucer breaks his narrative frame are legion, and we know in fact that silent reading was widely practiced by the end of the fourteenth century (see especially Saenger). Moreover, the vocabulary associated with listening that Lindahl singles out is often ambiguous. Thus when Chaucer implores "*herkneth* with a good entencioun" in the *House of Fame* (p. 2) he is not necessarily saying "Listen," but more generally "Apply the mind to what is said, attend"; see *OED*. Hearken, v. 3. The problem with Lindahl's premise for me at the outset is that the text by its very nature is "literary," and we have no external evidence to make it a transcript of a performance.

But that is not to deny the influence of folklore on the structure of the storytelling activity and even on the character of the audience and the nature of its varied responses. It is in these areas of interpretation that Lindahl is most effective. He sees, for example, a social grid with two modes of communication dictated by class. The first is elite communication, which was basically impersonal and reflected a long learned tradition as well as the established rules of rhetoric. It squares, as he points out later, with what Chaucer traditionally regarded as "auctorité." The folk mode, on the other hand, was spontaneous. It was centered "outside the boundaries of institutionalized learning" and depended on "popular concensus" (p. 8). Stories told orally will be finished only if they are approved by their audiences. They can be serious in intent, and, indeed, at their most significant they teach "the powerless to survive" (p. 11). For Chaucer, this popular mode was, in essence, what he called the world of "experience." It is the folk mode that Lindahl wants to examine, particularly for the strategies by which the pilgrims play their "earnest games" to express "their most negative and heretical thoughts" (p. 10).

The Canterbury pilgrims are organized in two "frames around the frame." The first of these is supplied by Lindahl, not by Chaucer—the parish guild. Although it is not entirely clear to me why we need this "frame," for which there is no textual warrant, Lindahl finds the parish guild an institution of great relevance to Chaucer's company of pilgrims beause it was essentially middle class and yet egalitarian in an economic sense. The second frame is the one we all know: the pilgrimage. Happily, Lindahl drops the guild as one of the two "frames around the frame," when in Chapter 3 he turns to the pilgrimage as both a source and a subject of oral storytelling. Showing, first of all, that both the profane and the sacred (game and earnest, ludic and pious) were "essential to the spirit" of the work (p. 32), he indicates that Chaucer, even despite himself (as attested by the Retraction and a certain polarization among pilgrims according to the intensity of their piety), casts his work in the "pray-and-play" ethic that prevailed prior to the days when pilgrimage became a subject for criticism by reformers. According to Lindahl, the *Canterbury Tales* are in this sense part of a very important formation of popular culture. They reflect the spirit of the feast, of the Corpus Christi plays, and, most important, of the entertainment of travel. Travellers traditionally are noted for telling tall tales, and most of the Canterbury pilgrims "lie with delight" (p. 39) as they engage each other in the fictional contest on the road to the truth of God. Lindahl then goes on to show how much of the *Canterbury Tales* reflects the content of oral fiction. He observes that many of the tales are concerned with travel (five begin on the road), many share with the folktale a setting that is ordinary and familiar, and most feature narrators that make themselves the heroes of their fiction. These are interesting observations but they are not systematically explored. One can think of numerous exceptions to these categories, and it is perhaps only with the application of one criterion at a time rather than all criteria at once that they hold up.

At the heart of Lindahl's argument is the view—notably contra Bakhtin—that Chaucer "reshapes literature into festival" (p. 45). The literary enterprise is thus not a subversive mechanism; rather, it reaffirms that which unifies society. Lindahl looks at nine popular festivals, noting their fundamental similarities: four are the revels of the *gentil* (that is, of nobles and bourgeois): *cour amoreuse*, London pui, may day, and love debate; five, on the other hand, are "mixed-class celebrations": mystery plays, feasts of fools, boy bishop, lord of misrule and mummings, ridings of St. George. These nine forms of festivals are shown as sharing a great many qualities with the *Canterbury Tales* (in fact, nine again). Thus, for example, all or nearly all the festivals—those of earls as well as churls—have a presiding figure, an autocratic ruler: the prince of the pui, the boy bishop, the queen of love, Harry Bailly. In only two qualities are the festivals unlike: first, those that represent the *gentil* compete for a prize, while those of the churls engage in occupational rivalry; and second, the elite games duplicate the social order, while those of the churls rearrange it (usually from the bottom up). Lindahl uses this interesting typology to demonstrate how game rules inhere in the *Canterbury Tales*. He also shows that at times Chaucer changes the rules. When, for example, Harry Bailly can't maintain his autocratic stance and reassumes his more churlish social position (e.g., in his challenge of the Pardoner), Chaucer gives us a prefiguration of the breakup of the festival world and intimates that "the older estates model is not adequate to describe the society of these fourteenth-century pilgrims" (p. 60).

In subsequent chapters, Lindahl expands on the folkloristic nature of the *Canterbury Tales*. He shows, for example, how they have the propensity to put "fantasy and reality into complex interrelation" (p. 63) and how this feature works when tellers are absorbed in their tales as is most palpably the case with the Pardoner. He also demonstrates that the power of the angry word in the churls' tales reflects the nature of angry exchanges among social equals, especially those of the lower classes, and that most such exchanges transpire within trade affiliations. In these and other reflections, Lindahl makes clear that he is looking at the influence of folklore from the standpoint of function rather than source or analogue (as has been the custom over the years). In line with that approach, he produces what he calls a "Folk Rhetoric of the Pilgrims," in which he attempts to furnish a guide for churls' talk analogous to the more customary rhetoric for elite speech.

Perhaps the most original contribution of the book, but also its most controversial, is the attempt to see the *Schwank* rather than the *fabliau* as the source of the churls' tales (especially as in the Miller's, Reeve's, Summoner's, and Friar's). A *Schwank* is defined as a realistic tale, relatively long (though tradition and Lindahl's examples would refute this characteristic), well-structured, concerned usually with eating, drinking, or sex, and humorous as well as mocking. As a form of folk humor, it was omnipresent in the Middle Ages. In Chaucer, the *Schwank* would be a tale told by churls about churls in which the teller identifies one of the characters with a rival class or trade. The story is marked especially by the reversal characteristic of festivals and holiday (a feature that would explain the resemblance between it and certain Corpus Christi plays). One important characteristic of a Chaucerian *Schwank* is how "the dupe reflects the personality of the teller's foe" (p. 129). The common traits of these churls' tales are anonymity, situational aptness, testing of the opposition, and ridicule by association. Lindahl argues somewhat circularly that while *Schwaenke* survive in modern folklore, the best examples we have of the common churls' tales in the Middle Ages are those in the *Canterbury Tales*. In his lengthy discussion of the four tales that allegedly are true *Schwaenke*, Lindahl shows how various oral features are put to use by Chaucer in constructing his narratives. The Reeve's Tale is seen as typical of the process, since it incorporates the viewpoint of the stereotyped Norfolk man, who was in fact a commonplace of the *Schwank*.

The argument that Lindahl advances is certainly interesting. The *Schwank* allows us to see more similarities among the tales in question than the classification of *fabliau* was ever able to do. It also accounts more adequately for the purpose of the tale (the lie to tell a truth, the requital, etc.) than does the sort of formal or narratological explanation that tradition has taught us to apply. Yet the new classification also introduces problems. For example, we have to search elsewhere to account for the more overt literary features. Thus, while Lindahl's analysis highlights the use of the Miller's Tale to embarrass the Reeve, and shows us how John is the typical victim character of the *Schwank*, it says virtually nothing about Alison and Absalon, or about the parody of the Annunciation, or about the sophisticated parody of the *hortus conclusus* and the allusion to the Song of Songs. The method unfortunately oversimplifies Chaucer's churls' fiction and reconstitutes it, with a folklore bias, as a new kind of "roadside drama," resurrecting the specter that we have worked so hard to dispel. All in all, here as elsewhere, Lindhal has brought some very interesting material to bear on our understanding of the churls' tales, but, at least as far as he takes the argument in this book, it cannot quite carry the weight that he assigns to it.

Leonard Koff relies basically on hermeneutics to reevaluate *Chaucer and the Art of Storytelling*. In a beginning chapter, he rejects the view that the *Canterbury Tales* presents the reader with an "inner meaning" which requires decoding. He therefore takes fundamental issue with both the New Critics and the Exegetes, both schools of interpretation that assume concealment and obscurity of meaning through irony. In his view, modern interpretation has unnecessarily darkened the fiction of the *Canterbury Tales* by converting its narrative design from one addressed to the listener to one addressed to the silent reader. A narrator, according to Koff, is a different kind of storyteller in print from what he is in person. The Chaucerian narrator is "real." He may not have been Chaucer, but then he was someone reading aloud as if he were Chaucer. Koff insists that "Chaucer substitutes cooperative story-making between storyteller in the text and audience, for which the performer, or the reader himself performing, is the public-voiced link" (p. 33). Readers accustomed to public performance, according to Koff, knew that the unity of a text was provided by the "constant presence of the storyteller with an identifiable storytelling manner as a discontinuous part of the text" (p. 16). The method of reading suggested serves to remove Chaucer from his fiction and to foreground the story proper.

Storytelling in the Middle Ages was, according to Koff, the art of "re-telling." The retold story was however not designed "in theory to distort the original" (p. 38) but, by recovering it, to make it public, to put it in the present, and to make it useful. Since stories were performed out loud, they were "published by being read" (p. 41), and the audience thus became an active participant in creating its meaning. Thus even the reader functioned in the form of the listener—he had to conceive of narrative as declaimed and not consumed privately. In a sense the reader had to do with the declaimed text exactly what the writer had to do with his *auctorité:* renegotiate its meaning. The author/performer was thus a "literary servant," the "transmitter" of the original meaning and the "spokesman" for his *auctorité,* but not the final arbiter (p. 47). As such he lays bare "the idea of the text" so that "its inner point is available" (p. 50). "Because these stories have been heard before, hearing them again aligns readers with the ancient and general human tradition the stories seem to embody" (p. 50). Reading Chaucer's narratives, therefore, instead of being a *private* decoding of the text, such as an allegorical reading of a printed text requires, calls for what Koff identifies as "parabolic listening," the kind of listening that we must do to understand parables. He connects this mode of listening with "the allegory of the poets," a demystified, secular search of the intellect to find the link between the natural and the spiritual order in the universe—a link which is enabled for the listener/reader by a good storyteller (p. 51).

The concept of "parabolic listening" leads Koff to an application of Gadamerian methodolgy which would allow the individual reader to decode Chaucer's indeterminate text as a personal act of interpretation. "Chaucer's narratives simply 'put the case,' the imagined situation, and ask that we interpret it" (p. 72). A story is consequently made and remade, every time that it is read; it combines past and present, and that is always the essence of its meaning. "*Life* becomes art when we read" (p. 71). Harry Bailly thus becomes a model for the reader by providing unabashedly personal readings in his responses to the storytellers. Each reader, like the Host, creates the kind of Monk he needs. The indeterminacy of Chaucer's text and its pluralism of interpretation are built into its framework. The very notion that tales become part of an agon among the pilgrims of telling, listening, and answering, allows the reader also to partake in this act. Koff, moreover, makes hermeneutic applications even within the stories. Chaunticleer, for example, when he foregoes the traditional meaning of *In principio* and leaps into the barnyard from his beam to "feather" Pertelote, has "stepped off a text" and has provided his own reading of the world ("the way a reader might"). Making the wider application to the hermeneutic process, Koff concludes that "Chaucer takes seriously the notion of standing on a text in order to understand the world just because such cockiness, such surefire and persistent reading of the world from an appropriated text, generates intellectual life, however misguided, however comic, however wrong" (p. 104). The subjectivity of this approach is, of course, overarching. It virtually frees the reader, along with Chaunticleer, to make any imaginitive leap that he desires and "feather" anybody. Reading is, simply put, a sport, not ever a discipline, and any attempt to arrive at a common understanding of a literary text is conceptually disallowed by this method.

I have attempted in the foregoing to summarize the first three chapters of Koff's book which provide the theoretical argument. He goes on in the remaining chapters to look at individual narrative situations in order to explore interpretive problems. In Chapter 4, he looks at the problem of "Who Speaks for the Wife of Bath?"; in Chapter 5, he contrasts voiced and voiceless performances in the Pardoner's and the Knight's tales (recalling in approach, though certainly not in method, what Jordan did with the Pardoner and the Nun's Priest); in Chapter 6 he explores through an examination of the Franklin's and the Prioress's tales the kinds of historicized readings that Chaucer's text, seen in its alterity, encourages; and, finally, in Chapter 7, he looks at what he calls "Chaucer's Leave-Takings" (i.e., Fragment X) as a way of encouraging cooperative readings which assume "the freedom of readers to read personally and to be judged accordingly" (p. 226). With the possible exception of Chapter 6, which among other things makes an interesting (though not original) argument for taking the anti-Judaism of the tale as a typological premise to test the religious piety of Chaucer's age, the book is an adventure in the indeterminacy of present-day criticism at its most self-indulgent. Perhaps the clearest instance of that position is in the discussion of the Wife of Bath. Because the prologue and tale continually shift in their view toward women, sometimes speaking in their defense and sometimes at their expense, Koff performs an imaginary exercise in which he conjures up the differences in meaning that would be rendered if a man or a woman were the performing narrator. Presumably the readings would give different emphases in accordance with the sex of the narrator: "For women, the Wife of Bath demonstrates masterful feminine wisdom"; "For men, the Wife is infinitely compelling" (p. 138); "For a man . . . the Wife's market analogies describe trading in the world as ascendancy and the sharing of power"; "For a woman . . . the Wife's analogies describe trade as play and allurement" (p. 134); "For a man, the Wife's conspiratorial circle may be both frightening and inviting"; "For a woman, the Wife's circle of 'Wyves' may be amusing" (p. 149). Quite apart from the fact that this conjectured performance difference is not presented as an extended contrastive interpretation for each position (one wonders by the way whether the gender of the conjectured audience wouldn't also have to be specified in this hypothetical interpretive experiment), this exercise of the imagination seems to set up oppositions that the text, in its wisdom, deconstructs. Who says that all women or all men necessarily read with the same sexual bias? If that were indeed the case, how could a man have written the Wife of Bath's Prologue and Tale in the first place?

Koff's book, I fear, despite its learnedness, takes the autonomy of the critic to the brink of his demise. In place of the dark interpretation of the ironist, who presents the reader with a verifiable if sometimes questionable exegesis, it provides the dark interpretation of "parabolic listening" which seems to exist at the whim of some imagined performance. It is also marred by a darkness of style which impedes understanding and risks the reader's exasperation. Its favorite device is the embedded sentence, whose Chinese boxes of parentheticals enclose ever smaller nuggets of meaning and make the sense of the whole so dense that sometimes its meaning cannot be recovered at all. Here is a typical instance:

If such remembered meaning is intended—and this is highly, though appropriately, speculative—then the Host has, like the Wife of Bath's own husbands, something to complain about, and Goodelief's "labbyng" tongue, like the Wife of Bath's—the Host tells us the name of his wife in his response to the Melibee—browbeats him. [p. 153]

Before leaving Koff's book, I feel compelled to note one further shortcoming, which, unhappily, it shares with all the other books covered in this review except Boyd's Variorum edition: the absence of a bibliography. Perhaps publishers, in order to reduce their costs, are no longer inclined to provide such apparatus, but when copious notes are supplied, as is the case in Koff's book, it is often a hardship to track down the first reference to a source that has been cited repeatedly. This is especially the case if the index fails to list the first reference to a work (e.g., the entry to C. H. Dodd in Koff's index). The bibliography remains a summary statement of the range of reference that a work embraces. It should not be allowed to be swept away by economies or neglect.

To read Laura Kendrick after Leonard Koff (as I did) is somewhat akin to reading the Miller after the Knight, or, perhaps more aptly, the Nun's Priest after the Monk. Here is a book about play that is also self-consciously playful, full of audacious interpretive moves, and, consequently, the liveliest, most keenly provocative book published in recent years on the *Canterbury*

Tales. The book, as its title indicates, takes Chaucerian play as its subject to discover what, in terms of modern psychological, psychoanalytic, and anthropological theory, making earnest out of game (and vice versa) really means. Demonstrating that this famous opposition deconstructs itself repeatedly, Kendrick sets out boldly to show just how laughter works as a metalinguistic sign in Chaucer's fiction. The reader is treated to a book that in its general appeal has a Chaucerian spirit about it. The voice of the author is never suppressed, but, by her own admission, it is frequently masked in the manner that critical writing encourages and even demands. What comes out of this interpretive effort is an exciting, controversial, often playfully revealing "page-turner," with suprises on almost every page. Chaucer's game and earnest have never been examined with so much zest, so much insight, and perhaps also so much interest in what Lee Patterson would call "negotiating the past." Critics may disagree with Kendrick's observations, and many will raise theoretical objections, as I shall, but I doubt that anyone will read the book and not be stimulated by the radiance of its intellect and the joy of its humor.

To explore the thesis of this book and to demonstrate its method, I can do no better than to jump into the middle of Chapter 2, "The Spirit vs. the Flesh in Art and Interpretation." Here Kendrick explores what she calls "the false 'no,'" which is silently voiced by critics, like Dryden, who "turn over the leaf" but linger long enough to summarize the obscene or salacious passages they are suppressing. It is Kendrick's point that even Augustine and Jerome in the process of rejecting carnality admit their interest in what they proscribe or, more accurately, allegorize: "The pleasure of Christian exegesis lies in finding ways not to have to give up the original sin entirely" (p. 28). In consequence, the critic who subscribes to "high seriousness" reads Chaucer's *sentence* without having to give up his "covert appreciation of *solas*" (p. 30). The act of sublimation is in effect an act of authorization, a reversal well known by Chaucer who, like his puritanic critics, wore a mask (of the fool, the churl, the naive rustic) to excuse the carnalities of his festive subversions. In a fastidious world—and Kendrick shows that Chaucer's world was

The *Canterbury Tales* for a New Age

indeed that—authors must play roles to get away with obscene statement and the depiction of erotic fantasies. Interestingly, Chaucerian critics have learned that trick as well. She cites in this connection Larry Benson's 1984 Chaucer Congress paper which warned critics not to overextend their own erotic fantasies in finding vulgar puns that Chaucer never intended. The effect, according to Kendrick, was that "Benson's denials enabled him, to everyone's amusement, to dwell at length on bawdy words" (p. 30). She adds a waggish Chaucerism of her own, "Even in this book, I might be said to be doing the same thing, under cover of scholarship—which does not make it any less scholarly, only more duplicitous" (p. 30). At a later point, in the chapter "De-*author*izing the Text," she examines more extensively the process of writing about Chaucer's game and laughter. Here she points out that plain speaking about such topics as "Goddes pryvetee" to a class of corruptible undergraduates is, for her, next to impossible. Speaking about it from a podium at a scholarly convention is a bit easier. Writing about it is easier yet. This is because the audiences in each of these situations becomes increasingly fictionalized. It is in this manner that critics—and Chaucer, too—deauthorize their observations. The game is, of course, endless. In writing this review-essay, an authorized practice in our world of scholarship, I am now masking my own pleasure as I sublimate the enjoyment of taboo words and situations that I read in Kendrick's string of candid summaries of obscene French fabliaux. Kendrick shows us experimentally and critically how we play the game of recovering Chaucer's games.

But recovering the process is only part of what this playfully astute book is all about. It tells us too what role Chaucer's play assumes in his poetry. The purpose of Chaucer's play is "mastery" (p. 43). Kendrick chooses to talk about this phenomenon by invoking evidence from developmental psychology. In quoting the text of a presleep monologue of a two-and-a-half-year-old, she shows that the rehearsal of a string of "don'ts" is a way for the unconscious mind to assume the power roles of the child's authorities. By playing all the roles, the child gains imaginative control over his world. The fiction writer does the same thing. Thus, for example, the Nun's Priest's fiction is a veiled effort of the narrator's quest for power over females. The fabliaux, likewise, empower the socially suppressed: all the fabliaux, according to Kendrick, are "variations on the Oedipal conflict" (p. 61), and their sport is ultimately with the cuckolding or castration of the father figure. As with the infamous "fart in the face" in at least two of the tales (the Miller's and the Summoner's), a child's revenge serves to displace, during festive play, the authoritative.

The book begins with an examination of what may be the most outrageously playful story in all literature, the Miller's Tale. The instance serves Kendrick as a paradigm. By citing the Miller's line about a husband who should not be "inquisityf of Goddes pryvetee," she demonstrates persuasively with the aid of some twenty-one illustrations from medieval art that the Miller's joke is ultimately a search "for forbidden or dangerous knowledge" (p. 9). The Middle Ages became increasingly obsessed about God's genitals. The various depictions of the Christ child included here, based on Leo Steinberg's trend-setting *Sexuality of Christ,* show the artist's gradual fixation on the child's penis and even on Mary's attention to it, either by fondling it or by covertly (and sometimes not so covertly) veiling it. What does all this have to do with the Miller's Tale? It shows how the churlish interpreter, in contrast to his gentle counterpart, reads "down." As all serious readers of Chaucer know, the Miller's Tale is in many ways a parody of sacred text. It is a veiled story of the Flood as well as the Annunciation, and it gets to its meaning in part through the perversion of the Song of Songs. What the Miller has done is to put together a burlesque medley in order to debase the interpretation of sacred images: Joseph becomes the impotent father, Mary the voluptuous wench. The sacred text has become desublimated; the euphemisms relating to Godhead, which are customarily preserved through "pryvetee," have become unmasked. In Kendrick's words, the Miller's story has removed "the verbal loincloths of exegesis and exposed the revitalizing energy of infantile, egocentric desire" (p. 19). This, typically, is the activity of festive game during carnival. It deauthorizes and disempowers the established order only, according to Kendrick, to reaffirm it. This is what Chaucer means by making game out of earnest.

Yet for all the zest and learning displayed by this often scintillating study of Chaucer's deep meanings concerning the structure and operation of festive play, one must finally come away from it with some disappointments. The interpretation of the Miller's Tale, as an instance, shows us that for all of Kendrick's exploration into psychoanalytic theory, medieval iconography, and developmental psychology, she hasn't really said anything that we haven't known all along. There are no radiant discoveries here, no daring new theoretical positions. Her view of festive play, despite her frequent reliance on Bakhtin, resembles the old, familiar model of Durkheim in the insistence on the reconstitutive power of play. And while I basically agree with that interpretation, I cannot find the sort of theoretical speculation in this book that also takes us beyond it. At base Chaucer may have been conservative in his view toward the institutions of his time, but he also voiced some fundamental discontents that did not simply assert themselves at moments of carnival only to reconstruct themselves. The book, moreover, comes dangerously close to reaffirming the old, shopworn "roadside drama" readings that Jordan and various deconstructionists have exposed as trivializing the power of Chaucer's text. The very nature of Kendrick's psychoanalytical approach forces her to look at characters as real people; for example, Harry Bailly is characterized as having "appreciated ... enormously" (p. 38) the Nun's Priest's Tale, or, on another occasion, as having real-life motives like provoking the Monk (p. 104). While Kendrick on various occasions recognizes the dialogism of Chaucer's text, her study is really designed, in Bakhtinian terms, to monologize Chaucer. We may see the Miller's Tale as deauthorizing the Knight, though actually Kendrick says very little about the intertextuality of those two tales, but in the final analysis by setting up the churlish speaker in opposition to the gentle, Kendrick oversimplifies the voicing of the text at large. If we depersonify the Knight and recognize that he is, in fact, an artifice of rhetoric and style, we come to see that we don't rely solely on the Miller to deconstruct his tale or his voice. The oppositions that are built into the text disturb us everywhere. It is the multiple voicing of Chaucer's text, not the creation of characters certified by psychoanalytic observations, that finally gives life to the opposition of game and earnest. In the final analysis, therefore, I find Kendrick's text a refreshing and enlightening reading of particulars, buttressed by an admirable range of reference, but not a book that truly extends our horizons.

I come away from this examination of the present state of *Canterbury Tales* scholarship with the impression that we are now in the midst of rethinking our premises and that we have yet to find approaches that will yield the solid learning and understanding that marked the post-War scholarship which is being displaced. In the current crop of theoretical, critical, and historical books, perhaps the greatest contributions are theoretical. It seems that we have not resolved the questions that realism and "roadside drama" approaches asked. While the most important new theoretical book among those examined here guides us to look at the *Canterbury Tales* as an assemblage of presentational styles, the critical approaches we have covered still see the work essentially as drama. No doubt this conflict will need to be argued out more forcefully and more systematically in the future. But I doubt that we shall ever again be content with the creation of such orthodoxies as held sway in the post-War generation. It is, in any case, reassuring that, at a time when radically new approaches are being tested, we retain the interest to document the text as fully as modern scholarship will allow and we understand the drift of our own history. With those efforts to guide us, we can confidently await "somme newe tydynges for to lere."

Works Cited

Auerbach, Erich. *Mimesis: The Representation of Reality in Western Literature.* Trans. Willard R. Trask. Garden City, N.Y.: Doubleday, 1957.
Blake, Norman E. *The Textual Tradition of the* Canterbury Tales. London: Edward Arnold, 1985.
Benson, Larry D., gen. ed. *The Riverside Chaucer.* Boston: Houghton Mifflin, 1987.
Corsa, Helen Storm, ed. *The Physician's Tale.* A Variorum Edition of the Works of

The *Canterbury Tales* for a New Age

Geoffrey Chaucer. Vol. 2: *The Canterbury Tales,* Part 17. Norman: Univ. of Oklahoma Press, 1987.

Curtius, E. R. *European Literature in the Latin Middle Ages.* New York: Harper, 1953.

Donaldson, E. Talbot. "Chaucer the Pilgrim." *Speaking of Chaucer.* London: Athlone, 1970. 1–12.

Fisher, John H. "Animadversions on the Text of Chaucer, 1988." *Speculum,* 63 (1988): 779–93.

Friedman, Albert B. *"The Prioress's Tale* and Chaucer's Anti-Semitism." *Chaucer Review,* 9 (1974): 118–29.

Gellrich, Jesse M. *The Idea of the Book in the Middle Ages: Language Theory, Mythology, and Fiction.* Ithaca: Cornell Univ. Press, 1985.

Gombrich, Ernst. *In Search of Cultural History.* Oxford: Clarendon, 1969.

Kane, George S. "John M. Manly (1865–1940) and Edith Rickert (1871–1938)." *Editing Chaucer: The Great Tradition.* Ed. Paul Ruggiers. Norman: Pilgrim Books, 1984.

Kittredge, George Lyman. *Chaucer and His Poetry.* 1915; rpt. Cambridge, Mass.: Harvard Univ. Press, 1970.

Lawrence, W. W. *Chaucer and the* Canterbury Tales. New York: Columbia Univ. Press, 1950.

Leicester, H. Marshall, Jr. "The Art of Impersonation: A General Prologue to the *Canterbury Tales." PMLA,* 95 (1980).

Lewis, C. S. *The Allegory of Love.* 1936; rpt. New York: Oxford Univ. Press, 1958.

Lumiansky, Robert M. *Of Sondry Folk: The Dramatic Principles in the* Canterbury Tales. Austin: Univ. of Texas Press, 1955.

Mâle, Emile. *The Gothic Image: Religious Art in France in the Thirteenth Century.* Trans. Dora Nussey. New York: Dutton, 1913.

Malone, Kemp. *Chapters on Chaucer.* Baltimore: Johns Hopkins Univ. Press, 1951.

Manly, John M., and Edith Rickert, eds. *The Text of the* Canterbury Tales. 8 vols. Univ. of Chicago Press, 1940.

Pace, George B., and Alfred David, eds. *The Minor Poems.* A Variorum Edition of the Works of Geoffrey Chaucer. Vol. 5, Part 1. Norman: Univ. of Oklahoma Press, 1982.

Panofsky, Erwin. *Studies in Iconology.* New York: Oxford Univ. Press, 1939.

Patch, Howard R. *On Rereading Chaucer.* Cambridge, Mass.: Harvard Univ. Press, 1939.

Payne, Robert O. *The Key of Remembrance: A Study of Chaucer's Poetics.* New Haven: Yale Univ. Press, 1963.

Pearsall, Derek, ed. *The Nun's Priest's Tale.* A Variorum Edition of the Works of Geoffrey Chaucer. Vol. 2: *The Canterbury Tales,* Part 9. Norman: Univ. of Oklahoma Press, 1983.

Ramsay, Roy Vance. "F. N. Robinson's Editing of the *Canterbury Tales." Studies in Bibliography,* 42 (1988): 134–52.

Robertson, D. W., Jr. *A Preface to Chaucer: Studies in Medieval Perspectives.* Princeton: Princeton Univ. Press, 1962.

Root, Robert K. *The Poetry of Chaucer.* Rev. ed. 1922; rpt. Gloucester, Mass.: Peter Smith, 1957.

Ross, Thomas W., ed. *The Miller's Tale.* A Variorum Edition of the Works of Geoffrey Chaucer. Vol. 2: *The Canterbury Tales,* Part 3. Norman: Univ. of Oklahoma Press, 1983.

Ruggiers, Paul G. *A Facsimile of the Hengwrt Manuscript of the* Canterbury Tales. Norman: Univ. of Oklahoma Press, 1978.

Saenger, Paul. "Silent Reading: Its Impact on Late Medieval Script and Society." *Viator,* 13 (1982): 367–414.

Smalley, Beryl. *The Study of the Bible in the Middle Ages.* Oxford: Blackwell, 1952.

Stenton, Sir Frank. *Anglo-Saxon England.* Oxford: Clarendon, 1943.

Stevens, Martin. "Chaucer and Modernism: An Essay in Criticism." *Chaucer at Albany.* Ed. Rossell H. Robbins. New York: Burt Franklin, 1975. 193–216.

Tatlock, J. S. P. *The Mind and Art of Chaucer.* 1950; rpt. New York: Gordian, 1966.

Houses and Their Heads

John Sutherland

Ruth Dudley Edwards. *Victor Gollancz, A Biography.* London: Gollancz, 1987. 782 pp.

J. W. Lambert and Michael Ratcliffe. *The Bodley Head, 1887–1987.* London: Bodley Head. xi, 365 pp.

These two books help focus on categories which are important but often underestimated in booktrade history of the nineteenth and twentieth centuries, namely house "style" and the ways in which the heads of publishing houses shape production to their personalities. Not all houses, of course, are equal. As a general anatomical observation, book production in Britain since the Victorian period has been dominated by a first division of very large firms (e.g., Longman, Macmillan, Blackwood, the two great university presses) and by a constellation of smaller, less dynastic, middle-sized commercial houses which are usually more adventurous and idiosyncratic. This second group has been notable for distinctive "styles"—both in physical appearance and in content. No one, for instance, could mistake a Graham Greene "entertainment" with its clean-cut John Ryder design and talismanic green binding for anything but a Bodley Head book; or a middlebrow Daphne Du Maurier romance with its "screaming" yellow dust jacket, a vulgarity mitigated by chaste Stanley Morison typography, as anything but a Gollancz book. Secker and Warburg, after catching *Animal Farm* on the rebound from more doctrinaire and timid publishers (including Gollancz) have specialized, among much else, in fiction of liberal critique (currently, Angus Wilson, David Lodge, Malcolm Bradbury). Chatto have sustained their links with the universities (especially Cambridge) and with Bloomsbury. Jonathan Cape, while publishing the cream of English fiction, have also cultivated a line in coarse-grained espionage thrillers (famously Ian Fleming's James Bond books). Faber, molded to the preferences of T. S. Eliot, publisher, have generally avoided fiction for canonical poetry, although very recently, under Robert McCrum, novelist, they have been in the forefront of publishing the new wave of young British novelists. Allen Lane's firm made such a mark on English literary culture that even today the word "Penguin" is more likely to be understood as denoting a paperback than a pedestrian bird. Each of these, and others like them, have been "general trade publishers," putting out a mixed list of fast and slow sellers, frontlist and backlist items, and books ranging from coffee-table glossies through cookery to children's stories. Nevertheless, the names Secker, Weidenfeld, Gollancz, Deutsch, Penguin, Cape, Hamish Hamilton, Chatto, Bodley Head each conjure a distinctive kind of "literary" book. And it is one of the recurrent anxieties of the British book trade that these innovative houses, on which the country's literary dynamism and heterogeneity depend, will be swallowed up either by home-grown giants or by buccaneering American conglomerates. Another crisis scenario sees them as in the process of being ousted by more narrowly specialized publishers with obtrusive "political" programmes, like Virago, Verso, or the Gay Men's Press. A third danger is perceived in the rise of the agent, a Mephistophelean figure whose role in life it is to break up the loyalty that previously existed between author and publisher.

Ruth Dudley Edwards's massive *Victor Gollancz* is ostensibly a biography, and she studiously avoids trespassing on the area covered by Sheila Hodges's house history, *Gollancz* (1978). But so egocentric was the founder that distinctions between house and head are meaningless. Gollancz the man, with all his drives, cosmic vision, and petty spots of commonness, *is* Gollancz the firm. Ideally the two books should be read together, the moreso as Hodges gives the crisper and more authoritative accounts of Gollancz's vexed but immensely fruitful relationship with Morison, and Dudley Edwards the fuller and less apologetic account of the Left Book Club venture. Ignoring the demarcations and taken with Victor Gollancz's own voluminous auto-

Houses and their Heads

biography, we are now in the welcome position of knowing more about this than any other comparable publishing firm. (Not that the competition is fierce. Middle-sized commercial publishers in Britain tend to be morbidly secretive, as anyone who has tried to winkle sales figures out of them will know.)

Two classes of outsiders have contributed disproportionately to the evolution of the modern British publishing industry: Scots and Jews. Racial theories for this are easy to frame. Both the Presbyterian and the Judaic traditions revere the book and the explicators of the book—whether Rabbi or dominie-minister. Compared to other long-ladder professions in British life, publishing is relatively open. It can be embarked on with small capital. Entry at ground level is easy and promotion by merit is rapid and generally unobstructed (nor unfairly assisted) by class or ethnic prejudices. British publishing, despite proverbial wisdom, is not (or not exclusively) a "profession for gentlemen." Or ladies, come to that; one of the more interesting current transformations in the book trade is the way in which women are increasingly occupying senior editorial and managerial positions, well in advance of the law, medicine, the City, or the Anglican Church.

Dudley Edwards gives an exhaustive but necessary account of Gollancz's Jewish background. His father, Alex Gollancz, was a well-off jewel merchant; a devout and highly respected member of London's tight-knit orthodox community of Jews. But in his own eyes (and eventually those of his son) Alex was, as a tradesman, a failure. His elder brothers were both University of London professors, and would eventually win knighthoods. Young Victor, following the secular aspirations of his family, was educated as a day boy at St. Paul's school in London. Sports, which traditionally take place on Saturdays in English public schools, were denied him by Sabbath regulations. He was prevented from taking up an instrument on the perverse but practical grounds that the Gollanczes were too good at music, and there are more important things in life than fiddling. Perhaps in rebellion, Victor developed in later life a love of opera that bordered on obsession.

The most singular feature of Gollancz's growing up was his

early and absolute repudiation of formal Judaism. It was, for the time and in the circumstances, a breathtaking assertion of individualism; as courageous and as spiritually formative as the teenage Mary Anne Evans's refusing to accompany her father to Church. But unlike George Eliot, Gollancz was no free-thinker or agnostic. It was, above all, discipline he kicked against. His favorite book through life was Wordsworth's *The Excursion* and he seems from birth to have been a Romantic for whom the ego was sublime and everything. In place of the religion offered him (in a very civilized fashion, it may be said) by his family, he cultivated a flamboyant Wordsworthian pantheism.

Gollancz's early destiny did not seem to be in publishing. He took a first-class degree in classical studies at Oxford and like all his generation was sucked into a World War in which, as a closet pacifist, he did not believe. He was saved by his clownishness. Too cack-handed even to serve as commissioned cannon fodder, he was seconded to the public school Repton, to teach sixth formers the beauties of classical literature, before they in their turn were chewed up by the insatiable war machine. Gollancz was clearly a school teacher of genius and despite the anti-semitism of the ethos might well have become a great headmaster. But he queered his pitch by insisting on teaching his boys classes in "civics"—instructing them, that is, in insubordination and habits of critical thought. These are not qualities admired then or now in public schools, and disgrace was inevitable. Gollancz went on to learn his publishing with the staid firm of Ernest Benn. He remained six years during which he was, as Dudley Edwards describes it, "at his worst . . . young, arrogant and out of control." Nevertheless, by 1927 he was in a position to demand partnership and, when this was prudently refused, he set up his own firm in his own name in 1928.

Victor Gollancz the firm transformed the practices of British publishing. Gollancz himself was unscrupulous professionally, poaching authors. He innovated patterns of cross-subsidization, by which the high-minded political, theological, and philosophical books that mattered to him were paid for by bestsellers by middlebrow favorites like A. J. Cronin, Dorothy Sayers and Daphne Du Maurier. Above all, he mastered the art of advertisement, which has always been regarded as somewhat vulgar by the British publishing establishment. He and Stanley Morison devised the famous yellow dust jackets and the heavy black lettering which gave Gollancz books instant eye-appeal and recognition. And until well after the Second World War, the firm advertised louder and longer than any other.

Gollancz understood that if you want to be noticed by a large number of people you must raise your voice. But it was not just a big slice of the market that he wanted so much as an audience, or a congregation. Having created a publishing apparatus he determined to use it in the 1930s as an instrument for the dissemination of ideas. In a decade dominated by propaganda he was to be a virtuoso. In 1936, he founded the Left Book Club, the most successful venture of its kind that Britain has ever known. Membership peaked at just under 60,000 in 1939, all subscribing to selections made by a committee of three comprising the marxist don Harold Laski, the communist John Strachey, and the agonizingly wobbly liberal-radical Gollancz. As a political educator, the LBC radicalized and informed a whole bourgeois elite. And the club's great virtue was that while its counterpart in Germany was being force-fed one book—*Mein Kampf*—the British intelligentsia had a whole library covering (at least notionally) the spectrum of socialist thought. There was serious talk of the membership of the LBC forming itself into a "party," or a political estate like the Trade Union Congress. But the LBC finally foundered on two rocks. The first was the blatant attempt of the Communist Party to take it over—which effectively they did by 1939. The second was the failure of the Anglo-Soviet Pact and the success of the later Soviet-German Pact, which destroyed Popular Front socialism in Britain, apparently forever.

LBC represented the high point of Gollancz's career and offered a Pisgah glimpse of what idealistic publishing can achieve. Like Penguin Books in the 1940s and 1950s and—to a much lesser extent—like New Left Books in the 1970s, LBC demonstrated that there is always a latent audience not just for reading matter, but for genuinely mind-opening and opinion-shaping books; and that publishing houses, at tantalizingly brief historical periods, can indeed become societies for the diffusion of useful knowledge, as Charles Knight once dreamed they might be.

The remainder of Gollancz's remarkable career was largely devoted to philanthropy and increasingly grand causes. At the end of the war he suffered an acute nervous breakdown, most sympathetically chronicled by Dudley Edwards, brought on by his sympathetic agony at the Holocaust. In one of the morally paradoxical leaps which characterized him, he immediately became an indefatigable advocate for German relief and reconstruction. In later years, he devoted part of his immense energies to programs for converting the Jews to Christianity. He founded or supported innumerable organizations working for world peace. Meanwhile, with his left hand, he continued to be a successful publisher. He was, for instance, one of the first to realize the importance of traveling to America for copyrights, where he found that country's less refined book trade to his taste. He pioneered, among much else, the publishing of intelligent science fiction in Britain in the 1950s and 1960s and "discovered" Colin Wilson, the *philosophe* of the Angry Young Man movement.

Victor Gollancz is a notable biographical achievement, and I would rate it as the best thing of its kind. It is not, however, without fault. Dudley Edwards's narrative is in some places pedestrian and transcribes far too much of Gollancz's correspondence. A more incisive and analytical approach would have been desirable—although the biographer's own defense that great men require long biographies is not without force. The convention of having such an essentially self-serving book published out of house would, I think, have been worth following here. A related flaw is the book's reluctance to take any truly critical line against Gollancz, many of whose social acts were appalling and political acts dishonest. He was not just occasionally but habitually crass, selfish, and unkind. The biographer's inclination is finally to pardon everything and excuse it with the sweeping gesture of her epigraph from Whitman: "Do I contradict myself? Very well, I contradict myself, I am large, I contain multitudes."

A question which is begged by this book is whether "creative" publishing in Britain is necessarily linked to megalomania and chronically immature personalities. Dudley Edwards quotes an illustrative anecdote in her first paragraph:

> A member of VG's staff once recommended that the firm publish Francoise Gilot's *My Life with Picasso*. Highly excited, Victor took the manuscript home and skimmed it, then telephoned his colleague to announce, "We can't publish this! Supposing someone wrote like that about Beethoven . . . or me!"

History will not, one is sure, record Gollancz as a giant of Beethoven's or Picasso's stature. But without such messianic self-delusion, could he have been a great publisher? Is innovative publishing typically the product of a kind of self-important infantilism that veers constantly between rage, transitory enthusiasm, and unbridled narcissism? The British satirical fortnightly *Private Eye* specializes in the retailing of the latest outrageousness (Gollanczisms, one might call them) of the *enfants terribles* of British publishing. And yet, once the snickering has died down, these are the men and women (Tom Maschler, Tom Rosenthal, André Deutsch, Carmen Kalil, George Weidenfeld, Liz Calder, Peter Mayer) who are, by any objective assessment, the trailblazing publishers of the day. Would they be less productive if they humbly rated themselves, as history rates the publisher, as nothing more than Literature's midwife?

Irresistible ego was Gollancz's strength. The corresponding weakness was that he could not delegate. Hence his career was interrupted by the regular breakdown of partnerships which restricted the growth of his firm and removed necessary checks from his own autocratic decision-making. The "board" to which he would allude for grand rhetorical effect was simply an occasionally mustered group of subordinates. Those who wanted to work with Gollancz were obliged to "humor" him; i.e., to submit. It was perhaps fortunate—though it grieved him—that he had no son to succeed him in the firm, so that it could descend to his daughter, Livia, to whom he could cede authority without Oedipal struggle.

Bodley Head, by contrast, is a firm whose character is entirely the outcome of inspired collaboration and teamwork. It was founded by two rather colorless individuals, John Lane and Elkin Mathews. Mathews was an antiquarian bookseller, who was soon thrown overboard. Lane—a clerk by training—was more durable, but no great mind or sensibility: "a poor fly caught in the amber of modernity," Beerbohm spitefully called him. The founders' main contribution to the success of their venture was an almost holy respect for "fine"—that is, sumptuously produced—books; this in an era when the trade's standards had been eroded by fifty years of mass production. The actual content of the Bodley Head list in its early years owes most to aesthetically inclined advisers like Richard Le Gallienne and Henry Harland, first editor of the *Yellow Book*. The subsequent disgrace of Wilde (who was arrested with a "yellow book" under his arm) and of Beardsley curtailed the firm's exuberance, but it survived and continued publishing licentious masterpieces, like *Ulysses*. Like many small publishers, it underwent a crisis of succession, which the superannuated and childless Lane solved by adopting a nephew, Allen Williams, on condition that he change his name to Allen Lane. This the young man did, and by 1936 had succeeded in reducing Bodley Head to penury, while elsewhere pioneering the overwhelmingly successful Penguin Books (whose elegance derives from Lane's Bodley Head training). The firm was rescued first by Stanley Unwin, then by Max Reinhardt in 1957. In 1973, Bodley Head was under financial pressure again and formed an awkward liaison with Cape and Chatto—the idea being that the trio could retain the individual flavor of their lists while pooling warehousing, office work, sales representation, advertising, and distribution. It did not work out as planned, any more than Secker and Warburg's "equal but separate" arrangement with the much larger Heinemann group worked out as planned. In May 1987, exactly on its centenary, Bodley was "acquired" by the American giant Random House. Reinhardt left to take with him the mission of producing Bodley Head books under the new imprint of his name. The history of Bodley Head is that of constant lurch from one financial or management crisis to the next. But through it all, the product— the Bodley Head book—has survived as a standard for the trade. Look at the Bodley Head *Ulysses* and compare it with the new

Garland edition and one can see how desirable that standard is. One cannot but admire Reinhardt's determination (aided by the eighty-three-year-old Graham Greene, now a Reinhardt author) to continue the tradition.

Unfortunately, *The Bodley Head, 1887–1987* is a house history of the old kind: anecdotal, unscholarly, thin on facts, jaunty in tone, and designed to appeal to the general reader. The author, J. W. Lambert, was former literary editor of the *Sunday Times;* he died in 1986, having written around three-quarters of the book. It was completed by another journalist, Michael Ratcliffe. The work was clearly commissioned to coincide with a festive anniversary for the firm, not its disappearance into Random House's alien maw. There remains an important (and now possibly complete) chapter of British publishing in the history of Bodley Head and one hopes that someone, some day, will properly write it.

The Vanishing Lives and Language of Victorian Poets

John Stasny

James Richardson. *Vanishing Lives: Style and Self in Tennyson, D. G. Rossetti, Swinburne, and Yeats.* Charlottesville: University Press of Virginia, 1988. x, 240 pp.

David G. Riede. *Matthew Arnold and the Betrayal of Language.* Charlottesville: University Press of Virginia, 1988. 239 pp.

The first three books published in the Virginia Victorian Studies monograph series on literature have been critical studies of poetry—in the opinion of the editor of *Victorian Poetry*, a simple matter of proper priorities. One approaches such studies not with the expectation that a critical epiphany awaits but that one has received an invitation to an exhibition of familiar art arranged by the curator with such provocative ingenuity, *dulce et utile*, that the exhibition itself may become a work of art. Was it Anatole France who said that the "critic is he who relates the adventures of his soul among masterpieces"? That Victorian poetry can provide adventures or, for that matter, masterpieces is, one suspects, a statement oxymoronic, equivocal, elitist, and, as Macbeth might have said, a tale told with an "empty signifier." Students of literature have learned, however, to endure lowered expectations. Critics are not "rigorous teachers" who profess to show us "the white star of Truth"; we live now where such a star no longer shines, where, as Geoffrey Hartman says, "wilderness is all we have." Criticism professes no vision of a Promised Land; it is, in Hartman's words, "contaminated creative thinking."[1] One must suppose that criticism comes, to paraphrase Pater, "professing to give nothing" but quality time "to [our] moments as they pass." We expect little that is True, but we anticipate a pleasant time amid "what is real in our lives . . . that continual vanishing away, that strange, perpetual weaving and unweaving of ourselves."[2] The two books under review here satisfy our anticipations.

James Richardson quotes in the introduction to *Vanishing Lives* the opening lines of section 121 of *In Memoriam* and focuses on "Dim / And dimmer," leading to the generalization: "Dimness is one of the most characteristic features of Victorian Poetry" (p. 4). One reads and pauses to conjure dim recollections and to remember, perhaps, *The Finer Optic* (1975) by Carol T. Christ and her discussion of "Tennyson's microscopic eye, the Pre-Raphaelite fidelity to minute detail" and in general the "preoccupation with the particular in Victorian poetry."[3] We have an apparent contradiction here that systematic thought might feel obliged at the outset to resolve. Richardson is aware of Christ's book; he cites it twice. However, in making his generalization about Victorian poetry, Richardson does not attempt a refutation, or qualification, of Christ's generalization—except in a note on page 232 that cites a note in a Gerhard Joseph essay which Richardson says "oversimplifies Christ's valuable book."[4]

Nor does Richardson in his "attempt to define mainstream Victorian" (p. 9) from early Tennyson to "the dim purity of [Yeats's] early work" (p. 143) even cite much less attempt any kind of refutation or deposition of fifty years of critical exploration of the nature of Victorian poetry from, say, Douglas Bush, Joseph Beach, Hoxie Fairchild, Alba Warren, Lionel Stevenson, E. D. H. Johnson, Robert Langbaum, Jerome Buckley, Morris Peckham, and J. Hillis Miller to the most recent feminist critics of Elizabeth Barrett Browning and Christina Rossetti or to W. David Shaw in *The Lucid Veil: Poetic Truth in the Victorian Age* (1987). A book that ignores Matthew Arnold's aspirations for poetry, relegates Browning, as a kind of minor Dickensian, to the "urban division of the Victorian Age" (p. 139), and does not even attempt to account for an uncharacteristic lack of Victorian "dimness" amid "The Pied Beauty" of Hopkins is not apt to achieve status as a significant extrapolation of insights devoted to aspects of Tennyson, Swinburne, Rossetti, and Yeats to Victorian poetry in general.

Richardson, however, is not writing revisionist literary history. He is practicing Saintsburyan criticism, and, as Jerome H. Buckley observed, "Saintsbury's attention to form may have led him to neglect the themes and attitudes we have come to consider characteristically 'Victorian.'"[5] In his introduction Richardson acknowledges that he is concerned with "habits, visions, and stances that are perhaps essentially preverbal. The psychological biases under consideration are less ideas than feelings, less feelings, even, than ways or forms or styles of feeling" (p. 9). His criticism describes not communicated thought but "an essential stratum of the *experience* of Victorian poetry" (p. 9; the emphasis is mine simply to note that Richardson's is quite different from Robert Langbaum's perception of the garrulity of Victorian poetry described in *The Poetry of Experience*). He is concerned with how a poem "*works*": "And whatever else it is, a poem is something that *works*. It is a program the brain loads and runs, with the difference that the brain gradually adapts to run it more successfully: the poem in effect runs part of the brain" (p. 23).

Richardson is critic as computer scientist; he examines a "language" called Victorian poetry, used to program not information or thought but a game. "Absent presence" might well be the name of the game. The phrase is, according to Richardson, "for Tennyson an irresistible oxymoron"; it conjures up "the chance lost and the life never lived [which] may be Tennyson's—and the Victorian age's most haunting absence" (p. 34). Richardson attempts to describe the vicarious experiences of those who "load and run" that game. The computer image is creative criticism in a characteristic contemporary mode—metaphor with dubious expository efficacy but with provocatively ambivalent and distracting imaginative appeal. Richardson comes close to what used to be rejected as the "ooh-and-ah school" of subjective criticism. There is a Saintsbury revival under way!

Early in his introduction Richardson announces his intention to devote a significant portion of his study to detailed metrical analysis, and, by way of "a few impressions," makes the first of his several references to Saintsbury's *History of English Prosody*—"the bird-like motion" of the *In Memoriam* stanza (p. 6). Richardson recognizes Saintsbury's authority: "A Victorian himself, he senses that nineteenth-century poetry is in some way an experience we move within, and that its momentum is a way of feeling and organizing time" (p. 69). Here it is "Saintsbury's *Impulse* to measure the velocity of poetry" that fascinates Richardson. What happens in a regular iambic line when the disyllabic words therein are trochaic; does a "two-syllable word crossing a foot boundary" speed up or slow down the line? One might use a stopwatch, Richardson suggests, but "both, especially in the Tennysonian context, seem correct in some ways" (pp. 50–51). Richardson solves the dilemma thus: "Whether the lines are slow or quick, they are moving, we feel, as fast as thy *can*. . . . Like Tennysonian time, the Tennysonian line can move slowly and quickly in the same moment" (p. 52). One trained to respect an Aristotelian law of contradiction has difficulty with such statements. One possessing only modest metrical discrimination and, I suppose, an uncultivated ear is apt to respond to such statements: "Why what a very cultivated kind of youth this kind of youth must be!" However, it is Richardson's aural acuity—impressionistic and subjective though it may appear to be—that evokes "a willing suspension of disbelief" for its hasty generalization about a monolithically "dim" Victorian poetry and makes this book actually a joy to read.

For instance, we acquiesce temporarily at least in a description of Browning's "failure to be a second Tennyson" (p. 15), in the suggestion that "the soulless perfection of Andrea del Sarto's art could easily resemble the sentimental smoothness of "Enoch Arden" (p. 17), and in the attribution of a characteristic difference between Tennyson and Browning—ignoring the matter of a dramatic persona—in the onomatopoetic description of the sound of bells: "The mellow lin-lan-lone of evening bells / Far-far-away" and the "Hy, Zy, Hine" of the vesper bells in "Soliloquy of the Spanish Cloister" (p. 19). We read with renewed fascination discussions of the technical bases of the most musical lines in English and the statistical basis of "a slight excess of pyrrhic over spondaic feet" in Shakespeare, Pope, Wordsworth, and Tennyson (pp. 69–75). An aficionado of all things Victorian will admire Richardson's comparison of Wordsworthian and Tennysonian moods apropos of *In Memoriam:* "The result exceeds its Wordsworthian original in poignance" (p. 90); he will admire the refutation of Auden's charge of stupidity: "In some ways Tennyson is a poet of deep inarticulateness, but he is an *emotional* intelligence of the highest order" (p. 90); finally, the aficionado will eagerly acknowledge that Tennyson is, indeed, a poet for our time: "To say that Tennyson's poetry is in flight from life is meaningless or at most only partially meaningful. Half of the truth is that our whole nature is to escape life because it is death. The other half, depicted more poignantly by Tennyson than by any other poet, is that life escapes *us*" (p. 95).

Richardson spends approximately the same amount of space on Tennyson at the beginning of his book and on Yeats at the end. In the middle are thirty-five pages devoted to chapters on Rossetti and Swinburne, which constitute a strange and unworthy interlude. It is significant that it is within these chapters that most of the editorial and stylistic problems occur. Index references, for example, are missed. Stylistic difficulties occur on almost every page. Richardson continues his impressive metrical analyses in these chapters, but on page 107, amidst analysis of the subtle matter of what "Vogel calls this 'stress-height rhythm,'" there is a sentence that might send one back to Joseph F. Vogel's *Dante Gabriel Rossetti's Versecraft* (1971), pages 21–25. Study and analysis seem to reveal that Richardson attributes to Vogel a position he does not take or that Richardson is saying exactly the opposite of what one might guess he intended to say. On page 110 there is a quaint comparison of Rossetti's loose sentence structure with the periodic sentence structure of Samuel Johnson (not cited in the index, by the way) that seems strange given the anticipatory Paterian elements Richardson attributes to Rossetti. In the chapter on Swinburne, Richardson, the phrase maker, describes Swinburne as "a poet of macroscopic abundance and microscopic restraint" (p. 131). What else is new?

Richardson's description of Yeats early in his career "delighting in the opening of dimnesses within dimnesses, an infinite regression for which there is also Rossettian precedent" (p. 151) and later experiencing an "evolution toward reticence" (p. 181) is also not exactly new. Richardson's virtuosity as an analyst of metrics, applying his skills to Yeats, makes scansion a vivid— almost dramatic—experience. He devotes four pages to "Adam's Curse," and he almost makes us see that "lines seem to come out of the left margin with a small surge" (p. 179). He concludes with an extended analysis of "Among School Children," drawing analogies between it and "Tintern Abbey" and "Tithonus." Yeats is concerned as Wordsworth and Tennyson were concerned, but "he is bent on heroic antielegy, an impossible denial of loss" (p. 225). This is Yeats's way of dealing with dim prospects and a dim future. Richardson does not know whether Yeats's dilemma "arises from deep faith or deep skepticism, and therefore whether it is a deeper faith or a deeper skepticism that made him half disbelieve it" (p. 226). That the dilemma between faith and doubt had been anticipated in the Victorian age is a critical commonplace. The "it" Yeats half disbelieved refers to "the choice between dancer and philosopher"; Richardson's choice is obviously discussing not the thought but the evocative movement of the poetry. He chooses an approach much neglected since the days of Saintsbury and his sensitive and impressionistic ilk. His book illustrates how much we have missed.

David Riede's *Matthew Arnold and the Betrayal of Language* discusses a poet almost completely ignored in Richardson's book. Perhaps Richardson has difficulty finding in Arnold the "dimness" characteristic of Victorian poetry. Riede too seems unable to find even a faint enlightening twilight in the world of Arnold's best poetry. There "all is night" and "Universal Darkness buries all": the "light [that] / Gleams and is gone" leaves a world "Where ignorant armies clash by night."

"Arnold's best poetry," says Riede, "is in a language . . . [that] is multitudinous, anarchic, caught between an age of certainties in which poetic style could express a unified ideology of faith and an uncertain future, in which no such unified discourse could be meaningful" (p. 215). The future of poetry, immense in the sense that Arnold foresaw, has not been and will not be realized.

Arnold, who abandoned poetry in an age he thought prosaic and uncongenial to poetry and who turned in a spirit of Victorian altruism to a critical effort propaedeutic to any possible poetically creative age, would probably have found Riede's praise of Arnoldian poetry incomprehensible: "To say that Arnold's poetry is prosaic, in the sense that it embodies the complexities of the living language, is only to praise it" (p. 215). Arnold's poetry is being praised for the defects Arnold himself found in it ("Preface to the Poems, 1853"): its "dialogue of the mind with itself"—"his overt purposes," says Riede, "are subverted by a corrosive subtext" (p. 29)—and for the fact that it does not "inspirit and rejoice the reader," that it does not "charm and infuse delight."

Language was Arnold's problem and betrayer: "Arnold was a man caught between two worlds, a past in which language generated 'a world of illusion, of divine illusion,' and a future for which an adequate vocabulary was yet unborn" (p. 4). Arnold's goal was ontological Truth, "to see the object as in itself it really is." Arnold, says Riede, recognized finally that "the truth of poetic language is subjective and arbitrary, but the truth of scientific language is absolute, and enables the writer to fulfil the purpose of Arnoldian criticism—to describe the object as in itself it really is" (p. 13). The truth of language that Arnold in the nineteenth century only gradually and reluctantly began to accept is the Lockian, empiricist, utilitarian view of language—the view Riede describes as possessing an "Iagoesque epistemology" (p. 19). Riede describes the triumph of that view in his "Introduction" (pp. 1–29); in his "Conclusion" (pp. 204–18) he describes the twentieth-century attitude toward language: "Since the triumph of the scientific outlook, language did not seem to embody truth, but only to reflect uncertainties, doubts, aspirations" (p. 205). Riede records—with citations from Michel Foucault, Walter Benjamin, M. M. Bakhtin, and especially from Geoffrey Hartman's *Criticism in the Wilderness*—a view of the world unsatisfying beyond Arnold's bleakest expectations of a darkling plain without horizon. "The best that was thought and said"—the tradition Arnold dedicated his criticism and his educational labors to perpetuate—turns out to be "simply a tradition of error" (p. 206). Borrowing terminology from Bakhtin, Riede attributes the inevitability of failure for Arnold the poet to his inability "to reduce the 'hetroglossia' of a multitudinous language to a unified poetic utterance" (p. 211). In his final paragraph Riede attempts a kind of rescue: "We can, indeed, excise the religious functions of poetry, doubt that its apparent power is necessarily a power for good, demonstrate the impossibility of an effective yet pure poetic style, show the inevitable intertextuality of all poctic utterance, and deconstruct all of Arnold's poetry—but still we cannot account for the mysterious power somehow inherent in words" (p. 217). This statement of critical agnosticism is a kind of act of poetic faith, almost an aesthetic Pascalian wager. Riede may yet be saved! But after reading a book-length deconstruction of poetic pretensions one wonders if criticism isn't endorsing—with as much arrogance and obtuseness and with paradoxical dogmatism—Jeremy Bentham's observation that so distressed the Victorians: "Prejudice apart, the game of push-pin is of equal value with the arts and sciences of music and poetry."[6] In our contemporary Benthamite wilderness, criticism of poetry seems idle and lugubrious, masochistic play at even a further remove from poetry and other modern equivalents of push-pin with which we wile away our moments toward oblivion. Strange are the ways of leisure-time activities!

Riede's book, however, is in fact quite a different book in the four chapters between the theoretical "Introduction" and "Conclusion." "Postromantic deconstruction" is an impulse throughout the book and is even found perhaps being deliberately and precociously practiced by Arnold's own Empedocles (p. 89), but what Riede actually gives us is a chronological survey of Arnold's poetic career with generous and extended commentary on specific poems, commentary that finds scholarly precedent and repeated authoritative support from authors of almost a score of books and many shorter studies as well. (The editor of *Victorian Poetry* is flattered to find that there are references—one safely conjectures—to every article published on Arnold in the twenty-five years of the life of the journal.) Riede's book thus becomes a wonderfully valuable introductory guide for a graduate student, for example, who is undertaking his first systematic study of Arnold and is seeking illuminating orientation.

Precisely what insights the experienced Arnold scholar, who has read all of Riede's sources, might derive from his book is, however, problematical. Riede, relying on Bakhtin's authority, observes that Arnold "produced a few remarkable poems that demonstrate the inevitable condition of literature in the wilderness. In language, so overused, so overpopulated, so teeming with multitudinous life, any poetry not written in a positively dead language must tend 'toward the condition of quotation, attenuated allusion and paraphrase,' must tend toward a bricolage dense with the traces of other writings and other forms of discourse" (p. 216). One might speculate that such also is the condition of criticism produced in the "wilderness." Perhaps Riede is—perhaps critics in general are—"belated" in a Bloomian sense. We get from Riede not a cogent critical argument, based on new discovery or systematic application of a potentially penetrating paradigm but rather almost a personal essay which, by insufficiently supported inference, attributes to Arnold in the nineteenth century an unconscious preternatural, anachronistic anticipation of late-twentieth-century attitudes. We get a Matthew Arnold created in the image and likeness of the critic himself. No matter by what "touchstones" of critical approach the effort "to see the object as in itself it really is" produces not even a Paterian or Wildean modified critical conclusion but rather a kind of critico-creative picaresque fiction in which the critic himself becomes the central figure. Riede's narrative is engaging because he has travelled so much in critical realms and because he holds our interest because he is so admirably articulate and witty.

Riede's book is actually a joy to read. A reviewer does not want to spoil the various treats in store for readers. All the same, he might, just for example, mention "a man's speech should exceed his grasp, or what's a Bible for?" (p. 14) or, in a reference to the opening lines of "Memorial Verses," "In a Bloomian sense such a mass murder of poetic fathers..." (p. 74). There are witty "one-liners" throughout the book. One is tempted to paraphrase the words attributed to Arnold's own niece, "Why, Uncle Matthew, Oh why, will not you be always wholly serious?" Paradox is used sometimes for the sake of paradox: in *Empedocles on Etna*—"one of the finest and most important utterances of the nineteenth century"—"the sum of its failures adds up to its success" (p. 93); *Sohrab and Rustum*, "very explicitly an effort to imitate the manner of Homer," on the other hand, "insofar as it succeeds . . . fails as a poem" (p. 103); "The Scholar-Gipsy" "may reasonably be judged a success precisely because it fails" (p. 147) as does "Thyrsis" which "becomes a moving poem more for its poignant failure . . . than for its forced and false success" (p. 156). This is fun even if a "success-amid-apparent-failure" man such as Andrea del Sarto or Rabbi Ben Ezra might inquire from Victorianists everywhere, "What's a guy to do?"

Years ago a generation of English majors were told in the very first sentence of an influential study: "We must first make a distinction between literature and literary study. The two are distinct activities: one is creative, an art; the other, if not precisely a science, is a species of knowledge and learning."[7] Richard D. Altick told many of us, "All literary students are dedicated to the same task, the discovery of truth."[8] In our "high seriousness" most still believed, I suppose, despite existential angst and all, that "Truth" was still to be found and that literature embodied truth, not as the world and science give us "truth," but as "Truth" resides in myth, communicated to us through the "natural magic" of language, wonderfully evocative, ingeniously ambiguous, but ultimately and ineffably, unequivocally the "Truth." Literary critics were prophets of an Arnoldian poetic millennium; theirs were voices telling us that in the wilderness we had no lasting homes. Now comes assertion and assumption, mostly unexamined, that we have only a permanent wilderness. We have a new generation of critics who write—who knows why—for a smaller and ever smaller audience among the inhabitants of the wilderness. Even for the "saving remnant" such books as those by Riede and Richardson—written, though they be, with contemporary sophistication, suavity, and verve—serve finally a purpose that is not entirely clear.

Notes

1. Geoffrey H. Hartman, *Criticism in the Wilderness* (New Haven: Yale Univ. Press, 1980), p. 8.
2. From Walter Pater's "Conclusion" to *The Renaissance*, quoted by Richardson in the first sentence of *Vanishing Lives* (p. 3).
3. Carol T. Christ, *The Finer Optic: The Aesthetic of Particularity in Victorian Poetry* (New Haven: Yale Univ. Press, 1975), p. ix.
4. See Gerhard Joseph, "Tennyson's Optics; The Eagle's Gaze," *PMLA*, 92 (1987), 420–28. Richardson refers to the following comment: "Where, however, Christ emphasizes a categorical Tennysonian penchant for stark individuation, I see a dialectical movement between particularity and indefiniteness" (p. 427n).
5. Jerome H. Buckley, "General Materials" in Frederic E. Faverty, ed., *The Victorian Poets: A Guide to Research* (Cambridge: Harvard Univ. Press, 1968), p. 16.
6. See Jeremy Bentham, *The Rationale of Reward* (1825), conveniently reprinted in *Victorian Poetry and Poetics*, edited by W. E. Houghton and G. R. Stange, 2nd ed. (Boston: Houghton, Mifflin, 1968), pp. 833–44.
7. René Wellek and Austin Warren, *Theory of Literature* (New York: Harcourt, Brace, 1949), p. 3.
8. Richard D. Altick, *The Art of Literary Research* (New York: Norton, 1963), p. 3.

Conrad as Nihilistic Conservative

Elizabeth B. Tenenbaum

Anthony Winner. *Culture and Irony: Studies in Joseph Conrad's Major Novels.* Charlottesville: University Press of Virginia, 1988. 132 pp.

A fundamental aspect of Conrad's thought informs Anthony Winner's analysis of *Lord Jim, Nostromo, The Secret Agent,* and *Under Western Eyes:* in the face of a cosmos that provides no basis for value or meaning, Conrad upholds the idea of moral civilization as a human necessity at the same time that he perceives it to rest not on fact but on illusion. Although this insight was convincingly established more than two decades ago in an essay by J. Hillis Miller,[1] its critical implications for both conceptual and technical aspects of Conrad's fiction as well as its potential relevance to contemporary debate over the nature and function of the culture of our own society certainly justify its expansion into a book-length study. Anthony Winner's intricately crafted prose, combined with the lucidity of his underlying hypothesis, gives us reason to expect his work to deepen our understanding of Conrad's multi-dimensional fiction—although perhaps at the risk of occasionally exaggerating the complexity of its narrative strategies. But the versions of Conrad's masterpieces that in fact emerge from Winner's explications disappointingly tend to reflect a more dogmatic, narrower vision of human possibility than most readers would find in the texts he discusses.

Making no attempt to define his use of the two key words in the title of his study, Winner employs both in widely ranging contexts. "Culture" (often preceded by the adjective "moral") is generally used with approbation to identify a traditionally based system of values. But it can also identify a body of admirable doctrines with little substantive effect on social behavior—e.g.,

"Up close, the heartland of culture emanates a moral unsavoriness not unlike the stench of rotted hippo" (p. 13). Surprisingly in a study as recently published as this one, Winner unselfconsciously employs the word "culture," without geographic specification, as synonymous with the traditional value system of the Western world.

The word "irony," on the other hand, is used broadly enough to cover any perception, occurrence, verbal construction, or other literary device that might call into question the assumptions or ideals upheld by Western tradition. Conrad is said "to conceive human action as taking place against the background of cosmic or general irony" (p. 6), and Winner argues that each of Conrad's four major novels "juxtaposes an unexceptional protagonist against the complex and equivocal irony that is the key signature of all human endeavor" (p. 43). When used in reference to literary technique, irony is likely to be ascribed to virtually any unexpected or paradoxical narrative choice: thus, for example, Winner finds in Conrad's characterization of the narrator of *Under Western Eyes* "the irony of a fundamental lack of an ironic temper" (p. 105). On the other hand, irony need not always reflect an authorial point of view, but can become in its own right the object of skeptical undermining. Thus, Winner maintains, Marlow's ironies are finally "contained tensely within an omniscient irony about irony itself" (p. 21).

While the irony of circumstance inevitably undermines human intentions, the conceptual irony that Winner regards as central to Conrad's art is as likely to dignify as to deflate the illusions that mortals create in an effort to give meaning to their lives. Conrad's characteristic stance toward culturally validated ideals is said to resemble romantic irony, "a moral and epistemological self-consciousness about the reality of what imagination can create" (p. 41). But most fundamental to Winner's study is a very broad conception of irony that defines it as the central shaping device of Conrad's major fiction, which paradoxically imposes "the artifact of moral culture upon the anarchistic facts of man's flaws and nature's indifference" at the same time that it insists upon the illusory nature of the culture that it embodies and protects (p. 92).

In progressing chronologically through the four novels that he explicates, Winner finds an increasing skepticism on Conrad's part regarding culture's capacity to provide an adequate basis for human existence, paralleled by an increasingly stark rejection of the possibility of establishing a viable identity without the support of a validating culture. His reading of *Lord Jim* identifies the first half of the novel as an equivocal investigation of "the truth of public value" and the second half as a repudiation of the romantic dream of independent self-creation. The crime against "moral civilization" that Jim commits in his desertion of the Patna is mitigated, Winner argues, by various suggestions of the insufficiency of the code of values against which he has transgressed. But Jim's subsequent efforts at heroic achievement in Patusan are seen not as a valid effort to compensate for a prior failure but rather as a second repudiation of the claims of Western culture.

Identifying the aspirations that take Jim to Patusan as a manifestation of "the early modern vision of self-creation," comparable, for example, to "the great Gatsby's desire to live out a platonic idea of himself" (p. 19), Winner suggests that even if Jim were permanently to have sustained his identity as the admired and trusted leader of Patusan, his retreat from the Western world would remain a betrayal of his own civilization: "By desiring to go it alone, Jim undercuts the bonds of moral community. These bonds may be illusions, but the illusion they represent may finally be the necessary paradox inherent in the maintenance of moral meaning in a dark world" (p. 19).

In order to support a judgment of Jim's endeavors considerably harsher than that provided by Marlow's narration, Winner argues that Marlow's ambivalence, no less than Jim's romantic dream, is part of Conrad's "treatment of the condition of Western moral order" (p. 26). Marlow's guarded admiration for Jim thus becomes for Winner a sign of Marlow's own inadequacy: "Indeed, Marlow's account of Jim in Patusan suggests in its near-envy a story told by one of the many overcivilized, overironic early moderns—the diverse kin of J. Alfred Prufrock—who covet the unmediated splendor of 'real life'" (p. 26).

Given the broad range of viewpoints that Conrad makes available for interpreting Jim's story, there would seem to be little basis for granting ultimate authority to any single perspective. But for Winner, all perplexities are resolved near the close of the novel by Marlow's citation of the views of an unidentified correspondent: "'You said . . . that 'giving up your life to them' (*them* meaning all of mankind with skins brown, yellow, or black in colour) 'was like selling your soul to a brute.' You contended that 'that kind of thing' was only endurable and enduring when based on a firm conviction in the truth of ideas racially our own, in whose name are established the order, the morality of an ethical progress" (p. 36). For many readers, the assumptions underlying this passage are among the most troubling in all of Conrad's work. But for Winner they seem to constitute an entirely valid corrective to Marlow's indulgence toward Jim's romantic dream: "The rigid restatement of the code places Marlow's allegiance and the question that underlies it firmly beyond the pale. Jim's faith and Marlow's willingness to entertain it involve a radical separation from the secular religion that ratifies our decency, honor, and truth" (p. 36).

Categorically rejecting the natives of Patusan as potential judges of Jim's identity, Winner suggests—by means of a metaphor rather startling in its context—that when Jim leaves his own civilization behind, he enters a vacuum that precludes any external validation of his achievements: "Can there be real sound where there are no actual ears?" (p. 29). A more cogent criticism of Jim's endeavors has been made in a recent essay by Hunt Hawkins, who suggests that Jim's efforts to achieve a valid identity in Patusan are doomed not because he has rejected his own culture but because he has not truly dissociated himself from it: "All his actions are taken not in reference to Patusan, but to a European idea of honor. . . . Jim is never fully able to redeem his sense of his own trustworthiness because he does not regard the trust of the natives, upon which he is so dependent, as equivalent to European trust."[2] An underlying question not addressed by either Winner or Hawkins, although highly germane to the judgmental conclusions of both, is the extent to which any human being is psychologically capable of a thoroughgoing transfer from one cultural framework to another.

In *Nostromo* as in *Lord Jim,* Winner contrasts the title character's initial circumstances, which offer him a basis for self-esteem through the fulfillment of externally imposed demands, with his subsequent efforts to establish a viable existence outside the framework validated by Western culture. When Nostromo loses his socially conferred sense of purpose, his disintegration demonstrates, far less ambiguously than Jim's jungle escapades, that the romantic ideal of independent self-creation bears little relation to commonplace psychological realities. Attributing to Nostromo a "pathetic fall from dependence into an independence of being he cannot manage," Winner observes that he "seems almost to wish to avoid the responsibility of character" (p. 48).

Winner's concluding summary of Nostromo's significance exemplifies the complex, paradoxical, sometimes even mutually obliterating meanings that he often attributes to Conrad's work.

> Gian' Battista contains the potential for efficient action that should be educated to serve a traditional moral ethos. At the same time, the Capataz exists beyond the pale of moral education; he is a simple fatality, a pretext for illusion. Mysteriously, the man is an absence and a truth. His position attracts derisive skepticism and hopeful idealism. He is nothing and everything. In a way, his reality resembles the artifice that much late-century and early modern art would create out of prosaic and hollow fact. [p. 68]

Winner's judgment of the Occidental Republic reflects the same emphasis on ambiguity and balance that characterizes his analysis of *Nostromo*'s title character. While ultimately proving undeserving of the faith that each initially inspires, both suggest that true achievement may be the product of illusion. Finding the novel's political vision less pessimistic than critics have generally claimed, Winner declares the work to be "as skeptical of skepticism as it is of idealism" (p. 69).

Winner's attempt to demonstrate a pattern of increasing doubt on Conrad's part regarding the efficacy of morally truthful illusions can easily be sustained through the first three chapters of his book. But his analysis of *The Secret Agent* reflects a vision so bleak as to render questionable the penultimate position that it holds within the structure of his argument. Accurately noting that "the irony that blankets the London of *The Secret Agent* seems far removed from the ambiguous interplay of sheltering illusion and innate disorder in *Lord Jim* and *Nostromo*," he tellingly observes that in *The Secret Agent* "almost every setting, character, and action mocks and is mocked by elusive moral judgments" (p. 70).

Winner's response even to those characters who embody positive moral values is considerably harsher than that expressed by certain other critics. (Compare, for example, Eloise Knapp Hay's description of Stevie, his sister, and his mother as "delightfully and nobly sensitive in their desperate circumstances"[3] with Winner's description of Winnie as "the demeaning picture of a charmlessness so complete as to suggest a grotesquerie of being itself" [p. 79].) Furthermore, Winner perceives the social order portrayed in this novel as pervasively as well as irremediably flawed: "the fact of outrageous injustice and the odious disjunction between things as they are and as they ought to be appear to demand nothing less than revolution," but the novel presents an image of anarchists that "mocks the very idea of radical action" (p. 75). Stevie is far wiser than the bomb-carrying Professor, Winner observes, by virtue of recognizing his own powerlessness.

Winner's effective evocation of the vision of utter futility reflected in so many facets of *The Secret Agent* creates a problematic context for the judgmental stance that he occasionally takes toward certain inhabitants of this novel's world. His tendency to alternate between a fatalistic cynicism that would render moral evaluation meaningless and an appeal to traditional ethical categories is particularly evident in his treatment of Mr. Verloc. Initially (and rather confusingly) he encourages the reader to perceive an analogy rather than a critical disjunction between the generously intentioned Winnie and her purely self-serving husband: "Mr. Verloc's omnivorous yet inert egoism is the debased but logical image of Winnie's limitations" (pp. 82–83). But a short while later, Winner categorically denounces Verloc's philosophically rationalized indolence by means of a concept drawn from traditional theology: "Mr. Verloc's force, like Sa-

Conrad as Nihilistic Conservative

tan's, is that of negation" (p. 83). Equally anomalous is a subsequent identification of Verloc's role as double agent as "an incarnation of the Schopenhauerian Will that undoes human intentions" (pp. 83–84), a puzzling assertion in view of the fact that in this novel all human intentions seem intrinsically doomed by contingencies that would appear to render ludicrous the very notion of a determining will.

In his concluding description of *The Secret Agent,* Winner observes that Conrad's "complex playing with the idea of civilization as fiction . . . now seems directed as much at the offensiveness of the fiction's raw materials as at the fictionality of true shelter" (p. 91). Nevertheless, he still perceives the shaping vision embodied in this work as a victory of the human imagination over the actual chaos of existence: "The flat faith and stolid order do finally hold meaninglessness and the horror of primal disorder at a remove. Language can still perform a protective work" (p. 91). Thus, Winner maintains, it is not until *Under Western Eyes* that Conrad finally repudiates his faith in the redemptive power of human effort of any kind.

The analysis of *Under Western Eyes* that constitutes the final chapter of Winner's study is subtitled "Irony and Women's Strength." But unlike the subtitles of his prior three chapters ("Irony and Dream," "The Irony of Faithful Service," and "The Irony of Home Truths"), this final pairing of subject and narrative stance reflects a conjunction that Winner perceives to be untenable. The train of thought that underlies the linking of stylistic, political, sexual, and metaphysical issues that Winner attempts in this chapter rests on a highly problematic dichotomy between masculine and feminine modes of perception. In his introduction to *Culture and Irony,* Winner explicitly dissociates himself from Conrad's view of women: "Conrad's irony—in one of its least engaging qualities—portrays women's moral romanticism as powerless to cope with the demands that realities place upon faith" (p. 9). But Winner's analysis of *Under Western Eyes* suggests that his own commitment to stereotypical sexual dichotomies may in fact be more rigid than Conrad's own.

The essence of Winner's argument seems to be that Conrad's choice of Russian autocracy as the subject for this novel requires him to confront a social reality too appalling to be rendered meaningful by the skeptical, masculine voice that shaped his previous fiction. Western civilization as portrayed in *Lord Jim, Nostromo,* and *The Secret Agent* justified Conrad's ironic affirmation by imposing at least the illusion of order upon human existence. But the Russia portrayed in *Under Western Eyes* is perceived by Winner to embody the ultimate negation of such order, "Conrad's fullest evocation of the darkness surrounding all the endeavors of moral civilization . . . the institutionalization of the cosmic irony that mocks and opposes man's hopes (pp. 116–17). The "masculine work" of protecting certain sheltering illusions cannot proceed in the face of such visible chaos. Thus, Winner maintains, the "special, and appalling, fact of *Under Western Eyes* is that heroic, manly irony collapses into futility and negation" (pp. 92–93).

Immediately after declaring this work to be "the most feminine of Conrad's major novels," Winner describes it as "Conrad's most gruelingly psychological story, and psychology here arises out of the defeat of reason and practicality and the enforced dominance of instinct, feeling, and sensibility" (p. 93). Personal relationships, he continues, are now given precedence over political concerns, and Razumov is subject to a "sensation of sheer bereavement" comparable only to the experiences of female figures in Conrad's earlier novels. Finally, Winner attributes to the male narrator of the novel "the combination of a kind of practical obtuseness with the civility, sensibility, and moral superiority that Conrad associates with women," proposing that Conrad created such a narrator because he believed "that only the ideal feminine truths at the heart of Western culture are capable of enduring and perhaps deflecting the fierceness of Russian cynicism" (p. 104). But Conrad's narrative substitution of idealism for irony is perceived by Winner to exact a high price, compromising "the moral discovery his tale demands" (p. 106).

If Russia is granted the capacity to emasculate both the protagonist of *Under Western Eyes* and the novel's narrative tone, it is also assigned the power to inspire the portrayal of female characters who are stronger, more independent, more outspoken, and more politically active than the women in Conrad's earlier works.

There may, as Winner claims, be considerable ambivalence in Conrad's newfound "faith in the force of women" (p. 106). But when Winner observes, for example, that Sophia Antonovna "incarnates the derangement of male and female qualities and spheres of action" (p. 109), his choice of language would seem to suggest a less than enthusiastic response on his own part to the challenging of traditional gender roles.

Winner's interpretation of the Russia portrayed in *Under Western Eyes* as the embodiment of absolute nihilism and moral chaos, which goes well beyond what is literally asserted in Conrad's text, may be seen as impoverishing the novel in several ways. The conviction that the political realities of Russia preclude "the kind of ethical balancing permitted by Western liberty" (p. 98) leads him to deny that any moral questions are raised by Razumov's predicament in the opening section of the novel. Subsequently, his image of Russia as a land in which no positive values can survive leads him greatly to oversimplify Conrad's contrast of East and West. To find in the ideological fervor of victims of Russian autocracy and in the complacent orderliness of the beneficiaries of Switzerland's longstanding bargain with fate an opposition that highlights both the strengths and the limitations of each would be impossible within Winner's conceptual framework.

Winner's argument encounters direct resistance from Conrad's text when, instead of exalting Switzerland as the antidote to Russia's evils, the narrator complains about Geneva's dreariness and hypocritical respectability. Acknowledging that he finds the narrator's criticism of Swiss democracy to be "troubling," Winner nevertheless attempts to defend his own hypothesis by attributing all political ironies in the novel to the need to question "the very possibility of moral meaning in a world that contains the fact of Russia" (p. 97).

Under Western Eyes constitutes a terminal point for Winner's paradigmatic analysis of Conrad's fiction because its male characters repudiate the ironic "artificing of faith" by means of which men, according to Winner, have traditionally protected women from the chaos of reality, while its female characters, finding an adequate basis for their existence in a passionate commitment to social change, cease to require the shaping power of cultural illusions. A hermeneutics that finds in this novel "the utter cynicism that will betray all mankind's works" (p. 91) can perhaps best be described as the imaginative construction of an illusory and perhaps not wholly necessary faith.

Notes

1. Miller, *Poets of Reality: Six Twentieth-Century Writers* (Cambridge: Harvard Univ. Press, 1966), pp. 13–39. No reference is made to this work in Winner's study.
2. Hawkins, "Conrad and the Psychology of Colonialism," in Ross C. Murphin, ed., *Conrad Revisited: Essays for the Eighties* (University: Univ. of Alabama Press, 1985), pp. 78–79.
3. Hay, *The Political Novels of Joseph Conrad: A Critical Study* (Chicago: Univ. of Chicago Press, 1963), p. 252.

Taking Comedy Seriously

Thomas M. Leitch

James Harvey. *Romantic Comedy in Hollywood from Lubitsch to Sturges.* New York: Knopf, 1987. xiv, 720 pp.

Harry Levin. *Playboys and Killjoys: An Essay on the Theory and Practice of Comedy.* New York: Oxford University Press, 1987. x, 214 pp.

Nancy Pogel. *Woody Allen.* Boston: Twayne, 1987. xvi, 247 pp.

Scott Cutler Shershow. *Laughing Matters: The Paradox of Comedy.* Amherst: University of Massachusetts Press, 1986. xii, 151 pp.

Richard Keller Simon. *The Labyrinth of the Comic: Theory and Practice from Fielding to Freud.* Tallahassee: Florida State University Press, 1985. xii, 260 pp.

Gerald Weales. *Canned Goods as Caviar: American Film Comedies of the 1930s.* Chicago: University of Chicago Press, 1985. x, 386 pp.

How seriously can we take comedy, which, after all, is designed to make us laugh? Nancy Pogel apparently takes the films of Woody Allen almost as seriously as the director himself does. In her new book, *Woody Allen*, she not only elucidates many of Allen's non-comic allusions (to Ingmar Bergman, to F. Scott Fitzgerald, to *Citizen Kane*) but adds some of her own. Allen's voice-over addresses to the audience in *Love and Death* don't simply stem from Allen's borscht-belt background but from "Tolstoy's first-person narrations and Dostoevsky's intimate authorial voice" (p. 72). Allen's use of the word *rose* in the titles of *Broadway Danny Rose* and *The Purple Rose of Cairo* "may indicate that Allen is not only using all of the heroic allusions associated with it, but may also be mocking the heroic pretensions associated with the term" (p. 190). More generally, she favors a thematic analysis which makes Allen's later films sound forbidding indeed:

> In *The Purple Rose of Cairo,* Allen highlights the philosophical concern with language as a "prisonhouse" that promises fulfillment but must continually frustrate it. Allen devises dialogues around a number of related questions: What are the possibilities for escape from determinate circumstances such as those described by Wittgenstein, where the limits of one's language are the limits of one's world? Can either film or reality be satisfying and authentic when each is so intertextual, when each is mediated by so many "others"—by interlocutors, perspectives, or pressures—by actors, plot, audience, producers, the ideology of a competitive society, individual self-interest, time, and history? Is meaning possible in the face of an overdetermination of meanings? Does knowledge or an understanding of the "rules of the game" make a difference? Is there such a thing as making a liberating decision when the limitations of language and experience may dominate the terms of the choice? Can art offer sustenance and the hope that may lead to risk taking and freedom, or does it merely exacerbate the problem by encouraging false illusions? [p. 203]

Not many films, comedies or not, could support the burden of these questions, which happily form a climax rather than a refrain to Pogel's discussion. Pogel treats earlier films like *Take the Money and Run, Bananas,* and *Sleeper* in one of two ways: either by discovering in them intimations of the thematic problems that reach full flower in the *Rose* pictures, or by noting briskly that often in these early films, "jokes take precedence over composition, lighting, color, and carefully controlled mise-en-scène" (p. 34). The progression she traces in Allen's career focuses on a single figure, "the American little-man character" (p. 2), descended from the characters of such humorists as James Thurber, Robert Benchley, and S. J. Perelman, and who is nearly always incarnated in Allen's films by the director himself. The little-man hero typically "feels himself to be a stranger in his own culture," but beneath his mask of incompetence and fear "lies a sense of innocence lost to time and the complexities of a fast-paced modern life" which allows comic artists who adopt this pose at once to "criticize their society and make fun of themselves" (p. 3).

The assimilation of the Allen persona to the little-man paradigm is a masterful stroke that allows Pogel to explain persuasively how he can present himself, in *Sleeper* and *Manhattan*, both as a comic figure and a moral exemplar. She acutely observes, for example, that the Allen hero is "too human" for the dehumanized world of *Sleeper* (p. 68). In the course of Allen's career, however—or at least in the course of Pogel's analysis—the little-man hero's relation to his world becomes less and less comic. In his later films, Pogel's Allen seems to rise above mere comedy. In *Stardust Memories*, "as a mature artist, he confronts himself, his audience, his critics, and his medium, and he deconstructs them all" (p. 150). A passage like this makes a strong case for the Philistine in *Stardust Memories* who gushed to Allen's hero, "I just love your movies. Especially your early, funny ones."

Pogel seems less comfortable with the early, funny ones than with *Zelig*, which she can describe as displaying "a saddened mood that at once interacts with and subverts the film's comic surface to produce an inconclusive and dialogic text" (p. 171). The term *dialogic* is borrowed from Mikhail Bakhtin, whose discussion of medieval carnival as a basis for comedy and for the multiplicity of voices and moods in the modern novel is central to Pogel's argument.[1] Despite the importance Pogel attaches to Bakhtin, she uses *dialogic* with a freedom that sometimes subverts its Bakhtinian associations. Bakhtin's carnival is a forerunner and a model for modern comedy; its chorus of inconsistent voices, many raised in irreverent parody, affirms the triumph of the human spirit over constraints that makes the carnival a prototypical comedy. In her passage on *Zelig*, however, Pogel sets the film's dialogic aspect against its comic surface, as if she felt obliged to rescue the film from its status as a comedy, even a sad comedy, by insisting how serious it was. Pogel's discussion not only makes Allen's earlier films seem more careless, more superficial, more inconsequential than his later work—as of course they are—it makes them seem more comic, or at least funnier.

But are the funniest films really the most comic? In Pogel's account the two terms seem remote and often opposed. Toward the end of her discussion of *Zelig*, she quotes Robert Stam on reflexive texts: "Unafraid of pleasure, the thrust of their interrupted spectacle is fundamentally comic, not in the sense of provoking hilarity, but in the sense of maintaining a socialized distance between the desiring subject and the text. They articulate the play of desire and the pleasure principle *and* the obstacles to their realization."[2] Pogel and Stam are of course entitled to define comedy in any way they like, but the socialized distance between the desiring subject and the text sounds less like a condition of comedy than an escape from comedy. Pogel may take Allen seriously, but she doesn't take comedy very seriously. In trying to rescue Allen's films from their comic matrix by straining to redefine comedy in a way that will make the films artistically and intellectually respectable, Pogel reveals a fundamental distrust of comedy that allows her to describe *A Midsummer Night's Sex Comedy* as "funny but profound" (p. 169). Aristophanes and Rabelais and Shakespeare aren't funny but profound; they're profoundly funny.

Pogel's trouble in defining the comic appeal of Allen's later films is less her responsibility than Allen's own. Of all Allen's films to date, *Annie Hall* and *Manhattan* come the closest to being profoundly funny; *Zelig* and *The Purple Rose of Cairo* (and *Hannah and Her Sisters*, which Pogel doesn't discuss) are probably better described as funny but profound. Like Chaplin fifty years earlier, Allen has developed an increasingly problematic relation to his comic roots; lately he hasn't seemed to trust comedy any more than Pogel does. Ten years ago Allen might have greeted Pogel's book with a satiric bray (remember the scene in *Annie Hall* in which he calls on Marshall McLuhan to deflate a posturing intellectual?). Now he's more likely to take it seriously.

But if we speak of taking comedy seriously, we need to look elsewhere than Pogel. The question is not how seriously we can take comedy (all too seriously, it seems), but rather in what serious ways comedy operates. And it is clear that these ways need not involve self-consciously serious themes. Daniel Moews has observed that Keaton's films "do not belong among the works of art possessing significant social themes. They do not fit into the schools of modernism, existentialism, or contemporary protest, and the attempt to make them fit, to force a social or philosophical commentary out of them, is to do violence to their real nature, to the fact that even though they are very intelligent comedies, there is in them no serious interest in ideas." Keaton's films, Moews contends, "are enduring masterpieces not for any highly individual means of expression, nor for any intense personal vision . . . ; rather they are classic because they so brilliantly sum up the themes and means of expression characteristic of their age."[3] Doing what it does superbly well can make a comedy serious, because providing comic pleasure is a very serious business.

Anyone who wants to take comedy seriously should be prepared for the striking indifference of contemporary critical theory to the problems of comedy.[4] It is tempting to conclude that poststructuralists do not like to laugh, or at least to admit that they do. But there are other reasons for the neglect of comedy by current theorists. Critics whose project is to deconstruct the premises that enable a given discourse might well be taken aback by comedies like *Duck Soup* or *The Palm Beach Story* that seem to have deconstructed themselves. Furthermore, since even the smallest comic unit, the joke, turns on a reversal, comedies seem always to be setting their audience up for a realignment of their expectations. Poststructuralists are uncomfortable with the whole idea of being set up, being made to react in a given way. Colin MacCabe has observed that when an audience watches *American Graffiti*, "we know, from the beginning of the narrative, that Curt Henderson will leave the town and yet . . . we hover, in suspense, over a decision which, once resolved, is obvious."[5] Every comedy constantly puts us into the position of being pleasurably surprised by developments we could have foreseen with perfect clarity; our pleasure therefore has as its requisite our willful blindness to the operation of the codes and conventions which produce it. Comic structures depend on arousing certain responses (tension, amusement, laughter) in prescribed sequences. Not only do comedies invite the audiences to laugh, they assume they will laugh only at certain times and in certain ways (during the punch lines, at the funny characters). An audience that does not respond with appropriate laughter may have the pleasure of using the comedy to illustrate an incisive argument, as MacCabe does with *American Graffiti,* but they are missing the pleasure that the comedy has prescribed for them. The aura of intentionalism that hangs over this prescription is at the heart of contemporary theory's distrust of comedy. It is impossible for critics to talk in good faith about why a comedy makes us laugh if they believe that the audience which the analyst projects is only a hypostatized ideal, that in fact there is no us.

Contemporary theory typically analyzes genres by deconstructing them, and it is not really surprising that so few critics would be engaged by the relation of comedy to satire, or to humor, or to laughter itself. But the questions raised by these issues remain provoking. What is the connection between laughter as a pleasure deliberately indulged and laughter as a convulsive experience suffered, as when an old-fashioned dentist gives us laughing gas? When Edgar Kennedy or Jean Hagen gets a pie in the face, to what degree is the audience's laughter a socially therapeutic response, to what degree an anodyne or opiate for potentially dangerous sentiments, and to what degree a genuinely subversive response that provides a pattern for further action? Does the answer to questions about the audience's experience of comedy depend on privileging a certain kind of comedy—mocking or accepting, naturalized or self-reflexive—as normative? But these questions are all distractions from the leading question about comedy, the most unfashionable question of all: what is everybody (or the hypostasized audience) laughing at? What's so funny?

This question seems to have dropped out of the discourse on comedy almost completely since Norman Holland's 1982 study *Laughing.* Evidently it remains a legitimate question only in film criticism, in which laughter is more closely allied to the comic than in literary criticism. Just as poststructuralists are suspicious of any genres which are defined in terms of a reaction they prescribe for an ideal audience (if I fail to laugh at a Three Stooges short, does that mean that it's not a comedy?), critics of many different persuasions are suspicious of theories of comedy that would conflate the audience's gelastic reaction with the nature of comedy itself. Audiences laugh at many things that are not comedies—the antics of their pets and children, their own slips of the tongue, the more picturesque misfortunes of others—and they may have many other reactions to comedy besides laughter. I can remember laughing only once at *The Purple Rose of Cairo,* but it still felt like a comedy to me.

Talking about what comedy is, however, is impossible without considering how it works. Whether we like it or not, theories of comedy have to postulate a normative audience. Deconstructionists aren't bothered by the entrance of this audience; in fact, they require such an ideal audience to deconstruct ('this is how comedy makes other people—not me—feel'). But other critics resist the affective approach to comedy more strongly. In order to talk about the operation of comedy as comedy, we need to discuss 'our' reactions to it without simply assimilating the mode to the sum of individual experiences of it. What is most surprising about recent work on comedy is the extent to which it does deal, however indirectly, with the question of what's so funny to the hypostasized audience, and its corresponding success in taking comedy seriously. Literary studies of comedy, for example, are often able to take the subject seriously despite their invocations of Bakhtin, who often stands in for a living theorist as a touchstone of comic theory.

In Harry Levin's *Playboys and Killjoys,* which is aptly subtitled *An Essay on the Theory and Practice of Comedy,* Bakhtin makes only a brief cameo appearance, a position he shares with dozens of other historians and theorists of comedy. Levin's discussion, urbanely assimilative and encyclopedic, acknowledges the importance of Bakhtin's theory of carnival but cannot linger over him or anyone else. Reading Levin often provides the same sort of experience as listening to a lecturer who, while pretending to remind us of things we already knew, is slyly feeding us information. It is an experience many readers will associate with Northrop Frye, and in his wide range of reference, his gift for the telling summary, and his ability to make convincing connections, often within a single paragraph, between such diverse comedies as *Ralph Roister Doister, Le bourgeois gentilhomme, The Beggar's Opera,* and *Dead Souls,* Levin surpasses Frye's cogent studies of

Shakespearean comedy and romance and recalls the synoptic brilliance of the *Anatomy of Criticism*.

At the same time, Levin adopts a very different attitude toward the theoretical implications of his analyses from the attitude Frye displays. Readers of *A Natural Perspective* and *The Secular Scripture*, made slightly tipsy on Frye's heady readings of individual texts, all too often awoke in the closing pages to find that they had been shanghaied into accepting Frye's anthropological archetypes as the motivating forces in those works. Levin's theoretical aims are far more modest. Citing the recent tendency of literary theory to depart from direct engagement with literary texts in favor of engagement with literary concepts, he offers as a corrective comedy's "unique and available record of practice, which can be observed empirically and theorized about in more general terms.... And it will be the strongest proof of the theory if, in its light, the practice is better understood and more thoroughly enjoyed" (pp. 7–8). Such a passage is as close as Levin ever comes to making explicit his anti-theoretical bias. Whereas in Frye, examples always seem to be offered for the sake of advancing the theory, Levin's theory seems almost to be offered in order to organize his examples. Trying to isolate the argument of *Playboys and Killjoys* is therefore rather like picking all the cherries and walnuts from a fruitcake in order to taste the cake without adulteration, perversely overlooking the fact that the cake was baked especially to enhance the fruit.

Still, Levin's argument, although frequently obscured by the examples and excurses with which his discussion is studded, is quite straightforward. He declines to define comedy except indirectly: it is not the same thing as humor, farce, or satire; it is not to be defined as anything that produces laughter, for "tickling can produce the same result by the slightest manual stimulation" (p. 10); it has never "managed to serve a utilitarian function" (p. 21); it is "written to be played upon a stage in the presence of an audience" and hence follows a form "shaped by performance" (p. 5); it operates in a dialectical relation with tragedy; its avatars resembles each other like Wittgenstein's games, defined through a family resemblance, and indeed games are "a genus of which comedy is a species" (p. 4). These observations prepare for an account of comedy which attempts to unite elements of structural and thematic analysis. These elements, which Levin grounds respectively in the audience's sense of superiority, their feeling of "sudden glory," Hobbes found constitutive of comedy and, in the sense of incongruity Kant found common to all comic situations, account for Levin's two central terms: the ridiculous, which implies the audience's superiority to the objects of their laughter, and the ludicrous, which implies a disposition "to share the fun with others" (p. 12).

Comedy, Levin contends, is based on "a dialectical interplay between the ludicrous and the ridiculous" (p. 13). He traces the synchronic development of the artless fool at play to the artful fool, the clown, and his playing to "comedy, bringing others—more pretentiously—into that charmed circle, reducing their pretensions to folly, and thereby effecting a transference from the domain of the ludicrous to that of the ridiculous" (p. 71). This impulse to free or mocking play generates the stock hero of Levin's comedy, the playboy like Synge's Christy Mahon—or like Pseudolus, Falstaff, or Macheath. And since "it takes two to make an argument" (p. 36) like the argument of comedy, the playboy is typically pitted against an antagonist who seeks to stifle, contain, or deny the impulse to play, some killjoy like Malvolio, Morose, or the *senex iratus* of Roman New Comedy and Molière's domestic comedies.

Having defined comedy in terms of two paradigmatic figures and its argument or plot in terms of their opposition, Levin proceeds to outline a series of increasingly complex relations they may assume. A comedy may turn on the revelation of playboys disguised by accident or by their own duplicity; or it may present a clownish playboy, a zany who is ludicrously attempting to ape the airs of some more respectable killjoy, often taking the form of a figure like Charlie Chaplin whose own nature is comically divided; or it may dramatize the generational conflict between playboy children and their killjoy parents, moving through courtship to marriage; or it may begin with marriage and show the adulterous affairs of the playboy, challenging the manners of a killjoy social order.

These terms and the plots they predicate are no more comprehensive or convincing than the more rigorous system Frye first advanced forty years ago, and readers who agree with Levin that "the territory [of comedy], for all the trudging through it, has never been very precisely or lucidly charted" (p. 6) are unlikely to be persuaded that his expedition has produced decisively different results. Who would think of refuting Levin's emphasis on the ludicrous and the ridiculous, or on playboys and killjoys, or on duplicities, zanyism, courtship, and adultery? Its value lies not in its logical necessity, its superiority to other theories, but in the way it illuminates what Levin aptly calls the practice of comedy and the pleasure we take in this practice. Levin writes of the way New Comedy transforms family and social tensions into matter for an audience's amusement:

Instinctively we sympathize with pleasure-seeking youth, looking through his eyes at crabbed age, feeling his distrust at whatever stands in the way of fulfilled desire. An Everyman in a hedonistic morality, suspended between Money and the Match, he is blocked on one side and abetted on the other. Inevitably, the agonistic principle runs counter to the pleasure principle. His relation to his seniors is negative, despite familial bonds; his relation to the servants is positive, athwart the social tensions. The former is a killjoy agon, financially grounded, tending toward satire. The latter is a playboy alliance, sexually animated, leading toward romance. Comedy is compounded of the interaction between the two, varying in its emphasis from one mode to the other. [p. 96]

Although this is not an especially original exposition of the typical themes and situations of New Comedy, it could hardly be improved upon as an analysis of how and why those themes and situations give audiences the kinds of pleasure they associate with comedy. Throughout Levin's discussion of the rise of tragicomedy and metacomedy, or his supplemental essays on protocomedy, city comedy, humor, and satire—the essay on humor especially sheds welcome light on the relation between humor and wit—Levin excels in indicating the ways in which audiences enjoy the materials of comedy. If he never directly addresses the question of what's so funny (a question he would probably find improper, referring its answer to the province of humor rather than comedy), his empirical approach repeatedly helps to reveal what's comic about comedy.

Perhaps the greatest strength of Levin's analysis is its persuasive command of the questions it raises. Levin has an answer for every question of comic theory he addresses. He rules on every dispute—comedy is distinct from the comic spirit, comedy is inseparable from stage performance, comedy is to be theorized empirically, but not through its effects on an audience—with an air of reasonableness that makes his conclusions seem inevitable, so that his own audience may have the impression of getting answers to questions they had never even formulated as questions. Two other recent books in the field take the opposite approach by raising questions they never satisfactorily answer. This inconclusiveness is central to design of one of them, Richard Keller Simon's *The Labyrinth of the Comic*. Like Levin's, Simon's goals are syncretic and comprehensive, and Bakhtin plays a much more prominent role in his argument. "Laughter," Simon quotes Bakhtin, "is one of the essential forms of truth concerning the world as a whole, concerning history and man. . . . Certain essential aspects of the world are accessible only to laughter."[6] Simon, following Bakhtin, is after much bigger game than defining comedy as tragedy's dialectical other; he contends that the comic perspective is the only truly comprehensive perspective because human consciousness itself is comic. Hence comedy is not a kind of game played on a stage before an interactive audience; it is a kind of awareness that plays a constitutive role in defining human life and human history.

Since Simon is one of those critics Levin gently rebukes as less interested in comedies than in the comic, his materials and procedures are very different from Levin's. Following Bakhtin's observation that novels are basically parodic and thus contain a greater comic potential than other literary modes, Simon's analysis avoids theatrical works entirely and focuses on four kinds of prose texts: self-reflexive English comic novels; philosophical critiques of comedy and irony (concentrating on Kierkegaard); scientific studies of laughter by Anglo-American psychologists (Darwin, Spencer, Dewey, et al.); and Freud's psychoanalytic account of wit in *Jokes and Their Relation to the Unconscious*. Deploring the fragmentation of modern comic theory among different academic disciplines, Simon attempts a rapprochement among the different interests of his four kinds of texts: "comedy as literary form, the comic as philosophic attitude, laughter as psychological response, joking as psychodynamic play" (p. 2). The subtitle of Simon's book—*Theory and Practice from Fielding to Freud*—closely resembles that of Levin's. But Simon sees comic theory and comic practice as much more closely connected. Throughout the dauntingly wide range of material he considers, the common ground is the reflexive nature of the texts, which are, as Simon says of his novels, "both provocations to laugh and studies of the laugh" (p. 1)—discourses about comedy whose presentational strategies are themselves comic.

Simon's title comes from Bergson's essay "Laughter," which both describes the comic as a labyrinth and offers its own discourse as a labyrinth without a center, a labyrinth whose putative goal is to provide "a straightforward analysis" (p. 9) of laughter, but which, failing to reach this chimerical goal, ends by confessing its failure, offering instead its readers the experience of wandering in a labyrinth whose techniques are comic:

"Laughter" is framed by a provocation to laughter and is itself a comic work—the labyrinth of the comic is a comic labyrinth. If we have made our way carefully enough in the labyrinth we should also be laughing. Bergson is testing us, for what is at issue is whether we can exit the labyrinth at all or will remain hopelessly lost in its mazes. But if we are laughing then our task has been hopelessly complicated, for it is by no means clear how much of the essay we should take seriously. . . . If the reader laughs, then Bergson is affirmed, for what he has had to say about laughter [that it cannot finally be grasped and analyzed] is correct. And if the reader does not laugh, does not see the repetition and inversion that closes the essay, then Bergson laughs at the reader, who has clearly not understood the argument, and once again, Bergson is affirmed. [pp. 9–10]

Although Erasmus and Cervantes portend the line of self-reflexive analyses of comedy on which Simon focuses (the *Praise of Folly* is a purer example of the pattern than any of the examples Simon analyzes at greater length), he begins his study with

Fielding, who makes explicit the connection Cervantes had seen between comedy and consciousness. Fielding marks the moment in history at which definitions of the comic were shifting from Hobbes's emphasis on the ridiculous and Addison's and Shaftesbury's on good-natured sympathy to theories of incongruity which were ultimately to lead to Kant's account of comedy in his *Critique of Judgment*. Unlike Levin, who advances a synthesis between ridicule and incongruity, Simon sees the second perspective as far more radical than the first. Fielding's perception, he contends, was that "consciousness itself was comic, comic because of its incongruous nature. This is an important moment in the history of laughter, for thereby the subject gains a new status—the comic is neither an unpleasant characteristic of men and women, which reminds us of our baseness, nor an incredibly rosy characteristic, which attempts to convince us of our loving kindness. It is, however, a fundamental quality shared by everyone" (p. 17). From this insight descend two traditions of comedy: the reflexive English comic novel, which reaches an apotheosis in Meredith, and the philosophical study of comedy and laughter by Kierkegaard and other analysts of Romantic Irony. It remained for later scientists and psychoanalysts to theorize the ways in which comedy and laughter were models of human behavior.

Simon pursues this ambitious and challenging theory with varying success. He makes such a powerful case for the self-reflexive nature of comedy in *Joseph Andrews, Tom Jones, Vanity Fair,* and *The Ordeal of Richard Feverel* (and for several other novels he names without discussing: *Humphry Clinker, Tristram Shandy, Pride and Prejudice, Nightmare Abbey*) that readers will probably be inclined to overlook points at which particular analyses strain. Simon persuasively argues that the narrator's project in *Joseph Andrews*, "to reform the reader's laughter . . . and thus to reconcile comedy with Christian morality" (p. 36), is constantly undermined, but he is less convincing when he argues that such disruptions in *Tom Jones* are controlled by the novel's structure as "comic architectural maze in prose" whose "order itself is dizzying" and which therefore produces "*orderly chaos*" (p. 62), and still less convincing when he describes Becky Sharp's life as recapitulating "the history of English comedy" (p. 123). The question is not whether these readings are defensible in terms of the evidence Simon presents, but whether they really advance and illuminate his argument that comedy is essentially self-reflexive. Although Simon's account of comic theory is apparently anti-thematic (the point of comic theory is not what it tells us about comedy but rather the comic experience it provides), his account of comedy is made thereby thematic (the point of comedy is not that it allows us to take pleasure in the incongruities of our consciousness but that it is about that pleasure) in awkward ways. Simon focuses so completely on the self-reflexive thematics of comedy that his examples of comedies, especially *Richard Feverel*, end up sounding self-reflexive but not funny, like the later films of Pogel's Woody Allen. His inclination to take Kierkegaardian irony as interchangeable with Kierkegaardian comedy extends to his later analyses as well, and by the time we come to his concluding chapters on physiological and psychoanalytic theories of laughter, the writers often seem ironic but not in the least comic.

In demurring from Simon's conflation of the comic with the ironic, I am placing greater importance than Simon would on the intimacy between comedy and humor or laughter. But this reliance on taste is unavoidable in a field whose central term has never been satisfactorily defined. When Simon remarks that "the real entertainment" of Fielding's novels is that "there are very few conclusions that can finally be drawn about this attitude to the comic beyond the sense that the comic's true value is the process, these wanderings about in the labyrinth" (p. 25), I can only protest that, although I agree with that judgment, attributing it to Fielding isn't what makes his novels entertaining for me. I'm amused by the experience they offer, not the way they theorize (or don't theorize) it. If Levin's generalizations move toward explaining how and why we laugh at comedies, Simon's move in the opposite direction, toward a history of comedy and ways of conceiving the comic.

This direction is almost inevitable given Simon's argument that consciousness is comic, for even the most straightforward consideration of comedy by a comic consciousness would gravi-

Taking Comedy Seriously

tate toward comedy itself. Academic readers can most easily rescue Simon from the irony of his own book being read as a comedy by recovering it as a history of the comic. But other readers, lacking any professional imperative to take Simon so seriously, may well prefer to read his book as a self-reflexive comic labyrinth, a reading he must surely have intended. The gradual broadening of the term *comedy* in his closing three chapters to a more inclusive but less analytically useful concept may be part of the joke he caps on his final page: "It is only when we do not take comic theory seriously that we can understand the complexities of its comedy and the meanings of its mockery" (p. 244). The implication that Simon has trapped his readers into taking him too seriously in undisclosed ways is a suggestion worthy of a comic practitioner like Fielding, though unsettling for a comic theorist like Freud.

Simon raises questions about the necessity for comic theory to adopt a thematic perspective (is comedy essentially about certain things, or does it treat non-comic things in a particular way?) and about the relation between comic theory and practice (are all comedies about comedy, and should all works of comic theory be read as comedy?) in ways that preclude any authoritative answers. A more narrowly focused study, Scott Cutler Shershow's *Laughing Matters,* turns on a single paradoxical question, the relation between two opposed impulses in comedy, the satiric impulse toward cynicism, derision, and critique, and the festive impulse toward optimism, affirmation, and celebration. Readers will recognize here Shershow's own version of Levin's elements of the ridiculous and the ludicrous, but Shershow relates them in a paradoxical way, opening several questions that never arise for Levin. He observes that "comic characters are, to quote Aristotle's formulation . . . , 'worse' than in life, but comic plots are 'better' than in life—more fortunate, more desirable, more inevitably joyful, than the unpredictable succession of events through which we struggle on the earthly stage" (pp. 17–18). What are we to make of this contrast? Does comedy tell us that if happy endings can befall such scapegraces as the heroes of comedy, they are bound to befall us as well? Or is the plot presented as something external to the characters' (and, by implication, the audience's) nature as a force which rescues them from their own baser natures? Or is the exaggeration of both plot and characters an invitation to a celebratory license, a suspension of certain kinds of judgment that the audience could never afford to make in their own lives?

In considering this question, Shershow points out that audiences for comedy foresee a happy resolution and so assimilate the hero's misfortunes as so many complications to be unraveled. Some audiences, of course, might go on to see the hero as at once contemptible and providentially favored by the conventions of the comic plot, but it is more likely that they indulge the hero's failings as necessary to their enjoyment or likely raw material for transformation by the plot. A more fundamental question, however, remains: if comic plots are unrealistically providential, in what ways can comedies be realistic? Critics have frequently dealt with this problem by defining a certain moment as privileged: for example, the opening situation, defined by the frustration of the principals' goals, or the complication, in which the force of authority threatens to suppress the community's impulse toward carnival. Since the comic catastrophe is seldom privileged as realistic, the audience watching a comedy has a double awareness of its action as realistically motivated and providentially artificial.

Shershow concentrates on the paradox arising from this double perspective:

The comic happy ending, contrived out of opposing approaches to reality, often evokes opposing interpretations and an ironic tension between them. Watching the fortunate resolution to which we always knew the characters were inevitably bound, the playwright may indeed invite us to feel what the classical critics demanded: that these feigned deeds "nevertheless could happen." But the playwright may also draw our attention to the ropes and pulleys of the deus ex machina and, indulging us with a beneficent vision of fate, may at the same time suggest "this is not the way it would happen." As the comic conception of character expresses an ambiguous cynicism, which either degrades or merely accepts the world as it "really" is, so the comic conception of plot expresses an ambiguous optimism. The happy ending magnifies the world with its infinite sense of the possible, and diminishes it with its ironic sense of the impossible. [p. 20]

Shershow proceeds to an analysis of two kinds of comedies, those in which the contrast between these two perspectives is made explicit and ironically central, and those in which the contrast is treated as a paradox to be resolved or overcome. In general he is more successful with the first group, which includes plays by Plautus, Machiavelli, and Middleton, than with the second (Euripides' *Helen,* the Second Shepherd's Play, Mayakovsky's *Mystery-Bouffe, Man and Superman,* and *Endgame*), which inevitably seems more tendentious and arbitrary. It is easier to construct paradoxes than to resolve them, and there is nothing in Shershow's later discussion to match the economy and authority of his remark that "Plautus' method . . . is founded in a certain duplicity. The playwright's mood is both complacent and indignant; he conveys an indulgent sense of holiday and a cynicism of everyday life" (p. 50). But his problems in resolving "the double comic motion toward realistic satire and idealizing fantasy" (p. 90), a motion whose theoretical roots are duly traced to Bakhtin, may be due more fundamentally to his decision to focus on two extreme versions of this conflict, the ironic opposition and the visionary synthesis, when many more complex relations between the two are possible, as we can see from the endings of Molière or Dickens. Shershow's book, more modest than either Levin's or Simon's, leaves its audience with just as many questions.

Shershow's survey of comic examples ends, like Simon's, just before the rise of motion pictures, and so raises the question of why literary theorists of comedy are so reluctant to consider film comedy. Levin, who doesn't even consider prose fiction, remarks that "it would be snobbish and self-depriving to ignore non-literary comedy, whether in the cinema, the circus, the puppet-show, the nightclub, the music hall, or the opera house, so long as it is acted—or, for that matter, danced and sung" (p. 7). But Simon's and Shershow's exclusion of film from their studies is more typical. More is at stake here than the decision to keep theories pure by remaining within a single mode of presentation, for literary and film studies—even on such a promising common ground as the theory of comedy—have never been completely comfortable with each other. Literary theorists, apart from noting that film is not literature, have often been suspicious of a medium which discouraged footnotes and encouraged extended plot summary, factual errors, and a chatty tone evidently addressed to buffs.[7] Over the past twenty years the academic study of film has produced an explosion of studies in representational theory, concentrating first in semiotics, then in psychoanalytic and political studies. But this purer strain of film theory seems so hermetic, so like a members-only club, that literary theorists who have not been trained in poststructuralism have avoided it. Literary criticism has been around long enough to have spawned a wide range of methods and tones, from among which a critic as canny as Levin can consider the "notebook" and the "treatise" before choosing the "essay" (p. 8). But film study has so far been rather self-consciously split between the higher criticism, which can seem forbiddingly high, and a bunch of books about the movies.

Virtually all studies of film comedy have fallen into the second category. Consider Gerald Weales's *Canned Goods as Caviar: American Film Comedies of the 1930s*. Here is a book which, although ostensibly dedicated to intrinsic analysis—it is divided into twelve chapters, each analyzing one film—includes an introduction that describes its author as "a methodology pack rat, an unrepentant eclecticist" (p. 2), and is never too busy for asides on the previous roles of the supporting comedians in *Steamboat Round the Bend* or the future career of the cinematographer of *Nothing Sacred*. Weales's book is emphatically and unapologetically a book about the movies.

Even given the figure of its title, there is something deceptive about the way *Canned Goods as Caviar* is packaged. That title indicates, despite Weales's disclaimer, a definite methodology uniting two points of view: an historical approach to studio production and an aesthetic approach to analysis. But despite his recurrence to these two viewpoints, Weales does not fulfill this implied program for several reasons. His opening remarks on the films' historical context are revealing: "Although all twelve of the movies can be—frequently are—watched with pleasure, I do not treat them as timeless art works. I see them as products of the decade in which they were made, which means that I sometimes discuss politics, social assumptions, contemporary trivia which are not immediately obvious nor of particular interest to audiences which, fifty years later, still find the comedies funny" (pp. 2–3). The miscellaneous quality of this list and its self-deprecating tone are borne out by what follows. Sometimes, as in his discussion of the mysterious provenance of the ending of *Nothing Sacred,* Weales's contextual remarks are pertinent and highly illuminating. Often, however, his idea of historical analysis involves recounting his own early impressions—discussing Billy Bevan's one-minute appearance as a bartender in *Bringing Up Baby,* he finds time to remark, "One of my best childhood memories of Bevan is his being shot out of a palm tree by besieging Arabs in *The Lost Patrol*" (p. 287)—or giving a selective filmography of every character actor featured in a given film. This last device becomes noticeable halfway through the book: Chapter 6 ends with the telling observation that "*Ruggles of Red Gap* is a comic celebration not only of a persistent American myth but of the art of the character actor" (p. 158). Eventually Weales's fascination with character actors gets a stranglehold on his commentary, and it reaches a sadly comic climax in his final chapter on *Destry Rides Again,* in which Weales interrupts the poker game which immediately follows the film's credits to give five pages of background material on the important players, proceeds to do the same with the other actors in the scene (seven more pages), and takes six more pages over the star, James Stewart, before proceeding to a breathless two-page gloss on the film's story. Although the *Destry* chapter is the longest in the book, these asides take up virtually the entire chapter.

But Weales's eclecticism, his refusal to fit the mold of either intrinsic analysis or New Historicism, and his discursiveness are frustrating only because they undermine the expectation that his project is an analysis of twelve films, an expectation that is of course encouraged by the organization of his book. Despite Weales's contention that his original impulse was "simply a desire to look closely and to discuss at length and without preconceptions a number of films that I admire" (p. 3), he is only intermittently successful—mostly in the first half of the book, before those cameos of supporting players take over—as a formal analyst of particular films. Nor, despite some impressive thematic discussions of *City Lights* and *My Man Godfrey*, is Weales especially committed to this sort of analysis. He begins a brilliant passage on *Steamboat Round the Bend* with the offhand remark, "If I were going to work thematically . . ." (p. 127), and dismisses attempts "to get to the seriousness at the heart of the hilarity in *Duck Soup*" by recovering the Marx Brothers as social satirists, turning instead to "the demonic element that made Artaud want to embrace them":

The unreality of the Marxes and their world, which makes it difficult to take their specific social comments seriously, becomes a vehicle for a deeper reality, the energy they generate in their collective endeavor to deflate, destroy, defuse, defenestrate everything around them and in their guiltless joy in the process. The audience, laughing with them, taps into that energy. There lies the truly subversive element in the Marx comedy. [p. 78]

Weales goes on to consider the ways in which *Duck Soup* differs from the Marx Brothers' other comedies. The climactic war provides "a structure that both contains and releases their malevolent energy," so that by the time the film concludes, as the brothers first capture Louis Calhern and bombard him with fruit (Groucho rejects his offer to surrender with the retort, "Sorry, you'll have to wait till the fruit runs out"), then turn to Margaret Dumont, who is singing the Fredonian anthem in celebration of victory, and bombard her,

the force that was stirred up by the musical mobilization and carried with such urgency through the war scenes simply keeps on going—past such mundane matters as apparent victory. The destructive energy does not choose sides. . . . In the earlier films, the Marxes have had antagonistic relationships with their settings and their subject matters. In *Duck Soup*, there is an alliance. War is the natural setting for meaningless destructiveness. The film has a shape, a movement, a texture that none of the other films has because it has accepted the evil implicit in what we have so often celebrated in the Marxes. [pp. 79–80]

This is not so much an analysis of *Duck Soup* as of our experience of *Duck Soup*, and by implication of Aristophanic comedy, Old Comedy, generally.

Weales excels in the sort of insight that slants away from the film at hand to the more general implications of comedy. Whether he is disentangling the way *May Man Godfrey* telescopes elements of five popular genres, tracing the relationship between comedy and "message" in *Mr. Deeds Goes to Town*, or examining the techniques by which *She Done Him Wrong* presents Mae West as "a sex figure who renders sex implausible" (p. 44), his focus is always on the relations particular comedies and kinds of comedy establish with their audience, and on the range of pleasures they provide. Though he never presents himself as a theorist, Weales is most provocative in his general intimations, which he advances offhandedly but with cumulative authority. He is disappointing only when he fails to confront the issues he raises, either because he has changed the subject or because he has run out of space, as in his book's tantalizing final paragraph: "The march of the women in *Destry* not only brought to an end a movie but a decade. And, quite incidentally, the kind of comedy I have been talking about in this book" (p. 327).

If James Harvey's new book, *Romantic Comedy in Hollywood from Lubitsch to Sturges*, pursues its particular insights more consistently than *Canned Goods as Caviar*, that is partly because Harvey has the luxury of twice as many pages. *Romantic Comedy* could probably have advanced its leading argument, complete with detailed examples, in a quarter of its space, but it is evidently not intended for readers who are in a hurry to get to the point. Even more obviously than Weales's book, Harvey's seems designed for film buffs rather than students of comedy. Knopf has produced the volume so sumptuously—it includes 175 beautifully reproduced photographs, mostly production stills—that it looks like a coffee-table book with an accompanying text of 300,000 words. Apart from framing sections on the two directors indicated in his title, Harvey consigns the main business of his book to a long section, "Directors and Stars, 1934–1939," which includes chapters on three directors (Frank Capra, Leo McCarey, Ernst Lubitsch in the thirties) and a greater number of stars (William Powell, Myrna Loy, Fred Astaire, Ginger Rogers, Carole Lombard, Irene Dunne, Cary Grant, Claudette Colbert, Jean Arthur). It therefore covers much of the same material as

Weales's book and depends even more for its appeal on the familiar anecdote and the appreciative précis. What could such a book—a movie fan's valentine to thirties comedy—have to say about the theory of comedy?

Quite a lot, it turns out. Harvey's leading interest is in the particular appeal of romantic comedy, which he identifies with screwball comedy, a term associated with the screwy and outrageous behavior of apparently normal characters (as against characters created by dedicated clowns like Chaplin, Keaton, and the Marx Brothers, who even looked funny). In fact, Harvey claims, "screwball comedy . . . named a style associated less with scattiness or derangement than with a paradoxical kind of liberation, with romantic exaltation of a very down-to-earth kind. This paradox was the peculiar, energizing complication that made the style so congenial to Hollywood—so expressive of both the place and the fantasy—and so magical to audiences in general" (p. xi). It is clear from the beginning that Harvey, whose first chapter begins, "Comedy was Hollywood's essential genius" (p. 3), is using screwball comedy as the exemplary Hollywood mode; by analyzing its appeal, he hopes to be able to explain something fundamental about the appeal of the movies.

The most closely argued part of Harvey's survey is its opening three chapters on Lubitsch, the Austrian expatriate who did more than any other single figure "to shape the spirit and style, even the substance, of Hollywood comedy" (p. 3). Lubitsch's contribution to American film, adumbrated by silent films like *The Marriage Circle* but not clearly apparent until the series of operettas that began with his first sound film, *The Love Parade,* was a tone "both dry and ardent, both dazzled and knowing" (p. 9), incarnated, for example, in the spectacle of Jeanette MacDonald singing "Dream Lover" in her lingerie. The contrast between the ceremonial formality and dignity of MacDonald's behavior and the subject of her song ("getting laid") produces an absurdity that, instead of undermining the performer or the conventions of her film, intensifies its affectionately good-natured tone: "The contrast between these genteel theatrical forms and their final, very ungenteel meanings only makes those forms

Taking Comedy Seriously

more treasurable to him—and to us, as he shows them to us. This wonderful joke—the identification of high aspirations with low cravings, of the most highfalutin forms with the most down-to-earth realities—is of course basic Hollywood. And though Lubitsch certainly didn't 'teach' this joke to other moviemakers any more than he originated it, he did teach them more than anyone else did about how to shape and repeat and perfect it" (p. 10).

In all of Lubitsch's movies, Harvey contends, this paradox of "ardency . . . ironized" underlies

> the fact that even when Lubitsch is working within a romantic genre, operetta or romatic comedy, he makes films that almost no one would think to call romantic. . . . Lubitsch focuses on something allied to 'love' but quite different from it. And it is that focus that makes his way of seeing things seem so distinctive, so unforgettable—a way of seeing that offers a quite unalienated and unmodish, a very direct, sensory, and particular sense of everyone's odd and disconcerting solitude. This intensely perceived solitude is at the heart of his comic vision. A central tragic fact for others artists is for Lubitsch the richest joke. In the world of his films, to feel strongly and passionately about anything, even in love, is to be alone. [p. 43]

This sense of intensity as isolation is what prevents Lubitsch's absurdist comedies from adopting what would become the distinctive tone of screwball comedy, which depends on "a deep belief in high spirits, in the ability of a joke or a song, a shared mood of elation or a witty inspiration, to transform and transfigure an unpromising environment" (p. 115) like the Depression Americana of *It Happened One Night*, the carping backstage milieu of *Twentieth Century*, the arena of domesticity in *The Thin Man*, or the earthbound intrigues of *The Gay Divorcee*. Lubitsch, by contrast, "is like the leader who brings people to the promised land but cannot enter it himself" because he never discovers the comic possibilities of freedom: "The Lubitschean spirit is too dry, too detached. He gave a triumphant, delighted form to the movies' spirit of skepticism. But the freedom and exhilaration, the sense of possibility and triumph, that qualified and even transformed that skepticism in the later great comedies were qualities beyond him" (p. 59). Lubitsch's films "lack that energy of opposition that infused the screwball genius as much as romantic love did. . . . He wasn't hopeful enough" (pp. 382, 389).

Harvey further defines the exhilaration of *It Happened One Night* and the other influential comedies of 1934 by contrasting it with the "pre-screwball" conservatism of comedies like *Platinum Blonde,* in which the proletarian reporter Robert Williams's decision to leave his rich society wife Jean Harlow for his fellow wage-slave Loretta Young "is framed too much in terms of things *not* working out. . . . His marriage to Harlow is a mistake . . . he should never have left his buddies or his job . . . happiness is in his own backyard" (p. 118). The riper, zanier, more adventurous spirit of screwball comedy gives romance the possibility of releasing the characters' (and the audience's) imagination and freedom in ways earlier comedies had never touched. In his survey of romantic comedy during the late thirties, Harvey consistently focuses on the ways in which different directors and, more often, performers release this energy in distinctive ways. Throughout these chapters, Harvey, like Weales, is at his best in the strong line, the telling sentence that captures exactly the appeal of a certain player or film. Cary Grant, "the only male star to spring full-blown and solo . . . from the screwball mode," is a hero who "manages at once to be a paradigm of masculinity and yet at the same time to elude and even to defy most of the categories of the masculine romance" (p. 301). Claudette Colbert "does for gold-digging what Lombard does for craziness: she makes it seem like something liberating" (p. 346). Irene Dunne is "a powerfully sensible woman with a passionate, even dangerous susceptibility for being amused, for 'going wild' " (p. 248). *Gone With the Wind* is "a kind of ultimate tough comedy, its vitality more a development of thirties movie comedy than of any historical romance tradition" (p. 282). *Stage Door* is "like going to wisecrack heaven" (p. 315).

Somewhere in the course of this bulky second section, Harvey's readers may well become suspicious about what kind of book they are reading. Harvey's way with an epigram whose penetration leaves practically no room for development, his fondness for affectionately detailed summaries of his favorite scenes from *The Awful Truth,* his persistently inductive tactics for advancing an argument, all suggest a tone and technique more appropriate to a collection of reviews than an extended analysis of Hollywood comedy. The pungency of Harvey's prose recalls that of Pauline Kael—no one's idea of a film theorist—whom Harvey quotes frequently. The dust jacket's announcement that "reading *Romantic Comedy* is like going to the movies" (a comparison often invoked on behalf of Kael's reviews, and an amusingly flat echo of Simon's argument about the relation between comic theory and comic practice) may be all too accurate; certainly trying to read Harvey's book straight through is like noshing on a fifty-pound drum of Raisinets.

This impression is confirmed by the organization of the book. Although the opening chapters really are about Lubitsch, and the closing chapters really are about Preston Sturges, the writer-director whose meteoric career in the early 1940s Harvey regards as the climax of screwball comedy, most of the chapters in between are misleadingly titled. Leo McCarey gets a chapter to himself, but his finest comedy, *The Awful Truth,* is mentioned only briefly there; a much more detailed discussion (fifteen pages) has just concluded the chapter on Irene Dunne. Jean Arthur's comedies are parcelled out among several chapters besides her own; so are Cary Grant's; so are Howard Hawks's. A chapter titled "The Screwball Years: The Leading Men," which begins as if it were going to be about Clark Gable, turns out not to be about anything in particular. The problem, as in *Canned Goods as Caviar,* is one of deceptive packaging. Harvey's chapter headings represent an ingenious attempt to disguise what is essentially a running commentary on a very large number of movies which are linked by the confusingly crisscrossed paths of a few repeating directors and stars.

All of these limitations ought to keep Harvey from advancing any very useful generalizations about romantic comedy or its relations to a broader comic tradition, but they don't, any more than Levin's empirical approach limits the resonance of his analysis. Levin's decision to get at the theoretical questions of comedy through the analysis of many comic plays may disappoint readers who were hoping for a book that articulated its theoretical concerns as fully as Frye's *Anatomy*, but not even the most unsympathetic reader would go on to invalidate Levin's approach, dismiss him as a reviewer, or call the book a blot on an otherwise distinguished career. An important part of the pleasure Harvey's book offers is the delight of replaying familiar and much-loved films in one's mind at his prompting, but Levin relies just as much on the same pleasure, reminding us of the delight we took the last time we read *Mandragola* or saw a production of *Le misanthrope*. The conventions of film criticism may make it more difficult for Harvey to establish his authority, but he establishes it in the same way. (And he jeopardizes it, when he does so, in the same way, as when he concludes his incisive analysis of Lubitsch's *Trouble in Paradise* with the remark that this film, the director's own favorite among all his films, "runs counter to Lubitsch's deepest and most persisting comic vision" [p. 54]—a judgment that would be inexplicable if it weren't required by Harvey's argument that "the idyllic strain" of the film marked "a dead end," a temporary detour in the development of Lubitsch's obsession with isolation.) His generalizations about particular films and their stars are so precise and perceptive that they shed light on larger issues raised by Hollywood romantic comedy and its relation to broader comic forms. Harvey observes, for example, that Katharine Hepburn's faltering film career was rescued by her portrayal of Tracy Lord, the arrogant heiress who is humbled first by the accusing male leads and then by her own misadventures in *The Philadelphia Story*—an observation which was made as early as the film's first release—but then adds:

It's the trouble with being a goddess, with being too magnificent. You lose the human touch. This was not only a consoling thought for the rest of us but an inspired solution (courtesy of Philip Barry) to the problem of Hepburn's career. Consequently, she spent most of the rest of it submitting to just such strictures—atoning before us all for the aristocracy she could never quite disguise or entirely throw off. That's one reason audiences liked to see her with Spencer Tracy. They knew *he'd* make her sorry. [p. 409]

A pattern is thereby established not only for Hepburn's forties performances but for the development of Hollywood comedy away from "the freedom and magic that belong to a sensible, down-to-earth, no-nonsense view of things" (p. 117)—preeminently the screwball heroine's triumphant view—toward the containment or chastening of that view set forth in *The Philadelphia Story* and Hepburn's first film with Tracy, *Woman of the Year*: "the high-flying independent woman brought finally and comically to ground by the solid, complacent, implacable male"—a development Harvey calls "the reverse of the old screwball pattern," the result of a new balance, or an imbalance, "between impiety and reverence, cynicism and sentiment, the city and the small town, busting loose and staying put" in which "the impious, irreverent, anarchic side seemed to lose out" (pp. 409, 405). The result was in effect a suburbanization of Hollywood comedy, which "shifted from a fantasy of freedom to a joke about entrapment: women by their nonsense, and men by their women" (p. 415)—a joke informing, for example, the title of the 1956 remake of *It Happened One Night*: *You Can't Run Away from It*. The Tracy-Hepburn comedies marked not so much "a return to the old magic" as "a gentrification of it.... *Adam's Rib* was less a fantasy of wit and love and freedom than of urban gentility and success" (p. 417).

Most of these passages come from a masterful chapter called "Decline of the Romantic Comedy," which spins a cogent historical analysis out of Harvey's observations about the changing sorts of pleasure forties comedies offer their audience. It is exactly this focus on specific kinds of pleasure that gives Harvey's generalizations, when he gets around to making them, their uncommon force. He has been discussing Preston Sturges for over a hundred pages (and more is still to come) before he allows himself to suggest that Sturges could be successful as a uniquely American director, capturing an audience whose taste for madcap comedy had largely passed, because "he cut through the knot of smugnesses and self-deceptions and half-truths that the idyllic Americanists had made of the American subject matter—and because he deals so directly with our love affair with innocence.... He finds a special and excruciatingly funny way to talk about American life—a way to express its strange and often panicking energies, even its peculiar decencies—without ever telling us comforting lies about it" (pp. 645–46). Even more telling is a passage on *The Awful Truth* (Harvey's favorite romantic comedy, as it is Cavell's):

> The screwball couple *are* plain people, figures of ordinary life in all but their fantasy trappings: in their common sense and downrightness, in their aversion to anything high-flown or disproportionate.... They are temperamentally conservative in this respect, with as acute a sense of how things will look to the neighbors as any small-town matchmaker might have. With this absolute difference: they concern themselves with appearances finally so that they can defy and rise above them. They immolate themselves like other great lovers—but for laughs. The skeptical and reductive comic vision—the wonderful wised-up voice of the movies themselves—becomes in them something overtly romantic: an element liberating and transcendent as passion is. And connected with passion: the life that stirs in this comic world is a passional one. [p. 240]

Harvey's conclusion that "laughter in all these great movie comedies *is* intimacy" (p. 313) explains why he takes romantic comedy as the essential Hollywood genre and ascribes to it the secret of Hollywood magic, as when he moves, in his final summary, from romantic comedy to generalize about the movies. "They were *about* common life—or at least its possibilities," he concludes; they "testified to the possibilities of American community, to the freedom of the city," and, especially through their zany and clearsighted heroines, "challenged the complacency of American life" and "suggested that we might grow up and live together with the kind of candor and risk and honesty that seemed specially, even dangerously American" (p. 678). No one has ever come closer to capturing the extraordinary appeal of Hollywood comedy.

Simon, discussing the relation of delight to moral instruction in *Tom Jones*, suggests that "while there is certainly much seriousness beneath the comedy, there is also much seriousness to the comedy" (p. 55). Recent studies of comedy, differing widely in their definitions of comedy, in their choice of comic texts, and in the kinds of analysis they practice—agreeing, evidently, only in their skepticism about theory—still manage to make a significant contribution to the theory of comedy by focusing on the seriousness to the comedy of Plautus, Congreve, and the Marx Brothers. It is a particularly healthy sign for comic theory that Weales and Harvey, agreeing that there was practically no seriousness beneath the Hollywood comedies of the thirties—and when there was, as in Capra's later films, it stifled the comedy—still find a great deal of seriousness in the comedy of such thematically inconsequential films as *Nothing Sacred* and *Libeled Lady,* and in the energies they liberate.

Notes

1. See Bakhtin, *Rabelais and His World,* trans. Helene Iswolsky (Bloomington: Indiana Univ. Press, 1984), pp. 5–12, and Pogel, pp. 222–23.

2. Stam, *Reflexivity in Film and Literature from Don Quixote to Jean-Luc Godard* (Ann Arbor: UMI Research Press, 1985), p. 253; quoted by Pogel, p. 186.

3. Moews, *Keaton: The Silent Features Close Up* (Berkeley and Los Angeles: Univ. of California Press, 1977), pp. 44, 38.

4. Of course there are exceptions to this rule—for example, Stanley Cavell's *Pursuits of Happiness: The Hollywood Comedy of Remarriage* (Cambridge: Harvard Univ. Press, 1981); George McFadden's *Discovering the Comic* (Princeton: Princeton Univ. Press, 1982); and several feminist studies of the comic butt as other. But the field is remarkably thin.

5. "Theory and Film: Principles of Realism and Pleasure" (1976), rpt. in Philip Rosen, ed., *Narrative, Apparatus, Ideology: A Film Theory Reader* (New York: Columbia Univ. Press, 1986), p. 188.

6. *Rabelais and His World,* p. 66; quoted by Simon, p. 15.

7. Factual errors in film criticism are common: Cavell deplores their frequency in *The World Viewed: Reflections on the Ontology of Film,* enlarged edition (Cambridge: Harvard Univ. Press, 1979), pp. xx–xxi, even though he notes many such lapses on his own part (see pp. x–xiii). The recent wide availability of films on videotape has presumably made it easier for researchers to get their facts straight.

Sex and Consequence

James Grantham Turner

Alice Browne. *The Eighteenth Century Feminist Mind.* Brighton: Harvester Press, and Detroit: Wayne State University Press, 1987. viii, 238 pp.

G. S. Rousseau and Roy Porter, eds. *Sexual Underworlds of the Enlightenment.* Chapel Hill: University of North Carolina Press, and Manchester: University of Manchester Press, 1988. x, 294 pp.

Peter Wagner. *Eros Revived: Erotica of the Enlightenment in England and America.* London: Secker and Warburg, 1988. xiv, 498 pp.

The new social history tries to rescue sexuality from the realm of biology or invariant "human nature," establishing it as a phenomenon that varied with time and place, that drew its meaning from social conditions, and that furthered ideological causes. It should be possible, according to this premise, to isolate a distinct sex-and-gender system for any period. Can we discover, say, a "Baroque" or "Enlightenment" Eros that influenced what lovers felt as well as what they said or pretended to think, that followed them as they crept between the sheets or collapsed onto the ottoman? And did sexuality *change* in the eighteenth century, between the Age of Libertinism and the Age of Sensibility? Many historians (literary and social) equate this period with an improvement in pleasure and freedom; others lament the imposition of new restrictions. But should the history of sexuality be written in terms of "freedom" at all? Should we not abandon a Whiggish model of history that conceals anachronism and self-congratulation? The essays in *Sexual Underworlds of the Enlighten-*

ment (on which I focus in the first half of this review) exemplify these issues very clearly.

The editors of *Sexual Underworlds*, a historian and a literary scholar with overlapping interests in the social history of medicine, explain their original goals as follows: to promote eclecticism and pluralism (inevitable in a multi-authored volume, surely), to shed reticence and ask daring questions "that could not be addressed just a decade earlier," and to come to terms with the pilot volume of Foucault's *History of Sexuality* "without discarding the older dyad of liberation versus repression."[1] This will be an agonizing task: the most important idea in Foucault's pamphlet was that we *must* discard this dyad, since the discourses of sexual liberation in the eighteenth and nineteenth centuries are really deployments of power more deep and intrusive even than the confessional. Rousseau and Porter have no desire to be left out of the post-Foucaultian age of "theory," but equally they value the comforts (and the stimulus to research) of an older and more Whiggish model of history as liberation, as "information" leading to "open discussion" and "frank debate," as the discovery of kindred spirits, the exposure of unnatural prejudices, and the revaluing of "underworlds." And they are particularly devoted to the notion of Enlightenment, tantamount to sexual "progress." Rousseau and Porter recognize the powerfully attractive self-image of the age, an image created by male *philosophes* and their fellow-travellers (La Mettrie and Diderot, Cleland and Bentham), in which hedonism and utilitarianism combine to promote the sexual happiness of the greatest number by any means that does not damage other people. But they also recognize the forces that destroy this image: Foucault's skepticism, the revisionist historiography that discovers deep anxiety over homo- and auto-eroticism, and—above all—the feminist challenge to male complacency.

Making sex speak has always seemed problematic. The Judaeo-Christian legacy of shame imposed an embarrassed silence, and yet for the Christian the sexual has always been irreducibly cognitive, bound up from the start with knowledge. As St Augustine put it, the sexual drive *rubescit videri* (blushes to be seen), but still *appetit sciri* (longs to be known); there is an epistemic component in sexuality itself.[2] This legacy is felt just as strongly in libertine encounters: the woman can enjoy sex only if her lover does not tell, while he can only enjoy it if he *does* tell. This is the ideology enforced (or exposed?) in Diderot's *Les Bijoux indiscrets,* where Mangogul's magic ring reveals the illicit sexual lives of every woman in the Court, producing an authentic, unmediated voice from beneath their skirts. Foucault suggests—using Diderot's tale as his paradigm—that to transform sex into discourse is to control it. But he probably underestimates the slipperiness of discourse and the anxiety that underlies Diderot's wishful fantasy: there *is* no language free from evasion, yielding direct access to the truth of the flesh. Words may be a spur to erotic action or a pathetic substitute, as the libertine himself realized: "But now, alas! for want of further force / From action we are fallen into discourse."[3] Foucault is quite right to insist that the historian of sexuality must confront the difficult relation of discourse and power, but he also exemplifies its problems. His working assumptions may undermine his theoretical positions. His most brilliant maxim suggests that, whereas hitherto the "discourse of sexuality" has been as coercive and tendentious as Mangogul's use of his ring, the new historian must make *the ring itself* speak. Thus he prolongs the discourse-as-liberation model that he is supposed to have demolished.

Rousseau and Porter declare at one point that to stimulate frank debate is their *ultimate* aim (p. x), but this seems unnecessarily modest. The book does establish certain methodological principles that should be, not "debated" endlessly, but accepted and internalized as standards for the enterprise. The quality of the scholarly verification, a necessary if not sufficient requirement for the genuine historian, is almost always high.[4] The whiff of solitary vice, which pours from the old limited-edition *Sittengeschichten* and bibliographies of Curiosa that used to pass for scholarship in this clandestine field, is almost never smelt. The design of the book itself drives home the essential point that sex must not be studied in isolation, but always in its complex relationship to discourse (ideas, languages, representations, genres, conventions) and to society—a society mapped out by power, divided into underworlds and dominant groups, peripheries and centers: the ten essays are grouped into sections on "Sex and discourse," "Sex and society," and "Sex at the margins." Sexuality is interpreted, by almost all the contributors, as an ideological construct, a socialized transformation of biology, rather than the neutral "instinct" or "pleasure" assumed by naive naturalism. But the editors still insist on the value of pure "information," and declare themselves unwilling to announce a "new conceptual blueprint" until all the facts are in, to claim or impose a new model of Enlightenment sexuality (p. ix). I would argue that these "facts" are always dialectically conditioned, if not actually determined, by the conceptual model of the investigator, and that all histories of sexuality—even the most innocent-seeming bibliography—are also ideological programmes for the construction of sexual identity.

The gender-distribution of the volume leaves something to be desired, though it is an improvement on earlier all-male collections. Five men hold down the fort of Discourse (Théodore Tarczylo, Peter Wagner, Randolph Trumbach, Paul-Gabriel Boucé and Rousseau himself), while Terry Castle joins two men (Anthony Simpson and Porter himself) on the theme of Society; both writers on the Margins are women, however (Lynne Friedli and Gloria Flaherty). The editors give pride of place to feminism among the revisionist challenges to the "Golden Age" view of eighteenth-century eroticism: "Golden age for whom?" As long as the double standard remained in place, emancipation and diversity for the male was "a new way of controlling women" (p. 4). Likewise

Eighteenth-century attitudes towards gender served only to heighten the differentiation of the sexual division of labour and to generate that idealisation, that angelification, of woman which found its apotheosis in the frail, feeble, but blameless Victorian wife. After all, the psychophysiological underpinnings of (the then crucial) sensibility stressed the mental and physical fragility of women, while the new social glorification of family life and natural motherhood . . . spelt out domesticity as the true woman's calling and the home as her shrine.

Such stereotypes "were not excrescences of the *ancien régime*, against which the paladins of the Enlightenment were committed

Sex and Consequence

to do battle, but were to a large degree the *creation* of the Enlightenment and its fellow-travellers from Addison and Steele onwards" (p. 4). Rousseau and Porter would presumably welcome all studies that throw light on how women understood their own sexuality and their own emancipation, such as Alice Browne's synthesis of "the eighteenth-century feminist mind." But at times I detect an undertow of hostility to these new forces. At one point they equate "feminist sectarianism" with the Moral Majority (p. 6). They are scrupulous to stress that one must not "conflate images of women as entertained by Enlightenment men with the real experiences of women themselves" (p. 5). But they find some truth in those male satirists who interpreted gynaecological consultations as lecherous assignations: they infer that women were actually gaining new sexual freedoms, freedoms "more impressive than recent feminist historians—all too ready to impose the role of victim upon women in the past—have credited" (p. 15, and cf. pp. 222–24).

The only meta-disciplinary piece in the volume, Tarczylo's polemic against recent French historians, begins with an attack on the conventional liberationist view of the eighteenth century, and on the "lascivious erudition" which takes the art and literature of a small hedonist elite as if it were objective truth, gloating over its sensuality while ignoring its "aesthetic and ideological conventions" (pp. 26–29).[5] He contrasts this gallant and faintly pornographic approach (exemplified by Apollinaire and the Goncourts) with the cold facts and hard analyses of the "Marxo-Freudian" school, which stresses the grim repressive conditions of life for the majority. Both are blamed for their simplistic handling of evidence. Legal records (the grist of the "hard" historians) may reveal changes in values and concepts, but they do not necessarily reveal actual behavior. Appeals to demography, another apparently objective source, collapse when other cultures and periods are brought in; the anti-masturbation campaign for example—prime evidence against the libertine view of the eighteenth century—*might* be explained by the late age of marriage, except that in the nineteenth century anti-masturbation hysteria increases while the age of marriage drops. And demographic statistics fail to allow for the massive differences in mentality and practice among different classes and regions. The hypothesis of a general repression comes to seem more and more reductive and self-fulfilling. The law, the church and the medical profession did not combine into a single repressive machine; we find instead "a multiplicity of intersecting relations, of momentary and limited connivances, of mutual exclusions" (p. 35). Each profession, each interest group, had its own conceptual and axiological structure for understanding sexuality. It is these mental systems that the historian must study. There *are* no ahistorical brute facts, separable from politics and ideology, and no objective criterion of the "natural" and the "free": "One man's liberty may be another man's repression" (p. 35). It is a great weakness of Tarczylo's essay that he limits his remarks to "man" and engages in a virility contest with his opponents; but his model of cultural analysis, and his arguments against "naive realism," are most valuable, and can be applied *a fortiori* to the politics of gender.

Indeed, the strength of this volume as a whole is its insistence on the complexity of the evidence, the conflict of competing models of understanding, the fluidity of boundaries, and the serious consequences of such clashes and misprisions. The historian Trumbach, for example, elucidates the position of women on the all-important boundary between respectability and the subculture of illicit sex, which could rapidly (and almost inevitably) degenerate into prostitution. How does the libertine text construct this situation, in comparison to the reality revealed in criminal records? For his test case Trumbach invokes another dichotomy, "the disjunction between the world of prostitution in the fantasy" of Cleland's *Memoirs* of Fanny Hill, and "the actualities of the legal sources" (p. 69). Though he takes the most frequently discussed of all erotic texts (contrary to the editors' wish to sidestep familiar examples), he certainly challenges the habit of reading fiction as evidence of reality, and thereby darkens the rosy picture of libertine sexuality upheld by "the older scholarship and the amateurs" (p. 73). In a pamphlet of 1749 Cleland documents the misery of the whore's life, but in the *Memoirs* of the same year he presents the brothel as "a little family of love," a golden-age community free of medical and financial problems, while Fanny's career with Mrs Cole (Mrs Cleo in one

Sex and Consequence 139

glorious misprint) translates easily into romantic marriage. Cleland's happy ending, a compromise between pornography and the novel of respectable courtship, thus conceals what an earlier bawdy text (not consulted by Trumbach) had cheerfully admitted: that once women cross the frontiers of "Erotopolis" or "Bettyland," the realm of illicit sex, they "never more return into their own Country."[6]

If we take an extreme position on "sex as discourse" (a Foucaultian phrase from the title of Wagner's essay), we might argue that both of these reality-effects—grim realism and arcadian eroticism—are produced by the genre itself, and that trial records merely add another discursive trope to this gallery of representations. It would be hard to sustain this ultraintellectual position in the face of Trumbach's evidence, however. Young women were decoyed into illicit sex, sacked from their jobs if pregnant, "almost stifled and killed" by their customers, threatened by landladies "with the grossest abuse," and "driven out in bitter anguish" to walk the street in constant danger of arrest (pp. 77–78). Pregnancy and disease together destroyed the possibility of alternative employment or relief: the Magdalen Hospital would only take her if she was young and "showed no sign of venereal infection"; the Lock Asylum would reject her if she was pregnant (pp. 78–80, 82). She was left to "inescapable grief," and the prospect of watching her own child die "with a black eye, a broken collarbone, and sick from whooping-cough" (p. 78). These moving testimonies are of course *texts*, taken from the victims' own depositions and inevitably expressed in the language expected by the court or the Foundling Hospital. They are scripts or scenarios, but scripts played out by the dispossessed, in a theater with no protective frame, and with life or death consequences. And they etch themselves into our reading of male libertine fiction, light-hearted visions of sex without consequences, prostitution "with the pain left out" (p. 79).

Trumbach does not argue for a complete separation of libertine fantasy and hard reality, however; many details of Fanny Hill's story *can* be matched in court evidence (especially the difficulties of her earlier years), and some seduced women *were* rescued into lives of security by determined efforts. He sees

Cleland's work as part of a larger revolution in gender roles, and links it ("distantly") to an overall improvement in the status of women. Before the 1690s, he argues, women in general were assumed to be actually or potentially whores, but in the age of politeness such gross misogyny was on the wane. Meanwhile, the growth of larger cities supported "a greater complexity than ever before of subcultures," including sodomites, Grub Street writers and prostitutes. Prostitution became a limited and specialized institution rather than a universal metaphor for the sex. Gender-identities were now constructed around the avoidance of these perverse extremes, Trumbach claims: "The sodomite's role was for men what the prostitute's was for women" (p. 73–74). This appears to mean that women in general defined themselves by absolute separation from and repudiation of the illicit—a familiar enough ideology to readers of *The Rape of the Lock* ("'Twill then be Infamy to seem thy Friend!").

We can appreciate Trumbach's method here: the psychoanalyst may study "Aphrodite builder of cities," but the true historian shows that cities build their own distinctive modes of sexuality. His arguments are vulnerable to several objections, however. Surely it is reductive to say that all women were feared as whores in the age of Petrarch or Milton, and surely it is the new libertine who proposes that "every woman is at heart a rake," that all women can be secretly conquered? This is what Richardson's Lovelace desperately wishes to prove, and what *Les Bijoux indiscrets* triumphantly proclaims. Furthermore, Trumbach seems unclear whether the sodomite and the prostitute operate in the same way on gender-identities. Certainly the crucial sodomy scene in Cleland's *Memoirs* does test the limits of sexual tolerance, since it is the only practice to be actually condemned by Fanny (though Trumbach fails to mention the injury that follows her denunciation, which seems like the text's revenge on her disapproval). But is the prostitute ostracized or contrasted to the "true" woman? Not at all: the new masculinity, as Trumbach describes it, requires that she be fervently pursued, celebrated, redeemed, integrated into "the sex" rather than isolated and opposed.

Lastly, does the low social status of those arrested, men as well as women, really prove that Fanny Hill's high-society career is pure fantasy? After an essay full of subtle and sympathetic readings, it is surprising to find this argument from omission: very few gentlemen show up in bastardy or brothel-going trials; therefore, illicit sex largely took place among the lower classes. Surely there is non-fictional evidence for the impunity of the upper-class male in sexual matters, the "civility" of constables coerced into releasing the high-born hooligan?[7] It was widely murmured that the Societies for the Reformation of Manners confined their attention to sinners below £500 *per annum*. Were there really no discreet brothels off bounds for the arrestable classes, occupying a higher rank than the places that show up in criminal records, though ever-fearful of sinking there—just as Fanny is afraid of disease after her Rochester-like excursion into the lower stratum of the "street-plyer"? Trumbach's paper is incomplete without an equally painstaking reconstruction of the life and circumstances of a figure like Mrs Needham, mentioned in countless texts and recommended by Pope himself, or "madam *Southcot* near old Dunkirk square; . . . only the lewd Quality f---k there."[8] By the end of the eighteenth century, a real-life Mrs Cole could describe, in print, the visit of the Viceroy of Ireland with his ceremonial guard, who stood in formation outside her door all night and much of the next day, an object of public wonderment.[9]

A number of these essays, like Trumbach's, explore "disjunctions," disputed boundaries, complex and sometimes painful dilemmas of classification. Friedli studies the phenomenon of women "passing" for men, especially in the armed forces, defining her subject as "gender-boundaries" and drawing on Gayatri Spivak's account of the unequal relationship between "the centre" and "the margin" (p. 234). Her method reflects her concerns: like other contributors, she crosses generic boundaries by juxtaposing and contrasting medical, legal, facetious and didactic texts, locating her subject in a network of scientific, social and epistemological ideas. Using some of the same examples, Castle describes the mingling of sexual identities in masquerade: "The Protean life of the city found expression in a persistent popular urge toward disguise and metamorphosis," Castle argues, and "through its stylised assault on gender boundaries, the masquerade played an interesting part in the creation of the modern 'polymorphous' subject—perverse by definition, sexually ambidextrous, and potentially unlimited in the range of its desires" (pp. 157–58). (Much of this essay, incidentally, is reprinted from her important book *Masquerade and Civilization* [1986].) Boucé explores a striking paradigm-clash with obvious implications for the social history of women, the debate over whether the mother's imagination has the power to stamp a deformity on the foetus (we might add that likeness was also explained this way, by those who refused to accept the mother's genetic contribution). Against a background of increasing restrictiveness on sexual matters, Rousseau gathers the shadowy hints of the homosexual and the "homosocial" in Richard Payne Knight and his circle, and decodes ambiguities in the outraged response to his *Discourse on the Worship of Priapus*. Simpson traces the confusion in the law—not knowing which statute to apply, or how seriously to take the offense—that effectively lowered the age of female consent from twelve to ten, and made it easier for rapists and child abusers to be acquitted. A surprising proportion of rapes were committed on girls between four and twelve, a situation caused by what we might call a paradigm-congestion, a disastrous convergence of urban geography, libertine ideology, legal incompetence and medical mythology: Simpson's explanation brings in the increase in paedophilic tastes, easy access to family members and servants in the smaller households of London, and the belief that syphilis (epidemic in the Metropolis) could be cured by intercourse with an uninfected child. Porter traces the ambivalent response to male gynaecologists, concentrating on those moralists and satirists who switch the genres, as it were—insisting that medical practices are really episodes from pornography. Wagner likewise documents the pornographic use of medical texts, both here and in the first chapter of his book. The final essay, Flaherty's "Sex and Shamanism," goes beyond the boundaries of Europe completely, anticipating Rousseau and Porter's projected volume on sexuality in other cultures; though she quotes extensively from Enlightenment ethnographers (mostly German), she uses them transparently, to reconstruct the magic sexuality of "wise natives" and "wise women."

Again and again we see that the conflict of codes is not a *post facto* phenomenon, an academic squabble over classification, but a living part of eighteenth-century experience. Paradigms had consequences. In the cultures described by Flaherty, male initiation could involve the excision of the left (i.e., female) testicle, or physical assaults on the mother; *pace* Rousseau, these accounts of homosexual and misogynistic rituals contrast sharply with Payne Knight's interpretation of ancient phallic worship as a benign fertility cult. If the initiation rite was not performed, Flaherty shows, biological males could be completely socialized as female (and eagerly sought as wives); then they could be slaughtered—after being further reclassified by the colonial invaders—as "sodomites." In urban civilization the results of category-slippage were scarcely less drastic. Cross-dressing women could be blinded in the pillory, displayed as fairground freaks, publicly whipped, or prosecuted for fraud—*not*, interestingly enough, for a sexual misdemeanor, except for one case in Germany; Friedli shows how Fielding goes *against* the legal consensus on the transvestite Mary Hamilton, by treating her in sexual and comic terms—a genre switch which effectively "preclude[s] a reading that constitutes gender roles as a site of struggle" (p. 240). (The same ideology led him to redefine Pamela as Shamela, we might add.) On the other hand, if female cross-dressers could be seen as wholly exceptional, they were celebrated for their virtue and military heroism.[10] And if they could summon up the effrontery and acting skill, they could mimic masculine identity and repossess the power to define themselves. Mary Hamilton was not broken by her four floggings, but appeared in Bridewell as an impudent beau, "very gay, with Perriwig, Ruffles and Breeches" (p. 239). Charlotte Charke managed to "explore a number of roles normally reserved for men" without adopting the conventional sexy breeches-part figure, and thus subverted the "closed reading," the "satisfactory reconciliation of cause and effect in the form of an 'official' explanation for her behavior" (pp. 240–41).

Nevertheless, the consequences of masculine ideology, of men's attempt to control how sexuality was perceived and managed, could sometimes be severe. Pregnant women in search of advice could hear themselves branded as adulteresses (Porter), and the distress of giving birth to a deformed child could be increased by men who blamed it on the evil power of her own mind (Boucé). Parents could see the rapist of their eleven-year-old daughter acquitted (Simpson). The court records prove that in London, for some periods of the eighteenth century, a quarter of *all* prosecutions for rape, and half of all attempted rapes, involved girls under ten. (The figures are lower in the provinces, where venereal disease was less prevalent.) The under-reporting of rape and child abuse must have been even higher than it is today, moreover; all the modern reasons for concealment applied equally then, Simpson argues, and in addition the victim and her family had to shoulder the cost and negotiate intimidating social differences. To these factors we must add two more: upper-class male impunity, and the libertine ideology. No doubt wishing to avoid the stereotype of the lustful squire, Simpson is careful to note that "there is no evidence that those rape victims who brought their case to court, and who were usually of the lower social strata, were typically abused by those far above them on a social scale" (p. 197; only fifteen "gentlemen" in the records he selected, though a number of cases do not give the defendant's occupation). Nevertheless, one of his multiple child-molesters was a substantial Anglican clergyman, and a very high proportion of victims were domestic servants: "Sexual exploitation of them by their masters was taken for granted. In rural areas the strong possibility of victimisation of this kind was recognized as an occupational hazard for young servant-girls bound for the capital" (p. 198). In these circumstances, it is astonishing that so high a number of employers *were* indicted: in 189 cases where social relations can be identified, Simpson finds thirty-five offenses by the master himself, thirty-five by other members of the household, and only eight by workmates. In addition, ten were raped by immediate family members. Sexual violence against subordinates must have gone largely unrecorded, though it may show up in the transcripts of other kinds of prosecution—for example, Trumbach's case-history of the fourteen-year-old decoyed into prostitution and "stifled and almost killed" by her first customer ("Squire Janssen"). The Royal pardon of Colonel

Charteris, after his conviction for rape, must have indicated approval from on high. Abuse of *very* young children was detested, but (to judge from the Magdalen Hospital records) a large number of prostitutes—evidently considered fair game—must have been below twelve, even though puberty came on later than it does today. And in any case, masculine ideology held that "woman" was made such by the first penetration, and proclaimed, in countless songs and fictions, that the female really *liked* to be overcome by violent men who brush aside all denial.

What does this say about the revolution in gender identities, the topic to which most of these essays turn? One of the most influential theses, pioneered by Trumbach among others, is that "eighteenth-century society saw the progressive development of affective relations within the family, and of more protective attitudes towards children" (p. 199). Having uncovered what the editors call an "isomorphism" between the high culture and the gutter, Simpson is understandably skeptical about this ameliorative model. Nevertheless, there is some evidence for the emergence of a new pattern of companionate marriage and a new breed of sensitive, modern men, who take an interest in their infants and discover every happiness in the home, now the focus of functions and pleasures previously hived off onto the mistress and the nurse. Browne has even discovered a young man, in a novel of 1764, who suffers agonies when his *mistress* gives birth, feeling that (like Jaffeir in *Venice Preserved*) he has betrayed a friend to the rack (p. 51). A new sentimental exaltation of woman as mother rises to absolute dominance in the later eighteenth century, Friedli argues, so that *every* "woman question" (from de Sade's crazed eroticism to Wollstonecraft's feminism) places the Mother at the center. I would suggest, however, that this creates new tensions in both sexes. Males made contradictory demands when they were drawn into the debate over breast feeding, and felt the jealousy of the new father when the child became a privileged rival. Both these feelings are sensitively captured by Samuel Richardson in the character of Mr B., the paradigmatic old-fashioned rake turned new man.

Trumbach at first seems to contradict his own thesis—set forth in *The Rise of the Egalitarian Family* (1978)—when he characterizes the new eighteenth-century male as a lusty whoremonger and homophobe. But it may well be that the Age of Sensibility, with its weeping men of feeling ("I am as weak as a woman," sobs Yorick at the grave of the kindly monk), is also an age of machismo; Lovelace and Hickman, Don Ottavio and Don Giovanni, are the same person. The young man affected by the screams of childbirth turns out to be concerned only with his *own* feelings, dismisses women and blacks as naturally inferior, and refuses his mistress's request for marriage in a tone both jocular and callous: he will "play" but he will not "pay."[11] The age that forces women to be both mistress and wife creates the equivalent tension in its males, who are just as much conditioned by the gender-fixing system. Already in the sixteenth century, Montaigne had declared that the roles of mistress and wife were so different that to combine them in romantic marriage is "a kind of incest" (III.v). Could not the child rape and virgin mania be precisely the dark side of the affective revolution? Eighteenth-century man was trained to respect and adore, to allow Motherhood a privileged space in which Father might seem an outsider, but also to "fuck everything that moves" (as a traditional libertine once boasted to me), to mark everything with what Cleland called "that peculiar scepter-member, which commands us all."[12] Certainly, he now identified himself by contrast, not just with the homosexual, but with the libertine. But this created a particularly ticklish situation. Firstly, this "new" masculinity made him more like the traditional female, defining himself in contrast not to a deficit but to an unruly *excess* of what was assumed to be his normal sexuality. Secondly, priapic individualism was still fashionable and attractive, associated with an aristocracy that still shared social and political hegemony. The feminist voices gathered by Alice Browne confirm that, even at the end of the century, libertine freedom for the male and extreme restriction for the female was still the norm:

The great difference now beheld in the external consequences which follow the deviations from chastity in the two sexes, did in all probability arise from the women having been considered as the mere property of the men; . . . when the plea of property had been given up, . . . it was still preserved in society from the unruly licentiousness of the men, who, finding no obstacles in the delicacy of the other sex, continue to set at defiance both divine and moral law, and by mutual support and general opinion to use their natural freedom with impunity. [p. 150]

For this sharp-eyed analyst, the historian Catherine Macaulay, primitive libertinism persisted even after the economic slavery of women had been ameliorated.

The physical violence documented by Friedli, Trumbach and Simpson is obviously the extreme case, but the model of unresolved tension (rather than benign evolution) also fits the violence of attitude that Porter explores. He identifies a tangle of ambiguities in discourse and in practice, confirming Tarczylo's vision of sexual history as "a multiplicity of intersecting relations." Pornography masqueraded as science, campaign texts like *Onania* or Mandeville's *Public Stews* "hover[ed] ambivalently between reform and titillation" (p. 208), and medical practitioners laced their writings with bawdy anecdotes. There was no consensus on how far the doctor's privilege allowed him to penetrate "the protective layers of privacy and decency surrounding patients in their normal social intercourse" (p. 210)—an intrusion obviously more problematic when the patient was a woman. Propriety itself was "double-edged," an enigmatic play between permission and transgression, concealing and revealing. Doctors were loath to make physical examinations (medical theory did not recommend it in diagnosis), so that any touching, however necessary in obstetrics, could be construed as a violation of decorum; fringe medicine, by contrast, put the utmost faith in touching, stroking, pressing sick infants against freshly hung corpses, and (Simpson's article informs us) raping children to transfer venereal disease. Meanwhile, the new cult of Sensibility, itself a product of increasing privacy, turned the entire body into a quivering, Sternean network of erotic sensors: "Blushing, the pounding heart, the racing pulse, the trembling hand, the tearful cheek—all became eloquent in a sign language of refined, suppressed sexual expression" (p. 215). This is the context for the complaint that male obstetricians are allowed "to have such intercourse with our women, as easily shifts itself into indecency, from indecency into obscenity, from obscenity into debauchery" (p. 217). But did social interaction shift *itself* through these gradations? Who were the agents of this change? Overwhelmingly, Porter shows, blame was heaped upon the wife.

It takes a particular mentality to cite the gynaecological manual as if it were pornography, to read the scene of consultation as a seduction: a nervous and schoolboyish amusement at the mention of the genitals (irrespective of the context), and a complete lack of empathy for the woman preparing for, or in the throes of, a childbirth which will certainly bring intense pain and might well kill her. The life of an adulterous countess was undoubtedly more pleasant than that of a prostitute in Bridewell, but she still had to "weigh well if she could bear pain, without alarming the family by her cries" (p. 222), to cope with the terrors of discovery as well as the "rack" of childbearing itself. Lady Bolingbroke had to consult with her doctor under cover of darkness—he found her "very much flurried, and almost fainting, [as if] under some great misfortune" (pp. 223–24)—while her husband's sexual adventures were the talk of Europe. Porter tends not to dwell on this aspect of his material, however, and stresses the unprecedented sexual freedom that women enjoyed in collusion with their doctors. He ends on a note of sympathy for the wronged and anxious husband.

The outrage of these pornographer-moralists is particularly fierce because "our women" were supposedly enjoying, in their touching-sessions with gynaecologists, what the double standard had always allowed their husbands: sex without danger, without opprobrium, without "consequences" either external or internal. At issue is the separation of the pleasure principle from biological procreation, a separation which could be purely mental (as in pornographic fantasy), but which constantly sought material expression. The more progressive theories of marriage, in seventeenth-century Puritanism and in the eighteenth-century "affective revolution," encouraged couples to build a strong erotic bond even during pregnancy or when child-bearing was impossible—a development which Defoe attacked, in the significantly named *Conjugal Lewdness, or Matrimonial Whoredom*,[13] with almost incomprehensible vehemence. But no respectable moralist campaigned for contraception, without which women could not begin to find real sexual freedom; this demand was made, however, by shadowy figures like the pioneering woman denounced by Defoe, a forerunner of Marie Stopes whom historians should research further. The fear that women might attain this "unconcerned" sexuality evidently sparked off the absurd attacks that Porter documents. A simulacrum of sex—even in conditions which no sensible person could find lubricious, and where no bastard children could result—aroused as much prurience and rage as the thing itself.

A general theme of these essays in fact, though insufficiently articulated, is the special status given to *representations*. Here the work of Castle and Friedli, on masquing and cross-dressing, is particularly relevant, though the concept of a dissociated but highly charged erotic simulation also helps to explain other phenomena discussed in the volume. The fantastic element in Cleland, for example, could be understood in terms of a culturally pervasive need for theatricality and display, for sexual "representations" under masculine control. The court records themselves reveal it: several of Trumbach's case-histories involve women arrested while "enacting lewd postures" for their clients, which confirms the frequent references in satire and pornography both to the codified "postures" of Aretino and to "Posture-houses" where these were performed in *tableaux vivants*. We can posit a general transformation of sex into spectacle or simulacrum, that casts the subject as a patron or stage manager rather than as a fully concerned and yielding participant, a potential victim in this age of exploitation and disease. Thus the Restoration rake cries out the name of the court beauty who spurns him, as he ejaculates into a prostitute—"Fancying at least I swive with Quality." And Boswell's excitement reaches new heights when he thinks of all the high-born ladies that his mistress Louisa has represented on stage: "Most courageously did I plunge into the fount of love, and had vast pleasure as I enjoyed her as an actress who had played many a fine lady's part."[14] Erotic experience, for Boswell, can be understood as a match between his current situation and some "scene" he has remembered from his libertine or heroic reading—though the connection is always a slippery one. Who is playing whom, when he enjoys her "as an actress"?

The most striking collective representation of erotic play, detached from real-life consequences and repressive codes, was the masquerade. But did it really promote sexual freedom—"particularly" for women—and dissolve the boundaries of gender, as Castle maintains? As with earlier carnivals, the crucial question is one of control: though they *could* slip away into insurrection, early modern festivals of misrule were generally licensed and consciously exceptional inversions of norms enforced all the more strongly after the festive time had elapsed. Evidence from seventeenth-century carnivals suggests a narrow boundary between festive tolerance and rage. When Jean-Jacques Bouchard visited the Roman Carnival with a group of *libertin* friends in 1632, he was delighted to be pelted with hollow eggshells filled with perfume—but the moment his group stepped out in *female* dress they were assaulted with real eggs and stones, and fled to escape injury.[15] To use Tarczylo's phrase, the "connivances" of carnival were "momentary and limited." And to the extent that the blurring of sexual boundaries did create freedoms, it released men as well as women from the restraints of politeness: in his "Stances sur sa Maistresse rencontrée en habit de garçon, un soir du Carnaval," Vincent de Voiture pretends at first to be in love with a boy, a Narcissus who has stolen his soul, his heart, his life, but he then turns this conceit into a pretext for physical intimacy—he will get back his stolen goods "if you allow me to search you."[16]

Castle does show that masquerade and travesty ran through the imagination of virtually every segment of this society, and allowed vicarious experience of "new realms of voluptuous disorder" (p. 161) including a range of modern perversities—often presented as accidents and thus detached from moral culpability. She shows, too, that representations of masquerades in fiction (simulacra of simulacra) *tried* to present them as "Congress to an unclean end," linking them to actual physical consequences of the grimmest kind: the father seduces his own daughter, and dies of horror after the discovery (pp. 161, 173). It is harder to prove that such things actually happened, however. We would

Sex and Consequence 151

expect the eighteenth-century masquerade—a scheduled indoors event, to which only ticket-holders could be admitted—to be more rigidly circumscribed and policed than its seventeenth-century predecessors; it seems implausible that such an event could "charm away the heiratic fixities of gender" (p. 157), not because they are fixed in some "natural" order, but because they are enforced with the utmost socio-economic power. If we examine some of Castle's sources, we find far less disorder than she claims. She mentions one masquerade at Almack's where men appeared as a procuress and as "Mother Cole," probably the idealized brothel-keeper from *Fanny Hill*. But despite this apparent intrusion of the lower stratum (which took place at the Pantheon, not at Almack's), the *Lady's Magazine* correspondent praised such events as a model of "propriety and decorum; . . . a masquerade is a more innocent entertainment than any woman of fashion's rout."[17] (Alice Browne also recognizes that masquerades "were popular with highly respectable people" such as Elizabeth Carter [p. 38].) The "risqué comments" directed at Harriette Wilson's party in 1814 (p. 164) turn out to be rather mild—"'we are admiring your feet and ankles,' said Mrs. Scott Waring"—and suggest a certain weariness with the pretense of disguise: "'But do, for heaven's sake, take off your mask, child: it really is such affectation!'"[18] This semi-detached attitude could be interpreted as a specimen of Regency decadence, except that similar remarks were directed at Sir Fopling's masquerade in Etherege's *Man of Mode,* as early as 1676 (IV.i).

Order prevailed even when sexual opportunities *were* part of the masquerade. Margaret Leeson's private ball of 1784, at which *tout Dublin* was present (the guests are described in a kind of Homeric catalogue of scandal for fifty pages), included a special surcharge on the two-guinea ticket for guests who wanted to sleep with her employees. It hardly "degenerated into an orgy" since it was a commercially regulated venture from the start. Impromptu seductions were frowned upon: Leeson describes with amused contempt an "impotent attempt to enjoy me in one of the recesses," the sixth that evening. At a previous masked ball—given by her most famous customer, the Viceroy—Leeson had appeared in a costume that wittily acknowledged her profession: she went as Diana, Goddess of Chastity, arguing that Cleopatra or Messalina "surely could not be deemed *masquerade*, as to be in masquerade is undoubtedly to be in an *assumed character*." But decorum still applied. When a male guest (dressed as Beelzebub) tried to feel the breasts of one of her attendant Graces—a gesture similar to that sanctioned in Voiture's poem on the Carnival—he was, like Lucifer, "husled out of Paradise, amidst the execrations of all the company, [and] afterwards degraded, totally ruined and turned out of the university."[19] It seems more likely, then, that masquerades functioned as a containment rather than a release of erotic simulacra, a Foucaultian control-by-proliferation, a guarantee that no real "assault" would take place and that the "polymorphous subject" remained only a fantasy.

It is tempting to suggest that male sexuality, in this age of great lovers, needed all the stage-management it could muster. Speculating how women could spend years in the army undetected, Friedli reminds us that half the male population would have been under sixteen, with unbroken voices: "standards of masculinity may not have been very high" (p. 250). The ideal of male good looks called for smooth pink cheeks, melting eyes, shimmering silks and (at least before 1770) a cascade of artificial curls. Meanwhile, as Browne shows, male moralists saw prostitutes as "gigantic women who stalk through the streets, *like grenadiers in disguise*, [exhibiting] wanton and ferocious effrontery" (p. 127, my emphasis). Such assertiveness was obviously a male prerogative. It was considered gallant, even "polite," to achieve sudden copulation in unexpected places. In Wycherley's comedies impromptu sex occurs twice while other speakers are on stage, and can thus be timed precisely; the whole business takes less than a minute.[20] This Punch-and-Judy coupling may be a farce convention in this case, but even the memoirs of refined voluptuaries show that speed of execution was a matter of pride: "I obtained the last favors with my hat still under my arm and my sword at my side"; "I attack, I pillage, I fire my pistol shot, I move camp."[21] In the more stately setting of the bed, men seem to have measured the quality of their sexuality by the number of repetitions they could achieve. The military and the erotic both aspired to the

Sex and Consequence 153

condition of rapid-fire artillery. Key pornographic texts of the seventeenth and eighteenth centuries explicitly conclude that the "image of Venus" enjoyed in the memory is far superior to the act itself.[22] No wonder Aphra Behn complained that masculine desires "like lightning flash and are no more"—a condition she links directly to the ideology of disengagement: " 'Tis a fatal lesson he has learn'd, / After fruition ne're to be concern'd."[23]

The obscene poetry of the Restoration is obviously an extreme paradigm, but it does point to the nexus of experience and ideology that underlies this preoccupation with frenetic performance. The misogynist satire of Richard Ames and Robert Gould, for example, denounces copulation as a "slimy Drudgery," a "short Bliss,"

> thought[,] begun and finisht in a minute;
> And when the eager short liv'd transport's o're
> We lie like Fishes gasping on the shore.[24]

Gould projects a terrified vision of female sexual voracity and loathesomeness, and anticipates the virginity-mania of the following century:

> But for that Charm who is it that wou'd care,
> Meer Lust excepted, to approach the Fair?
> Why are we Fond, why Languish and Adore,
> But to have something none e'er had before?
> To be the first that Crops the Virgin Flower?[25]

The ideology of the insatiable woman is obviously much older than the 1680s. But the renewed virulence of such themes in Restoration satire suggests a new anxiety created by a distinctly modern and urban social arrangement—a free competitive market with infinite possibilities for infidelity and sexual exchange, a sea of sex where the male could be just one of "a dozen of Pricks."[26] The simultaneous arousal and fury generated by this perception of sexual availability are expressed not only in texts, but in the violent practices of brothel-goers and upper-class roisterers—multiple rape, "tumbling," face-slashing, the insertion of burning candles or fireworks—which survive even in the politer circles of eighteenth-century France.[27] Rochester shows that a comforting eroticism *could* be snatched from the midst of this violence, though it is significant that, in order to praise Love as "That Cordiall dropp Heav'n in our Cup has throwne, / To make the nauseous draught of life goe downe," he must create a female persona (p. 84). For contemporaries like Gould, and at times for Rochester himself, love *is* the nauseous draught. Only rarely can he combine the extreme of erotic tenderness and neurotic abuse, as in "A Ramble in St James's Parke." Here he imagines his mistress "Full gorged . . . With a vast meal of nasty slime / Which your devouring Cunt had drawn / From Porters backs and Footmens brawn," but then identifies this state of liquefaction with "pleasure," with "The secretts of my tender houres / . . . When leaneing on your faithless breast / Wrapt in security and rest / Soft kindness all my powers did move / And Reason lay dissolv'd in Love" (p. 67).

Elsewhere, Rochester polarizes the sexual response into an uncontrollable amorphous dissolving (in the arms of the beloved) and an insensate priapism which makes him no more than a "Dart" for spearing virgins or a "*Fucking-Post*" for common whores (pp. 30–32). Both—and this is the irony of the poem's title—are fundamentally "imperfect enjoyments." The body-in-love, as opposed to the state of priapic contempt, is totally deliquescent, totally sexual, completely unspecialized: "I dissolve all o're, / Melt into Sperme, and spend at ev'ry Pore." He is excited in the first place because "Her Hand, her Foot, her very look's a *Cunt*," and responds in kind. This polymorphous arousal is something like the angelic sex described in *Paradise Lost*, and very much like the condition to which he aspires to bring the other person; his mighty phallus would hitherto "invade" woman and man alike, since "Where e're it pierc'd, a *Cunt* it found or made." But the crucial element of control is lost when his mistress orders him to "throw / The *All-dissolving Thunderbolt* below"—that is, to concentrate his efforts, to serve her pleasure by becoming *more* Priapic and *less* polymorphous. In Rochester we discover the prehistory of the diffuse and quivering Sternean body, created— as *A Sentimental Journey* makes clear—by a self-controlled withdrawal from sexual engagement: the "sentimental" eroticization of all social intercourse is deployed and intensified by genital abstinence or impotence.

It would be unwise to take these seventeenth-century texts as reportage, of course, but they did exert a great influence on the eighteenth-century "discourse of sexuality" and on the identity formation of the male, as Boswell makes abundantly clear. Even Defoe quotes the scandalous Rochester *against* the scandalous pleasure-seeking wife—a paradox that the poet himself would have enjoyed. Indeed, we might almost say that the modern notion of Sex as a specialized voluptuary system—a chain of priapic triumphs multiplied according to a technique of permutation, an abstract pursuit of pleasure detached from psychological or gynaecological consequences—is a product of the tensions they express.

If we add together everything we know about child abuse, rape, prostitution and male hostility, and set it within the all-but-unbreachable walls of the double standard, then the whole field of illicit sexuality comes to seem like a Gulag Archipelago for women, policed by men. It is not easy, after reading the Rousseau/Porter volume, to maintain a simple libertine-liberationist model, and among all the contributors, only Wagner feels able to state, *tout court,* that "the eighteenth century adored . . . sex" (p. 46). Friedli reminds us that sex and gender are contested areas, and Tarczylo asserts that "sexuality remains one of the places where the battle of castes, of classes and of ranks is played out indefinitely" (p. 41). (We don't need, however, to accept his conclusion that sexuality is nothing but a "pretext" and a "chimera" and its history impossible to write—a flashy exaggeration that his own work mercifully belies.) Nevertheless, we should heed the editors' warning not to make women *completely* the victim and men completely the insouciant Lovelace or hypocritical Yorick. Rousseau and Porter are right to discern that feminist interpretation of the period has divided into two camps, one wholly pessimistic, the other recognizing that, despite the horrors, women did manifest an unprecedented verve, creativity and cultural leadership at this time.[28] The *salon* is clearly a healthier place than the Victorian drawing room. And even the most masculine texts may be "unwittingly" sympathetic to women, as Castle discovers in a lewd poem by Fielding. We should not underestimate the power of fantasy to redress the balance, the capacity—even in rank pornography—to create images of freedom that can be turned against male hegemony. By its stress on simulation and transgression, and its valuation of Wit and improvisation, libertinism *may* have undermined the apparent fixities of gender and sexual morality. Fanny Hill's respectable marriage *is* a defeat for the double standard, and we should not overlook real-life equivalents like Catherine Sedley, who married respectably after being mistress of James II, and who could tell her children frankly and humorously that "if any body call either of you the son of a whore, you must bear it for you are so, but if they call you bastards, fight till you die."[29]

It is essential in any history of sex and gender to draw on women's own writings, as do Friedli and Castle in these essays and Browne in her book. (Despite the call, in an earlier Rousseau/Porter collaboration, for deeper study of female novelists like Manley, Haywood and Charke, the other contributors to this volume pay little attention to women's representations of sexuality.)[30] Eighteenth-century women's voices generate a welcome complexity, because they spoke on both sides of the debate over sexual freedom. Castle tends to stress the liberating force of the masquerade for women, adopting a sophisticated version of the Whig model: like Porter, she characterizes the eighteenth century as an age of greater sexual freedom and "new modes of intimacy," anticipating "the Protean future of desire" and offering "unprecedented sensual release" for women (pp. 169, 174–75). Harriette Wilson, for example, declared that "I love a masquerade, because a female can never enjoy the same liberty anywhere else" (p. 169). Though this was written after 1814, we can find literary evidence for this liberating effect as early as Behn's *The Rover* (1677), where female characters use the Carnival as a means of escaping parental control, taking the initiative in conversation, and teasing men about their secret sexual fears (I.ii); the Carnival-scene also gave Behn some discursive liberty, since it allowed her to depart from the male-authored text she was adapting for the stage. Castle does not cite Behn, but she does discover several respectable witnesses from the eighteenth century: "Besides obvious demi-mondaine figures like Wilson and Margaret Leeson, such distinguished women as Mary Wortley Montagu, Fanny Burney and Elizabeth Inchbald acknowledged a fondness of [*sic*] masquerade privileges" (p. 169). Wortley Montagu appreciated the "perpetual masquerade" of the veil in Turkey, and discovered in the Venetian carnival "a universal liberty that is certainly one of the greatest *agremens* in life" (p. 179). But what exactly constituted this freedom, this "subversive—if temporary—simulacrum of sexual autonomy" that Castle almost calls "a feminist counterpart to the brothel" (p. 169)? Wilson certainly did meet lovers at other masqued balls, but here she stresses the socio-dynamic rather than the sexual: a freedom to move about the room and to initiate conversation that we now take for granted. She certainly did translate her personal dynamism into a discursive freedom best expressed in the dazzling first sentence of her *Memoirs:* "I shall not say why and how I became, at the age of fifteen, the mistress of the Earl of Craven" (I.5). But again, this is not simply a sexual revelation. By *refusing* to give details after making the readers' ears tingle, Wilson is not merely drawing a veil of hypocritical privacy: she is exercising the right *not* to treat an illicit liaison as a sexual experience. Her motive was not that of the "woman of pleasure" conjured up by libertine fiction, but the need to escape a tyrannical father, and she left the Earl because the avoidance of *ennui* was more important than financial security or sexual satisfaction: "Craven was a dead bore."

Wortley Montagu, again, may have enjoyed the imaginary freedoms of masquerade, but she is no less aware of the effects, in the real world, of the double standard. Her unpublished poetry is particularly eloquent: the dark "Epistle from Mrs Yonge" chokes with indignation at the punishments inflicted on the erring wife and the impunity of her brutal and adulterous husband; and the light-hearted ballad "The Lover" is equally clear-sighted about the impossibility of finding a man mature and discreet enough not to exploit her vulnerability by turning her private pleasure into an acknowledged conquest. Writing to her future husband, she sums up the different meaning of sexual adventure for males and females in this society: "'Tis play to you, but 'tis death to us."[31]

Masquerade and exotic fantasy *did* allow women to redefine sexuality as "play," or—in the terms of this essay—as representation without commitment, under the control of the presenter. But there is no evidence that it actually softened the restrictions on women, the absolute separation of "good" and "bad," and the painful experience of being condemned, irreversibly and without reference to any other moral criteria, for errors on which men would be congratulated. Browne cites the words of Laetitia Pilkington, a victim of this unequal treatment who did her best to redress the balance by writing memoirs: "Is it not monstrous that our seducers should be our accusers?" (p. 148). Even the brothel-keeper and masquerade queen Margaret Leeson, a thoroughly public persona whose audible *double entendres* convulsed the Dublin theatre audience, was not naive enough to assume a general liberationist position. Her *Memoirs* open with a hard-hitting and eloquent denunciation of the double standard from which she materially profited.

Browne is suitably outraged by the notion that a single physical slip would doom a woman forever, irrespective of her personal qualities—an ideology "obviously impossible to reconcile with respect for women as rational moral beings" (p. 59). But she also shows how some women maintained the double standard, and how some men claimed to be ready to relax it, blaming women themselves for maintaining it so strictly: one reviewer of *La Nouvelle Héloise* preferred it to *Clarissa* because the story of Julie, a heroine despite her affair with St-Preux, corrects the harshness of "the female world, who generally resign over to vice and wretchedness those of their own sex who have once deviated from the paths of virtue." As Browne notes, this complacent position fails to account for the sexual precariousness of "good" women and the realities of a male-dominated society: the same critic reviews *Clarissa* without mentioning the rape, and puts Clarissa's refusal of Lovelace down to "false delicacy" (pp. 68, 141). But many women *did* uphold the conventional distinction between the respectable and the fallen. Elizabeth Montagu remarks, of a man who *had* married his mistress, that "the age is

Sex and Consequence

wicked when men make w----s, but it is shameless when they marry them; from infamy to virtue there is no return" (p. 143). (In practice, as Browne points out, Montagu was kind and discreet in helping a friend hide her affair.) By the late eighteenth century divorced women could legally marry their lovers and regain respectability, but Jane West cannot accept this: "The duchess who has violated her marriage oath, who is discarded by her husband and married to her gallant, is but the same creature who is transferred at Smithfield to a new purchase" (p. 173).

In these cases it seems that the male establishment, individually or collectively, *had* eased the system of sexual apartheid, and that it is women who call for a tightening-up. Does this mean, as the critic implied, that the whole structure of the double standard is a fantasm kept up by female prudes? It would be hard to maintain this interpretation in the face of Browne's evidence; she shows that women did indeed have much to lose and much to fear. The category "respectable" did protect women in some ways—not because they were necessarily better treated by newly sensitized men, but because it guaranteed a minimal financial security, civility and access to a circle of friends. Browne shows that many women supported it as a way of marking themselves off from the general sexualization imposed on them by men (p. 140); they feared that to abandon the distinction would be to have *all* women treated as men currently treated whores. (The extremity of male violence was thus interpreted politically, like the threat of rape today, as part of the conditions that determine all gender relations, even the most genteel.) In practical terms, Browne reminds us, to be classed as bad "made it impossible to earn a living in any of the few ways open to middle-class women" (p. 141). Some of her most interesting examples come from one institution that actually did attempt to rehabilitate the victims of the double standard: the Magdalen Hospital for repentant prostitutes. Those younger women lucky enough to escape infection could arrive at a better life than dying on the streets, but at the cost of their status, identity and moral complexity. Those who supported rehabilitation (and many opposed it) tended "to reduce the women in question to stereotypical victims or whores, who must be completely innocent or completely guilty" (p. 72).

(Browne contrasts this polarization to the moral complexity allowed to fictional characters like Clarissa or Julie.) Even the innocent were assumed to have passed into another world, cut off from any identity they might have enjoyed before their "fall." Horace Walpole recalls that, on one visit to the hospital, he actually recognized someone from his own social class, the "niece" of his friend Sir Clement Cotterel; the shock of the encounter was so great that she fainted (p. 144). In another case-history, an upper-class woman "endeavour[s] to wash out the guilt of her former crimes, by her tears and repentence, and prepare[s] to enter the world afresh, in the humble character of servant; for . . . her friends are firmly resolved never to see her more, nor to afford her any relief or assistance" (p. 145). In a fictional example, the redeemed female (like a federal witness to the most dangerous crime) is offered a new life in Ireland, where she will be known by nobody (p. 165).

Sexual ideology did not operate alone, then; it was thoroughly interlocked with class privilege. To pass into the demi-monde was to be *declassée*, isolated from one's peers, placed under a kind of house arrest. For the young Wortley Montagu it was "death"— if not literally, in childbirth without proper care, then socially. One moralist seriously proposed (using classical and Biblical antecedents) that women who transgress strict chastity should be considered "foreign."[32] Jane West compares an adulterous duchess to a Smithfield Market purchase—a horse, or perhaps one of those proletarian wives who could be sold "at twopence-farthing the pound."[33] Women were excluded from the political nation, and upper-class women (unlike the female proletariat) played only a marginal part in the economic nation. But they had one precious asset: membership, even leadership, in the social nation, "The World." Freedom of manner, seductive flair, and expertise in the finer points of love were the keys to success in this world—and the occasion for instant expulsion. This is true, not only in the England of *The Rape of the Lock*, but in supposedly libertine France: a figure like Mme de Lursay in Crébillon's *Les Egarements du coeur et de l'esprit*, whose sole function is to "form" the young aristocrat by educative seduction, must still operate completely within the code of chastity, and owes her social position to her official reputation. Striking exceptions obviously leap to mind, such as the irrepressible Leeson or the mistresses of the royal family—those who benefit from an exceptionally forceful and impudent style or from a social status so high that it transfers impunity as it were by touch. But such anomalies or paradigm-clashes generated a considerable strain, as we sense when reading the gross and violent satires directed against the mistresses of Charles II. And individual advancement to a royal bed did not alter the general politics of gender, as was clear to Mary Robinson (Browne, p. 154); she evolved from the Prince of Wales's mistress into a prolific feminist novelist and critic of masculine ideology.

How far the nexus of sex and class governed decoding practices and habits of perception can be judged from two late Restoration examples. The cavaliers who respond to the Carnival scene in Behn's *Rover* are perplexed because they cannot reconcile the women's apparent sexual forwardness with their fluent and witty style: they are afraid that this "free" style can only belong to a person of "free" (i.e., upper-class) status, who will therefore not be "free" for sexual adventures.[34] The editors of the *Athenian Mercury*, the popular predecessor of eighteenth-century "ladies" magazines, apply a similar double take to a desperate letter from a female correspondent, pleading for advice about her lover's fickleness. Textual interpretation leads directly to assumptions about class and sexuality:

If the Querist had not *specify'd* her *Character* and Quality, it might have been guess'd at without much *difficulty*, by her way of *Spelling* and *Writing*. Whoe're she be, she's *miserable enough*, being infected at once with the two greatest *Plagues* of her *Sex*, *Prostitution* and *Love*. . . . Why shou'd the poor *cheated Creature* expect *Impossibilities;* that a *Man* shou'd continue to be *true*, when he has more than all he desires: Or how can she wonder that any is *false* to her, when *she* has been already so to *Virtue?* . . . She might full as reasonably hope a Man shou'd *fall to[o] agen* upon the same *Dish* on which he is already *surfeited*.[35]

Flippant dismissal alternates with thunderous sermonizing. Two issues later, however, the letter is resubmitted with the spelling and grammar corrected—and the response is utterly different.

The tone is now respectful, the appeal to religious values is tactful and understated, the correspondent is assumed to be able to "give [her]self the liberty of thinking," and the whole affair is interpreted as a situation redeemable by marriage.

But we cannot simply impose a two-tier system on history, assuming that sexuality belonged to the lower stratum while the respectable classes remained above such things. For sexual adventure was simultaneously associated with the vulgar depths and the fashionable heights, the "underworld" and the Beau Monde that converted erotic lawlessness into sublimity.[36] As the eighteenth century progressed, in fact, the ardors of heroic love were reappropriated for the marriage bed, in that fusion of sex and sensibility that Jean Hagstrum has documented so well. It might be argued that the Age of Sensibility moves away from the sexual into hyper-refinement and sublimation; certainly Browne shows the increasing prevalence of the idea that "fallen" women from good families must have been the victims of force or fraud, since truly feminine women are too delicate to feel illicit desire. But women were no less subject to contradictory demands that centered on their sex. Sensibility was no less "double-edged" for women than for men. The controlling paradigm in the later eighteenth century was not just Motherhood, as Friedli suggests, but the simultaneous insistence that women be wholly the rational mother and wholly eroticized. Critics like Wollstonecraft urge women to place a wedge between the two, and denounce Sensibility as a vicious attempt to equate the totality of woman with erotic stimulus and "libertine reveries." As I argue above, Sensibility is better understood as a simultaneous denial and deployment of sexuality; but Wollstonecraft's argument should not be ignored. Browne cites evidence from didactic writers, including Wollstonecraft's *bête noire* John Gregory, to show how every detail in the production of "delicate" young women revolved around sexuality or attractiveness to men (pp. 30–32). In this context, it is easy to see why radicals had to adopt a stringent and austere anti-sexual doctrine—and were attacked for leading a life of sexual freedom that contradicted this principle.[37] Browne argues, in fact, that eighteenth-century feminists were trapped by the need to make common cause with conservative women, laying a heavy emphasis on female chastity and male depravity; this made it harder for the radicals to attack the core of their oppression, the double standard (p. 154). An alternative is hinted at but not developed by Browne in her remarks on Mary Astell: on the one hand, Astell had to break away from the gallant eroticization that trivialized women; on the other hand, she benefited from "new comic portrayals of witty and autonomous women," which gave a new satiric bite to her traditionalist calls for Virtue and Patience (p. 100). The worldly libertine code, just as much as the Sentimental, could be rescued and turned into a woman's resource; the issue, once again, is the control, expropriation, and "play" of representations.

"The double bind of demanding that women be both seductive and chaste" has always been part of gender ideology, of course, and Montaigne had expounded it sympathetically.[38] But it is "completely articulated in the eighteenth century in a way that it is not in earlier periods" (p. 34). This intensifies the problem of women's control over representations, because in polite society, governed by the codes of Worldliness, the absolutely essential distinction between reputable and fallen women had to be absolutely invisible. Eighteenth-century costume did not mark any distinction between prostitutes, upper servants and "ladies," who followed precisely the same fashion codes and (in certain decades) the same verbal codes (p. 35). "Propriety and fashion sometimes worked against each other," Browne points out in a memorable understatement; "Elizabeth Montagu defended an acquaintance's morals by saying 'She wants to have the *bon ton*, and you know the *bon ton* of 1756 is *un peu équivoque*'" (p. 40). Already in the Restoration a fictional prostitute could attribute her fall to this equivocal style: "Brisk and Airy (which our dull Grandmothers would have call'd Wanton and Impudent) is long since become the Character of a Well bred-woman; to be a Miss, was both a pleasant and thriving Undertaking"—though after falling into the hands of a procuress she is "in a worse Servitude than the most wretched Gally-Slaves."[39] Serious commentators in the following century could assume that prostitutes came, not from the hardworking proletariat, but from upper servants and the lower middle classes, those with aspirations to gentility without the means to support them (p. 127). The ambiguity of fashion disturbed women themselves, and fuelled their demand for stricter enforcement of the chaste/bad distinction. Sarah Trimmer, in words that hover between mean-spirited blame and protective compassion, calls upon the upper classes to establish a dress code whereby "the outward appearance of every woman [would] secure the respect due to circumstances and character; and we should no longer see the modest virgin, with dishevelled hair, inviting the insults of libertines" (p. 142).

For both genders, then, sexuality was permeated by discourse, by performative trope, by representation. But this in no way removes it from the hard questions of political analysis—what, to whom, for whom? Discourse has no *intrinsic* relation to power or impotence: the same words may be spoken in different theaters, theaters of repression, liberation, or the compromising "license." They may be expropriative or compensatory. Strong self-characterization by women may regain control over conceptual boundaries or blur them, may give women access to the "center" or keep them dreaming on the "margins." There is no automatic link between hyper-masculine statements and the oppression of women; they could express male hysterias and fears. On the other hand, there is no automatic comfort to be gained from the idea that representations are mere fictions. Wollstonecraft denounces Milton's Eve as a kind of harem-fantasy, more relevant to male desire than to women's real concerns; but the issue is still profoundly relevant to her campaign, since these projections *are* enforced as models of female identity. Fictions propounded with authority were all too easily internalized, as Mary Hays saw very clearly:

Half the sex, then, are the infamous, wretched victims of brutal instinct; the other half, if they sink not in mere frivolity and insipidity, are sublimated into a sort of—what shall I call them?—refined, romantic, unfortunate, factitious beings, who cannot bear to act, for the sake of the present moment, in a manner that should expose them to complicated, inevitable evils! . . . And beside which these refinements, however factitious, are, in time, incorporated into, and become a part of, the real character.[40]

Male unreality produces inauthentic "factitious" females; and "it is from chastity having been rendered a sexual virtue, that all these calamities have flowed" (*ibid.*).

Whatever answers we put forward, one thing is clear: the historicity of sexuality resides in its problematic connections and consequences, as they are articulated by feminism both in the past and in our own day. Not that men should adopt a pseudo-female position uncritically, or attempt to conceal their own identity and concerns. But feminism has set the agenda. Peter Wagner's *magnum opus*, to which I finally turn, seems at first to participate in this historiographic movement, but on closer inspection it proves to be an anachronism.

In his Rousseau/Porter essay Wagner declares his subject to be "sex *as* discourse" (my emphasis), and in the Introduction to his large book he announces an ambitious socio-cultural project. He attacks the simplistic equation of "pornography" with sexual stimulation, pointing out its historical variability and the multiplicity of its functions: "disorientation," literary mimicry, entertainment, didacticism, protest against Church, State and "middle-class morality," the transgression of all kinds of taboo. Erotic texts not only "reflect the society that produced them," but "had in turn a telling effect upon the economic and political thought and deeds of their time" (pp. 6–7). In the body of the text, however, this socially engaged and dialectic model is almost entirely abandoned. Apart from a couple of incidents of sexual violence during the French Revolution, Wagner offers no evidence of clandestine texts acting upon society. He repeatedly falls back on the stimulus definition of pornography, and focuses on the most explicitly genital passages within his chosen texts, rather than exploring their wider implications. He lapses, too, into naive reflectionism: the dildo "was apparently not only known but also in demand and, *consequently*, a subject of literary comment"; "if the prostitute became a cherished topic in literature . . . it was *because* [London and Bath] were swarming with ladies of pleasure" (pp. 29, 133–34; my emphasis). He does not broach the complex interrelation of sex and discourse, and simplifies the Foucaultian thesis he is ostensibly testing (Foucault's "incitement" is equated with an increase in the *volume* of erotic publishing). His promise to tackle "middle-class morality" and transgression leads to a tautology, since the only restrictions he deals with are those against pornography itself. Despite its claims, Wagner's compilation belongs to what Tarczylo called "lascivious erudition," rather than to the new history of *mentalités* and discourses.

Wagner's method is almost invariable. Having arranged his texts and pictures in a rather shaky taxonomic scheme—some chapters are defined by their target ("Anti-Religious Erotica," "Matrimony and the War of the Sexes") and others by their medium or tone ("Poetry and Facetiae"), so that the same examples show up in several places—he then describes them one by one. He outlines the circumstances of publication (normally relying on other scholars' research), and then gives a summary of the contents that is often little more than a check-list of the sexual practices covered, or a coy paraphrase of the obvious: "The lustful clerk is secretly eyeing the shapely bosom of the young sleeping beauty beside him. . . ." "[The gouty husband sleeps by the fire, but] the young wife, in the background, being in heat—so to speak—has no need of a fire while she is being serviced by a young gallant. . . ." "Randy Roger appears and sets to work . . ." (pp. 60, 145, 176). In many cases he will also reprint the most "spicy" or "juicy" passages (his words), but these extracts are not then subjected to further literary or sociological analysis: transcription replaces interpretation, and a new text is immediately brought on, a new candidate for solitary enjoyment.

On the few occasions that Wagner does offer a value judgment the effect is quite bizarre. The sophisticated *Contes* of La Fontaine and Godard de Beauchamps's amusing *Histoire du Prince Apprius* are dismissed as "coarse" or "childish, if not primitive" (pp. 171, 195). The cheerful, billowy females in Rowlandson's erotic engravings are pronounced "grotesque" and frightening. And the seventeenth-century dialogue *L'Ecole des Filles,* one of the founding texts of philosophical libertinism, is solemnly condemned for "a claustrophobic atmosphere, a loss of psychological depth accompanied by an idealisation of sex, and an anarchic message"

(p. 227)—though Wagner's summary reveals that he has not properly read it.[41] On the other hand, the crudest texts are summarized with obvious relish and without value judgment, while a hideously misogynistic satire like Gould's *Love Given O're* can be presented as an example of "ribald fun," "innocuous bawdy works on the war of the sexes and marriage, stressing laughter and entertainment rather than social criticism" (p. 156). (Though he claims to have read Felicity Nussbaum's study of Gould and his contemporaries, Wagner still cites his 1682 poem as an anonymous work of 1709.) Alice Browne's book could also be accused of methodological shortcomings, since she does reduce her primary texts to card-index summaries and defines her reading too narrowly, ignoring recent work by radical feminists like Moira Ferguson. But Browne compacts her texts skillfully, fitting them into a comprehensive network of social and ideological connections. Wagner puts his texts through a kind of meat grinder, isolating the "good bits" and promoting an ideology of sex as fun for everybody, problematic only when attacked by "unenlightened" or "Victorian" prudery.

Though Wagner insists on the importance of *Rezeptionsgeschichte* in his Introduction, he produces very little evidence for it (apart from re-editions of the lewd texts themselves). He is particularly cavalier about female readership, which he evidently associates with the "sentimental"—dismissed as boring and unreadable because it fails to include explicit descriptions of "erotic encounters" (pp. 203, 218–19, 245–46). (He assumes that the "modern reader" has no patience with sentiment and high-flown diction, even from the pen of Fanny Hill, being "used to hardcore scenes in text and film presented in a realistic and obscene vocabulary.") Rather than investigating what eighteenth-century reading was actually like, he provides a generic "natural" or liberal reader from his own imagination: "Scatology was an unquestioned part of erotic folklore, and did not disturb eighteenth-century readers in the least" (p. 182). Swift's "so-called dirty poems" (p. 189) are the main examples discussed (though the rest of Swift's work is strangely neglected). But had he read Laetitia Pilkington—as he claims to have done, despite confusing her with Constantia Phillips—he would have known that her mother actually "threw up her dinner" after reading Swift's *Lady's Dressing-Room*.[42] Alternately, Wagner creates a "middle-class," "Puritan" or "bourgeois" reader utterly shocked by "so-called" obscenity, repressing all forms of "natural" expression. This straw person, invoked at every turn, obviously contradicts the most interesting of Wagner's claims—that the "bourgeois mentality" itself created pornography (the aristocracy did it and the middle classes wrote and read about it) and dominated every aspect of works like the *Memoirs of a Woman of Pleasure* (pp. 3, 131, 243, 255).

In his Rousseau/Porter piece and on his dust jacket, Wagner claims that his long-announced book is only an "introductory" study, less "scholarly" than the Sorbonne thesis on which it is apparently based. This modesty is not kept up, however. Wagner frequently complains about other scholars' "failure" to consider the clandestine material and about "unreliable" bibliography. Unfortunately his own book swarms with errors, contradictions, redundancies and omissions.[43] He rebukes the "sadly disappointing" Hagstrum for ignoring both the pornographic materials themselves and the existing scholarship on them, assuming that they would have been directly relevant to Hagstrum's theme of "love in the literary culture."[44] But Wagner throws very little light on the all-important relation between sex and sensibility; and though he brings Socratic Eros into the Introduction, the body of his book—like the earlier scholarship he recommends to Hagstrum—makes virtually no reference to the concept or the experience of love.

Wagner's general complaint, legitimate in itself, is that scholars neglect the complex but illuminating relationship between high and low culture, what Boucé calls the "secret nexus" between canonical literature and these libertine or scandalous texts. As we read through this massive book, however, we come to realize that Wagner is largely unqualified to demonstrate this nexus himself. Literary terms like "epic" are used in ways that suggest no grasp of their meaning (pp. 163, 222, 226). Though Wagner complains about "reducing textual ambiguity to mere sexuality" (p. 263), he shows very little interest in textual ambiguity (he uses "equivocal" and "ambiguous" as euphemisms for "sexual"), or in any other literary feature for that matter: on the rare occasions that he cites an erotic poem of real stylistic merit (like Richard Savage's *Progress of a Divine*) or a skillful parody like *The Members to their Sovereign,* he fails to respond to its charms. These clandestine texts are crowded with literary allusions, and offer innumerable opportunities for identification, comparison and analysis. None is taken. When educated readers encountered the position taken by "Jenny" with "Roger"—"Subtle Lechers! knowing that / They cannot so be got with Brat. / I grant, indeed, they may, with Ease, / When resting on their Hands and Knees" (p. 177)—they would recognize a travesty version of Lucretius's *De Rerum Natura* IV.1263–77. But Wagner never mentions Lucretius, neither here (p. 177) nor in a section explicitly devoted to classical writers on sexuality. When Lord Lucian interrupts his wife in the arms of her *castrato* music teacher, having "heard [her] cry out in an extatic tone of voice, 'Give what thou can'st, and let me dream the rest'" (p. 31), we enjoy a near perfect illustration of the "secret nexus," one that reminds us that a canonical author like Pope himself balances between propriety and scandal. (These are of course the words of Eloisa to Abelard after his castration.) "His Lordship was too well read in Pope, not to know where that line was, and the occasion of speaking it" (p. 31); Wagner, however, passes the whole allusion over in silence. Again, when he summarizes John Armstrong's *Oeconomy of Love,* he pays no attention to the play of Miltonic and Thomsonian effects; he assumes that features like the prose "Argument," rather than alluding to the format of *Paradise Lost,* are simply "designed to facilitate the finding of special, titillating passages" (p. 15).

When Wagner does apply himself to canonical figures, the result is not fortunate. Apart from his scatology, Swift appears only as a "harsh and condescending misogynist" and as a mid-eighteenth-century "novelist" (pp. 160, 250; no evidence is cited in support of these opinions). Defoe is reduced to an "incipient pornographer" whose "allegedly moral" concerns are nothing but a prurient sham (pp. 134, 210). Pope is mentioned in the most desultory fashion, except in the Conclusion when *The Rape of the Lock* is put forward as a test case for the "nexus" theory and a justification of the whole project. He tells us, with an air of triumphant revelation, that the poem contains many *double entendres* and that lap dogs were thought to lick their mistresses' "love-grottoes" (an allusion noted by virtually every commentator on the poem in recent years).[45] On this basis, he concludes that Belinda actually *was* raped. Fielding is assumed to be a thoroughly good fellow, of course, and Richardson is naturally a lecherous prude and "a bigot at heart." Wagner can now reveal "Richardson's essentially prurient pizzicato of sex throughout *Pamela*," which is "basically a series of erotic episodes": the disguise scene is "essentially the titillating description of a striptease interposed with occasional moral reflections and dialogues," and Pamela's terrified collapse and cold sweating "must have caused chuckles with any reader who had some knowledge of erotic fiction and jargon" (pp. 210, 217, 307–09).

But why should this matter? Sex *is* a great pleasure, after all, and sexual fascination *does* play a central part in Richardsonian fiction; isn't it merely a matter of taste how the theme is interpreted and emphasized? It matters, I suggest, because these failures of literary judgment are interlocked with failures of empathy and historical imagination, and effectively endorse the masculinist ideology that separates "pleasure" from "concern" and brackets the victimization of women as a trivial side issue. To be fair, Wagner does go on to sketch the hard economic situation of the serving-maid and the ostracism that would follow seduction; but this does not stop him, in the same breath, from calling Pamela's concern with virginity "excessive" and "obsessive," and Richardson's morality "unbelievable." He does sporadically recognize "downright brutality," "cruel and unenlightened" medical beliefs, bad treatment of male homosexuals, and degrading sadistic elements in libertine writing, and he does sometimes question his own assumption that "Enlightenment" is synonymous with the acceptance of pornography. But these declarations are belied by the actual conduct of the book and its sex-shop catalogue method. His summary technique allows him no ideological distance, and paraphrase is at times indistinguishable from endorsement: "Fanny's defloration by Charles . . . may be painful for her, but she had been longing for it" (p. 239). Johnstone's *Chrysal* "excels in scenes of sensuality and sexuality [which] establish a picture of a society interested in the pleasures of the senses"—even though these scenes include rape and murder (p. 218). The rape in *L'Histoire de Dom B.*—quoted in loving detail—is assumed without question to "heighten the reader-voyeur's stimulation" (pp. 236–37). The Marquis d'Argens's *Thérèse philosophe* is described purely in terms of Enlightenment hedonism, ignoring an important scene in which the Abbé reveals the social arrangement that sustains his upper-class libertinism: he explains that, to keep his mind clear while researching, "j'avais une petite fille, comme on a un pot de chambre pour se soulager, à quoi je faisais une ou deux fois la grosse besogne."[46] He discharges into her without concern, whereas with Mme C., his social equal, he is careful to prevent pregnancy by *coitus interruptus*.

Wagner recognizes, in a brief aside, that the sex-as-pleasure ideology was "for men, to be sure; women had to bear the consequences" (p. 255). But he shares the pornographer's indifference to the issues of pregnancy and childbirth, and he dismisses concern with women's guilt and post-coital embarrassment as a repulsive and tiresome burden, part of the "puritan bourgeois moralism" that ruined English culture; "Puritan preachers," we are told, "had harped on the sinfulness of *enjoying* sex" (pp. 280–83).[47] Wagner cites few female authors (and has read even fewer), and does not explore the most striking paradox to emerge from libertine literature: that virtually all the hard-core texts produced and consumed in Europe from Aretino's *Ragionamenti* to Cleland's *Fanny Hill,* as well as genteel erotica like the "Tale," are male attempts to imagine, fictionalize, expropriate and control *female* sexuality. Control over representations, once again. Wagner's general inattention to women's concerns belies the superficial unisex phrasing of his Introduction, where he glosses the Platonic myth of the divided androgyne: "Erotic literature is one of the recognisable attempts of man to find his/her missing 'half' after the cutting, so to speak" (p. 4). It is tempting to suggest, on the contrary, that libertine discourse *is* the cutting.

Notes

1. Unless otherwise indicated, citations from the joint editors come from their Preface or Introduction. Their notes form a valuable resource for the historian of sexuality, including thirteen articles and five collections by the editors themselves (separately or together). Porter elsewhere cites ten more of his articles and six more collections he has edited.

2. See my discussion of Augustine in *One Flesh: Paradisal Marriage and Sexual Relations in the Age of Milton* (Oxford: Clarendon Press, 1987), esp. p. 47.

3. John Sheffield, Earl of Mulgrave, "The Appointment" (also known as "The Perfect Enjoyment"), in *The Gyldenstolpe Manuscript Miscellany*, ed. Bror Danielsson and David M. Vieth (Stockholm: Almqvist and Wiksell, 1967), p. 234.

4. Rousseau's own essay makes several valuable contributions—he makes a good case for Richard Payne Knight's *Discourse on the Worship of Priapus* as a radical Enlightenment text (though he does not mention that the *libertins érudits* of the seventeenth century had already studied ancient sexual religion); he reconstructs a whole circle of dilettanti, patrons and (more or less fraudulent) scholars; and he raises an important question about the relation of sexuality to aesthetic taste—but the central hypothesis, the importance of Knight's "personal sexuality," does raise the question of evidence. Rousseau does not actually claim Knight as a homo*sexual*, but he insists that he was entirely homosocial, and that he "obviously connected anticlericalism to homosocial desire or sodomy." The subject may be "close to the heart of the matter," but it is certainly "not discussed": there is not the slightest hint of homoeroticism, either in Knight's own writings or in the hostile private communications of those who detested him. Rousseau's evidence shows that he frequented women sexually, that he preferred "the luxurious displays of Rubens" to the simplicity of Raphael, and that he sustained friendships with at least two women; Rousseau tries to prove that one of these, Judith Damer, was lesbian, but wisely he does not try the same argument with Knight's "Favourite," Emma Hamilton.

5. The essay is translated from the French by George St Andrews.

6. Charles Cotton?, Εροτοπολις: *The Present State of Bettyland* (London, 1684), p. 152, referring particularly to the alumnae of girls' boarding schools. Other passages also connect the real-life perils of sex with self-alienation: a woman swallowing mercury to cure venereal disease remarks "the Pleasures of my Youth have sowr Sawce, for I am undone and never shall be my own woman again" (p. 171).

7. Trumbach makes a similar argument with regard to bastardy cases and the seduction of servants in a paper given to the Symposium of the McMaster Association for 18th Century Studies, 1984; in recent research, however, he recognizes the problem of upper-class impunity (private communication). For "civil" police and riotous aristocrats, see my "The Properties of Libertinism," in Robert Purks Maccubbin, ed., *'Tis Nature's Fault: Unauthorized Sexuality during the Enlightenment* (Cambridge: Cambridge Univ. Press, 1987), p. 81.

8. Alexander Pope, *Sober Advice from Horace;* author unknown, "The Last Night's Ramble (1687)," ed. Harold Love, in his *Restoration Literature: Critical Approaches* (London: Methuen, 1972), p. 309.

9. *The Memoirs of Margaret Leeson, Written by Herself* (Dublin, 1797), III.4–10.

10. The male biographer of a female soldier in the American revolutionary army, Deborah Sampson, even makes up a feminist speech for his heroine: woman's state is "a prison, where I must drag out the remainder of my days in ignorance" (Herman Mann, *The Female Review* [Dedham, 1797], p. 108, cited without ref. by Friedli, p. 243). Males associated with female soldiers could be treated with great contempt: George Washington was declared female by a British newspaper (Friedli, p. 245), and in the previous century James Strong, author of a poem in praise of the women who helped defend Lyme Regis against the Royalists, saw his work published with mock commendatory poems by Royalist (and misogynist) enemies (*Joaneriados, or Feminine Valour Eminently Discovered in Westerne Women* [n.p., 1645], repr. in 1674 with extra poems including "On the Masculine-Feminine Poem of Mr. *James Strong*, Poet Hermaphrodite" [ff. b3-v]).

11. Richard Griffith, *The Triumvirate* (London, 1764), II.56–68; Browne does not mention these details, nor does she explore the bizarre circumstances of the relationship—the mistress had been a college chum of the narrator's, brought up as a boy and unaware that she was a woman at all.

12. *Memoirs of a Woman of Pleasure*, ed. Peter Sabor (Oxford and New York: Oxford Univ. Press, 1985), p. 183.

13. (1727), ed. Maximillian E. Novak (Gainesville, Fla.: Scholar's Facsimiles and Reprints, 1967), pp. 151–53. See p. 133: wanting to prevent conception "is neither more nor less than acknowledging that she would have the Pleasure of lying with a Man, but . . . would not be confined at home, or loaded with the Cares of being a Mother," and p. 164; "'tis scandalous to the last Degree; 'tis seeking the Man meerly as such, meerly for the *frailer Part*, as my Lord *Rochester* calls it" (i.e., in "The Fall").

14. "The Last Night's Ramble," p. 310; James Boswell, *London Journal, 1762–1763*, ed. Frederick A. Pottle (New York: McGraw Hill, 1950), p. 149.

15. Jean-Jacques Bouchard, *Journal*, ed. E. Kanceff (Turin: G. Giappichelli, 1976), I.143–44.

16. Vincent de Voiture, *Lettres* (Amsterdam, 1657), pp. 492–96.

17. "Mentor," in *The Lady's Magazine,* IV (1773), pp. 94–95; cf. Castle, p. 163.

18. Harriette Wilson, *Memoirs* (1825; London: Navarre Society, 1924), II.610, 623.

19. Margaret Leeson, *Memoirs*, III.15–74. Castle seems to have read this text carelessly (p. 166); the reference to a naked couple has nothing to do with masquerade (Leeson, III.12), and the later masquerade (mentioned with no page reference) was not "given by Moll Hall" but by Leeson herself, though Hall encouraged it and attended as "Mother Cole" (III.31).

20. *The Country-Wife* IV.iii; *The Plain Dealer* IV.ii.

21. Duclos, cited in Peter Brooks, *The Novel of Worldliness: Crébillon, Marivaux, Laclos, Stendhal* (Princeton: Princeton Univ. Press, 1969), p. 23; Andréa de Nerciat, cited in Patrick Wald Lasowski, *Libertines* (Paris: Gallimard, 1980), p. 74. Several of my generalizations in this paragraph ("polite" encounters in public places, pride in speed and repetition) derive from Wald Lasowski (e.g., pp. 30, 73–74).

22. E.g., Nicolas Chorier, *Aloisiae Sigeae Toletanae Satyra Sotadica de Arcanis Amoris et Veneris* (1660–1668), ed. Bruno Lavagnini (Catania: Romeo Prampolini, 1935), p. 214; Julien Offray de la Mettrie, (*La Volupté* (1750), in *Oeuvres philosophiques* (Berlin, 1774), II.197, 227–28, 232, 234, 239.

23. See my discussion of Behn in "The Culture of Priapism," *Review*, 10 (1988), pp. 30–31.

24. Richard Ames, *The Folly of Love, or an Essay upon Satyr against Woman* (London, 1691), p. 12.

25. Gould, *Love Given O're* (London, 1682), *passim*, and *A Satyrical Epistle to the Female Author of a Poem, Call'd Silvia's Revenge* (London, 1691), pp. 9–10; Gould continues with a quasi-pornographic description of female arousal (quite different from the rest of the poem) and concludes that his desire is entirely caused by the thought that he is breaking the "shell" of virginity.

26. John Wilmot, Earl of Rochester, *Poems,* ed. Keith Walker (Oxford: Blackwell, 1984), p. 61 (cited hereafter in the text). I am not suggesting that the "sexual market" actually *was* free in this way for women, but that it could be so perceived; Behn, for example, sees it as a bargaining-floor or game of chance, but one in which women are handicapped or forced to play by harder rules.

27. Cf. John Garfield?, *The Wandering Whore* (London, 1660), p. 7 ("drinking healths over the dead drunk party, til the merciless Candle fir'd her Furbush quite away, the flame whereof was quickly abated by drawing a codpiece engine, and giving her two or three Coolers"); *Spectator,* 324; Wald Lasowski, *Libertines,* pp. 71–72.

28. See pp. viii, 4–6, 15, 140, 216, 221.

29. Cited in Antonia Fraser, *The Weaker Vessel: Woman's Lot in Seventeenth-Century England* (London: Weidenfeld and Nicolson, 1984), p. 407.

30. G. S. Rousseau and Roy Porter, eds. *The Ferment of Knowledge* (Cambridge: Cambridge Univ. Press, 1980), pp. 197–98.

31. Cited in Patricia Meyer Spacks, "'Ev'ry Woman is at Heart a Rake,'" *Eighteenth-Century Studies,* 8 (1974–75), p. 28; the line is wittily taken from L'Estrange's fable of the boys and the frogs, "and if we had the wit of the frogs," Montagu continues, "we should allwaies make that answer." Browne, like Spacks, cites Wortley Montagu's later disapproval of girls who "declare that if

they had been born of the male kind they should have been great rakes, which is owning they have strong inclination to wh-ring and drinking, and want only the opportunity and impunity to exert them vigorously" (p. 147); but her objection is probably to the coarseness of the rake persona rather than to the idea of libertine relationships *per se*.

32. John Turner, *A Discourse on Fornication, Shewing the Greatness of That Sin* (London, 1698), pp. 24–26. The occasion for the treatise was what Turner considered a general laxness and acceptance of extramarital sex—it wasn't foreign enough.

33. Cited in Keith Thomas, "The Double Standard," *Journal of the History of Ideas* XX (1959), p. 213. Trumbach, in the conference paper cited above, suggests that lower-class wife sales may have been a way of regularizing a change of marriage partners with the consent of all three parties—and thus an anticipation of modern marriage practises.

34. Again, this expands upon a point made in "The Culture of Priapism," p. 34.

35. *The Athenian Mercury,* IX.3 (Dec. 20, 1692). In both versions the author says that "all my Friends" advise her to leave him, which could (if the letter is genuine) count against my thesis that illicit sex led to social isolation for women. I am most grateful to April London for bringing this and the next passage (IX.5, Dec. 27, 1692) to my attention, and suggesting this interpretation.

36. See my articles "The Libertine Sublime: Love and Death in Restoration England," *Studies in Eighteenth-Century Culture*, XIX (1989, forthcoming), and "'Illustrious Depravity' and the Libertine Sublime," *The Age of Johnson*, 2 (1988), pp. 1–40.

37. Browne, 109, 170–72, 182. The topic is well analyzed in Janet Todd, *Sensibility: An Introduction* (London and New York: Methuen, 1986), esp. ch. 8 ("The Attack on Sensibility"), and in John Mullan, *Sentiment and Sociability: The Language of Feeling in the Eighteenth Century* (Oxford: Clarendon Press, 1988), esp. ch. 2 ("Richardson: Sentiment and the Construction of Femininity").

38. In *Essais* III.v. The anonymous (probably French) author of *The Secret History of Pandora's Box* (London, 1742) makes good use of this passage: contrasting the high moral achievement of chaste women to the triviality of their education, which offers them "nothing that is grand and sublime," he adds in a footnote that "*Montaigne* cries out loudly against the manner of educating the sex. 'We enure them, says he, from their infancy, to the soft business of love. Their dress, their behaviour, their knowledge, their speech, all their instruction tends only to this end. Their governesses impress no other image on them but the countenance of love . . .'" (p. 36).

39. Author unknown, *The Night-Walkers Declaration, or the Distressed Whores Advice to all their Sisters* (London, 1676), p. 5. The description of economic hardship that follows has a realistic ring to it, and would form an interesting supplement to Trumbach's research.

40. Letter to William Godwin, cited in Browne, p. 151. (I have regularized punctuation.)

41. Wagner calls the young married interlocutor "an elderly person" and dates *L'Ecole* to 1688, confusing the original publication of 1656 with the prosecution of a lost English translation, and compounding the error by giving the same date to Pepys's famous reading of it (pp. 373–74).

42. See Wagner, pp. 347, 445 (he actually assumes that Phillips *is* Pilkington under an assumed name); and see Pilkington, *Memoirs* (1748–54), introd. Iris Barry (London: Routledge, 1928), p. 416.

43. Names appear wrongly (e.g., Hildebrand Jacobs, John Brown, John Banks), and translations or adaptations are cited without proper reference to their originals (e.g., Claude Quillet's *Callipaedia,* Antonio Vignale's *Cazzaria,* on which the eighteenth-century *Libro del perchè* is based). Texts are mistranscribed: at the climax of one poem, for example, a mouse jumps out of the farmer's wife's "Meeve," a non-existent word which Wagner may have taken to be slang for vagina; if so, he misses the comic point, since the original, reproduced alongside and clearly legible, says "Sleeve" (pp. 174–76). The tone and stance towards the reader change: Wagner assumes that we need to be told that William Hogarth produced a series called *The Rake's Progress,* and that aristocratic men kept mistresses, but when recounting Parisian gossip he slips into an insider's character, dropping references to "the Dubarry" and "poor Cagliostro"; his account of literary texts is quite minimal, but in the chapter on visual art he suddenly becomes a connoisseur and analyst of detail. (His grasp of art history is not impressive, however: he discusses Hogarth without reference to three important paintings [the Fitzwilliam *Before* and *After,* and *Sir Francis Dashwood Worshipping a Female Nude*], ignores Fragonard's painting altogether, lists Boucher among French engravers whose work is now "forgotten," chooses plates from the crude popular version of d'Hancarville's *Douze Césars* rather than the deluxe edition, and talks about "attractively painted" figures in a print.) He seems to change his mind on several issues: Freudian psychoanalysis is dismissed in some places and embraced in others; sometimes Rochester is assumed to be the author of *Sodom* and the Beggar's Bennison records are assumed to be genuine, but elsewhere doubt is (rightly) cast. Though some of his notes are useful, there is a large amount of redundancy; three different footnotes in the same chapter, for example, give a long list of Nerciat's works (with the dates changed in one case), and the full references that encumber the notes (not always consistent) are duplicated in the immense bibliography.

The book appears, in short, to have been compiled over many years and never properly edited: on the one hand, he refers to a work "already mentioned" that has evidently been cut from his final version (p. 42); on the other hand, he tells us that Vieth's is the standard edition of Rochester's poems (replaced by Walker's in 1984), and that the sodomy scene "has never again appeared in modern editions" of Cleland (pp. 241, 359), even though the full text has been available since 1985 in two reputable paperback editions, one of them (Penguin) by Wagner himself. Nor is Wagner's reading complete. Among the case-histories published by Curll he omits the interesting attempt of Mrs Weld to obtain a divorce because of her husband's psychosomatic impotence (her lawyer had to rebuke the court for not taking the subject of female sexuality seriously). In the field of French erotica, his discussion of La Mettrie is wholly inadequate, and he fails to mention La Mettrie's favorite libertine poet, Chaulieu. Several indecent poems discussed in the Rousseau/Porter volume fail to appear in this book (for example, Fielding's poem on the masquerade), nor does he seem aware of Fielding's Miscellany piece "Some Papers . . . Concerning the Terrestrial Chrysipus," which continues the genital humor of the "arbor vitae" series, or Pope's libertine-bachelor writings. Among actual pornographic works, he leaves out Alexis Piron's *Ode à Priape*, both in its original form and in the garbled version published by anti-Jacobites as the work of Prince Charles Edward. Even in his chosen field, he omits several works by Cleland that contributors to Rousseau/Porter put to good use, and informs us that the 1750 bowdlerized *Fanny Hill* "is lost" (p. 376).

44. See pp. 3, 322, 381. Wagner's sniping at other critics began in his review-essay "Researching the Taboo: Sexuality and Eighteenth-Century English Erotica," *Eighteenth-Century Life*, VIII.3 (May 1983), pp. 108–15, where he accuses Hagstrum, Eagleton, *et al.* of (i) believing that popular erotica are inferior to the greatest literature of the age, (ii) "turning a blind eye" to French clandestine texts, and (iii) trying to persuade us that Richardson is readable.

45. Wagner actually misses some of the sexual references in the poem; see my "Pope's Libertine Self-Fashioning," in David B. Morris, ed., Special Issue on Alexander Pope, *The Eighteenth Century: Theory and Interpretation* XXIX (1988), pp. 133–37.

46. Jean-Baptiste de Boyer, Marquis d'Argens, *Thérèse philosophe* (1748; Paris: Euredif, 1975), p. 80.

47. This absurd view of Puritanism is attacked, not only by every writer on the subject since the 1940s, but by Wagner himself in his final chapter on America.

Clarity and Opacity in Elizabeth Bishop

Thomas Gardner

Robert Dale Parker. *The Unbeliever: The Poetry of Elizabeth Bishop.* Urbana and Chicago: University of Illinois Press, 1988. xi, 170 pp.

Thomas J. Travisano. *Elizabeth Bishop: Her Artistic Development.* Charlottesville: University Press of Virginia, 1988. xi, 228 pp.

Most of us who care about the poetry of Elizabeth Bishop (1911–1979) would agree that we are in the midst of a significant rethinking of how to read her work. Where once she was praised, if grudgingly, for her "elegance, grace, precision," she is now beginning to be seen as a poet of openness and struggle, one for whom "the question is the final form."[1] Helen Vendler's early account of the way a sought-for "domesticity" is, in Bishop, constantly eroded by the "strange" or inscrutable helped initiate this revision.[2] Vendler has gone on to suggest, more recently, that these qualities are set productively in tension with each other: "Bishop made a new sort of lyric by adhering to a singular clarity of expression, simplicity of effect, and naïveté of tone while making the matter of her poetry the opacity and inexplicability of being. . . . The combination of somber matter with a manner net-like, mesh-like, airy, reticulated to let in light, results in the effect we now call by her name—the Bishop style."[3] By insisting that the "clarity" of Bishop's manner be read in some sort of conjunction with the "opacity" of her matter, both of the valuable overviews of her work under review here can be said to join in this recent re-imagining of her work. That they differ in how they describe this balance shows how much an open question that project still is.

Travisano proposes that Bishop's response to "the bewildering complexity of life" (p. 26) went through three different stages. Her difficult childhood, he suggests, encouraged an early celebration of an introspection that "ignores or blocks out essential realities" (p. 19). In the "reticent and enigmatic fables of the isolated soul" found in the Northern poems of *North & South*, Travisano sees "a struggle for peace and fulfillment within the confines of a wholly imagined world" (p. 20)—confines, he asserts, that are both sought after and, in the best of these poems, discovered to be "dangerously constricting" (p. 21). Travel, he suggests, forced Bishop out of that "prison." Furnishing her with objects and landscapes that remained stubbornly resistant to "the soul's implicit desire to appropriate them" (p. 58), Florida and Brazil not only gave Bishop a rich and unlikely source of material but pushed her to develop a new technique capable of recording that engagement. Quoting Bishop herself, Travisano describes the innovative technique of her second-stage poems—the Southern section of her first book and *A Cold Spring*—as an attempt "to dramatize the mind in action rather than repose," that action often being "the quietly changing attitude of the observer as it responds to the object observed" (p. 63). "At the Fishhouses," for example, a poem about her native Nova Scotia seascape written during this period of travel, follows "the subtle turns of the eye (and mind)" (p. 128) as Bishop dramatizes both her impossible "yearning for immersion in this sea" and the recognition that "no familiarity will render it comfortable or tame" (p. 126).

Eventually, in Travisano's account, Bishop made an even greater turn away from the security of enclosure and, in the poems of her last two books, *Questions of Travel* and *Geography III*, began to work out a way of engaging the shifting realm where "public and private history intersect" (p. 133). These poems often work by encouraging the tendency of "enclosures and frames . . . to open dramatically, both outward and inward" (p. 188), such reversals usually exposing a series of difficult questions about the writer's own "latent assumptions, commitments, and predilections" (p. 176). Thus, in a poem such as "Brazil, January 1, 1502," Bishop, in noting the shared "mental set" of Portuguese explorers and modern tourists, comes to see

Clarity and Opacity in Elizabeth Bishop 181

that the attempt of her own poem to render a bewildering landscape possessible "exposes . . . [an] unconscious complicity in the rape of a land" (p. 140). Similarly, the child in her late "The Waiting Room," discovering suddenly "the insubstantiality of the boundaries upon which we smugly rely—the boundaries between selves; the boundaries between cultures" (p. 186), finds her insistent attempt to name and place herself opening dizzily out upon "the blank strangeness of being" (p. 187). The mind-in-action, that is to say, even as it becomes the mind groping and questioning, tracks the vistas opening before it.

This clear and useful account of Bishop's development for the most part confirms rather than overturns the progression sketched by earlier writers. Even more valuable, I think, are the references to Bishop's letters and early essays woven throughout Travisano's account. Particularly striking is his piecing together a theory to explain Bishop's technique of "'timing' the unfolding of a poem so that it seems as if the poem was being composed on the spot, with the poet 'thinking as [s]he writes,' so that the symbolic import of the images presented dawns on both the speaker and the reader only gradually" (p. 154). Following the lead of a letter Bishop wrote to Marianne Moore in 1938 about attempting to write "according to a *theory* I've been thinking up down here—and of a combination of Poe's theories and reading 17th century prose," Travisano convincingly works that early "theory" out by linking a reference to Poe in a 1948 essay (his ability to delay indicating the symbolic implications of his images) with a reference to Hopkins and baroque prose in a 1934 essay written as a student at Vassar. Hopkins's poems, for her, made a drama out of thought, much in the way that baroque prose did, often stopping when still incomplete in order to show, in Bishop's words, that "the poem, unique and perfect seems to be separate from the conscious mind, deliberately avoiding it, while the conscious mind takes difficult steps toward it. The process resembles somewhat the more familiar one of puzzling over a momentarily forgotten name or word which seems to be taking on an elusive brain-life of its own as we try to grasp it."[4] This is a wonderful piece of reconstruction intimating that, for Bishop, delaying closure might mime the mind's difficulty in fixing an intuited wholeness that grows increasingly elusive and alive as one attempts to grasp it. Bishop's "manner," this should convince us, tracing the difficult steps of engagement, is not as simple and direct as it appears.

This idea of the mind working toward a perfection that remains separate and elusive seems to explain more than Travisano realizes, especially about Bishop's early fables. Rather than reading those poems as flights from engagement, might we not see them, more in line with the rest of Bishop's work, as describing a potentially rich recognition of the difficulty of grasping the elusive? Without as yet having the technical means to record a movement from that awareness into an unfolding action, the figures in these early poems *are* set apart from the world (in that they naively trust its tools no longer) and yet, by holding themselves in that acknowledgment of difficulty, are also poised to embark on just the charged, groping journeys Travisano has described in the later poems.

Let me give two examples. Bishop's "Man Moth," part underground modern man, part moth drawn to the light, when venturing to the surface reads the moon in a way that sets him apart from the rest of us:

> He thinks the moon is a small hole at the top of the sky,
> proving the sky quite useless for protection.
> He trembles, but must investigate as high as he can climb.

The radiance streaming through suggesting to him that the sky is simply a temporary, eroding boundary, the Man-Moth "climbs fearfully, thinking that this time he will manage / to push his small head through that round clean opening / and be forced through, as from a tube, in black scrolls on the light." That is, he expects that when he has confronted the failure of that blue, too-easily accepted boundary, he will skid out into what we have seen Travisano label, in a late Bishop poem, "the blank strangeness of being." It is true, of course, that the Man-Moth fails to scribble himself across that radiance, but his return to human subways—which he rides "facing the wrong way"—seems to me not the "self-incarceration" (p. 30) or flight to "escape anxiety" (p. 31) that Travisano describes but rather a sign that Bishop was not yet able to imagine the poetic manner by which one might face the failure of boundaries, and could only posit a charged, troubled awareness of the *potential* insight generated by that encounter. So, too, we might take the 1938 story "In Prison," in which the narrator dreams about how his "real life" will begin in prison, not as the account of the "potential cowardice" of retreating from "the tumult and confusion that the world of accidents thrusts upon one" (p. 26) that Travisano sees, but as another way of imagining, but not arriving at, a world in which the authority of man's descriptive abilities has been jostled and put aside. What will the prisoner read there? One very dull book, on a completely foreign subject, whose "terms and purpose" have been eroded: "Then I shall be able to experience with a free conscience the pleasure, perverse, I suppose, of interpreting it not at all according to its intent."[5] That this is a world the prisoner has not arrived at yet, and that Bishop has not yet developed the "mind-in-action" manner that might allow her to experience such authoritative structures suddenly turned elusive, doesn't mean that she lacks confidence or nerve in these early poems; it means, as Travisano has indirectly let us see, that she lacks an adequate technique.

It is a mark of the difference between the two books under review here that Parker's *The Unbeliever* takes as central to its sketch of Bishop's career the very fables—Parker calls them "allegories of imagination"—whose strategies Travisano saw as excessively limited and, in time, necessarily abandoned. Parker reads these fables differently, seeing that the "distinctive refusal of belief" (p. 30) illustrated by these poems—Bishop's inability to rest contentedly within conventional constructs of the world and her exploration of the compensations offered by uncertainty, suspension, and uprootedness—is what produced the masterpieces of her more mature work. Where Travisano sees the slips and reversals of Bishop's manner as a record of increasingly difficult encounters with more and more personal subject matter, Parker suggests that the slips and reversals of the manner-matter mismatch *generate* her poem's insights. From this point of view, the strategies employed by these early fables are central; though they are deepened and extended, they are never set aside.

Parker reads "The Unbeliever"—an extension of Bunyan's remark on the anxiety of unbelief: "He sleeps on top of a mast"—as a fable about imaginative compensation. In contrast to a passing cloud, "secure in introspection," who assumes that the reflection he stares down at is a marble pillar rising to support him above the sea, and in contrast to a drifting gull, "tower[ing] through the sky," who is convinced he is the winged top-piece of a commemorative tower, the unbeliever:

> sleeps on top of his mast
> with his eyes closed shut.
> The gull inquired into his dream,
> which was, "I must not fall.
> The spangled sea below wants me to fall.
> It is hard as diamonds; it wants to destroy us all."

The unbeliever, Parker argues convincingly, refuses the illusion of security and "savors the thrill of the precarious" (p. 33). That thrill is chosen; it is, in fact, indulged in in order to "vault our imaginations forward" (p. 33). The sleeper's vision of a "voracious diamond sea" comes as a dream, for Parker, because, like the Man-Moth's vision of the moon, it is a kind of wish—a terrifying opening out beyond all certainty that Bishop, in these early poems, could engage in only by labeling it fantastic. And yet, Parker makes the case, the state of mind arrived at is no retreat into fantasy. As with Dickinson, Bishop's "concern is not to find solutions but rather to seize the thrill of suffering without them. . . . Bishop's unbeliever finds more in his tipsy metaphor of unbelief than she suggests anyone can find through belief" (p. 35). As Parker sees it, "wish" is the most fitting label for Bishop's early poems—he includes all of *North & South* in this phase—for it usefully captures the thrill-producing mismatch, or tension, between the desire for some impossible perfection and the unbeliever's realization that such mastery remains elusive: "only a wish." "*Wish* is the world—or manner of imagination—in which those who do not believe and who do aspire will find the most that pleases them. The world of *have* they find confining. They aspire to more than they can have, and they cannot believe they will ever reach what they aspire to, so that only *wish* is left to fill the space between satisfaction in the here and natural, and faith in the hereafter and supernatural" (p. 41). This formulation strikes me as exactly right; Parker has seen this difficult first book with a subtlety that will surely affect the way these poems are read.

Like Travisano, Parker sees a second stage in Bishop's work initiated by the experience of travel—particularly by the sense that "travel cannot be an innocent act. It must be questioned. It doesn't present us with an inert place" (p. 75). In Bishop's middle two books, the traveler's experience of "the intransigent resistance of place" (p. 77) or of "the settled disillusion of ordinary, public space" (p. 82) produces the same sort of generative tension that the impossible wishes of her first stage had. Travel, at its most basic, acts out the impossibility of the wish for possession: "have we room / for one more folded sunset, still quite warm?" Travel points toward what we impossibly desire, acknowledges "the evanescent place [inevitably] slipping away before she can trap it in poetic capture" (p. 82), and, in the very best of these poems, rides that tension toward what Parker describes as a kind of "rest[ing] in awe" (p. 84) of the unrecoverable. In his reading of "At the Fishhouses," Bishop gradually works her way from land to sea, attempts to "dive in," but, on sliding away from that attempt into ellipses, finds herself caught up in "a startling hesitation, as if both the length of her reluctance and the piling up of her repetitions measure the force of what she hesitates before" (p. 81). Her meditative entry exposed as impossible, Bishop, Parker convincingly argues, gives voice to the "allure" of losing one's language to the ungraspable in this "intimately self-conscious poem . . . dissolving, finally, in the watery mystery of its own contemplation" (p. 84).

Parker's third stage, the use of "retrospect" in the personal poems of Bishop's last book, follows logically from his analysis of wish and travel. Just as travel acts out both the wish to possess *and* the impossibility of that dream, so memory—we can "see" the past only as we admit it's gone—makes its way by exploiting that built-in tension. Like wish and travel, "retrospect" richly questions itself. As Parker puts it, such poems, in Bishop's hands, "stretch out . . . hope by anticipating its collapse." Though a bit sketchy in its details and fairly close in its responses to the standard readings of these poems—like Travisano, for example, Parker sees "The Waiting Room" as an analysis of someone "popped free" of "the presumption she can know who she is" (p. 134) and launched into "the bare existentialism of identity [which] exceeds the reach of her language" (p. 144)—this chapter does make a case for the continuity of Bishop's investigations. Clearly, the forced suspension of certainty was a consistent attraction in each of the controlling metaphors of her career.

Aside from this important argument, a second strength of Parker's book is his attempt to provide a larger context within which to read Bishop. Where Travisano usefully buttressed his readings with selections from her letters and early essays, Parker turns for support to such figures as Whitman, Dickinson, O'Connor, even Hemingway. I found the Whitman comparisons to be the most striking. Claiming parallel concerns rather than a pattern of influence, Parker uses Whitman's "As I Ebb'd with the Ocean of Life,"

> Aware now that amid all that blab whose echoes recoil upon me I
>   have not once had the least idea who or what I am,
> But that before all my arrogant poems the real Me stands
>   yet untouch'd, untold, altogether unreach'd

to convincingly argue that each "tries to defeat the impossibility of making a new literature by trying to make a literature that centers on the recognition of that impossibility" (p. 67). That linkage leads Parker to a number of useful insights about contrasting responses to the problem of "unbelief" visible in the very language of each poet: where Whitman "oscillates between . . . the private apocalypse of unbelief . . . [and] the public arias and orations of belief" (p. 68), for example, Bishop can be seen responding to the same situation by creating a language whose insistent indirection pointedly signals its distance from the "real Me" by calling attention to the "limitless deferral" (p. 69) of all its attempts at contact.

Such passing insights into the way in which the ever-so-slight slippages, self-mockings, and silent revisions of Bishop's manner of speaking put into play her awareness of being's inexplicability make me wish Parker had given more sustained attention to this subject. For they suggest not simply that wish, travel, and retrospect thrillingly question themselves, but that description, analogy, and narration might as well. And if that is true, perhaps we are ready for a full-scale examination of the way our simultaneously opaque and clear, mismatched language itself encourages Bishop's "sinking or sliding giddily off into the unknown."[6] With the issues raised by these two significant, if quite different books, we are well on our way to such an analysis.

Notes

1. M. L. Rosenthal, *The Modern Poets* (New York: Oxford Univ. Press, 1960), p. 235; Bonnie Costello, "The Impersonal and the Interrogative in the Poetry of Elizabeth Bishop," in *Elizabeth Bishop and Her Art*, ed. Lloyd Schwartz and Sybil P. Estess (Ann Arbor: Univ. of Michigan Press, 1983), p. 132.

2. Helen Vendler, "Domestication, Domesticity, and the Otherworldly," in *Elizabeth Bishop and Her Art*, pp. 32–48.

3. Helen Vendler, *The Music of What Happens: Poems, Poets, and Critics* (Cambridge: Harvard Univ. Press, 1988), p. 299.

4. A portion of this essay is available in *Elizabeth Bishop and Her Art*, pp. 273–75. I quote from this version.

5. My attention was called to this passage by an unpublished essay by Jacqueline Vaught Brogan, "Elizabeth Bishop: *Perversity* as Lyric Voice."

6. Elizabeth Bishop, "The 'Darwin' Letter," in *Elizabeth Bishop and Her Art*, p. 288.

When England Became Victorian

Stanley Weintraub

Richard L. Stein. *Victoria's Year: English Literature and Culture, 1837–1838.* New York: Oxford University Press, 1987. xiii, 314 pp.

Marlene A. Eilers. *Queen Victoria's Descendants.* New York: Atlantic International Publications, 1987. v, 245 pp.

The Victorian mood was Victorian well before the accession of Alexandrina Victoria in mid-1837, which creates a problem in coverage for any book calling itself *Victoria's Year*. Richard Stein's artificial year becomes a Jovian one, stretching from the early 1830s into the 1840s, and creating his opportunity for collecting partly related essays on early Victorianism under an umbrella title.

The probate of the will of Victoria's predecessor, William IV, which publicly disclosed the large number of illegitimate children for whom he had made provision, Stein notes wryly, gave *The Times* the opportunity to praise the late King's consideration as further evidence of his "social and domestic virtues." To Stein this "straining to adulate domesticity, especially where its existence is so dubious, is a kind of parody of Victorianism, before the fact" (p. 5). In reality it validates social hypocrisy as an English continuum. Victoria and Albert would ban divorced women from the Court, and the young Queen barely survived the embarrassment and scandal, in 1838, of accusing a Lady-in-Waiting to her mother of an unmarried pregnancy and having Flora Hastings, of the ballooning belly, die instead of liver cancer. Meanwhile her Prime Minister and her Foreign Minister, Lords Melbourne and Palmerston, hopped in and out of the beds of nubile but undivorced gentlewomen with more agility than discretion. One rule was unshakable. Embarrassments that get into the newspapers are punishable; those that do not, do not exist.

The Queen herself represented a new opportunity for English self-congratulation on the persistence of uprightness. She was a woman, and represented the respectable rather than the rakish side of the double standard. One official writ, as yet unsure of her reigning name in 1837, was dated "In the Year of our Lady." One thing was certain: she was a monarch of untainted virtue, having been brought up under what was close to house arrest by an ambitious mother, the German-born Duchess of Kent, whose opportunity to rule as regent had been spoiled by William IV's being "tinkered up" by his doctors to live a month past Alexandrina Victoria's eighteenth birthday.

That she "was almost unknown to her subjects" on her accession is a non-fact which Stein accepts from the always imaginative Lytton Strachey, who wasted little energy—he had little enough—on biographical research. Princess Victoria was a very popular figure, made much of—to her mother's indignation—by William and his undervalued Queen, Adelaide (whom Victoria adored). Even the Duchess of Kent, for her own purposes, had taken Victoria on grand tours of the great English houses, stopping here and there for her daughter to be adored by enthusiastic villagers and slum-dwellers. At the Opera, Victoria distracted attention from the stage; at the opening of the Royal Academy's annual show no one looked at the pictures, and the artists, rivals often at each other's throats, turned their competitiveness to doing her honor. None of this visibility emerges in Stein.

The confusion about her reigning name lasted little more than a day, although much is made of it. Perhaps, Stein hypothesizes, the name *Alexandrina* "was struck off to dispel associations with her German family, to make her seem a more genuinely native monarch.... One periodical writer even reported that she was named Victoria in honor of the victory at Waterloo" (p. 5). It takes very little to discover the origins of her name. The Queen's reigning name was that of her mother, who, although German, had been given the French version of it, Victoire—hardly, as alleged, a connection with Napoleon's defeat. Alexandrina was in honor of the Russian Czar, her token godfather. George IV, who despised his younger brother Prince Edward, Duke of Kent, had refused to permit his unwanted niece to carry any of the "English" names her parents had requested—Georgina, Charlotte, Elizabeth, or Augusta. Few royal infants past or present have been christened with so few names. The Princess—fatherless at eight months of age—began life as a deprived child in more ways than one.

When Stein comments upon writers treating Victoria in 1837 as "simply an unknown, a blank for commentators to fill as best they can," he associates lack of information—she was only eighteen, and largely out of the public eye—with uncertainty about the prospects for her reign. "When the adjective 'Victorian' was coined," he concludes, "it came to be associated with a widespread sense of confidence, direction, and identity" (p. 274). It happened sooner than that. It did not take many months after her accession for her name, however un-English in origin, to go into the language. We are wont to give tags to concepts, to concretize them. Stein sees the first adjectival use in the second volume of *Punch* (1842), in an article titled "The Victorian, in contradistinction to the Elizabethan Style." There were other signs of recognition that a new age had begun, not merely a new reign. Yet unmentioned is the light, low, four-wheeled carriage with collapsible hood and elevated front seat for the driver, named "Victoria" *by the French* as early as 1844.

The plethora of bays, falls, rivers, harbors, peaks, valleys, and towns named for the Queen in an increasing crescendo suggests something of the changing state of her reputation as well as the burgeoning of the Empire. There was no Royal Geographical Society requirement that she be topographically venerated at such absurd lengths. While Stein sees the first place-name in her honor as occurring in the year of the Crystal Palace, 1851—the christening of the colony of Victoria in Australia—he should not have had to go much beyond "Victoria's year" of 1837–38 to find earlier examples. Victoria Island in the Canadian arctic was discovered and named by Thomas Simpson on 25 August 1838; Victoria River in Australia was discovered and named by Captain Stokes in 1839; Victoria Land in Antarctica was discovered and named by Sir James Ross on 12 January 1841; and the town of Victoria on Hong Kong Island (Queen's Town since 1840) was christened by Sir Henry Pottinger, the colonial governor, on 26 June 1843. There was even a great Amazonian floating water lily named for her in 1846, and an asteroid given her name by the discoverer, a Mr. Hind, in 1850.

Primarily a literary study, *Victoria's Year*, though ranging well beyond the Coronation in 1838, uses its literary (and some visual) materials to evoke those characteristics of the early Victorian years which separate it from its predecessor decades. In many cases this proves an oversimplification. England did not change because a young girl succeeded two elderly uncles. The same Liberal prime minister, Viscount Melbourne, continued in office with his government. Owing to Victoria's youthful willfulness and ignorance of procedure, he continued long after he should have given way to the Conservatives and Sir Robert Peel. Literature did not change because Victoria read Dickens and had not read a poem of Wordsworth's when she acted upon advice and made the writer, long past his prime, Poet Laureate.

Nor did the pronounced Evangelical strain that had already affected manners and morals of the middle and lower classes emerge with Victoria. And what Stein calls the "shift from the heroic to the domestic" does not really occur, although the familial values exemplified by Victoria and Albert did create what he calls "domesticity elevated into the form of a myth."

Victorian values of family and faith and frugality were part of the parallel Evangelical culture now given prominence because a young queen with a young family had replaced elderly and sleazy kings with no morals and spendthrift impulses. Yet side-by-side was also a revival of the chivalric, selfless, Arthurian ideal that represented a century-long reaction to grimy, selfish industrialization and materialism. It was an artificial medievalism in which even Victoria and Albert participated, notably in the costume ball to create interest in the silks of Spitalsfields. To that occasion the young Queen and consort came attired as Edward III and Philippa, memorably limned in Sir Edwin Landseer's full-length portrait of the pair. That this dimension of Victorianism would inspire works ranging from Tennyson's *Idylls of the King* and

Rossetti's Pre-Raphaelite medievalism, to the *fin de siècle* works of William Morris, Burne Jones, and Aubrey Beardsley, and that it was emerging out of the same early Victorian setting, is one of the paradoxes of the extended Victorian "year." (In the 1830s, Stein writes, "Tennyson did not find contemporary life entirely congenial to myth" [p. 71]). Even Landseer would paint both dimensions, Stein calling attention to his "great pictorial study of the royal family, *Windsor Castle in Modern Times* (painted in the early 1840s)," in which the emphasis is upon a new domesticity in monarchical life: "the Queen and Prince Albert are depicted as ideal wife and husband, surrounded by dogs, children, and the game he has just brought in from hunting" (p. 73).

"No wonder," Stein comments approvingly, "*Blackwood*'s refers to her in December 1837 as 'the best beloved and worst painted Queen'" (p. 61). Victoria had then been Queen for only six months! She would be Queen for sixty-four years, and would be the most-painted monarch in British history, some of the pictures badly painted indeed, but many others striking examples of nineteenth-century portrait and narrative art. The standing portrait of the young Queen by Thomas Sully, the Charles Robert Leslie portrait of Victoria kneeling at her throne at the Coronation, the blowsy, romantic, loose-haired portrait by Winterhalter that her young husband loved, would prove *Blackwood*'s condemnation to be premature as well as spiteful. To borrow a bias out of its historical frame, especially if the language is colorful, salty, and quotable, is always tempting. Often, as here, the result is to borrow errantly, accepting as fact what were only slanders from an age of press viciousness and innuendo that makes our media seem very tame.

Another example of the temptation taken is in the characterization of Victoria's coronation. William IV had ordered some fiscal prudence into his own coronation because the nation had inherited his brother's massive debts. "Sailor Bill's" ceremonies were labeled, in terms of the coin no longer with us, the "Half-crownation." Without even noting that, Stein wants us to remember it in remarking that "the Penny Coronation" of Victoria "lacked some of the pomp it should have had, and this was seen as an offense to both queen and nation, a degradation of [the] present festivities and failure to venerate the past" (p. 265). Borrowing a cheap political attack without identifying it as such conceals the fact that spectators at Victoria's lengthy and elaborate coronation had to be in their seats by three in the morning, and that the rites were not over until mid-afternoon. Was more ritual than that humanely useful or necessary?

The problem of *Victoria's Year* is its use of literary materials out of real social and historical context. The age—even Victoria's first decade—was so complex and dynamic a time that many labels fit it, each an oversimplification. Dickens called another decade the best of times and the worst of times, and we can use either, or both, to characterize the later 1830s and the early 1840s.

"Victoria books" are plentiful in the decade now following the marking of the centenary of her Golden Jubilee in 1887 and the 150th anniversary of her accession in 1837. They range from a gushy one about her last Royal Physician, Sir James Reid, whom she abominated (*Ask Sir James*, by Michaela Reid), to a life of her bohemian sculptress daughter (*Princess Louise*, by Jehane Wake) that goes easy on the bohemia. There is more scandal in Marlene A. Eilers's *Queen Victoria's Descendants* than in all the other recent Victoria books put together, and the potential as well for a slew of further books. Yet necessarily, there is no continuous narrative. It is a royal genealogy which begins with Victoria's children and goes on to the present day. In the process we learn about Victoria as ineffectual mother, and Victoria, through her propensity to seek out dynamic marriages for her brood, as grandmother to prewar royal Europe.

Many of the capsule biographies suggest melodramatic stories for the *National Inquirer*. This is also a genealogy that is spiced by wit. Of Princess Victoria Melita of Edinburgh and her first husband, Grand Duke Ernest Ludwig of Hesse and By Rhine, Marlene Eilers writes, "Their birthday was almost the only thing the couple had in common" (p. 103). Victoria's great-granddaughter, Lady Iris Montbatten, we are told, had to go to work after her divorce, and among other things sold brassieres, posed for a bubble-gum advertisement, and was arrested for passing a worthless check in a Washington, D.C., shop. Some stories keep us hoping for more, as we learn of grandsons who became Nazis, homosexuals, insurance salesmen and other things Victoria would have deplored. Yet there is one authentic success story. A great-great-grandson, of whom nothing was predicted other than that he would become "Juan the Brief," is the effective and admired head of state of a socialist constitutional monarchy that succeeded a ruthless military dictatorship. Queen Victoria would be pleased about King Juan Carlos of Spain.

How (and how not) to Explore the Burneys: Questions of Decorum

Betty Rizzo

D. D. Devlin. *The Novels and Journals of Fanny Burney.* New York: St. Martin's Press, 1987. viii, 118 pp.

Slava Klima, Garry Bowers, and Kerry S. Grant, eds. *Memoirs of Dr. Charles Burney, 1726–1769, Edited from Autograph Fragments.* Lincoln: University of Nebraska Press, 1988. xxxix, 233 pp.

" 'Why when & where,' interrupted Mr. Seward, 'are these Burneys to stop?'
" 'No where, said Mrs. Thrale, till they are tired, for they go on just as long as they please, & *do* what they please, & *are* what they please. There never were such people before, I believe, in the World.' "
—Fanny Burney's Diary Manuscript, August 1781, f. 1512

The Burneys, a wonderful family, famous in their own time two hundred years ago, are currently undergoing an explosive revival. The revival is in large part the result of the work of Joyce Hemlow, whose authoritative 1958 biography of Fanny Burney was succeeded by her splendid edition of *The Journals and Letters of Fanny Burney (Madame d'Arblay), 1791–1840,* published in twelve volumes from 1972 to 1984. The Hemlow edition was possible only because the manuscript versions of Fanny Burney's letters and journals had survived after having been thoroughly edited for earlier published editions by both their author and her niece, Charlotte Barrett. From these manuscripts, restoring both the omissions and, in the case of alterations, the original text and providing comprehensive notes has been the task of Hemlow and a number of sub-editors and is now the task of Lars E. Troide, a veteran of the great Walpole letters project, who from the Burney Papers project at McGill University has just issued a superlative first volume, *The Early Journals and Letters of Fanny Burney* (Clarendon Press, 1988), covering the years 1768–1773, and who in a series of subsequent volumes will republish the letters and journals to 1791, Hemlow's starting point. Almost as pronounced as the interest in Fanny Burney has been the interest in her father, Dr. Charles Burney, two biographies of whom, emphasizing respectively his musical and his literary achievements, were published by Percy A. Scholes in 1948 and Roger Lonsdale in 1965. For the Burney Papers, A. F. V. Ribeiro has edited for publication the letters of Charles Burney to 1784, and Slava Klima is editing the remainder of his letters. Klima's recent edition, with Bowers and Grant, of the extant portions of Charles Burney's autobiographical writings to 1769 is considered here. We have begun to acquire important materials and soon will have many more from which we can learn considerably more than we know now about both the Burney family and their works.

A second important factor contributing to increased interest in the Burneys is the renewed attention, much assisted by feminist criticism, directed toward Fanny Burney the novelist, whose reputation is rapidly regaining the heights it enjoyed in her own time. Whereas not very long ago only her first novel, *Evelina* (1778), was generally available, now editions of all three of her subsequent novels are or soon will be in print. And three critical studies of her work appeared in 1987: Kristina Straub's *Divided Fictions, Fanny Burney and Feminine Strategy;* Judy Simons's *Fanny Burney;* and the effort by D. D. Devlin considered here. Further explorations of Fanny Burney's work are in preparation by Margaret Doody and Julia Epstein.

We have before us two of this company of new books about the Burneys to consider, one so entirely critical that its judgments are based only on the published letters and journals without reference to the manuscripts, and the other largely concerned with text, the unpublished memoirs of Charles Burney, which his literary daughter first attempted to edit and then at last replaced with her own *Memoirs of Doctor Burney* (1832) in three volumes. Each of the books under consideration, however, involves both the Burney family and the problem of the development of Fanny

Burney's writing; a proper discussion of both books therefore necessitates some rehearsal of the Burney family history and of the careers of father and daughter.

Charles Burney in 1751 was forced by bad health to retreat to the provinces, was never rewarded by one of the plum musical posts he coveted, and was forced to support his family, when he did return to London in 1760, by teaching as many as fifty lessons a week at a guinea apiece—travelling in his carriage from seven or eight in the morning to eleven or twelve at night and writing in his study through the family dinner hour. Though disappointed of reward as composer, conductor, and even performer, Burney's ambition remained such that in spite of family responsibilities and teaching obligations, he applied himself to the attainment of a Mus.D. degree at Oxford in 1769 and to the writing of a history of music, and at last attained his goal when in 1776 the first volume of his *History of Music* appeared and he emerged an established literary man. In the meantime, after the move from Norfolk in 1760 and the death of his beloved wife Esther in 1762, Charles Burney brought up his brood of eleven children and stepchildren in Poland Street, Queen Square, and after 1774 in St. Martin's Street, where the best musicians and singers of the day gave concerts attended by the most musical members of London society.

Fanny Burney grew up, therefore, though without formal education, knowing a great deal of the world. She was nevertheless in the equivocal position of the daughter of a mere *performer*. Furthermore she had no dowry—and after the publication of *Evelina* in 1778, when she was twenty-five, she was known to be a clever girl with a satirical eye for character who had published an excellent novel, full not only of sentiment but also of humor, and sometimes low humor. It is no wonder that she held off unwelcome advances by preserving an inflexible social decorum. After her refusal in 1775 of the unlucky Mr. Barlow, a lover unforgettably anatomized in her journal—that is, after she knew she could never marry simply for an advantageous establishment, and understanding that her father could not provide for her—she assumed the burden of becoming not only an author but a recidivist author. It was her way of remaining at home without burdening her father, but she had a great price to pay. The Burney family as a family had no entré into London society. Each member had to make his or her own way, so that at the peak of their success only Charles and Fanny Burney went out into the fashionable world while the second Mrs. Burney and the remaining children moved in quite different middle-class circles. Both father and daughter, however, understood that their livelihoods depended upon their acceptance in society, which in turn, as they were each in their way instructors of the young, depended not alone upon their formidable talents and graces but also upon the perfect decorum of their behavior and the impeccability of their reputations. D. D. Devlin gibes at Fanny Burney's avoidance of Madame de Staël after she learned of her equivocal relationship with the Comte de Narbonne (she had done the same with Madame de Genlis because of her similar arrangement with the Duc de Chartres), but at the time Fanny Burney's only security was a pension from the Queen, who loved her for her perfect propriety. It was for entirely serious reasons that Fanny Burney was always concerned for her own decorum. One result of her concern was that quite in keeping with the opinion of the time, like Richardson, Fielding, and other serious writers of fiction, she preferred to identify her works as histories, epics, or anything but novels, an attitude which Devlin also deprecates.

There was yet another reason for the careful decorum observed by both the famous Burneys: a reckless and impetuous streak in the family produced scandal after scandal, which had to be concealed from the world and glossed over by a surface of apparent familial rectitude—and this with all the world coming into the house. Charles Burney and Esther Sleepe apparently managed to conceal the fact that their first daughter Hester, the musical prodigy of the family, was born a month before they married in June 1749. In 1777 the second son, Charles, then nineteen and a brilliant Cambridge scholar, was sent down for having stolen books from the University library and was subsequently denied ordination by the Bishop of London. And in 1798 the eldest son James, who had already aborted his naval career, left wife and children for his half-sister Sarah Harriet; in the five years of their life together it was Fanny Burney who devised the explanation that "to their great regret James had separated from his wife, and . . . Sarah had gone to keep house for James for the present."[1]

Yet this was a family worth protecting. Charles Burney was later able to boast, "The eldest son was a seaman and a circumnavigator with Cook and Fourneau—the 2^d son admitted in the Charter house and became one of the best scholars in the kingdom. My eldest daught^r the best performer on the Harp^d & Piano forte in her day; my 2^d daughter the best Novelist for variety of characters, correct language, & purity of morals, wch we can boast, perhaps in the English language. The 3^d had the best taste in all the Arts" (Klima, p. 144, n. 3).

Fanny Burney was her father's great ally in keeping the family scandals secret, and her devotion to the family can be gauged by the manner in which she accepted immolation at Court as Second Keeper of the Robes to the Queen (the ultimate accolade to her propriety) for five years from 1786 to 1791, in exchange only for her happiness, her health, and almost for her life, in the hope that her presence at Court might result in favors for those she loved. (It did not, but in 1791 she herself received a pension of £200 which subsequently enabled her to marry the penniless emigré Alexandre d'Arblay.) Like her father she had achieved her success by eschewing, in the heart of fashionable society, every conceivable indiscretion. The two most famous Burneys were notable then for their professional and social successes and for their sterling reputations, and the thin lines they walked contribute much to the interest of their letters, their journals, and their memoirs.

Although both the *Memoirs* and *The Novels and Journals of Fanny Burney* treat the Burney family and their writings, the two volumes provide many contrasts. Devlin attempts a critical exploration of the connections between his subject's journals and her novels, and, resorting only to those journals in print and not to the manuscripts (except in one case when he found a useful unpublished bit quoted by Hemlow), he has not concerned himself about possibly incomplete texts. Conversely, Klima, Bowers, and Grant have produced a text consisting mostly of previously rejected and unpublished bits of Charles Burney's autobiographical writings. This is a great enough contrast, but the greatest difference between the two books lies quite simply in the fact that for any study of the Burneys, critical, biographical, or textual, Devlin's book is virtually useless, whereas the other volume is invaluable.

To be fair, Devlin does provide a few useful passages (see pp. 25–37), deriving largely from Pottle's examination of the way in which Boswell composed his journal and comparing Fanny Burney's journalizing to Boswell's. But in the rest of the book he is consistently wrong about everything. Though he presents himself as a magister, cutting down silly recent critics of his subject, he is sweeping out new brooms with an old one, reaffirming the judgments and value systems which have conspired since her death to keep Fanny Burney a minor, even an irrelevant figure. He thereby demonstrates a last-gasp sexism, an anticipated historicism, and an elitism of which he seems altogether unaware.

The first problem for Devlin is Fanny Burney's subject matter. What could be more boring than a novel about a woman in society? Then he identifies as the theme of her earlier novels the passivity of the heroine which, he believes, operates so completely in *Evelina* that there can be in that book no cause and effect,[2] no clear logic of character, "since a young woman cannot initiate action, cannot be mistress of her fate, but must reveal her helplessness and simply suffer one incident after another to unfold and involve her in spite of herself" (p. 93). For Juliet in the last novel, *The Wanderer,* however, prudence is no longer enough, and she makes her way alone. If Devlin had been a good reader of the novels and if this were indeed the case, his preference for *The Wanderer* on the grounds of the autonomy of the heroine would make him something like the feminist he fancies himself to be.

Admittedly, autonomy for a woman in Evelina's day was a great deal less dramatic and absolute than autonomy for a man, but *Evelina* is nevertheless a *bildungsroman* which brings its protagonist to a maturity (and to a worthiness to marry Lord Orville) that enables her to recognize when to act, even when against convention and apparent prudence. She is advised by her mentor, Mr.

Villars, in a passage quoted by Devlin, that "fortitude and firmness, when occasion demands them, are virtues as noble and as becoming in women as in men; the right line of conduct is the same for both sexes."[3] And thereafter we find her storming upstairs alone to a man's room, quite regardless of convention, to stop a suspected suicide attempt; meeting, for excellent reasons, the same man secretly alone; and contesting her father's most solemn injunction to quit his presence and his life with both a positive refusal and a persuasive argument. Fanny Burney's point is that good judgment is far more important than either prudence or convention, that true decorum is something quite different from these. Evelina learns when to follow convention and when to eschew it; her heart has always been perfect but her judgment has needed forming. Cecilia and Camilla, heroines of Fanny Burney's next two books, are also quite willing to act but must learn when and how to do so. Juliet in *The Wanderer* is set the most dramatic task, survival with honor when quite alone, nameless, and penniless in a strange place.[4] But the difference is one of degree, not kind, and in no way represents Fanny Burney's conversion on the point.

The rest of the problem of subject matter is Devlin's apparent conviction that Fanny Burney's great preoccupation with society is dull. His solution is to justify his own interest in her by setting a great value on her growing political awareness, specifically of the French Revolution. Not that he isn't always on the lookout for something showing historical awareness on her part, noting, for instance, that her court diary contains much of her most entertaining writing (p. 57). Her description of the Hastings trial in 1788 is rated "one of the finest long passages in her journal-letters," even though "she had no interest in the state of Denmark—no interest, that is, in the politics of the trial or the reasons for it" (p. 32). He faults her for never mentioning the French Revolution for four months following the fall of the Bastille. But then, at length, she produces *The Wanderer*, a novel about a victim of the Revolution. She has finally acquired a true political consciousness; and here is Devlin's second reason for asserting the superiority of her last novel.

By this time surely Fanny Burney no longer needs defense for having taken as her subject the social fabric which was at once her milieu, her battleground, and her laboratory; nor need the intricacy of the fabric be denied, the politics involved in maintaining it and surviving in it ignored. The arrangement of the social structure for the purpose of the intermingling of families to facilitate marital and political alliances, an intermingling accomplished both in small familial groups and in extended private and public entertainments, required a continued thought, planning, and vigilance which traditionally have been assigned to women. The results, however, have been denigrated as though they occurred of themselves, or at least deprecated as a minor achievement far inferior, for instance, to the male contribution to what is virtually the same business but is transacted not at the assembly or the dinner table but in Parliament. In Fanny Burney's time, whenever women were actually observed transacting business, their heads together at balls or card parties or tea tables, they were at best pitied for their inferior interests and at worst labelled old cats. One can learn a great deal about how all this worked by studying Fanny Burney's journals, but not if one is still denying that "society" is an important subject and insisting that "politics" is more important.

Devlin manages the Hastings trial all right, but collapses when he tries to interpret a social scene. In 1791 Fanny Burney was in Bath with her bluestocking friend Mrs. Ord, who didn't want to visit Lady Spencer, the most fashionable *and* the most worthy of the nobility, because she had with her her errant daughters Lady Duncannon, suffering from a strange paralysis of possibly dubious origin, and the Duchess of Devonshire, then, though no one outside her family circle yet knew it, pregnant by Charles Grey and about to be banished to the Continent. With them was Lady Elizabeth Foster, the Duchess's companion and the Duke's long-time mistress and mother of two of his children, and the children. The decorous Lady Spencer loved her daughters dearly and defended them faithfully but loathed Lady Elizabeth, whom she now had to tolerate because Lady Elizabeth was to accompany the Duchess in her exile. Desperate to keep up appearances in Bath, Lady Spencer sought the countenance of the impeccable Fanny Burney for her little family, and to a considerable extent, an extent far greater than Mrs. Ord approved or advised, she gained it. What was Fanny Burney to do and how could she snub Lady Spencer?[5] Her recourse was to be as civil as possible and not to believe all Mrs. Ord said, or at least to purport not to believe it. With Lady Spencer's two daughters she was civil and avoided intimacy, and Lady Elizabeth she eschewed as much as possible. Devlin's account of the incident (which omits the Duchess entirely) isn't even close: "There was an awkward moment in the summer of 1791 when two English adulteresses, Lady Duncannon and Lady Forster, appeared at a party given by Fanny Burney's friend Lady Spencer" (p. 64). And so on. Who is related to whom? And when does decorum demand more than a simple application of standards?

Again, in 1783 Devlin's sympathies were all with "poor Mr. J—"—distinguishable enough to us as Edward Jerningham, the "mighty delicate gentleman; looks to be painted, and is all daintification in manner, speech, and dress" of Fanny Burney's journals, when he interrogates her as to whether she has read *Les Liaisons Dangereuses*.[6] "In a rapid but aggressively defensive retreat," says Devlin, "Fanny Burney disposes of the novel, its author and poor Mr. J— . . ." (p. 63). Devlin apparently does not recognize Jerningham's question as improper and offensive, representing a prod of a kind his victim not infrequently suffered, for gentlemen did not always think that a woman novelist could have retained the purity of the usual lady. *Her* only recourse was to rebuff him in order to teach him a lesson: "I only spoke to him in answer, after this little dialogue."

Devlin has an odd way of introducing some of the more interesting characters in Fanny Burney's world. These make their awkward appearances in his pages as "a certain Dr. King," "a Russian called Pogenpohl," "a Colonel Goldsmith" (elsewhere correctly identified as Colonel Goldsworthy), "a certain Mr. Hutton," "a young man called Mr. Barlow," "a Mrs. Pringle," and so on. This belittlement of important characters persists in the index which includes none of the above, instead presenting a list compiled from the names of every modern scholar mentioned in the notes and various people mentioned in the text who have been consecrated by the *Dictionary of National Biography*. Ten pages of this small book are devoted to recounting the story of Mr. Barlow's unsuccessful suit, and yet he is not in the index; nor are any of the Burneys except Fanny and her father; nor is Mr. Crisp. To give Devlin credit, he cannot be beguiled by a title; one seeks in vain as well for Lady Spencer, Lady Duncannon, or "Lady Forster," the King or the Queen. (One finds, however, Lafayette, Napoleon, Narbonne, Robespierre, Madame de Staël—and Choderlos de Laclos, the author, though unnamed in the text, of *Les Liaisons Dangereuses*.)

All of this is depressingly familiar, as is Devlin's second major problem with Fanny Burney's work, his reluctance to discern art in it. Devlin views Burney, both the journal writer and the novelist, as a child of nature. In his second chapter Devlin states that "Fanny Burney came to fiction via fact," and he attempts to demonstrate that his subject was first and foremost a writer of journals—instructed therein by her male mentor, Daddy Crisp—and that *Evelina* is in fact the same thing, "a love-affair with a wedding at the end" (p. 87) imposed. "*Evelina* is successful," he writes, "because its letters, 'written from the thoughts that occur to the Pen at the moment,' are successful, and because in it the art of the journal-letter and the art of the novel are the same thing" (p. 22):

> Modern criticism does not always know how to handle such common things [the stuff of *Evelina*] because it forgets that their origin is in the letters and diaries; it looks for the sophisticated techniques of fiction to account for the novel's success and creates them when it does not find them. It searches for the coherence of a novel instead of watching for the art of a journal-writer. [p. 87]

Truly, *Evelina* and Fanny Burney's earlier writing style benefited from her years of sprightly journal writing, but Devlin's reductive account of the novel's origin evinces ignorance of the facts. Though he does once refer to the fifteen-year-old Fanny Burney's funeral pyre of early writings, he seems unacquainted with the long passage in her *Memoirs of Doctor Burney* where she describes her life as a young writer, at ten scribbling "almost incessantly, little works of invention; but always in private," and soon after her mother's death, in 1762, "converting into Elegies, Odes, Plays, Songs, Stories, Farces,—nay, Tragedies and Epic

Poems, every scrap of white paper that could be seized upon without question or notice," then in her fifteenth year burning her entire stock, including the "History of Caroline Evelyn," the mother of Evelina. She was left, however, with so animated an impression of that tale that "irresistably and almost unconsciously, the whole of A Young Lady's Entrance into the World, was pent up in the inventor's memory, ere a paragraph was committed to paper."[7] Plot, structure and theme preceded writing. Needless to say, this differs markedly from Devlin's account of *Evelina*'s genesis.

Inevitably Devlin's attitude toward the novel results in acerbity towards critics who have found structure and meaning in the book, and he rebukes an array of them, including Edward and Lillian Bloom, Joyce Hemlow, Patricia Spacks, and Susan Staves:

> Symbolism and satire, like irony, thematic structure and the rest have to be found, or how shall we talk about the book? . . . . Some recent feminist writing throws more light on *Evelina* and the other novels, and recognizes the closeness of the fiction and the journals, though here, too, the wish to see Evelina and Fanny Burney as totally representative figures makes it difficult for these critics to see the trees for the wood of theory. [pp. 90–92]

Well, commitment to theory apparently leads Devlin to deny Burney irony in her work: "She was not an ironic writer. . . . Irony is almost as absent from her journals and novels as satire. . . . Satire is a form of aggression and Fanny Burney's instinct and method led her to hide" (p. 62). If Devlin cannot see the pervasive irony and satire in Fanny Burney's work, no citing of examples could convert him. In fact she employed an ironic reservation of mind, which refused obeisance to the social powers who courted her, as her stay against shyness. Both irony and satire are often implicit in the situations she draws. She is being satiric of Lady Louisa Larpent in *Evelina* when she shows Lady Louisa totally indifferent to Evelina until she learns "who she is." She is being satiric of the young bloods in that book when she shows them practicing every foolish fad including making bets on bizarre contests, racing in their phaetons and taking a vast interest in cookery; then, devastatingly, she mentions that they also attend Parliament—these, the law-makers of the nation! What is the very opening of Fanny Burney's 1768 journal but ironic? Examples abound:

Why, permit me to ask, must a female be made Nobody? Ah! my dear, what were this world good for, *were* Nobody a female?

No! 'tis impossible! this style is too great, too sublime to be supported with proper dignity—the sublime & beautifull how charmingly blended!—Yes! I *will* desist—I *will* lay down my pen while I can with [honour].[8]

And what could be more gently satiric that her portrait of Edward Jerningham singing to his own accompaniment upon the harp with a small-voiced fineness so that "it required a painful attention to hear him. And while he sings, he looks the gentlest of all-dying Corydons!" The vulgar Mrs. Bowdler calls out, "Pray, Mr. Jerningham, can't you sing us some of your own poetry?" At which the observer remarks, "I really feared he would have fainted away at so gross a question."[9]

Devlin's unwillingness to see Fanny Burney's true subject as worthy of consideration and the unwillingness to see her art as art are disastrous for his book. And he should have confined his strictures to Burney's journal style and method and refrained from touching upon the question of what she wrote or did not write about. Although he has never seen the full journals of the court years, still to be published, he allows himself this statement: "In these [court] years especially she seldom allowed herself to assert her 'real and undisguised thoughts' " (p. 57). As it was just Fanny Burney's real and undisguised thoughts on delicate questions which she tended to expurgate from the journals, he ought to have bolstered such a statement with a note recording his visits to the manuscript sources in question. In support of his thesis that her journal-writing was her proper genre, he says that in the worst depression of her court years, "when she most needed to survive, her customary life-saver—the act of writing—failed her" (p. 57). Strangely three pages later he shows himself entirely aware that at the time she was writing three or four tragedies.

But let us leave Devlin with a note about his *most* annoying habit, the supposition that he can clear the whole thing up with the simplest of dicta, at the same time, no doubt, showing up the offensive verbiage of feminist critics and their fellow travellers. Of his four chapters, the first is a demonstration of his favorite thesis, "The dates of her novels are important," a thesis which reappears once in that chapter and which concludes the book— *Quod erat demonstrandum.* It means that there is an inevitable change between each novel and the next. The chapter is actually, however, an essay on Fanny Burney and the French Revolution. The second chapter opens with and repeats another reductive statement, "Fanny Burney came to fiction via fact," and attempts to prove that point. The third chapter, apparently intended to contribute to a non-existent political discussion by demonstrating that it would be difficult to say just how radical or conservative Fanny Burney's political opinions actually were, proceeds by instead comparing the educational theories of Hannah More and Mary Wollstonecraft to suggest that these were virtually indistinguishable. Here is a point, oddly enough, which has already been made by Mary Berry almost two hundred years ago and noted by Ellen Moers in *Literary Women.*[10] Perhaps, though he does not mention her, Moers is one of those recent feminist critics who have thrown some light on *Evelina.* Despite the encouragement lent by Mary Berry and Ellen Moers, the fact that sixteen pages of this slender book are dedicated to a discussion of two women other than his subject is baffling, though it may be Devlin's offhand demonstration that he can "do" any woman, an impression he shores up by frequent references to Jane Austen. His fourth and last chapter, in which Devlin alludes to Fanny Burney's fiction, features another frequently iterated thesis, that "*Evelina* was born of the diaries and journals," and proceeds by devoting fourteen pages to *Evelina,* five to *Cecilia,* four to *Camilla,* and seven to the favorite *The Wanderer,* before concluding with the general thesis, "The dates of Fanny Burney's novels are important."

The book edited by Klima, Bowers, and Grant represents the finest of textual work. In the years after her father's death in 1814, Fanny Burney, now Madame D'Arblay, intended to edit the memoir of his life which he himself had left in the belief that

Perhaps few have been better enabled to describe faithfully & exactly, from an actual survey, the manners & customs of the age in wch he lived, than myself: ascending from those of the most humble cottagers, & lowest mechanics, to the first Nobility, and most elevated personages in the kingdom, with whom circumstances, situation, & accident, at different periods of my life, have rendered me familiar. . . . A book of this kind, though it may mortify & offend a few persons of the present age, W^d be read with avidity at the distance of some centuries by antiquaries & lovers of anecdotes, though it will have lost the piquancy of personality. [pp. 9–10]

Was Fanny Burney right in her judgment that her father had failed his purpose? It was this judgment that caused her in the end to scrap his book almost entirely and compile her own from his materials. Her first impression—"What a Labrinth!"— yielded to "He seems to have burnt nothing: things the most common & useless being hoarded with those that are most edifying, secret, or interesting."[11] For four years she labored, marking excisions, writing in emendations, discarding unwanted portions. In the end she reluctantly concluded that her father's own version of his life simply was not worthy of him and could not be redeemed. She found the juvenile incidents, when not enhanced by his recital of them, "trivial to poverty, & dull to sleepiness," what respected his own family "utterly unpleasant—& quite useless to be kept alive," his recollections of early life in London and Lynn details of events and people now of no interest, and his notations of his great life in London society a disappointing list of engagements only, without detail (pp. xxvii–xxviii).

We are fortunate to have before us what the editors estimate to be perhaps half of the discarded writings of Charles Burney for the relevant years, so that we can judge Fanny Burney's conclusion for ourselves. When she projected her father's memoir, the great model in her mind was Boswell's life of Johnson. During her labors on his manuscripts she wrote as a comment to his statement already quoted above from page 10, "Had health, spirits, & native vigour favoured the execution of this project, no memoirs of the time, or none but Boswells Johnson would have contained equal instruction with Entertainment—but alas, they all failed in its execution."[12] And so she believed. She admired

Boswell's life for its wealth of incident, all tending to aggrandize Johnson's natural powers and emphasizing how, humbly though he had been born, he was idolized by the fashionable and great. Exactly thus did she wish her father displayed. But she had long disliked Boswell's "loquacious communications of every weakness and infirmity of the first and greatest good man of these times."[13] In her memoir of her father she set to work, using a purple version of Johnsonian prose as her standard, to apply to her father's life the best of Boswell's technique without the worst.

The great service that Klima, Bowers, and Grant have done is to provide an accurate and authentic text of all the bits of Charles Burney's autobiographical writings that survived his daughter's cutting and discarding for the period 1726–1769, roughly corresponding to the events considered in the first of her own three volumes of his memoir. The extant bits were reassembled from three major libraries—the British Library, the Osborn Collection of the Beinecke Library, and the Berg Collection of the New York Public Library. The index written by Charles Burney himself enabled them to know what had been lost as well as how to order what had been saved. They have provided expert bridge passages and superlative notes. The volume is also enhanced by a remarkably accurate index.

For anyone expecting a continuous narrative, the volume will naturally constitute a shock. The various fragments, of which there are 117, sometimes begin or end unceremoniously in mid-sentence, and we will probably never know what "ludicrous misfortune" befell "the fat & facetious Harry Hatsel" in the "extensive garden totally wild" of Arne's apartments at Marble Hall (p. 61). And what did the intrepid Mrs. Mackenzie do to the interloper who sneezed in the clock case (p. 126)? Nevertheless, from the fragments presented and connected here, we can judge for ourselves between the advocates of the father's and the advocates of the daughter's memoir.

The editors of the father's memoir are of the opinion that Fanny Burney's "own *Memoirs of Dr. Burney* [actually, from the title page, *Memoirs of Doctor Burney*], published in 1832, is a very poor substitute for what she destroyed." They note its "prose of turgid preciosity very different from her early style," her creation of her father as a Sir Charles Grandison, and the criticism of John Wilson Croker that she ought to have presented her father's memoirs as she found them and ought not to have devoted so much space to herself (p. xxix). A consideration of the kind of alterations Fanney Burney made when she wrote her own version of the memoirs is illuminating. A comparison between the two memoirs was not within the scope of the editors of this edition, but their notes, referring to parallel passages in his daughter's work, facilitate such a critical discussion.

Charles Burney's memoir is written, or dashed off, in an informal, sometimes incorrect, and frequently graceless style which almost certainly he intended at one time to revise and which, once he was incapable of revision himself, he expected his daughter to revise. One of Fanny Burney's major concerns was that the memoir be written with a correctness and elegance of style meant to emblemize both the correctness and elegance of her father's life and of the entire Burney family. In one instance she provides what she claims to have been her father's own account of an interlude in Lincolnshire, although his actual account differed. (One of the reasons for her revision is to provide an account of her father's old friend Molly Carter.) Charles Burney's actual account reads:

When I arrived at Elsham, I found there, beside Mr T. and his Lady, his brother, Mr Robt Thompson, M^r Le Grand, and 5 or 6 young Ladies of the neighbourhood. I had the honour of being introduced to the acquaintance of all the families that visited at Elsham: such as the Pelhams, the Andersons, the Gores, & the Carters. Four of the Miss Gores, and Miss Molly Carter were inmates. Miss Philly Gore, a great beauty, & Miss Carter, very young, intelligent and handsome, though very pleasing, did not discover herself to be possessed of so large portion of wit, as that for wch she has since been so justly celebrated.

I continued here during the month of $Sept^r$ Octr and part of Novr and never passed my time more pleasantly in my life. It was one continued series of mirth, amusement & festivity. [p. 51]

But Fanny Burney writes:

Miss Molly Carter, in her youth a very pretty girl, was, in the year 1745, of a large party of young ladies, consisting of five or six Miss Gores, and

How (and how not) to Explore the Burneys 213

Miss Anderson, at William Thompson's Esq., in the neighbourhood of Elsham, near Brig. Bob Thompson, Mr. Thompson's brother, Billy Le Grand, and myself, composed the rest of the set, which was employed in nothing but singing, dancing, romping, and visiting, the whole time I was there; which time was never surpassed in hilarity at any place where I have been received in my life.[14]

Here the style has been emended and additional information provided, either from a lost portion of Charles Burney's manuscript or from his daughter's memory. The principal change, however, is the suppression of the fact that Charles Burney, then an apprentice of Thomas Arne's, was apparently sent to Lincolnshire to provide music for the party, and was delighted with a general social acceptance which achieved for him "the honour of being introduced to the acquaintance of all the families that visited at Elsham." His daughter wishes to make him appear a member of the Elsham social set.

Here we have one of the distinguishing differences of the two memoirs, for the father is utterly honest about his status and his ambitions while the daughter is willing to alter his very text in order to maintain family pride. Consistently she suppresses details calculated to lower the family and adds details calculated to exalt it. Where her father plainly, exultantly, describes the manner in which he had the good fortune in Chester to become apprentice to Thomas Arne and go with him to London, even to the detail that his father had not the hundred pounds which at first Arne required, Fanny Burney seeks to euphemize the odious term *apprentice*. Charles Burney writes:

Mr Arne spoke out, and said he would take me to town as an apprentice, for £100 premium, & exempt my father from all further expence.
  This proposal we sh^d have eagerly embraced, if the £100 c^d [have been furnished]. [p.42]

His daughter writes:

Dr. Arne ... was so much pleased with the talents of this nearly self-instructed performer, as to make an offer to Mr. Burney senior, upon such conditions as are usual to such sort of patronage, to complete the musical education of this lively and aspiring young man; and to bring him forth to the world as his favourite and most promising pupil.[15]

Whereas Charles Burney is proud of his brother Richard's success as a dancing master, which enabled him to take a large house in Hatton Garden and give balls there, Fanny Burney forbears naming her uncle's profession and gives the impression that somehow his frequent balls (at one of which her parents met) were social occasions. She does not mention her Grandfather Burney's appearance as an actor at Goodman's Fields Theatre from 1729–1731.

But her red pencil was perhaps even more ruthless when she happened upon examples of the Burney penchant for light-heartedness, surely an innocent enough trait in her father which she may have come to dislike and distrust in her brother Charles (the prototype of Lionel in *Camilla*). There is some justice to the charge that she presented her father as Sir Charles Grandison. She ignores his anecdotes of a giddy youth, as when at Bath the Bishop of Raphoe's horse, in a race for sport, failed to clear a five-barred gate: "The B^p was hurled into the Air & seemed to fly into the next field while his horse remained stationary; wch was quite as good a joke to me as Harry Hatsels misfortune had been at Marble Hall. I thought I sh^d never compose my muscles again: to see a B^p try to leap a 5 bar gate and fail! was a joke at my time of life, a far ridere a morto" (p. 76).

Charles Burney was twenty-one at the time. He was eighteen when he arrived in London with Dr. Arne and played the excellent trick on his brother Richard, whom he had not seen for years, of impersonating for some weeks a friend of his own named Mr. Arnold. His daughter does not refer to this incident either, but perhaps most telling is the difference in accounts of the string-on-the-toe awakening device: As her father tells it, "In the height of Summer, I robbed my sleep of a few hours in order to meet some other boys at a Bowling-green: and used to tie a string to one of my great toes, wch I put out the window of my room, by wch I was waked as soon as it was light, by an apprentice at next door" (p. 31). Compare Fanny Burney's rendition: "On quitting Shrewsbury to return to his parents at Chester, the

How (and how not) to Explore the Burneys 215

ardour of young Burney for improvement was such as to absorb his whole being; and his fear lest a moment of daylight should be profitless, led him to bespeak a labouring boy, who rose with the sun, to awaken him regularly with its dawn. Yet, as he durst not pursue his education at the expense of the repose of his family, he hit upon the ingenious device of tying one end of a ball of pack-thread round his great toe, and then letting the ball drop, with the other end just within the boy's reach."[16]

Fanny Burney is also particularly ruthless when dealing with her father's comical anecdotes, which characteristically she finds both low and pointless without his animated recounting. She must have read with nothing but distaste his account of his old playmate Dick the Barber who "intoxicated with Ale and Village Importance, had enlisted for a soldier! When entering into all the debaucheries of the Military of Petty France, he had not been six months in the Capital, before he merited by his ill conduct 100 Lashes for his first offence, as a specimen of the discipline to w[ch] he had subjected himself" (p. 29). She ignores such passages as that about Underwood, the town clerk of Lynn, who having been challenged for satisfaction by Alderman Holley, "called on his enraged antagonist and addressed him in the following manner: I am very sorry, M[r] Alderman that I have offended you, & I beg your pardon: if that will not be sufficient satisfaction for the offence (turning round, he says) pray Sir kick—consider my wife & family" (p. 123). She would of course eschew such expressions as "M[rs] Mackenzie . . . had not been long out of the straw" (p. 125) or the apparently celebrated anecdote Charles Burney told of his Welsh housekeeper who exterminated the bugs in his bedstead by pouring boiling water into the joints: "Ay inteeet! (says she, with a sigh) I caave them a little waarm trink, I can assure you" (p. 147). And yet the reminder that Charles Burney was a gifted mimic and a glimpse into the matter and style of some of his anecdotes provide the answer to the question that baffled London on the publication of *Evelina:* how had this twenty-five-year-old girl met such a variety of low characters and mastered their dialects? The answer is that she too was a fun-loving Burney who had listened avidly to her father's stories and had not yet learned that the world professes to prefer some distance between high thinking and low comedy. As she grew older, she gave her readers cause to regret the gradual disappearance of low humor from her novels, precisely as it disappeared from her father's memoir.

As she tried to obliterate the low humor, so of course she removed the more racy or blunt of the characterizations her father gave of his acquaintance. She emphasizes the respectable friends her father made at Fulke Greville's seat, Wilbury, in his youth but fails to mention "Duke Hamilton, whose manners and character were not to be copied, but avoided.... Mr Young of Dunford, a strong marked character, for swaggering, meanness & lying" (p. 72). Although she gives an accurate appraisal of Arne's mean-spirited treatment of young Burney, she omits, of course, this passage:

He never c^d pass by a woman in the Street, to the end of his life, without Concupiscence, or, in plain Engl. *picking her up*, if her look was not forbidding, & impracticable. It has frequently happened in walking home with my Wife of a Night, if we have by some accident been separated for a few minutes, that she has been accosted by the D^r with that design, ere I c^d overtake her or he know to whom she belonged (p. 103).

To what does all this adduce? It is fair to say that we have here two entirely different memoirs of Charles Burney, each written for a different purpose. Charles Burney was right when he wrote that "a book of this kind ... w^d be read with avidity at the distance of centuries." It was new in *respectable* memoir to give such details as how an ordinary practical man might respond to a challenge, how Arne could not pass a woman in the street without propositioning her. But compared to Boswell's life of Johnson, probably Charles Burney's model, his work is too hastily noted down, too unfinished, not fully detailed. Fanny Burney chose another aspect of Boswell's life, the veneration which Johnson patently received by almost all he encountered. Her account is full of information, but information selectively taken and therefore rarely honest. She is thinking not only of readers generations hence but of the critics of and the reputation of the Burney family.

Ultimately it is her sense of decorum, or the decorums, which ruled her decisions. In life she wished to impose a perfect decorum retroactively upon the actions of her father. In art she had come to believe in the decorum dictated by genre. The novel might incorporate low comedy, but she wrote something higher than the novel and maintained that she did by keeping in her later fiction an almost (not quite invariable) uniform sobriety. The prose of her latter years, which we judge to be overinflated, is intended to characterize the elevation of her genre, whether fiction or memoir.

Because she never lost her light touch or her sense of comedy, what we ought to regret is that she all but ceased to write comedies for the stage and eschewed the writing of mere novels which might have had low characters. *A Busy Day,* a comedy written as late as 1800–1801, is a triumph of idiosyncratic comic characters, each with a different style and dialect, and many of them deliciously low.[17] But a comedy was one thing, a memoir of her beloved father another. To "rank" the two memoirs is perhaps a mistake, for they are so very different. But if we had to have only one, and if we could have either one complete, we would undoubtedly choose Charles Burney's, for its honesty, its delightful freshness of detail, and its vitality. We would have to regret, however, that it remained in some ways only a sketch, and while we disagreed with Fanny Burney's complaint that many of its anecdotes are about insignificant people and events about whom we would care nothing, we would regret the absence of details about the great personages her father had known, the famous salons he frequented, and the secrets he must have learned. We owe a profound debt to the editors of the fragments of his book for showing it to us in as complete a state as is possible and for focussing the image of a man at once loveable, ambitious, and uncompromisingly modest and honest.

Notes

1. Joyce Hemlow, *The History of Fanny Burney* (Oxford: Clarendon Press, 1958), p. 285.
2. A reference to Ian Watts's theory in *The Rise of the Novel* that action in the novel is regulated by cause and effect.
3. *Evelina*, Book II, Chapter xviii.
4. Sarah Scott's novel *The History of Cornelia* (1750) is a prototype of this novel, suggesting that Fanny Burney's plot is not altogether radically new.
5. The Burneys were probably better able to understand Lady Spencer's dilemma and her need to seek countenance for her daughters when they themselves allowed Sarah Harriet, after she had left James, to become governess to the grandchildren of their old family friend Mrs. Crewe.
6. *Diary and Letters of Madame d'Arblay (1778–1840)*, ed. Austin Dobson (London and New York: Macmillan, 1904–05), I, 350.
7. Fanny Burney D'Arblay, *Memoirs of Doctor Burney* (London: Edward Moxon, 1832), II, 123–26.
8. *The Early Journals and Letters of Fanny Burney:* Volume I, 1768–1773, ed. Lars E. Troide (Oxford: Clarendon Press, 1988), pp. 2, 4. The last word is an uncertain reading.
9. Dobson, *Diary and Letters*, I, 351.
10. Ellen Moers, *Literary Women* (Garden City, N.Y.: Anchor Press/Doubleday, 1977), p. 190.
11. From letters of 1816 and 1817 quoted in Klima, Bowers, and Grant, p. xxvi. On p. xxv Fanny Burney's reference to her father's writings as "Manuscriptural" is quoted.
12. The editors appear to believe (p. 12, n. 1) that Fanny Burney added the sentence "disingenuously . . . as if CB were writing," but surely she intended the sentence as an editorial comment.
13. Quoted by Devlin, *Novels and Journals*, p. 37.
14. Fanny Burney D'Arblay, *Memoirs*, I, 19.
15. *Ibid.*, I, 10–11.
16. *Ibid.*, I, 10.
17. Tara Ghoshal Wallace's edition of *A Busy Day*, never performed, was published in 1984 by Rutgers University Press.

Redefining Norris and Recovering the Primary Story

Joseph R. McElrath, Jr.

Barbara Hochman. *The Art of Frank Norris, Storyteller.* Columbia: University of Missouri Press, 1988. x, 150 pp.

The beauty of an encounter with an interpretive monograph is that, as its author executes the definition of *the* topic upon which falls the restricted focus, the reader too can jettison what are, for the moment, peripheral concerns. The reader, ready to adventure for a while with a new mentor, has the pleasure of turning from the well-known to trace out a new line of thought; since it is only *a* line of thought, the reading experience also provides a temporary escape from the complexity of addressing the whole of a multifarious subject such as the entire canon of Frank Norris. It is a working holiday, but a holiday nonetheless, since the initial demand made is so simple: as with a thematically focused novel, one reads the "plot" to see how its central conception emerges, content with illuminations of aspects of the canon and hoping that, when viewed in retrospect, the individual elucidations will combine in a brilliant effect. Fine measurements are taken *after* one has divined the gist in its entirety. Then one reflects upon its larger implications and how well they fit. All of which is to say that I found myself giving Barbara Hochman's volume two readings, and I came to two conclusions. I would suggest that others measure the achievement in the same way. The value of this study will prove greater if one initially refrains from quibbling and is not distracted from viewing the overarching design.

A critic choosing to write "the big book" which contends for the honor of the "definitive study" of Norris will not, of course, provide this type of reading experience; and the reviewer will immediately ask a different question than that posed to a monograph. This question will be, was the whole portrait executed with the proper wide-scope perspective and with all-encompassing specificity? While Hochman's title may invite this kind of interrogation, *The Art of Frank Norris, Storyteller* soon reveals itself as instead concerned with interrelated parts rather than the whole. For example, only five short stories and nine of the literary essays are treated. Four of the seven novels receive chapters of their own, with special attention given to a fifth, *Blix*. Paragraph-length treatments are the fate of *Yvernelle, Moran,* and *A Man's Woman,* as is usually the case. In short, over 300 writings by Norris have been sifted through a relatively fine mesh. Offered up are the data immediately relevant to Hochman's thesis; and she proves that the dimension of Norris's art described is, indeed, an important one. To echo William Dean Howells regarding *McTeague,* there are "little miracles of observation" along the way.

The first positive readjustment in viewpoint offered by Hochman will be found in the title. Don Graham made a contribution along the same lines in *The Fiction of Frank Norris: The Aesthetic Context* in 1978, stressing the notion that Norris was an artist and, from at least his high-school days on, had interests congruent with such a primary identity. Graham gave these concerns, and Norris's turn-of-the-century experiences that went with them, an appropriate emphasis in his research and analyses. The consequence was an original reading of the works made possible by an extraordinary sensitivity to *fin de siècle* aesthetic allusions. Hochman's approach is less contextual and more oriented to the intrinsic qualities of the texts and to Norris's personality *during* narration: that is, she yet more boldly presses the point regarding the artist in question via the initial emphasis on the concept of *Storyteller,* which takes the reader to several vantage points from which to view both Norris and his works. It eventually becomes a trope, as not only Norris's narrative acts are scrutinized, but the story-telling of *the characters themselves* is identified as a major means by which their psychologies are both revealed and evaluatively indexed by Norris for the reader. One of the eye-openers here is how many of the characters have an identity-establishing "story" of their own to tell others or recapitulate to themselves. These scenarios as well define life, as the characters visualize their relationship to it. Hochman compiles a disarmingly large catalogue, and one now really cannot again read Norris the same way: the most reluctant will find themselves finally forced to take this phenomenon into account when considering characterization, point of view, and theme.

Initially, though, Hochman's term is simply signalling her allegiance to the implications of Graham's study by orienting her reader to a modified conception of Norris which has been emerging since the mid-1970s. Her point is that, first and last, Norris was the type he autobiographically described in 1902 in "Story-Tellers Vs. Novelists." That is, he should be approached as story-teller.

On the face of it, this may seem less than a profound observation. No one has *denied* that he was a fictionalist by predisposition and conscious commitment to the profession that he energetically practiced. But the fact is that, in much of the literature on Norris and even in descriptions of his style, one may easily receive the impression that he was a philosopher working in a literary medium rather than a thoughtful writer—that the ratio between philosophy and art in his canon resembled that of Emerson's and Thoreau's. In addition, Norris has appeared more closely related to these artful metaphysicians than to his anti-metaphysical contemporary, Stephen Crane. In 1962, Warren French judged Norris a "scion of the American transcendentalists" whose Thoreau-like Vanamee leads the reader down the true path to the central theme of *The Octopus*. In 1966, Donald Pizer took a different tack, picturing Norris in a variant but related ideational context. His *Novels of Frank Norris* elucidates Norris's work in terms of the ethical evolutionary idealism of Joseph LeConte, and thus brings into view a philosophical consistency greater than that previously envisioned. William B. Dillingham, in 1969, inverted the picture of a metaphysically oriented intellectual: he stressed the anti-intellectual intellectualism of a Norris preoccupied with the sub-rational, or instinctual, in man in *Frank Norris: Instinct and Art*. The 1960s, in short, yielded a Norris amidst the streams of intellectual history in nineteenth-century

America, with the conceptually dense *Octopus* as his masterwork relatable to like touchstones. One does well to remember that interdisciplinary American Studies programs were then in vogue, and that books such as Leo Marx's *The Machine in the Garden* not only documented a keen interest in measuring the evolution of key concepts, but invited scholars to go forth and do likewise. The various grand conceits of *The Octopus* provided a bridge from *Moby-Dick* to *The Great Gatsby* or *Grapes of Wrath*, allowing one to measure the durability of certain American *weltanschauungen*.

None of this focus-on-the-*philosophe* and the waning/waxing of philosophical traditions at the turn of the century is carried forward in any significant way in Hochman's study. While Norris's thought of course receives consideration, Hochman first strips away long-honored categorizations, so that she may begin with a fashioner of tales and then follow where the evidence leads. Of the three studies from the 1960s noted, Pizer's has proven the dominant influence. Its continued vitality will be seen in Kevin Starr's 1986 introduction to the Penguin *Octopus,* when he tires of splitting hairs and declares that Pizer has already rendered limpid what some find a turbid novel. And yet, one notes that Joseph LeConte appears not at all in Hochman's index. Thoreau too is absent. Dillingham's notion of the centrality of instinct as well receives very little play.

The radical break from tradition is even more dramatic as Hochman marks a climax in the grousing heard among critics vexed by that terrible term, Naturalism. Hochman proves to be the liberationist critic, proceeding immediately to minimize as much as she can the relevance of the "naturalist" tag, and striving to dispatch it the way mid-century critics did "muckraker." Hers is the widespread exasperation articulated by Edwin Cady in 1970. In *The Light of Common Day,* his conclusion was that "it is probably true that there are not finally any naturalists. . . . Norris, Jack London, and Dreiser talked brave naturalism but never uncompromisingly wrote it." While she does not cite Cady, the implications of her monograph effect a parallelism; she is not far from his sense that beneath and around those writers' "commitments were governing, antinaturalistic loyalties to man" (p. 51). Hochman's affinity is repeatedly displayed as she finds characters in Norris's works who could have, or do, counter the deterministic "forces" of life traditionally identified as naturalistic. Her Norris tells psychologically focused stories in which the characters determine their own fates via behaviors which establish what becomes the "necessary."

Despite the clarification of Norris's inarguable primary definition as fictionalist, there are difficulties involved in moving toward the image of a less naturalistic Norris. She admits the formidable obstacle: it is what Hochman, like her predecessors, terms the discursive narrator who sounds "the iron note" repeatedly. Indeed, the concepts and imagery employed by Norris *are* naturalistic by even the most minimal standards of measurement. How to get around that? Two routes are taken, the first having already been blazed by others, as she indicates on pp. 2–3 and 129 (notes 5–6).

There are many passages in the works featuring language that is 100 percent deterministic but which are interpretable as expressing Norris's *characters'* points of view—rather than Norris's own. That is, although Hochman does not use the term, the narrative technique of indirect discourse employed by Zola and by Stephen Crane is often utilized by Norris. The language of the narrator is in the third person singular as the familiar imagery appears, but it is the character's consciousness rather than Norris's—or, a discursive narrator's—that is revealed. At particular moments in *Vandover and the Brute,* for example, we find that it is *Van*'s sense of impotence before the "engine" of life, or *Charlie Geary*'s hard-Darwinism attitude, that is disclosed. Norris records *their* sense of forces or natural laws governing their conditions—or, he assigns them attitudes which are not necessarily his own at that moment. In short, *they* participate in their own ways in the naturalistic sensibility circa 1900—and for good reason. Self-absorbed Charlie can thus justify his predatory personality with his amoral, survival-of-the-fittest "story" of the-way-things-are; he is the hero of his "plot." Van has a convenient "tale" about how the determining forces work, excusing his steadfast refusal to modify his view of life or his self-indulgent life-style; he is the pathetic victim finally requiring nothing less than a supernatural intervention, *à la* Gounod's *Faust,* if he is to be "saved."

Still, while clarification of this kind minimizes the problem, the discursive narrator *qua* naturalist is not eliminated from the works. *That* Norris, so to speak, remains in the texts. The direct-statement, formulaic glosses on the action are undeniably there, explaining things naturalistically with what, nearly a century later, appears to be millwork regularity. The route Hochman next takes, then, is not so simple as the first. Indeed, many readers may find it a rocky one. It does not lead to her overtly bifurcating the writer's personality or to diagnoses of post-Freudian *malaise;* and yet, her reading of the texts makes necessary the perception of a split sensibility as she differentiates between what the story *per se* of *Vandover* or *McTeague* reveals and what is declared in the voice of a naturalistic ideologue addressing the reader. She often finds the import of one in conflict with that of the other; and thus, since Norris is in control, the dialectic in the texts suggests a contradiction within his own vision.

By way of making an appropriate reading/interpretive response to such cruxes, Hochman does two things. She identifies Norris's contradictoriness as what it apparently is. She also opts for the critical exercise of choice regarding which meaning generated is of signal importance. In a nutshell, that meaning is not the formulaic one having to do with the irresistible determinants of heredity, environment, and chance—or the image of man as Carrie Meeber-like "wisp." Rather, the contrary theme traced-out and celebrated for its superior worth has more positive implications. It is that the acceptance of, and positive adaptation to, the flux of life is possible. Moreover, such is the means of transcending or avoiding the pathetic and sometimes horrific consequences that overtake the characters who will not countenance change, or modify their expectations and behaviors to fit new conditions, or take the risks involved in developing strategies of coping. That is, Norris's characters *can* "save themselves" and do not *have to be* ground beneath an engine of life. At the other extreme, they do not have to become like Charlie Geary and the other inhumane villains who resemble engines riding down their contemporaries, visualizing determinisms as their apologias for doing so.

To cite a simple example of the choices Hochman makes, she rejects the narrator's explanation of Trina's obsession with money as a simple consequence of her heredity. The justification is to be found in much fuller, non-discursive aspects of the narration, where this naturalistic saw related to an unalterable necessity is belied by a complex characterization defying the reduction that has occurred. Hochman finds a Trina whose primary trait is profound insecurity—fear of change and the risk of loss that goes with it. It is exacerbated by events after she leaves her parents' home: neurotic symptoms begin to appear even before Marcus Schouler deprives the McTeagues of their main source of income. Like her compulsively orderly father, she seeks to freeze life in a convenient, safe, permanent form via organization, a rigid insistence that things and people conform to the setting/plot that *should be* those of her life's story, and the forestalling of loss of any kind. The stasis she obsessively attempts to maintain is the measure of her divorce from the dynamic flow of experience which requires adjustments along the way—adjustments that her husband and she do not make. As with Mac carrying his bird cage into the Sierras and then Death Valley, both have a hard time with the notion of "letting go" of old arrangements when conditions change. In *McTeague, The Octopus*, and *The Pit* there looms large a considerable cast of characters with a like aim manifesting itself in various ways but always to the end of denying the protean character of life by bringing it under control. This rage for order that the many characters display—usually to their own disadvantage but also to socially destructive ends—assumes clear definition under Hochman's hand. The majority of examples easily conform to the paradigm which manifests itself in simple terms via ritualistic behavior and refusals to accept the hazards of positive decision-making, as well as in complex manipulations of experience of the kind attempted by Vanamee in *The Octopus*. One may reject some of the interpretations, or certain aspects of them, but the paradigm for what is typical for Norris's characters appears to be verified.

Having measured negative experience in Norris's works in terms different from those employed by the discursive narrator, Hochman turns to the more positive developments in the fiction in order to reapply, and thus further verify, her thesis. That too appears to work, in the majority of cases. *Blix* concludes with

Condy and Travis not attempting to prolong their idyllic, essentially adolescent experience of love and life; their little gaieties behind them, as Norris phrases it, the hero and heroine of this *bildüngsroman* move forward to the unknowns of adult experience with some trepidation, but appear ready to develop strategies to deal with the unpredictable demands that will be made upon them, professionally and personally. Defeated in his attempt to control life according to his terms, a frustrated and guilt-ridden Ward Bennett of *A Man's Woman* turns from the present and the future, obsessively recreating the past in the memoir over which he labors—until, aided by Lloyd who also reshapes her expectations of life, he escapes into the present where he adjusts to things-the-way-they-have-become (and are still becoming). Annixter in *The Octopus,* as domination-driven as the hero of *The Pit,* largely transcends his self-absorption and fear of being manipulated by others—to find that risk-taking is attractive since the possible benefits are inestimably fine. The theme is traceable in *The Pit* as well, though Hochman's view of Page and Landry Court as the primary vehicle for its exposition is dubious; Don Graham's explanation of the relationship between the story of Laura and Curtis Jadwin and the sometimes parodic echo that is the Page-Landry subplot seems closer to the mark. True, the juveniles do bring the positive developments of *Blix* to mind; but it is Laura who has escaped from the role of Ruskinesque "housewife," and those of multiple scenarios of life fashioned by romantic artists, to begin the development of what Norris terms "identity." At the close, she appears to be developing a personality of her own at last, rather than persisting in the search for a story-book model to which to conform. *Blix* is again echoed as Laura and Curtis leave the old order (or disorder) symbolized by their mansion and Chicago, ready to try a new way. That is, the same paradigm can be applied in another manner to this novel, should one not find Hochman's reading appropriate.

And thus the ultimate value of what is available here. Though there are some "stretchers," Hochman is truly on to something. It pays to experiment by moving beyond a traditional reading of Norris as naturalist, even if one eventually chooses to return to a view of the author within the context of Naturalism.

But, what of that discursive narrator sent into the wings? Must he remain there without the limelight, and must one make a choice: between the Norris who may be today termed both simplistic and fustian; and the Norris who appears so enlightened in his thought on human behavior? Put another way, why cannot Trina be hereditarily predisposed to hoarding, and anal-retentive to boot, in addition to being motivated the way Hochman sees her? Must Mac's fear of abandonment, or of the loss of cherished behaviors, preclude naturalistic emphases of the kind made by the discursive narrator? Then there is the discursive narrator's repeated use of the descriptor "pliable" when evaluating the hero of *Vandover*. Hochman observes that Van's problem is actually a *lack* of pliability; his stock reaction to radical alterations in the repetitive rhythms of his life Hochman finds typed when he was eight, in his paralysis before the death of his mother. Change is associated with traumatic loss; Van is rigidly unresponsive to opportunities for readjustment which may eventuate in negative developments, and he resists adaptation to the new configurations of experience. This *is* generally the case in the novel—and thus the "long slide" imagery of the work. Hochman's analysis is correct.

But on second thought, one may quote ornery Annixter when he is not ready to throw in the towel: "maybe it is and then again maybe it isn't." For, in a second sense, the discursive narrator is also correct. Van *can* get used to anything so long as it does not require a display of the *positive* pliability—self-originated, renovative adaptations—of the sort that Hochman has in mind. In the negative sense of the term "pliable," he is indeed the ultimate conformist whose minimal exertions ever take the line of least resistance, with each situation defining for him what the easy way is. For example, Toby is wrong when declaring what happened during Van's shipwreck experience was "regular murder"; there was nothing "regular" about the chief engineer's drowning of Brann. To protest, though, is to complicate his life; and Van "shut[s] his teeth against answering." Then he consumes oysters, an omelette, and a pint of claret "with delicious enjoyment." Conformation to what appears the "official" version of the event obviates the troublesome and immediately allows for pleasure. Is it possible that Norris was thus deliberately fashioning a dialectic of sorts, inviting the reader to consider "pliability" both as accurate and ironic in its import?

Once the discursive narrator is brought back upon stage, Naturalism itself merits reconsideration in light of what Hochman has shown. There are four essays in which Norris clarifies his sense of the meaning of the term; and they may be profitably reviewed after finishing *The Art of Frank Norris, Storyteller*. The review, "Zola's *Rome*" (1896), quickly puts one in mind of Hochman's distinction between the formulaic naturalistic glosses and the stories *per se*. While Norris notes how Zola is "faithful to the gospel of Naturalism" when giving attention to the heredity of Benedetta in *Rome*, the word choice, "gospel," mildly suggests that Norris, like Hochman, has heard it all before. More important, while duly observing this ideological element, Norris only notes it. He gives the lion's share of attention to Zola's storytelling, which left him "breathless." He had found the novel "crammed with tremendous and terrible pictures, hurled off, as it were, upon the canvas, by giant hands wielding enormous brushes." A few weeks later, in July 1896, appeared "Zola as a Romantic Writer"—in which Norris again touched only lightly upon the ideological, with a reference to Jacques Lantier who is "haunted by a heredity insanity." That's it. The emphasis instead falls upon how, in the plot of a naturalistic tale, characters "must be twisted from the ordinary, wrenched out from the quiet, uneventful round of every-day life, and flung into the throes of a vast and terrible drama. . . ." The historically focused finale of the essay distinguishes between Zola's writings and both old-style romances and realistic fiction (Howellsian): Naturalism is a new form of Romanticism, "this drama of the people" set in a modern milieu. Norris hardly reduces himself to the type suggested by the ideological narrator described by Hochman. Indeed, Norris's definition of naturalistic art is remarkably fluid: in "Frank Norris's Weekly Letter" of 3 August 1901, he offers a new image, superseding that of 1896. Naturalism now stands between Realism and Romanticism—synthesizing the best from the opposed traditions. Norris thus appears much more the literary historian than the deterministic thinker. Hochman's interpretation, then, can be further bolstered. For, the *littérateur* rather than the *philosophe* stands forth.

At the same time, though, one returns to the fact that Norris was familiar with the ideology and did embrace it in his own fashion. In the 1896 review of *A Summer in Arcady: A Tale of Nature*, we find him employing the voice of the discursive narrator as his own when describing James Lane Allen's handling of the sexual nature of the relationship between his hero and heroine. The naturalistic language anticipates that of *McTeague*: increasingly randy Hillary and Daphne "are little better than natural, wholesome brutes, drawn to each other by the force of nature, . . . irresistibly, blindly, moved only by an unreasoned animal instinct." The modern reader will not be inclined to dismiss the content of the phraseology, for Norris is thus celebrating Allen's frankness. He appreciates his willingness to picture positively a natural development in non-Victorian terms; he admires Allen's "naturalistic point of view" on man as a sexual creature in a novel then appearing as naughty as it now appears innocuous. Norris is quite up-to-date regarding our mores today—as he was in "'Man Proposes': No. 2" the same year. It is a comic treatment of the sexual crisis developed in the second chapter of *McTeague*.

In short, there are instances in which one profits from taking seriously the language viewed as old chestnuts. One really should not sweep them aside, especially since the review of *A Summer in Arcady* positions one to read in a new way Norris's attitude toward Mac's traumatic, first experience of arousal in chapter 2 of *McTeague*. The traditional reading is that Norris participates in Mac's hysterical response to the vile "monster" suddenly awakened; but his use of naturalistic imagery to summarize approvingly Allen's uncensorial depiction of the same awakening invites the notion that "something else" is transpiring in *McTeague*. Indirect discourse may be more present in chapter 2 than has yet been observed, just as it is patently being utilized in the description of Van's attitude toward the sexual "brute" within his personality. Mac and Van do not think the way Norris clearly did in

1896 or in 1901 when, in "A Plea For Romantic Fiction," he straightforwardly identified "the mystery of sex" as worthy of literary investigation.

When Hochman turns from *explication de texte* to her secondary consideration, the autobiographical significance of the discursive narrator, it turns out that those lamentable chestnuts she finds contradicting and obscuring the more important themes are useful in another way. For, as the characters reveal themselves through *their* stories of the-way-things-are, so does Norris-the-storyteller. Via the naturalistic glosses, he attempts to exercise his own control over what Faulkner termed the "furious motion of being alive." The furious, which is ever susceptible to blurring as it is imaged, could be conceptually tamed via the Zolaesque formulae. Allusions to the winds of chance, the genetic inheritance from an alcoholic father, a too-pliable nature, irresistible environmental forces, the appointed movement of wheat through its appointed grooves, and like formulations provided a "temporary stay against confusion." They offered Norris a stability, a conceptual clarity, and a fixed definition amidst the flux of experience being pictured in the works. The "literature" and "life" relationship in Norris's mind, so often considered by his interpreters, thus receives a promising illumination: that literature served a life-shaping function for him. The canon, as the Freudian critic will quickly note, thus becomes the chronological record of Norris's attempts to come to terms with the fluid nature of reality which so many of his characters would not accept. Confirmation of this reading by Hochman develops gradually. If true, the logical outcome concerning a maturing, more confident Norris would be the gradual reduction of the discursive narrator's ideological explanations, which Hochman sees occurring in the later works. Speculating on what he might have gone one to, had he not died at thirty-two, Hochman extrapolates to a Norris even less formulaic because better adjusted to the often shapeless flow of events.

Will this biographical interpretation be accepted? At present, that seems unlikely. "Simplicity in Art" (1902) suggests that a change in style was on the agenda, for the aesthetic values articulated in that essay contradict his big bow-wow work in *The Octopus* and *The Pit*. Perhaps fuller analysis of the canon will provide more verification of Hochman's interpretation of Norris's personality development; closer descriptions of the 1901–02 writings may possibly win the day. But, given the way that *The Octopus* has been read for decades, Hochman will still have a difficult time eliciting assent to her assertion that the discursive narrator pronouncing naturalistic formulae had paled. One thinks especially of the critics who may not countenance the idea that Norris employs indirect discourse; they will most likely see the discursive narrator just as present in the later works as he was in the earlier ones.

Further, that narrative voice, ever eager to comment on the force represented by the wheat in the last novels, carries a good deal of weight in Norris criticism, as well as in larger circles represented by works such as Ronald E. Martin's *American Literature and the Universe of Force* (1981). Those who have developed their interpretations of theme by, in effect, approaching *The Octopus* as a leitmotif enhanced by a plot (rather than a plot complemented by a leitmotif) will not take kindly to a diminution of that narrative voice which repeatedly articulates the "epic of the *wheat*" and interprets it. The wheat, with which the discursive narrator appears infatuated, has the status of a main character in the interpretive literature. Indeed, one might waggishly complain that it has been interpreted too often as the hero of the novel. Thus, the many critics viewing Vanamee and/or Presley as *confirming* what the discursive narrator has stressed concerning the benign qualities of nature typed by the wheat will not, one suspects, be willing to sacrifice a major source of evidence for such a reading.

But even those who share Hochman's view of Presley *not* being Norris's spokesman will not be able to discount the significance of the discursive bombast. Critics in what Richard Allan Davison has lightheartedly but earnestly dubbed the "Vanamee vanguard" will, as they continue to champion the visionary shepherd as seer, not be alone in resisting the downplaying of the ideological pronouncements. Those who agree with Hochman's diagnosis of Vanamee's malady-ridden psyche will probably balk as well. Finally, even readers who suspect that the leitmotif of the wheat simply got out of control and flawed an otherwise fine novel about life in the San Joaquin Valley may hesitate—despite the truly positive service rendered by Hochman as she brings the much more engaging stories of the human characters to the surface of the text of *The Octopus*. Her sweeping away of all of that damned wheat, so that one can see the human beings more clearly, is the rarest of all gestures in literary criticism, an act of kindness. Once dusted off, the actual main plot—concerning human behavior rather than a *zeitgeist*'s—does stand in high relief as what it is. That is, Hochman is correct in seeing what is *most* important; but she still needs to devise a way of putting the relentless commentator on the wheat into perspective. That Norris himself distinguished between the "wheat motive" and the "story," or plot, in a November 1901 letter to Isaac F. Marcosson is a promising starting point.

This monograph, then, is remarkable not only for the many new observations it offers but for the way in which it raises unsettling questions concerning the works examined and the rest of the canon. It provides many challenges meriting positive responses from other interpretive storytellers (as the trope turns), now that Hochman has offered her scenario. And one wonders what Hochman herself will find next as she further examines the implications of her own conclusions, in the larger context of the whole canon. One hopes that she will also go on to test her notions in a more macrocosmic way by comparing the practice of other naturalists, and that she will consider the possibility of expanding her concept of Naturalism itself. It should be allowed a broader definition than that to which it is presently restricted. The restrictions seem a part of the problem with which Hochman has wrestled. The author who dubbed works as different as *McTeague* and *The Octopus* naturalistic, and who described so genteel a novel as *A Summer in Arcady* with the same word he applied to Zola's, should not be boxed in the way he has been for decades. Hochman's analysis opens many new possibilities for a better definition of Norris; it also draws one to the promise of someday making the term Naturalism more an aid than a hindrance in the fashioning of American literary history.

Worry, Wogs, and War

Kinley E. Roby

Cecil D. Eby. *The Road to Armageddon: The Martial Spirit in English Popular Literature, 1870–1914*. Durham: Duke University Press. 1987. x, 286 pp.

D. C. R. A. Goonetilleke. *Images of the Raj: Southeast Asia in the Literature of Empire*. New York: St. Martin's Press, 1988. x, 182 pp.

Wendy R. Katz. *Rider Haggard and the Fiction of Empire: A Critical Study of British Imperial Fiction*. New York: Cambridge University Press, 1987. x, 172 pp.

In *An Autobiography* Ingmar Bergman writes, "Most of our upbringing was based on such concepts as sin, confession, punishment, forgiveness and grace. . . . This fact will have contributed to our astonishing acceptance of Nazism." Not at all astonishing. Ethnic monotheism in its several manifestations has invariably provided, as Joseph Campbell repeatedly illustrates in *The Masks of God: Occidental Mythology*, "throughout the breadth and length of the history of religion in the West, the chief occasion for a sordid, sorry chronicle of collision, vituperation, coercion, and spilled blood." The invasions of Greece and, more catastrophically, of the Levant by aggressive herding populations, structured in a patriarchal order, who entrusted that order to their gods, brought with them group-specific ethnic monotheism in which the revelation of truth confers on those adherents a special blessing or set of blessings, from which nonadherents are absolutely excluded.

One result of the imposition of these tribal or clan belief structures on large populations, either by force of arms or proselytizing, has been the laying of a groundwork for endless strife—not only between adherents and non-adherents but within the group of adherents itself as, inevitably, factions with special interests lay claim, again exclusively, to an interpretation of the revelation or the laws. Such interpretations support their depredations, carried out in the name of or under the protection of their god. The Levant invasions by virulently aggressive and culturally intolerant populations of cattle-, sheep-, and goatherders produced over time three systems of monotheistic belief—Judaism, Christianity, and Islam—which would profoundly affect the West. The "spilled blood" followed, and follows still.

It would be impossible to read the books by Eby, Goonetilleke, and Katz without coming to the conclusion that the first and fundamental cause of the physical, psychological, social, and political mayhem recorded in the history of British imperialism, both at home and abroad, and vigorously, sometimes shrilly, advocated in a stunningly large segment of a vast literature published in Great Britain between 1870 and 1914, is adherence to a form of ethnic monotheism that justified and even encouraged bellicosity, xenophobia, and cultural myopia. All this was matched with a boastful, self-righteous, grandiose, and bullying aggressiveness that, supported by a superior industrial technology, resulted in the annexation of immense geographical areas and their indigenous peoples in the name of profit and God.

That it was a debased, co-opted, unintelligent form of Christianity that provided the impetus is of little consequence. It was the version subscribed to by the overwhelming majority of the population and the one exploited and publicly supported by a frighteningly large number of churchmen, teachers, writers, and politicians. It was the one that allowed H. H. Monroe's sister, who was not criminally insane, to accompany her brother to Victoria Station on his way back to the front and the fighting at Somme and to shout across the barrier as he boarded the train, "Shoot a good few for me." She meant Germans, of course, but almost anyone not English would have sufficed. As it worked out, someone shot him instead, a development not provided for in the imperial romances of the day.

Two short passages of scripture from the many available, one from the Old Testament and the other from the New, will serve to illustrate where the impetus for empire originated. The first is from Isaiah 54:2–3: "Enlarge the place of your tent, and let the curtains of your habitations be stretched out; hold not back, lengthen your cords and strengthen your stakes. For you will spread abroad to the right and to the left, and your descendants will possess the nations and will people the desolate cities." The second is from Matthew 24:14: "And this gospel of the kingdom will be preached trougout the whole world as a testimony to all nations; and then the end will come." This sort of thing requires little explanation. If the record of history is anything to go by, people die for metaphors all the time, kill for them even more frequently, and luxuriate in culturally sanctioned abominations of every sort.

In looking at the literature between 1870 and 1914, which all of the books under scrutiny have done in their various ways, one is almost stunned by the bombast, bluster, boasting, and aggressive posturing in it. One is even more struck by the anxiety, dread, distrust, psychological pain, and outright hysteria that is also there. The latent content of the national neurosis that deepened after 1870 to the psychotic acting-out that began in August 1914 and went on for four horrific years is everywhere evident in the texts Eby, Goonetilleke, and Katz explore.

The fostering myth is of an England whose empire encompassed the world, established by the natural superiority of the English race and underwritten by an approving God who has given His (definitely not Her) chosen people the solemn task of grabbing as much of the earth as possible, bringing light to the dark places of it and Christianity to the "subject peoples." In contrast, the latent content of the myth is of a pervasive individual confusion and profound personal alienation, of incipient guilt and deep self-doubt verging on self-loathing, as the writings of George Orwell, Joyce Cary, E. M. Forster, and Paul Scott make abundantly evident. The violence, the exploitation, the degradation visited on both master and man by the functioning of the empire expose the myth for what it is, a lying mask of virtue and prowess covering an egregious, cowering, and pathetic folly. Of course, no cultural condition is so simple that it can be accounted for by any single named cause. But the point about religion is worth making, nevertheless, because over and over again in the imagery, in the appeal to first principles, in the unexamined assumptions underlying the action, the faith of their fathers comes shining through.

If they do nothing else, Eby's, Goonetilleke's and Katz's books make two things abundantly clear. When it comes to the treatment of cultural issues rooted in the national psyche, there is little difference between so-called serious fiction and popular fiction. The combined outpouring of high and low art draws on a common source of inspiration existing in the cultural bases of the community from which it springs and to which it addresses itself. And a national cultural neurosis, apparently, like murder, will out. The books arrange themselves in an interesting way. Eby is primarily concerned with popular literature, although his book ranges over a variety of topics. Goonitelleke explores "the permanent works of literature about the Raj" (p. 3). And Katz unpacks H. Rider Haggard, whose trunk of improbabilities from *King Solomon's Mines* (1885) onward brought him astonishing acclaim, a huge reading audience, and an incalculable opportunity for destructive mischief. The kind of mischief meant is of the sort that would naturally emanate from the mind of a man who could and did record in a diary entry of January 1916, "In some ways I think the war is doing good in England." The result of their efforts is a surprising commonality of judgment, with Eby and Katz far more critical of their subjects than Goonetilleke, who exhibits a gentle tolerance for the shortcomings and excesses of his subjects—Kipling, Woolf, Forster, Orwell, and Scott.

Ruskin got things off to a rattling good start in 1866 in a speech delivered at the Royal Military Academy. "All the pure and noble arts of peace are founded on war," he said. "No great art ever yet rose on earth, but among a nation of soldiers." He was just getting warmed up: "All healthy men like fighting, and like the sense of danger; all brave women like to hear of their fighting, and of their facing danger" (Eby, p. 1). That such dangerous claptrap, passing as social Darwinism, could be aired in a public place is surprising enough. That the speech could have been made in a time of general peace for Great Britain is even more perplexing. But that it could have been made following the carnage of the American Civil War and all the horrors that it entailed argues strongly that Ruskin should have been committed. As Eby points out, however, the spreading social Darwinism of the sixties made it possible for a respected scholar such as Ruskin, and he was not alone, to advance such a theory and gain a respectful hearing. War came to be seen as a testing ground for national character. And as though to drive home the idea with shot and shell, the lightning Prussian defeat of France in 1870 convinced the English of the possibility of a future war, a war that would be fought along entirely different lines from those which existed in the Napoleonic era.

Eby looks at popular literature between 1870 and 1914 in order "to isolate and interpret the tides of militarism and xenophobia which prepared the public for the Great War of 1914–1918" (p. 9). The writers to whom he gives particular attention are H. G. Wells, William LeQueux, Henry Newbolt, William Barrie, Rudyard Kipling, Arthur Conan Doyle, Rupert Brooke, and George Thompkins Chesney. If some of these are not household names, it is only because it is no longer 1910. We are familiar with Wells and *The War of the Worlds*, but fewer of us know Chesney's *The Battle of Dorking*, an invasion novel first published in *Blackwood's Magazine* in May 1871 and reprinted in a sixpenny pamphlet which sold 80,000 copies. In the first year following the publication of the story, nine books were published repudiating Chesney's vision of an England ground under the German heel. But Chesney had touched an already-raw nerve of anxiety in the English public. A host of invasion narratives followed, and for the next forty years the English terrified themselves with tales of Germans, Russians, Frenchmen, and even the Chinese landing at Dover. It was not only in fiction that this sort of semi-hysteria flourished. Music hall songs, brass bands, boys' magazines, sermons, politicians' jeremiads, even hymns—"Onward, Christian Soldiers" is a well-known example—fanned the flames of super patriotism and muscular Christianity.

Eby tells us that these invasion narratives appeared with such regularity and were read with such interest that when war finally came, it arrived "like an ancient prophecy at last fulfilled" (p. 9). T. H. Huxley, coming at the problem from another direction, spoke and wrote glumly about humanity's future. He thought society and nature worked at cross-purposes. Herbert Spencer authored the possibly misconceived and certainly misapplied phrase, "survival of the fittest." When Wells came along, he sensed the "bizarre appeal which apocalyptic literature had for an audience raised on the Bible" (p. 39). Both Kurtz in Conrad's *Heart of Darkness* and the narrator of *The War of the Worlds* "found his meliorist assumptions, bred by civilization, displaced by scenes of unforgettable horror" (p. 43). And these futuristic novels, particularly of the sort written by Wells and Richard Jeffries, pictured a world wiped clean of the human race or literally bombed back into a preindustrial age.

But perhaps no other segment of society was so drenched in a literature of war propaganda, drilled in xenophobia, and raised as champions of jingoism as that which came to manhood around 1914. Eby asserts that "boys' magazines consistently prepared their readers for wars in the future" (p. 73). Probably more sinister in its long-term effects were two youth organizations. The first was the Boys' Brigade, founded in 1883 in Glasgow by Sir William Alexander Smith, who was looking for a way to control the rowdy working-class boys in his Glasgow Sunday School (Eby estimates that there were about two million boys who were alumni of the organization, not counting the hundreds of thousands who belonged to other groups that were offshoots of the Boys' Brigade). The second was the Boy Scouts, launched by Robert Baden-Powell in 1907. B-P, commander of the Mafeking garrison during the Boer siege, founded the group partly in response to the wishes of Lord Roberts, his former military commander, who wanted rifle shooting and martial arts made compulsory in schools, universities, and the Boys' Brigades in order to prepare them to join the Territorial Army he was trying to form. One week after the declaration of war, Lord Kitchener, yet another veteran of the Boer War, was busily organizing the New Armies for slaughter at the front. He wrote to B-P, "What a splendid thing this war is for you!" (Eby, p. 71).

Two other influences impelled B-P toward the scout movement—his book, *Reconnaissance and Scouting* (1884), and his friendship with Ernest Thompson Seton, who had written *The*

Birch-Bark Book of Woodcraft Indians. In 1907, B-P wrote *Scouting for Boys,* which may be the third-ranking bestseller in the English language after the works of Shakespeare and the Bible. Together with the public schools, Scouting served a sinister purpose prior to the Great War by helping to prepare the minds of thousands and thousands of boys to accept the war and the sacrifices war required as an unquestioned responsibility. Those same boys were not trained to question anything that institutional authority demanded—especially if that authority were draped in school colors or the flag.

Children of both sexes, as well as their parents, were conditioned by a series of plays and entertainments carrying similar messages. In 1904 James Barrie, a profoundly disturbed man, brought *Peter Pan* to the London stage with thunderous success. It became a children's classic in its first performance. Over the ensuing years thousands upon thousands of children were taken by their enraptured parents to see the play. No one seemed to notice the "sinister features of the play . . . the gratuitous violence, the repudiation of adult and bourgeois values, the blatant appeal to do-or-die patriotism, and the necrotic messages," such as Peter's being dressed in cobwebs and autumn leaves (p. 131). Even Wendy's rallying message to the boys who were prisoners on the pirate ship went unchallenged: "I have a message to you from your real mothers, and it is this, 'We hope that our sons will die like English gentlemen'" (Eby, p. 135). Mr. Darling, the rational man, is relegated to the doghouse.

It seems impossible to take issue with Eby's summary statement that popular literature and "its impregnation with xenophobic and paranoid warnings of Armageddon did assist in creating a climate of popular opinion that almost unanimously cheered the decision of Parliament to declare war on imperial Germany" (p. 128). It seems, looking back on the period, inevitable that disaster was a-making. Added to the sycophancy of the aspiring middle class who wanted their sons to become gentlemen and were unwilling to raise their voices in criticism of the gothic follies that passed for education in the English public schools, was a pervasive decadent romanticism fostered in those schools. Such romanticism encouraged permanent intellectual adolescence as an ideal and fostered a general paranoid delirium involving sadistic/masochistic persecution fantasies and spying fetishes.

How could it have been otherwise in a culture that raised its ruling class to believe a vital parallel existed between children's games and life, that fostered an endemic siege mentality, that harped with hysterical insistence on English superiority, and that gave its allegiance to a value system that measured success in terms of force? Is it really any wonder that the declaration of war was greeted with almost universal approval by the British public of every class and economic station?

G. M. Young, the English historian, is reputed to have lectured his students, "Read until you hear the people speak." Goonetilleke is convinced that, at its best, British colonial literature makes the voices of the Raj audible. He also asserts boldly that the best colonial literature will help both the British and those who were colonial people to understand themselves better. He admits that the challenge for the literary critic (and, I would add, the reader) is great. The English critic must liberate himself "from the imperial culture to which he belongs, while an Asian critic has to face the problem of freeing himself from his colonial heritage" (p. 3). The modern reader must be equally alert.

A Sri Lankan, Goonetilleke comes at the issue of imperialism the opposite way from which western readers usually encounter it. Perhaps not surprisingly but, for me at least, disturbingly, he is of the three writers the least condemnatory. In fact, he repeats what has been said many times by other commentators: that Leonard Woolf's *The Village and the Jungle* remains the best work of fiction in English about Sri Lankan life. Even his treatment of Rudyard Kipling is gentle. Goonetilleke insists with initial sternness that T. S. Eliot, Bonamy Dobree, C. S. Lewis, Nirad C. Chaudhuri, and Shamsul Islam have either sidestepped or discounted Kipling's politics. "But I think Kipling's politics have to be faced squarely: they lie behind, if not in the forefront of, his writings and pervade his work" (p. 20). This confronting is very softly accomplished. Goonetilleke finds much in Kipling to admire and is satisfied to call him "an extraordinarily liberal imperialist" (p. 42). He particularly likes *Kim* and regards it as "a unique masterpiece" (p. 56) with only *A Passage to India* in the same class. He finds nothing patronizing or condescending in *Kim:* in his view the Llama is the true hero of the story, the theme of which is spiritual quest rather than the less challenging search that Kim makes for personal identity or mastery of the Game, in which the English seek to indoctrinate him.

Goonetilleke considers the Llama "an absolutely original creation of Kipling; he has no forerunners and, so far, no descendants in English literature" (p. 47). Joyce Cary's Mister Johnson seems equally original and a product of a similar split within his creator. Of course, Johnson is hanged and the road-work ended, whereas the Llama has his vision and may win Kim away from the Game. But the split is there. Both novels reveal their authors' inability to close the division between the western mind and its African or Asian opposite. True, in the "Ballad of East and West" Kipling gives as gospel that East and West don't exist between "two strong men" standing face to face, but *Kim* denies it. The problem is that Kipling can't find a way for Kim to follow the Llama and remain an Englishman. T. S. Eliot couldn't "surrender" to Buddhism for much the same reason, although he wished to remain a European. Neither man seems ever to have caught on to the fact that the hindrance was internal and not external.

Goonetilleke looks to the Elizabethan period for the beginnings of both "the exotic as well as realistic traditions of literature about developing countries" (p. 7). And he sees imperialism as the energy that produced a desirable social revolution in India, Celon, and Burma. While granting that "self-interested economic motives" formed the primary impetus for imperialism, he finds in it a degree of altruism and political motivation (p. 5). The Raj for him is a distinct unit of space, a finite period of time, which produced its own literature. *Blackwood Edinburgh Magazine* was its voice, and Kipling, Woolf, Forster, Orwell, and Scott its important interpreters. On the whole he finds their work admirable and worthy of preservation; they were the recorders of "a new moral order" (p. 6). If he has read Edward Said's study of orientalism, he has dismissed its conclusions.

Katz is much less sanguine than Goonetilleke. Her study of

H. Rider Haggard is a withering attack on imperialism, made almost exclusively from within Haggard's writing, which she describes as being intimately, intensely linked to his historical era. For her, his was the voice of imperialism in the period leading up to World War I. She makes a compelling case for saying so. By working with writers who practiced a "high art" form of the novel, Goonetilleke is able to appeal to qualities in the writing that takes attention away from underlying issues of racism, distorted views of the nature of life based on crippling neuroses, as well as unexamined assumptions involving a broad spectrum of social issues—such as "going native," as Kipling has it. With Haggard, by contrast, the raw stuff of imperialist thought is spread out for clear viewing. It is not a pretty sight, but it certainly is diverting.

Haggard was an almost ideal conscript to the imperialist cause. He was born in 1856 on a 400-acre estate in West Norfolk in a period of agricultural prosperity. His childhood and adolescence were happy and privileged. But the depression of 1870 ended it all and sent the nineteen-year-old Haggard to South Africa just in time to play a minor role in the struggle in the Transvaal among the Zulus, the Boers, the English. He raised the British flag over the Transvaal in April of 1877. And by a wonderful irony, the negotiations which led to the return of the Transvaal to the Boers in 1881 were conducted in the farmhouse to which Haggard had recently brought his new bride.

Haggard was deeply humiliated by the outcome of the negotiations. He wrote that he "suffered the highest sort of shame, shame for my country" (Katz, p. 12). It had all come together: the privileged and entitled child, who had been driven out of his home and had landed on his feet in a foreign country where his status was insured by military force, saw that force defeated and the land which he considered to be England's by a kind of divine right lost to the perfidious Boers. Disgusted and financially pressed, he returned to England in 1882 to study law and to begin writing. With *King Solomon's Mines* (1885), his first successful novel, undertaken after his having read a favorable review of *Treasure Island,* he was launched on a literary career. In the next year and a half he wrote *Alan Quartermain, Jess,* and *She,* all to an excited and enthusiastic reception by readers and critics.

He had progressed from a very junior colonial bureaucrat to an ostrich farmer to a lawyer to a novelist. From 1886 onward he wrote a spate of novels set in far-off places, contemporary novels set in England or Europe, and nonfiction books about agriculture, the Salvation Army, and coastal erosion. In 1895 he ran for Parliament on the Unionist ticket, lost, and vowed never to run for office again. He hated the political realities and called them "indirect corruption" (Katz, p. 14). He did not like having to defend his political and social theories in a public forum. He much preferred to express them through the medium of his fiction.

And what theories! Coming together in his fiction are a congeries of ideas and attitudes that are the ideological underpinning of the imperial age. He draws together sundry elements of class conflict, domestic policy, party politics, foreign policy, racist ideology, and imperialist idealism, the last being "the erection of a monumental image of the state as an object of reverence wholly idealized" (p. 25). The imperialists in general sought to transfer the allegiance of the working class away from its class and to the nation. They sought the achievement of unity as the outstanding characteristic of imperialism and through it to solidify the state's power, "justify its practices, and mythologize its greatness" (p. 21).

To underline the kind of totalitarianism toward which imperialism tended and to which Haggard's fiction gave encouragement, Katz quotes Viscount Milner on the political liberalism that opposed the imperialist views: "'The influence of representative assemblies, organized upon the party system, upon administration—"government" in the true sense of the word—is uniformly bad'" (p. 24).

But how did the works of a second-rate yarnspinner have any influence for either good or evil on the body politic of England? Katz responds by asserting that, while Haggard may have a minor place in the history of literature, he was of considerable cultural influence. She further suggests that "a dynamic relationship exists between late nineteenth-century imperialism and the literary climate of Great Britain, the development of romance literature being the most striking by-product of this relationship" (p. 4). Robert Louis Stevenson, W. E. Henley, Rudyard Kipling, H. Rider Haggard were all rank imperialists and all reached, through writing and editing, millions of readers over a very long stretch of time.

The ideology espoused by Haggard and the others solidified over time into a recognizable imperialist ideology and gained enough currency to become settled as the typical system of beliefs of British society. Haggard's characters, in Katz's reading, crave a world of excitement and sensuousness to replace the monotony and emptiness of their own lives. Haggard's fiction, most especially his romances, surrounds the vanishing rural world with nostalgia. It avows the existence of absolute truths. It sentimentalizes the Africans, the child, the past, and nature. It systematically distorts reality in order to bring a false and fleeting relief to the disaffected. His romances satisfy a desire for power and exhibit a logical congeniality with messianic interpretations of Empire and with notions of ruling-class stability, both of which depend upon *a priori* truths.

In Haggard, as in the writings of Stevenson, Kipling, and Kenneth Grahame, there is a marked ambivalence toward freedom. Katz points out that, in *The Wind in the Willows*, Rat is persuaded not to go to sea with the seafaring rat, that Long John Silver and Mr. Hyde are both "free" men, and that, in *Kim* and the *Jungle Books*, aimless freedom brings on anarchy. The monkey people exhibit the consequences of just such freedom. There is no doubt that Haggard's authoritarian, imperialist vision was messianic. He once told the Anglo-African Writers' Club, "I don't believe in the divine right of kings, but I do believe in a divine right of a great civilizing people, that is in their divine mission" (Katz, p. 50). That mission, as he wrote elsewhere, was to conquer and hold in subjugation.

Like Milner, Haggard mistrusted majority representation and the party system. He also disliked bureaucracy. Just what kind of government he did favor is uncertain. He had a vague notion that governments should "take a firm hand" and should be made up of "men," a character rather than a gender specifier. He saw imperialism as an agent of moral regeneration. In his novels there is everywhere projected a deep sense of insecurity, masked by aggression. His heroes are freebooters, and, like so much of the popular art of his time, his novels show a "fervid preoccupation with manhood"—Manhood narrowly defined in public school terms of being able to absorb punishment without flinching and to "play the game."

Haggard's heroes are part of the defensive reaction of romantic fiction against Darwin. They deny their biological origins and reject the tyranny of factory whistles and machine-dominated society. Like other fictional heroes of the period, they grow increasingly virile and physically aggressive, and they become addicted to foreign places. Realistic fiction in the hands of Hardy, Flaubert, Gissing, and Bennett took the opposite direction, portraying characters less and less free, less and less able to control their environments.

Beneath Haggard's ideal of the hero as a figure whose secular actions bear a religious significance and who comes as a stranger-hero to a dead or plague-ridden land (the white man's arrival in the land of the black; see *Allan Quartermain*) lurks a profound fatalism. He believed in "an ultimate and pre-existent order" (p. 87) in the universe. He always and fundamentally required the support of an ulterior frame of reference, a rationale for life, a fatality. His heroes represent and believe in a transcendent universal moral order, and his villains believe in chance—which is another way of saying that he lived in fear of freedom. His beliefs led to the creation of a literature that in "its excessive dependence on watchwords and formulas, its sanctioned prejudices and antipathies, goes a long way towards fostering a limited moral consciousness" (p. 154).

Had his been a solitary voice grumbling on the fringe of the national culture, it would not be worth deciphering. But Haggard's voice articulated the disordered dreaming of a vast population who found no other way to deal with the complexity of modern industrial life, the falling away of religious belief, the increasing conflict between classes with essentially conflicting interests, the fading glory of world domination, and the general conviction that things were worse than they used to be. No other way except to turn away from the problem, assisted and encouraged by political and class leaders eager to exploit the disorder for personal advantage, to convert individual anxiety, frustration, anguish, and doubt into a national hatred and project it outward toward France, Russia, China, and, fatally, Germany. Spilled blood, the holocaust of the trenches, and wholesale destruction followed.

Plantagenet England on Display

Jean F. Preston

Jonathan Alexander and Paul Binski, eds. *Age of Chivalry: Art in Plantagenet England, 1200–1400.* London: Royal Academy of Arts, in association with Weidenfeld and Nicolson. 1987. 575 pp., 748 plates + 123 figures.

A magnificent exhibition took place in London during the winter 1987/88: the galleries of the Royal Academy, a very eighteenth-century building, were transported into the Middle Ages. Splendid gothic-looking props suggested gothic pointed arches within the classic rooms, which were filled with medieval books and objects of all sorts. They all were "made in England" during the gothic centuries, 1200–1400. Anyone lucky enough to see this exhibition must long remember the dazzling effect of so much color and variety—whether in stained glass windows (at a suitable height for really seeing what they represent without craning the neck) or the sparkling Crown (#13) bedecked with pearls, sapphires and rubies, part of the dowry of Blanche, daughter of King Henry IV. And nearly a hundred manuscripts of different kinds, some of them historical documents (starting with a 1297 confirmation of Magna Carta as #1), some of them literary or theological texts, and many of them illuminated manuscripts, their gold leaf shining.

The catalogue of this exhibition is not only a reminder of the occasion, but a book to be kept and pored over afterwards. With more than forty scholars contributing to the descriptions, it contains too much information to digest quickly, and is in any event far too heavy to carry around the cases. It is a vast exhibition catalogue containing twenty-eight prefatory essays by twenty-six different scholars, before the catalogue proper even begins on page 194. Eight European countries lent objects, and there were a dozen loans from the United States (all from New York or Baltimore). About one hundred and sixty lenders in the United Kingdom, from the Queen down, both public and private, added to the richness. Every one of the seven hundred and forty-eight exhibits is illustrated, often in color, and there are also one hundred and twenty-three illustrations to the prefatory essays; so *Age of Chivalry* is sumptuous indeed, and a medievalist's delight whether or not the reader was able to see the exhibition.

From the title of the exhibition, one might imagine that *Age of Chivalry* would contain a good deal of arms and armor, and that manuscripts would be of the Froissart variety—only English ones of course—with miniatures of battle scenes. But this is not the case: the scope is far larger, and the materials shown are very wide-ranging. Of the twenty-eight preliminary essays, one of the shortest is by Claude Blair on "Arms and Armour," pages 169–70. Other short articles include topics like "Decorative Wrought Iron," "Pottery," and "Tiles"; these are not exactly chivalric, but give some idea of the scope of the coverage. There were accounts, documents, and texts for the historian, coins for the numismatist, seals for the sigillographer, pictures of cathedrals and other buildings for the architect, and literary texts for the Middle English enthusiast ("Sir Gawain and the Green Knight" has pictures which also interest the art historian, as do manuscripts of Chaucer, Gower, or Hoccleve, #718–21). There was something for everybody interested in Medieval England, be they historian, literary critic, musicologist, art historian, craftsman, general scholar, or curious tourist. The article on "Manuscript Illumination of the 13th and 14th Centuries" is one of the longer preliminary essays, pages 148–56, jointly prepared by Nigel J. Morgan and Lucy Freeman Sandler, the authors of consecutive double volumes in the series *Survey of Manuscripts Illuminated in the British Isles* edited by Jonathan Alexander. So we can be sure that the manuscripts are authoritatively selected and described by experts in their special fields. Often these descriptions incorporate new research, as the writers are specialists in their areas and keep abreast where they do not themselves lead the way.

Plantagenet England on Display 249

One of the attractive features of the exhibition was the juxtaposition of items brought together from afar. Sometimes this consisted of two separated parts of the same object, such as the Ramsey Psalter, five folios of which are in the Pierpont Morgan Library in New York (M302) but a much larger section of which (one hundred and seventy-three folios) lives in Austria, in the Benedictine Abbey of St. Paul, St. Paul im Lavanttal. It was exciting to see the two parts reunited as #565–66 in the same case of Section XIV. One longed to turn pages, and examine more than the two openings exhibited. Here the catalogue is muddling: one page is reproduced in color (7 x 5 inches) and one in black and white (3 x 2 inches), without a clarification of which is the New York and which the Austrian miniature; the difference in size makes them hard to compare (both are reduced from an original of nearly 11 x 8 inches). The next item is another East Anglian Psalter (#567), the Peterborough Psalter sent from Brussels. Here the very small reproduction ($3\frac{1}{2}$ x $2\frac{1}{4}$ inches) in black and white is very different from the full-page color reproduction on the cover of Lucy Sandler's book, showing the very distinctive green and red ruling. Perhaps it was considered that this Psalter was well enough known, or sufficiently reproduced elsewhere, for a small black-and-white picture to suffice. But there are larger color reproductions of the equally well-known Tickhill Psalter (#568) lent by the New York Public Library, and the De Lisle Psalter (#569) from the Bodleian. It was wonderful indeed to see all these and other Psalters displayed alongside each other. Here again the tiny $3\frac{1}{2}$-inch x 2-inch, black-and-white plates of Gorleston (#574) and Ormesby (#573) are too tiny to compare details; Luttrell (#575) has a larger plate, in color. All are big books, and the catalogue can only be a reminder. More thirteenth-century Psalters were gathered in earlier cases, and later ones in the "Edward III" section. The index lists their disparate numbers under "Psalters," bringing them together for the reader.

Five great thirteenth-century Apocalypses (#347–51) are brought together: Paris, Morgan, Trinity (Cambridge), Bibliothèque nationale, and Douce (Oxford). Another four Apocalypses are dispersed in different places in the catalogue: the

Lambeth Apocalypse of comparable date (#438) is in the section "Medieval Artists and Their Techniques" because it is open at a monk painting a statue of the Virgin and Child. Three fourteenth-century Apocalypses are scattered in other places: #11 is under "Kingship," and shows a Coronation text and miniature, in the same hand as the preceding Apocalypse texts and commentary, all here discussed. Under "Pilgrimage" #40 is open at scenes from the life of Edward the Confessor, bound with an Apocalypse, described but not illustrated; #203 is under "Towns and Merchants" because it displays miniatures in the *Gesta Infantiae Salvatoris* preceding an Apocalypse, probably illustrated by the same artist, and here related to other manuscripts, too. These examples illustrate the selectors' problems of choice, where only one opening can be shown from a multi-content manuscript, but more than one text or miniature are exhibition-worthy. An item description of the whole manuscript can therefore be more informative to the reader in his study than to the viewer at the exhibition; several catalogue descriptions are far more valuable for putting that particular manuscript in relation to other manuscripts—a scholarly function—than for describing the one opening shown for the general visitor to the exhibition. These comments make the catalogue valuable to scholars afterwards.

Catalogue illustrations can be very generous. Item 564 is a retable from a Suffolk church, and it has four illustrations; only on careful examination does one realize that the first plate is a reduced black-and-white image of the whole, the fourth a large colored plate of a detail, the second a comparable panel painting from Paris (not in the exhibition), and the third a detail of the Paris panel, in rather dark color. Incidentally, these two non-exhibited plates are numbered "Figures 131–132." Most of the other "figures" accompany the introductory articles, where references to figures 131 and 132 are very hard to find (they are on page 448).

Plates do vary in size, so that plate 1 of Magna Carta, 1297, is ridiculously small, reduced to about quarter size; other documents also (#443–45) have plates far too small to read. The Missal of Henry of Chichester (#108) was lent by the John

Plantagenet England on Display

Rylands University Library of Manchester, and has a 7-inch x 5-inch colored plate; this is repeated as a 9-inch x 5½-inch color plate on the back cover, where it is not identified. The manuscript description refers to the manuscript as a whole, rather than to the exhibited page or plate, so there is no explanation of the three small lions grimacing on the steps of the throne, before the Virgin and Child adored by a cleric, presumably Henry of Chichester himself (as the book is his Missal).

The exhibition had wonderful things to see—such as the Gittern (#521) with very detailed carving of the wood, with foliage and figures. This was a real show-stopper in the exhibition, but even a colored plate reduced to about a quarter of the size can give no idea of the delicacy of the carving. The misericords come off better; it was thrilling to see half a dozen of the best, brought together from Lincoln, Worcester, Chester, and Oxford. Here the black-and-white plates, though reduced, give a very good idea of the originals. Hand-drawn maps from time to time usefully show the geographical relationships of the various workshops.

This is one of the areas where the links between different media can be so interesting: misericords have a lot in common with drolleries in margins of manuscripts. The same English sense of humour pervades painting and carving. A good example of such a link is the Swinburne family silver pyx (#571), and a Book of Hours (#570) made for Alice de Reydon, a member of the Swinburne family. Both have Nativity scenes which are very close in design (figure 25 on page 53, compared with plate 570). The catalogue is useful at showing interrelationships both visually and descriptively.

Sometimes the arrangement seems confusing. There were three manuscripts of Matthew Paris, in three different rooms (#315 in room 9 for "Henry III," #346 in room 10 for "Edward I," and #437 in room 12 for "Medieval Artists and Their Techniques"). It would have been nice to have put them together. Overall the arrangement was odd: a mixture of topic and chronology. Some rooms, and some chapters, were devoted to a single reign, others to a subject such as "Kingship," "The English Church," "Peasants," or "Cathedrals." Section 7 has a wonderful assemblage of "Lords lying on high on their graves," in effigies and in stained glass; these representations are vivid and realistic both in stone and glass, and the plates splendid. But why is there an Annunciation to the Shepherds, in color, in the middle (#228)?

I noticed a couple of mistakes that slipped through: #356 talks of the Alfonso Psalter, while #357 spells it the Alphonso Psalter. And page 297 informs us that "the Gothic style of architecture . . . was brought from England to France in the 1160's and 1170's"; presumably the "from" and "to" should be reversed, as it is generally thought that Gothic began in France and spread to England.

There is an excellent bibliography, some 2500 entries in twenty pages of four columns each. The references in the item descriptions are ingeniously simple: "Morgan 1977" can refer to N.J. Morgan or F.C. Morgan whose works are listed fully in the bibliography, and "Bennett" can be A. Bennett, J.A.W. Bennett, or B.T.N. Bennett, but the year clarifies which one is meant. For example, "Bennett 1986a" refers to a specific article by Adelaide Bennett, published in 1986, the title listed in full in the bibliography; "Bennett 1986b" to one by J.A.W. Bennett, also published in 1986 and listed in full in the bibliography. In the English way, authors have only initials rather than spelled-out first names; this used to be such a nuisance in card catalogues, but is less so in these days of on-line computer searches.

The year 1988 was a spectacular one for outstanding manuscript exhibitions and catalogues. Another English catalogue is the Bodleian's *Duke Humfrey's Library and the Divinity School 1488–1988;* despite its title it contains descriptions of well over a hundred pre-1500 manuscripts, with a number of black-and-white plates. A small American catalogue, *Saints, Scribes and Scholars,* is a thirty-two page record, with eight plates, of the exhibition of manuscripts at the Free Library of Philadelphia in 1988. A splendidly full catalogue of twelfth-century manuscripts, not limited to bibles, is Laura Light's *The Bible in the Twelfth Century,* for Harvard's exhibition at the Houghton Library; the thirty-nine exhibited manuscripts have full codicological descriptions and commentaries, with twenty-five black-and-white plates. Even fuller is *Time Sanctified: The Book of Hours in Medieval Art and Life*, the catalogue by Roger S. Wieck of his show at the Walters Art Gallery in Baltimore, with essays by Lawrence R. Poos, Virginia Reinburg, and John Plummer, containing a wealth of new matter and well over a hundred black-and-white plates and forty in color. Here at last is a definitive work on Horae in English, of inestimable value to any describer of these manuscripts. Barbara A. Shailor analyzed the ingredients of a codex for the Beinecke exhibition, *The Medieval Book;* this catalogue will be especially useful for teaching codicology and manuscript description, as it has over a hundred manuscripts of many kinds, selected to illustrate their variety, with numerous plates (eight in color). Also in 1988 came an exhibition on loan from Scotland, *The Glory of the Page: Medieval and Renaissance Illuminated Manuscripts from Glasgow University Library;* this was shown in Toronto, Houston, and Richmond as well as in Glasgow. There are about one hundred and twenty manuscripts and about a dozen early printed books, all described with interesting commentary in the excellent catalogue by Nigel Thorp, with forty-two color plates, as well as many in black and white. But all these catalogues are dwarfed by the huge *Age of Chivalry,* in size, in splendor, in width of coverage, and in overall value to the scholar. Whereas the other catalogues are of manuscripts mostly in single collections, *Age of Chivalry* is the opposite; it is a bringing together for the first time of related manuscripts from many different sources with art objects of all kinds. Similar trends can be seen in misericords, ivories, tiles, embroidery, stained glass, and manuscript decoration. Scattered objects are brought together (some from unexpected places like Norway) to throw new light on both familiar items and related pieces.

The exhibition was an unqualified success, with crowds of people on each of the six successive days I was able to go. The catalogue is certainly one to keep and belongs in any research library. It is packed with a mass of information about a great many objects and interrelationships. Art flourished in England during these two centuries. Despite the losses during the Reformation and Civil War destructions, there still remains much to be proud of—and this catalogue is one of the few places where the

Englishness of England's medieval achievement in art can be seen. Jonathan Alexander and Paul Binski, both expatriate English art historians now teaching in the United States, are indeed to be congratulated on their awesome achievement in locating, assembling, describing, illustrating, and placing in context seven hundred and forty-eight very English medieval manuscripts and works of art. Their *Age of Chivalry* catalogue is a book of lasting value.

Author, Intention, Text: The California Mark Twain

Guy Cardwell

Union Catalog of Clemens Letters, ed. Paul Machlis. Berkeley: University of California Press, 1986. xi, 465 pp.

Mark Twain, *Early Tales and Sketches, Vol. 1, 1851–1864*, eds. Edgar Marquess Branch and Robert H. Hirst, with the assistance of Harriet Elinor Smith. Published for the Iowa Center for Textual Studies. Berkeley: University of California Press, 1979. xxii, 789 pp.

Mark Twain, *Early Tales and Sketches, Vol. 2, 1864-1865*, eds. Edgar Marquess Branch and Robert H. Hirst, with the assistance of Harriet Elinor Smith. Published for the Iowa Center for Textual Studies. Berkeley: University of California Press, 1981. xx, 763 pp.

Mark Twain, *Adventures of Huckleberry Finn: Tom Sawyer's Comrade*, eds. Walter Blair and Victor Fischer. Published in cooperation with the University of Iowa. Berkeley: University of California Press, 1986. xxii, 451 pp.

Mark Twain's Letters, Vol. 1: 1853–1866, eds. Edgar Marquess Branch, Michael B. Frank, and Kenneth M. Sanderson; associate eds. Harriet Elinor Smith, Lin Salamo, and Richard Bucci. Berkeley: University of California Press, 1988. xlvi, 616 pp.

Edward Gibbon, according to Henry Digbe Beste (1829), was permitted by the Duke of Gloucester, brother of King George III, to present to him the second volume of *The Decline and Fall of the Roman Empire*, the prince having earlier accepted the presentation of the first. Gloucester received the author "with much good nature and affability" and remarked as Gibbon laid the new volume on a table, "Another d-mn'd thick, square book! Always scribble, scribble! Eh! Mr. Gibbon?"

The editors of "The Mark Twain Papers and Works of Mark Twain" have now presented to scholars eighteen damned thick, square books made more or less in accord with Greg-Bowers bibliographical principles, six additional volumes in "The Mark Twain Library" (derived from these scholarly texts and intended for the general reader), and two relatively extraneous publications under the heading "Other Mark Twain Project Publications" (meant for whoever is concerned). The numbers keep changing, always mounting upward, but seventy of the scholarly volumes (those in critical editions) were recently projected. The addition of popular volumes would, one supposes, run the total a great deal higher. Clearly this is a project of exceptional magnitude and importance in the history of scholarly publishing, one that will run through many years and through many generations of editors. If present plans are fulfilled, editors will end by reprinting all of the published writings and by printing for the first time all of the literary remains of Samuel L. Clemens.

The appearance in mid-1988 of volume one of Twain's letters (1853-1866) serves, then, as the occasion for a partial account of the editing of Mark Twain prefaced by a brief survey of relevant features of the quarrelsome modern history of the creation of what are usually called "critical" or "eclectic" texts of American authors. A hint of the complexity of the issues attendant on the publication of texts of Mark Twain is suggested by noting that by 1968 five volumes of correspondence were planned with two volumes to appear in 1971, three more in 1972; in 1980 it was estimated that the letters would fill twenty volumes; and in 1982 three volumes of the letters were advertised by the University of California Press to be ready in the fall of that year. The first of those volumes has just now reached print. Although a second volume in expected momentarily, history indicates that, in these highly problematic matters, moments can stretch into eternities.

Editorial practices may be said to have been a matter of scholarly concern in the Western world for more than three hundred years; yet, significant as the development of textual bibliography in America has been over the past four decades, the critical editing of American texts (meaning primarily of nineteenth-century American texts) is a recent phenomenon and is still evolving. At present, descriptive, analytical, and textual ("scientific") bibliography have little to do with the usual reprinting of texts for popular consumption. In fact, so far as the non-critical texts published by university presses are concerned (with the exception of "clear" texts made from critical texts), their preparation does not seem to have been greatly influenced by the methods and practices of the bibliographers. It may be argued that, primarily because of rising costs, editing is permitted by many presses to be increasingly slack with respect to such details as accidentals, notes, lists of works referred to, and indices.

According to *Professional Standards and American Editions: A Response to Edmund Wilson* (1969), an abortive attempt in the direction of critical editions was initiated in 1948–1949 by the "Definitive Editions Committee" of the American Literature Group of the Modern Language Association. (Bibliographers today continue to speak of a "definitive" edition but not, as some earlier ones did, of a "definitive" text—*ça n'existe pas*.) This committee, which must have had little understanding of what it was getting into, failed to raise money and so did not engage in any publishing ventures.

Using seed money from the American Council of Learned Societies and the MLA, a second attempt towards critical texts was made during the years 1963–1966. In 1967–1968 the newly authorized National Endowment for the Humanities made available to the Center for Editions of American Authors of the MLA a grant of $300,000. (Beginning in 1976 the CEAA was renamed the Center for Scholarly Editions, still later the Committee on Scholarly Editions. It is usually referred to here as the Center.) The learned ship was at last afloat, though, as things developed, it was leaking at numerous seams. Money for the Center, for editors, and for presses doing the actual publishing has come from the federal government and from a variety of other sources. The Center itself has changed its nature over the years. At first it allocated funds from the NEH; later, editorial projects applied directly for grants. According to various editors, the Center also changed its tone, becoming less prescriptive, less rigid, more open to different kinds of editing.

The granting of those first funds from the NEH became a focus for one of the most bitter ideological-monetary squabbles in American literary history. Edmund Wilson, a versatile, nonacademic man of letters, at the time the best known of America's "public" critics and highly respected by most scholars, began the affray but was joined promptly by a modest cohort of sympathizers, both lay and academic. The wrangling which followed—not yet altogether over—was, then, not strictly a conflict between town and gown. It was exceptionally virulent and involved name-calling, displays of ignorance, and a profusion of factual inaccuracies. The case may be conveniently reviewed by drawing upon Wilson's *The Fruits of the MLA* (1968; originally published in the *New York Review of Books*, 26 September and 10 October 1968) and the MLA reply *Professional Standards and American Editions*. These pamphlets include, somewhat corrected and made more temperate, many of the documents which had appeared earlier in periodicals.

Wilson had in mind a project for publishing selected American "classics" for general use. The books would resemble those in the French Pléiade series or in one of several other European series. Almost everything should be edited anew, he thought. He contradicted himself by calling for the publication of everything by major writers, though not by minor ones, then demanding that what he took to be unsuccessful works be omitted from the canons. Certainly the texts should be readable. He approved the application by Jacob Epstein, the publisher, to the Bollingen Foundation for funds to bring out "in a complete and compact form" the principal American classics, saying in a letter of 18 August 1962 that he had been trying for years to interest some publisher in the idea. The Bollingen Foundation decided that the project was not within its scope, but the new NEH, or so Wilson believed, first set money aside for it, then "whisked the funds away" because the MLA managed to have the grant suppressed in favor of its own project for reprinting the American classics in accord with the principles of textual bibliography.

So far as American writings are concerned, probably the most spectacular "respectable" publishing success of our time has been achieved by the Library of America. The Library nods politely towards the bibliographers by using clear texts of critical editions that happen to be available at reasonable prices; otherwise it makes no attempt to print either diplomatic editions (exact reproductions) or critical editions. Instead, it selects the best available text of the work to be published, makes obviously necessary emendations, adds a minimum of apparatus, and prints handsome, well-bound, reasonably priced books on acid-free paper. These books offer, one judges, no competition to the volumes given the MLA seal of approval; and they fill a popular need. (The first Mark Twain volume sold approximately 25,000 copies within a very few months.) In them the Wilson ideal may be said to have been belatedly realized.

Lewis Mumford, who himself edited a volume of Emerson's essays and journals in 1968, brought the disagreement over editorial practices into the open when he published a review entitled "Emerson behind Barbed Wire" in the *New York Review of Books* for 18 January 1967. In this essay he attacked the critical edition of *The Journals and Miscellaneous Notebooks of Ralph Waldo Emerson*, published by the Harvard University Press. (Editorial policies were fixed, and three volumes of this series were already in print and three more in process by the time the MLA Center was established.) Mumford charged the editors with printing too much trivial material, including material that Emerson had asked to be destroyed, and with squandering a subvention on a pedantic text that was made unreadable by the use of no fewer than twenty diacritical marks. Mumford's essay provoked both agreement and dissent and gave Wilson an immediate incentive to lead a highly public assault, conducted mainly in *The New York Review of Books*, on "MLA editions." To ensure that what might otherwise have been an ephemeral vendetta would not go unremembered, Wilson gathered—with a few revisions and added remarks—pieces hostile to the MLA into the pamphlet mentioned earlier. On its side, the MLA assembled and reprinted in a pamphlet (mentioned above) the more effective ripostes made on its behalf.

Wilson generated initial support for his opposition to the MLA by addressing a letter to thirteen persons of importance in the worlds of literature and scholarship and to President Kennedy. He received sympathetic replies from thirteen. Perry Miller, of Harvard, was the only respondent to equivocate: he mentioned "the difficulties of preparing authoritative texts" but concluded that "the project on Hawthorne, to cite only this one, . . . is perhaps more 'academic' than the average reader needs."

As the quarrel widened in letters and essays, a number of scholars voiced resentment at the tone as well as the substance of Wilson's animadversions; and it is true that a splenetic temper marked his complaints. He satirized the MLA as an organization and spoke of its pretentious ineptitude. He believed that the bureaucrats of the MLA—abetted by their allies in Washington—were making ill-judged and sterile publications that obstructed republication in any other form. He also complained at length of the defects of Justin Kaplan's *Mr. Clemens and Mark Twain* (1966) as representing another department of the American literary industry: Kaplan was not an academic but "the competent journalistic hack" who, like the mediocre professor, "can make a reputation for himself by seizing on some well-known author." Most professors were, it seems, academic hacks, selfishly motivated, afflicted with parasitical careerism, trying to clamber up the ladder towards recognition and respectability. This opinion apparently applied especially to those attached to state universities in the Middle West, for Wilson wrote derisively of the editing that was then being done at Ohio State University, the University of Iowa, and Indiana University. He took Howells's *Their Wedding Journey,* edited at Indiana University, to be "the reductio ad absurdum of the practice of the MLA" and rather meanly ridiculed the celebration that was held when it was published.

Turning from the Middle Western editors, who were to him very small game, Wilson brought a worthier opponent under his guns—Fredson Bowers, of the University of Virginia. Wilson was, he said, on friendly terms with Bowers; nevertheless, he charged him with being the "great Demiurge behind all this editing" and quoted a critic who remarked that in editing *Leaves of Grass* Bowers "had done everything for it but read it." Bowers was the general textual editor for the Centenary Edition of Hawthorne, published by the Ohio State University Press. Wilson termed *The Marble Faun* "the masterpiece of MLA bad bookmaking": the volume was impossibly weighty, the paper was bad, the textual introduction and textual notes were excessively voluminous, and the historical introduction contained useless information. Although some variants recorded were of interest, Wilson wrote, the mass of apparatus accompanying the text was not; its only value was for the gratification of "the very small group of monomaniac bibliographers."

Pursuing a remark made by Mumford, Wilson objected to having a writer's "garbage" served up to the public, considering this to be a sign of pedantry. University libraries like to preserve garbage; candidates for the doctorate use it for their own purposes. This greed-for-garbage is indicative of a failure to discriminate; and discrimination is needed to distinguish between interesting drafts and uninteresting resources: "But of anything like discrimination these MLA editors do not have a gleam, or if they have, they are afraid to reveal it."

A stung and stinging swarm of professors and of academic bureaucrats answered Mumford and Wilson in personal letters, in public letters to the *New York Review of Books* and other periodicals, and either at length or by allusion—open or covert—in extraneous essays and articles. William M. Gibson, then Director of the CEAA and heading those responsible for the unreadable Emerson, denied knowing what had happened to the money supposedly allocated by the NEH to Epstein's projected series and gave assurance that there was no serious difference between Mumford's views and those of the MLA editors: it is only a matter of realizing that a scholarly text must precede a clear (readable) text, he insisted. Full collation and full reporting are essential to produce "the ideal text—the text the author wanted."

Several of the scholars writing about the construction of texts tended to misuse words like "definitive" and "ideal" simply because they had not absorbed the Greg-Bowers vocabulary, misconceived the nature of texts, and failed to understand the role of subjectivity in editing. Their positions were likely to be inconsistent. Gibson, for example, suggested a perfect correlation between textual bibliography and exactitude by his use of the word "ideal" and by his certainty that editors can produce what the author wanted. Ambivalence is hinted, however, when he falls back upon "instinct": "The editor . . . by a kind of instinct that is acquired only after long immersion in the thought and feeling and style of his author may be able to detect, and emend, printer's misreadings."

The importance of the scientifically prepared text was a topic frequently recurred to. Bowers, though he did not enter directly into the controversy, argued the importance of the cumulative effect of changes made in an author's accidentals. Gibson argued characteristically that errors in texts give writing "a different texture" and that alterations in nuances of meaning may be crucial, as in the interpretation of poems. Without properly prepared texts, no one could say whether a work is moderately accurate, and no authoritative text would exist on which to base reprints.

M. H. Abrams, of Cornell, and Morton W. Bloomfield, of Harvard, well-regarded scholars, saw the issue as unnuanced, querying whether Mumford and Wilson wanted to make available texts the author did not write or wrote only in part. Oscar Cargill described Wilson as a critic who once displayed brilliant promise but whose graph "has shown a bearish trend in the last two decades" and who has now dipped into the abyss of an ill-tempered attack on the MLA.

Wilson's conviction that academic editors were not intelligent enough to discriminate (yet should discriminate by printing some variants but not others) drew irritated replies. His view that professors exploit authors for the sake of professional advancement and are jealous of intruders in their fields led Gordon N. Ray, President of the Guggenheim Foundation, to protest that the Wilsonian "attack derives in part from the alarm of amateurs at seeing professional standards applied to a subject in which they have a vested interest." The American learned world had come to full maturity since the Second World War, Ray added, and animus like Wilson's, displayed in field after field, had been discredited. In the long run, "professional standards always prevail."

By virtue of his position as Executive Secretary of the MLA, John H. Fisher assumed the role of a major spokesman for scholars, scholarship, and literary criticism. He preferred not to correct the many factual errors made by Mumford and Wilson nor to answer Wilson's attacks on individuals; his wish was to put the matter in perspective. Only two editions of American authors, he wrote, can stand without major revisions and additions—those of Sidney Lanier and of Emily Dickinson. (The edition of Dickinson has in fact come recently under sharp attack.) No other existing editions are correct or complete enough for scholarly use. The text of Emerson depreciated by Mumford is intended for thousands of scholars all over the world. What Mumford and Wilson take to be garbage ought to be printed: because "artists are the barometers and seismographs of a culture, the better we understand them, the better we can understand the ambiguity of experience. Such understanding is the only justification for literary criticism. The way we achieve such understanding is by reading everything an author wrote—as he himself wrote it."

Gibson had explained that the Center did not favor giving lesser work of lesser writers the complex treatment given to major writers, nor did it favor furnishing financial support for such effort. Fisher added the explanation that the CEAA had committed itself to nine authors because "these are indisputably major figures." (Washington Irving, Stephen Crane, and William Dean Howells were among the nine, and other authors, William Gilmore Simms among them, were added as university presses undertook to republish them.) Provided funds became available, the Center would "like to add Cooper, Poe, and Henry James." (Three volumes of a Poe edited in accordance with obsolete and in fact hardly discernible principles had been printed by the Harvard University Press before it discontinued the series.) Fisher also reviewed some of the circumstances under which the "Constellation" series proposed by Epstein lost the funds allocated to it by the NEH. The MLA invited Epstein to meetings, informed him of its relevant activities, and urged him to arrange for the republication of prepared texts. Epstein and the then Executive Secretary of the MLA became members of a committee of the NEH which recommended that $300,000 be made available to initiate the MLA project and $50,000 to initiate the Constellation volumes, provided appropriate machinery for the administration of the project could be arranged. Because no such machinery was developed, the funds were not made available.

Exchanges having to do with the editing of Mark Twain are of special immediate interest because of the focus of this review. Wilson cited a student-editor at the University of Iowa, one of a team of thirty-five engaged in the editing of Twain's published works, who thought the entire project "a boondoggle" and complained that eighteen students were reading *Tom Sawyer* "word by word, backwards" to ascertain answers to such momentous questions as how many times "Aunt Polly" is printed as "aunt Polly." This, even though the Hinman Collating Machine showed no serious problems in the state of the text.

Paul Baender, both a general editor and the chief textual editor at Iowa, explained that, while scholars at his university were editing Twain's published works, others at California were at work on the unpublished papers. He then tried to justify the Iowa method of proofreading and charged Wilson, as had others, with inconsistencies and lack of editorial principles. John Gerber, chief general editor of the Iowa project, calculated that approximately fourteen volumes would take care of the unpublished papers being edited at California (now it is estimated that the letters alone will fill twenty volumes) and assured Wilson that the texts made available in cheap editions would contain no footnotes or other paraphernalia inserted by the editors other than a short introduction and explanatory notes. (In fact, the paperback *Huckleberry Finn* contains more than two hundred pages of apparatus.) It is apparent that in 1968 the editors at Iowa, to mention only that group, knew little more than did Edmund Wilson about where they were heading. Poets, as Shelley put it, "are the mirrors of the gigantic shadows which futurity casts upon the present": scholars, one judges, are less vatically sensitive.

Frederick Anderson, of the Mark Twain Papers at Berkeley, made some telling points about editing that probably came as news to Wilson. Anderson noted, for example, the need for the principled selection of a text, as when there are several manuscript versions to choose from. (He could have added that a principled choice is needed whenever two or more versions of a text—whether manuscript or printed—are available and that even if only one text is at hand, unless a diplomatic edition is desired, principles should control each correction or emendation.) He also defended the presentation of *all* of Twain's previously unpublished works, rejecting the idea of relying on editorial judgments to decide what might be of interest to the ordinary reader. (When Anderson himself published an edition of the first volume of Twain's notebooks in 1975, he printed only "representative selections" of the thorny, generally uninteresting notes that Clemens made as *aides mémoires* when he was learning to be a pilot on the Mississippi. It is also true that the editors at Berkeley do make decisions about what to print and what to omit in the case of some of the volumes printed for the general reader in "The Mark Twain Library.")

Wilson went to a good deal of trouble to examine scholarly volumes and to reply to professorial assaults on him. He happily called attention to errors in proofreading and to grammatical blunders, and he took pointed exception to features in the scholarly volumes that he did not like. On examining *Mark Twain's Satires and Burlesques* (1967), edited by Franklin R. Rogers, he concluded that these papers have no interest whatsoever: a reader already knows that Twain published "so much uninteresting clowning that there can be very little point in salvaging any he rejected." On looking through *Which Was the Dream?* (1968), edited by John S. Tuckey, he recommended that "Three Thousand Years among the Microbes" be omitted from the canon as "rambling, labored and boring." Tuckey, he held further, was inadequate in his explanatory treatment of "The Great Dark." Nevertheless, Wilson anticipates with interest the coming publication in three volumes (none of which has as yet appeared) of Twain's *Autobiography*. Replying to the call for exclusionary editorial judgments, Frederick Anderson chided Wilson for wanting "Three Thousand Years among the Microbes" omitted and queried whether he would object to the publication of the Autobiographical Dictations if he found passages less interesting than anticipated.

The work done on critical editions of American authors over the past two decades has demonstrated that Wilson was simply wrong to think that all such editions are either unreadable or otherwise incompetently made. Assuming that one accepts the privileged role of the author, as Wilson assuredly did, empirical evidence also indicates the unacceptability of the implication that texts reprinted according to old-fashioned publishing-house standards are quite good enough: such texts sometimes preserve hundreds of departures from the author's text and generally add new errors. On the other hand, rationale, methods, and praxis of modern bibliography were by no means so veridically certain and immutable as suggested by most of those who answered Wilson. (Gibson did, in fact, apologize for the "prescriptive and even magisterial tone" of the Center's 1967 "Statement of Editorial Principles.")

Rancorous internecine warfare within bibliographic ranks has been frequent, not so much over Greg-Bowers principles as over details of praxis—details that have to be worked out afresh for each text published.[1] Certain large, tacit understandings by presses and by academic editors have been arrived at: for one, no edition resembling the unreadable, expensive Belknap Emerson from Harvard has been attempted; for another, largely because of the costs involved, university presses have in general learned to think twice before they plunge into multi-volume, "scientifically" edited projects.

No one would now hold with Samuel Johnson that the use of type and the publication of works by their writers preclude "conjectural criticism." If the rationale for textual criticism holds, bibliography should flourish, for modern printing methods and practices preserve old forms of corruption and generate complex new ones. Disagreement among bibliographer-critics also flourishes. Dissatisfied comments are made about the practice with respect to details for almost every volume of each critical edition of an American author as it appears; and, a graver matter, profound differences over rationale have made themselves known.[2]

Reverberative questions about the assumptions and policies of bibliographers have been raised within the academy. It has been argued repeatedly that the manuscripts of numerous nineteenth-century authors, including Mark Twain, are essentially drafts, meant to be refined by the author and by others en route to the form given them in print. Acceptance of the conception of a text as a cooperative enterprise has obvious bearing on the choice of a copy-text. A reply to this argument by G. Thomas Tanselle is that an editor must be cautious about attributing authorial intentions or preferences to alterations "simply because they were passed, in one fashion or another, by the author."[3]

A common related argument is made that although a verbal change in a short poem may be important, in a long prose work the few corruptions likely to occur will be of little moment to the reader. This assumption has frequently been rebutted by the citation of examples of corruption occurring in quantity. Bowers reports that even though the first printing of Hawthorne's novels had the author's approval, there are thousands of accidental variants between the manuscript and first printing; this means that "the real flavor of Hawthorne cumulatively developing in several thousand small distinctions can be found only in the manuscript." If variants are few, they may nonetheless be important, for, it has been argued, some aspects of a novel are not repetitive. In such instances, if anything is omitted or obscured, it is lost forever.

Tanselle, among others, holds that editions of several kinds have their special uses. It is also widely recognized that strict objectivity is not possible; subjectivity is both inescapable and necessary at every turn. Greg himself, who is, as Tanselle notes, flexible, practical, and expedient, insisted that textual criticism may never be reduced to a code of mechanical rules. Paul Maas warned of "the tyranny of the copy-text." Although Bowers is more skeptical than is Greg about letting the editor's judgment enter into choices among substantives, he notes that in a critical edition, "editorial responsibility cannot be disengaged from the duty to judge the validity of altered readings in a revised edition." The editor tries to produce a text close to "the author's original and revised intentions." Disciples speak of avoiding "inconsistency and uncontrolled subjectivity." Subjectivity is thus a readily conceded or a grudgingly acknowledged feature of editing.

Wilson's allegations that MLA-sponsored editions were produced by self-serving petty bureaucrats and academic mediocrities who lacked the capacity to discriminate or to exercise aesthetic judgments did not pass unchallenged. Editors must be as objective as possible; yet they must be, and presumably are, possessed of capacities and skills that give them the right to make subjective judgments. A single editor needs (or a corps of editors needs to possess collectively) a thorough knowledge of publishing and printing practices and of the author's life, handwriting, methods of composition, and habits of revision.

By this view editing is not "a mere mechanic art" nor are textual bibliographers "vile mechanics." Vinton A. Dearing offered up a brief hymn to the Euclidean joys of editing: he sees a Petrine "new heaven opening"; he hears the Jobian "morning stars sing together and all the sons of God shout for joy." James Thorpe asserts more soberly that "all textual decisions have an aesthetic basis or are built on an aesthetic assumption and it is idle to try to dissociate textual grounds from aesthetic grounds as the reason for our choice."

Not all bibliographers, to be sure, experience work-induced religious-aesthetic ecstasies. After serving for a period as an editor for the Center, Paul Baender—though he defended the editions produced as a major achievement—indicated that textual editing had its drawbacks. For a person of his disposition, he decided, it finally becomes intolerable.[4]

Disagreements within the academy about such things as subjectivity-objectivity are intensified when edited volumes are scrutinized. Baender, who describes some of Wilson's remarks as "cheap shots of no argumentative value," identifies as comparable the "stylized clichés" used by Hamlin Hill in an article entitled "Who Killed Mark Twain." Even so, he writes that those who examine the books before the Center awards them its seal of

Author, Intention, Text 269

approval have at times been fussy, dogmatic, arrogant, inconsistent, and unknowledgeable as to the ways of the authors whose texts they inspected. Furthermore, Baender criticizes adversely the Northwestern-Newberry edition of Melville's *Pierre* for its documentation of trivia and for Hershel Parker's contribution to the "Historical Note."

All scholarly editions appear to have had their problems.[5] There have been changes in editors, in editorial practices, in publishers, and in presses. Most presses seem to have suffered disappointments with respect to the regularity with which manuscripts have been submitted to them. The cost of scholarly editions and the lack of interest exhibited by possible purchasers have given ammunition to critics attached to the Wilson camp, enabling them to scoff at claims that texts made by trained bibliographers are important to thousands of scholars and readers all over the world.

The Washington Irving edition lost the sponsorship of the University of Wisconsin Press. A reviewer has charged that editorial practices for the different volumes have been inconsistent; some of its volumes are not indexed; its notes are badly done; its policy is inconsistent from volume to volume with respect to the choice of a copy-text; and its introductions are uneven in merit. Its editors are accused, moreover, of mishandling such details as Latin phrases and the names of English peers.[6]

Wilson was not the only one to view the Hawthorne unfavorably. A scholarly reviewer considered the critical apparatus for *The Marble Faun* to be cumbersome and repetitious; the analysis of internal bibliographic evidence to be tendentious and narrow, without regard to pertinent linguistic and lexicographic evidence; the "normalization" of variants often to run counter to Hawthorne's artistic and linguistic intentions; and the adherence to a predetermined editorial practice to result in the inadequate handling of problems special to *The Marble Faun*. This is to mention only some of the problems with a volume supposed to serve as a model for the editing of American texts.[7]

One must add, to palliate adverse criticisms, that reviewers who have criticized the Hawthorne volumes or volumes in the other editions sponsored by the MLA have nonetheless considered the editorial achievements to be full of interest and the books to be monuments to scholarly industry.

The Belknap Emerson, the efficient cause of the Wilson-MLA polemics, came to a quiet, somewhat inglorious end. It was completed in sixteen volumes. received NEH assistance, kept its editing practices unchanged, and was awarded the CEAA seal of approval for its later volumes. A highly selected, one-volume, clear-text edition of the journals appeared in 1982. On the adverse side, as typesetting for the critical edition was very costly, the price was high and sales did not go well. Press runs were cut back from three thousand copies to twenty-five hundred, then two thousand, and finally fifteen hundred. An additional expense was entailed by the need to reset in order to print the clear-text volume of selections. To the best of my knowledge, no press has since undertaken so nearly unreadable a critical edition.

Twayne Publishers, which took over the edition of Irving and the selected letters of William Dean Howells, brought books out more slowly than they would have liked and sold fewer of them than they had predicted. Instead of printing a hoped-for 2,000 to 3,000 of the Irving, they printed on average 750 copies, and they found it necessary to increase prices. Except for some help from the NEH, the press would have lost money on the series. Wisconsin, which sold the rights to the series to Twayne when the NEH did not approve a request for a grant, had similarly meager sales.

New York University Press considered the technical details of the production of its Whitman to be unusually difficult, the repeated applications for grants to be necessary but burdensome, and found that, while manufacturing costs mounted, sales declined from about 2,000 to 1,000 copies per volume. The Indiana University Press received help from a foundation or it could not have afforded to publish the Howells: in 1983 no volume had sold as many as 2,000 copies, only six as many as 1,000. The Press has licensed a limited number of reprint rights to other publishers.

Editorial offices for the Thoreau Edition were moved from Princeton to the University of California at Santa Barbara, but the Princeton University Press continued to be the publisher. Replacing experienced editors with new ones who know

Thoreau well has been a problem, and funding has offered difficulties for both the editorial office and the Press. Perhaps in part because Thoreau published only two books in his lifetime and because the published selections from his writings were edited and cut in unacceptable ways, sales have been relatively good, running from about 2,500 to more than 9,000 for some volumes. A paperback edition of *Walden* sold approximately 27,000 copies.

Systemic problems of sales and money beset the University Press of Virginia, which published the edition of Stephen Crane, edited by Fredson Bowers. During publication, print runs were cut from 3,000 to 2,000. The Press received no outside help, had disappointing sales of permissions to other publishers, was only partly successful in efforts at remaindering unsold copies, and took a large direct loss on the project. Apparently the series received only one notice by a reviewer who knew Crane well; and this reviewer of the first two volumes published was sufficiently unhappy about the editing to raise serious questions. Why not print the canon in chronological order? Why not check the entire canon before arriving at solutions for single works? Why did the editor miss a printing of an abbreviated *Maggie*? Why not place the voluminous editorial matter at the backs of the volumes? Should an editor regularize Crane, a writer who was careless in the preparation of his manuscripts, inconsistent in punctuation, spelling, syntax, and grammar? Bowers is said to show great diligence and to be at times ingenious in his textual introductions; but "at others, he is embarrassing," as when he tries to explicate the psychology of a prostitute and thereby defend a textual reading. This reviewer also criticizes severely the general introductions to the volumes, which are by other scholars, not by Bowers.[8]

A great theoretician is not necessarily a great practitioner, but that texts made by Bowers, the master, should be subject to harsh criticism must raise some concern about the state and validity of textual criticism. The lay person asks with the Persoun, "if golde ruste, what shall iren do?" or, "*Quis custodiet?*" The intent of nearly all criticism of this sort is not, however, to destroy the institution—textual criticism is left intact; critics are expressing dissatisfaction with the execution of principles that they more or less accept. Their demand is for similar but better editing.

Vexing theoretical questions are, nevertheless, posed from time to time and are debated by bibliographers. Are the hypotheses of bibliographers adequate? Are eclectic texts either desirable or possible? The intimated field of inquiry is a large one and could be expanded indefinitely, but fortunately a capable bibliographer, Tanselle, supplies a thoughtful *vade mecum* to the progress of textual criticism and the debates about it.

Greg established the fundamental principles of scholarly editing of post-medieval literature in "The Rationale of Copy-Text" (1949). For the purposes of the editing of American texts, the most important addition to Greg was made by Bowers in "Some Principles of Scholarly Editions of Nineteenth-Century American Authors" (1962). Greg's theory of copy-text was "scientific in its central impulse," but as Tanselle indicates, his recommendations on moot points tend to be flexible, expedient, and pragmatic—more so than those of Bowers and of a number of the epigoni—especially the earlier American ones. The *Grundprinzip* of the Greg-Bowers theory is that the author's intention or, as Bowers sometimes puts it, the author's final intention, must control choice of copy-text and serve as a guide for emendations.

In the course of the debates that have arisen, supposedly solid principles for editing have come, in some eyes at least, to resemble quicksand. For practical and psychological reasons the author's "intention" has been an obvious target for discussion. Textual bibliography both inflates and makes impossibly definite a bafflingly indefinite word. Does Mark Twain positively intend to have his wife excise his socially offensive opinions and his vulgarisms or does he simply suffer her to do so? Should the vulgarisms that William Dean Howells deleted from *Huckleberry Finn* be restored to the text? When Twain did not rebel against having his spellings and punctuation "normalized" by copyreaders did he approve of what was done? If the scholarly editor wishes to recapture Twain's "final" intentions, should he print at least in notes late emendations made by Twain in the Barrett copy of *Life on the Mississippi*? Did Twain intend to have editors condense and rewrite? Was it only "to accommodate the publisher's convenience," as the California edition of *Huckleberry Finn* puts it, that he authorized the removal of the "Raftsmen's Chapter" from *Huckleberry Finn*? What if his intentions—like those of Emerson that were disregarded by his editors—with respect to unpublished papers were *purement et simplement* not to print? Certainly his intentions, if the word means anything, were not consistently aesthetic: they could be primarily commercial. Does anyone ever know what someone else intends? Is the author himself always sure?

The "author" proves to be little more stable than are his intentions. There is the whole great, amorphous, modern problem of the nature of "the Self," together with less daunting uncertainties. Who, or what, is the author? When Hawthorne's preferences are not observed in a copy-text, should editors repunctuate or should they instead try to preserve the intentions of Hawthorne's publishers? When Twain encouraged others to bowdlerize or otherwise to edit him, did an inclusionary principle set in that made them co-authors? When he accepted for book publication a text that had been macerated by Mary Mapes Dodge for use in her magazine for children? When he let Charles Webster write chapter titles for *Huckleberry Finn*?

To speak of "the author," as "author" is conventionally defined, is clearly imprecise; and the more one takes into account the social nature of literature, the more imprecise the practice becomes. What if others than Twain revise his language, his punctuation, and his ideas? Choose his illustrations and the format for his books? What of the languages he uses, his characters, images, literary conventions, and meanings? Is a written discourse a social production rather than a virtuoso individual performance? Is a novel in the largest sense of the word intertextual?

Tanselle gives historicist-pragmatic answers to such queries. Morse Peckham, unhappy about editorial work he attempted, attacked Greg's central assumptions, called attention to the possibility that the author is an organism, not an individual, and charged linguistic hypostatization and literary hagiolatry. He denied that substantives and accidentals can be meaningfully segregated, and held that the reconstruction of a text representing the author's intentions is neither a meaningful nor an attainable goal.

Tanselle agrees with Peckham on some points but rejects his conclusions. The editorial goal is one of historical reconstruction, and the scholarly text has special status: the author possesses "some individuality" because he "initiated" the discourse; and the editor "should be cautious about attributing authorial intentions to alterations because they were passed . . . by the author." For practical purposes, Tanselle seems to dismiss the enormously complicating word "final" prefixed by Bowers to "intentions" and to take a synchronic view of the text as an event frozen in history: it is not a series of social intentions.

Setting aside any reference to the author's helpers and revisers, the word "author" offers internal difficulties. Critics distinguish the historical writer from the fictional narrator and from the agent whose actions account for the features of the text. Introduction of the word "initiator" in place of "author" does not appear to simplify matters or to add decisive weight to the argument. The question remains as to whether the "initiator" is discrete, can be decisively removed from the series, the tradition. Is the editor justified in trying to reconstruct a particular stage in the history of a work by placing himself "in the frame of reference of the author"? Critics operating on the pragmatic level but interested in "the sociology of the text," in the institutions of literary production, ask why the scholarly editor should be less scrupulous about the physical form—the type face, margins, binding, and so on—of the presentation of the original than he is about the text. Does it matter if the author was alienated from his work, as was Mark Twain? Are all authors items in the tradition and bound by it, if less obviously so than is the African tribesman who carves a granary door in such accord with social expectations that every incision may be, to use Roland Barthes's term, *lisible* by tribal viewers?

It appears to be at least possible that we accept the Greg-Bowers rationale either as a matter of convenience or because we accept a now frequently discredited Renaissance-Romantic view of the uniquely valuable expressiveness of the artist: there is nothing universal or more than transiently exact about this conception. The initiator and his intention would be seen very differently by a Romantic poet, an Egyptian scribe, a Romanesque sculptor, or a follower of Giotto.

That the text itself is in process of dissolving or has dissolved is not a matter for surprise in view either of history, the new hermeneutics, or of changing attitudes in religion, philosophy, and science. Quantum mechanics revised our conceptions of time: it is said that some suspect that what we do now not only alters the future but also alters the past. The existence of a world independent of our interests is doubted. If indeterminacy stalks abroad, what may be called "the ontological situs of the text" is naturally in question. The modernization and adaptation of texts were standard procedures in the Middle Ages and beyond: "A text was a living thing, which could be adapted, added to or extracted from according to the needs and inclinations of those who wanted to use it." Scholars for the past half-century, in contrast, have been obsessed with the related ideas of accuracy and authenticity, possessed by a need for "total faithfulness to the author's copy."[9]

Even the Romantic Jean Paul Richter took the relativist position that thought is a form of exercise, never absolute or final, that the viewer must "complete the painting." Approaching our own time, Valéry speaks of the decomposition of a text which takes place when one attempts to separate form and meaning. To the hermeneuticist a text is not so substantial as to decompose only when put to the Cartesian knife: cultural history dissolves it, turns it into a shimmering mist of concepts and affects. A kind of Heisenberg principle operates: the object observed is altered by the condition of being observed. The New Criticism considered the text to be a whole, autonomous and anonymous, but in general, as the author has grown shadowy, so has his text.

In terms of ordinary logic, if the author disappears, taking his intentions with him, the Greg-Bowers text vanishes, too. Nevertheless, influential modern critics—William K. Wimsatt, Monroe Beardsley, Wayne Booth, M. H. Abrams, John Reichart, and E. D. Hirsch among them—retain belief in a normative text and think that the role of the critic continues to be to elucidate the author's purposes; but this is not the most fashionable view.

Structuralists, phenomenologists, feminists, and psychoanalytic critics tend to see the text as a function of its readers.[10]

Nietzsche deconstructs causality, reverses the hierarchical world of ordinary causation by seeing "effect" as occasioning "cause": we experience pain, and pain causes us to discover the pin. "If either cause or effect can occupy the position of origin, then origin is no longer originary: it loses its metaphysical privilege." Opening up the subject of *Rezeptionstheorie*, of an aesthetic of reception, Hans Robert Jauss (1967) emphasized the impossibility of returning to earlier literature "as it was," of the necessity for new interpretations, and of the importance of the role of all those who are exposed to literature and recreate it.

The elevation of reader above writer reverses the hierarchy in the Nietzschean way. A number of critics have said, or have been thought to have said, that all interpretations are equally valid. Meaning is the experience of the reader or at best results from the cooperation of dominant reader and subordinate text. Harold Bloom describes all readings as misreadings and insists that the human subject is the ground or source rather than the effect of textuality. Roland Barthes asserts that the birth of the reader is at the cost of the death of the author: the work is an intertextual construct, a "product of various cultural discourses on which it relies for its intelligibility—and thus consolidates the central role of the reader as a centering role." It is language that speaks, not the author.

Jacques Derrida declares that the possibility of meaning something by an utterance is already inscribed in the structure of the language; but he restricts the implications of his thought by extending to the system of signs what Saussure says of language: *langue* "is necessary for speech events (*parole*) to be intelligible" and "the latter are necessary for the system to establish itself." Thus each "shows the error of the other in an irresolvable alternative or aporia."

At least partly comparable opinions about reader and text by critics of several persuasions may be piled like Pelion on Ossa. Michael Riffaterre takes the text to be the collaborative creation of author and reader: they *encoder* and *décoder*; together they make the text (*message*) what it is. Geoffrey Hartman concludes that the Renaissance notion of unique works of art "fades away into nostalgia." Michel Foucault considers the author to be "a fiction created, more or less, by Saint Jerome." J. Hillis Miller says, "The reading of a poem is part of the poem." Stanley Fish argues that "the reader's response is not *to* the meaning; it *is* the meaning, or at least the medium in which what I wanted to call the meaning comes into being." For Fish, the normative impulse is not from the text but from the community whose assumptions determine the kind of literature the reader makes. The formal features of a work are the product of the interpretive principles for which they are supposedly evidence.

Modern phonology joins in destabilizing the printed text. A printed version of a novel omits such phonemic aspects as stress, timbre, speed, and juncture. If an author writes by hand, the printed text omits holographic shadings. And if readers must play an active role and fill in the empty spaces, so listeners to speech itself are not "passive recipients of sets of acoustical signals which have all the necessary information for their decoding and interpretation": the listener adds hypothesized phonetic signals to acoustical signals in order to arrive at "a reasonable syntactic and semantic interpretation of the message."[11]

The first MLA bibliographers were innocently sanguine about their publishing victories to come, the triumphs they would achieve by applying infallible principles of editing to the American classics. Now, by virtue of its most fundamental conceptual assumptions, traditional textual bibliography appears to be epistemologically infirm, set against the grain of powerful current beliefs. Objection has been made, as well, to some of its detailed procedures. Although understandable in view of printing-house practices, the distinction made between accidentals and substantives is surely one of convenience, not grounded in either authorial intention or artistic integrity; it creates serious difficulties. As we have seen, the problematics of the field are so serious that author, intention, and text have all become words that may be used with confidence only if their meanings are stipulated.

It is possible for the texts produced by bibliographers to be inferior to what was available before, as seems to be true of *Ulysses: The Corrected Text* (1986); but so far as I know nothing of this sort has been suggested for any of the Mark Twain volumes. The reader must be a devotee of the Victorian-expectable to prefer the version of *The Mysterious Stranger* trumped up by A. B. Paine, Twain's official biographer, and Frederick A. Duneka, an editor at Harper and Brothers, to the incomplete versions written by Mark Twain.

May American bibliography be redeemed? Probably not fully, so far as theory goes; but for practical purposes, I think those who defend it may be justified, and this is not altogether a matter of avoiding aporia by the ruthless cutting of a Gordian knot.

Certain arguments may be advanced. It is easier for a reader to posit an initiating author who has intentions than it is to imagine an infinity of readers who invent an infinity of works. This is true even if the reader, or critic, accepts wholeheartedly that a text is a socially composed network of meanings. As Jonathan Culler puts it, "it makes a better story to talk of texts inviting responses than to describe readers creating texts." From a different perspective, Wolfgang Iser holds that essence and meaning belong to "the process in which textual structure and the reader's ideation interact"—in effect, the reader's ideation must interface with something. Furthermore, we must consider that paradigm shifts as described by Thomas Kuhn have occurred and doubtless will occur again. We may at some point find ourselves living once more in a determinate world where Platonic absolutes have meaning, where we may reasonably entertain the Miltonic, author-centered, elitist assumption that what matters is the writer speaking to his fit audience, though few.

We like the idea of having something tangible at hand to start the reader on his invention of patterns and meanings; and I myself find it hard to believe that, practically speaking, the reader is not better served by being offered texts made in accordance with some principles, theoretically justifiable or not, rather than by being handed texts printed from other texts, helter-skelter. Whether the scholarly reader who is not a bibliographer needs apparatus that may be scrutinized in order to follow, though imprecisely and haltingly, in the tracks of the editors is debatable. But when one has compared one or two unedited paperback reprints of nineteenth-century American authors with carefully edited texts, he becomes keenly aware that the differences are important and that we must be grateful to the scholars who participate in the work and to the individuals and institutions that support it.

A. B. Paine, the first of the major editors of Mark Twain, sat on the Papers, like a dragon on a gold hoard, for twenty-seven years after the death of Clemens. For him, problems of exactness or of copy-text hardly existed; he felt free to modernize, combine, omit, and rewrite. Although his procedures were not extraordinary for his period, they now seem thoroughly irresponsible, especially when he concealed what he had done. Paine wrote books and essays on Twain, made use of the great mass of the Papers and published excerpts from them, but did not bring them into anything resembling satisfactory order.

To a much lesser degree, the editorial disabilities of Paine were also those of Bernard DeVoto and of Dixon Wecter, the second and third editors of the Mark Twain Papers. By modern standards, they were without bibliographical principles. They were not very accurate in transcribing, and Wecter, particularly I think in editing *The Love Letters of Mark Twain* (1949), selected and cut with abandon. He also expressed some of the most grotesque historical and aesthetic judgments in all of the literature on Mark Twain. Both DeVoto and Wecter, like Paine, dipped into the Papers at will to mine the mother lode for marketable items.

Paine, with the approval of Clara Clemens Gabrilowitsch (later Samossoud), Clemens's only surviving daughter, and of Harpers (who owned Clemens's copyrights), made the Papers unavailable to scholars: the intent was to protect a partly false, relatively insipid, more than life-sized image of Mark Twain. DeVoto strongly opposed this protective attitude, opened up the Papers to scholars, and went beyond Paine in determining what was actually in them. After coming into sharp conflict with Clara over what might be published, he resigned his position, and Wecter became editor and literary executor.

Under Wecter's executorship the Papers were moved from the Widener Library, at Harvard, where DeVoto had placed them, to the Huntington Library and Art Gallery, in San Marino, California. In 1949, when Wecter left the Huntington to become a professor of history at the University of California at Berkeley, he took the Papers with him. Wecter died in 1950. He was succeeded by Henry Nash Smith, an unusually competent and responsible scholar, though not a bibliographer. At the death of Clara in 1962, the Papers were acquired permanently by the Bancroft Library.

In 1963 Smith turned the Papers over to Frederick Anderson, his assistant, who died in 1979. At Anderson's death, Smith was again pressed into service for a brief interregnum before the appointment in 1980 of Robert H. Hirst to be what is now known as Director of the Mark Twain Project. Significant advances had been made during the editorships of Smith and Anderson; but the Project was still very much feeling its way. No comprehensive plan had been fully settled upon; editorial procedures were only slowly being worked out; and volumes were published that may eventually have to be redone.

Enormous and intricate complications arose in connection with an initially quite separate proposal first made in 1961. This proposal was for the reprinting in good texts of Twain's previously published works. The editing was to be undertaken at the University of Iowa under the general editorship of John C. Gerber. Innumerable difficulties of all conceivable kinds ensued. The work proceeded by fits and starts; relationships were established with the enterprise at Berkeley; and after two decades of uncertain existence, the Iowa project was, as I understand it, absorbed by Berkeley.

Perhaps the chief evolutionary trends that may be discerned in the editing of Twain's Papers have been in the direction of a planned comprehensiveness, away from incomplete, topical, thematic publications, away from the use of academic generalists in supervisory capacities, and towards the use of a team of variously trained experts, accomplished as a group in all necessary aspects of editing, including the use of the unparalleled resources available at the Bancroft Library for providing biographical and historical-explanatory notes. Some questions remain, some objections may be entered; but to this reviewer, a non-bibliographer who must be for that reason tentative, it seems that the present editors at Berkeley have begun to triumph over all technical difficulties. They have a plan; they have established principles; and they have had experience in adjusting their practices to fit new conditions.

Even after all of the Twain letters are published, the *Union Catalog* compiled by Paul Machlis will continue to be helpful to scholars. At present it must be indispensable to the editors at Berkeley. The volume lists more than ten thousand letters, all written during Clemens's lifetime, either by or on behalf of Clemens, his wife, their daughters, or Isobel V. Lyons, Clemens's secretary from 1904 to 1909. The design of the work is eminently sensible, and the computer format must have made it economical to produce. The most unusual feature of the presentation—one which could have implications for other publications—is the inclusion of a microfiche in a pocket at the back of the volume. The microfiche contains a place list, date list, source-date list, source-address list, and writer list.

A few of the decisions about what should go into the volumes published in the two major series—the Works and the Papers—necessarily remain partly arbitrary, one of a number of reasons that it is beneficial to have the entire project controlled by Berkeley. Should an essay go into *Early Tales and Sketches* or into a volume of short writings treating religious topics? *Early Tales and Sketches* is part of the Works series; nevertheless, it contains pieces that were never published before. The first two of five proposed volumes of these sketches print—usually in chronological order—152 short pieces written between 1851 and 1865. They range from juvenilia to sketches that may no longer be thought of as apprentice work. When completed, the series will bring together more than 400 items.

Gathering these early writings from often elusive sources was a Herculean labor. The editing, too, was difficult. It entailed the examining of such materials as manuscripts, clippings, newspapers, journals, and scrapbooks. Some items occurred in a number of versions, complicating the choice of copy-text. The textual apparatus, the headnotes for each item printed, the explanatory notes, and the indices—all products of ingenuity and long labor—add to the usefulness of the volumes for the scholar. Taken together with headnotes, explanatory notes, and footnotes in other volumes published by Berkeley, they give information on the life of Clemens that is not to be found in any biography. Soon these volumes will constitute the best available life.

The Textual Introduction to Volume I is rich in details related to Twain's self-censorship, his practices in revising texts for different audiences, and the attitudes that various editors took towards his work. For what seem to be adequate reasons, the editors attempt to print original versions even when later versions revised by Mark Twain are available. This is a choice with which some, of course, may quarrel.

The sheer bulk of Clemens's journalistic writing is intimidating. To a reader who is not an undeviating Twainian, one who reads other authors and has other interests, the overriding question is whether editorial devotion should culminate in publishing *everything*. Do we need *all* of these apprentice pieces? They are usually short, often fleetingly topical, mostly trivial, and—one regrets giving the appearance of lacking a sense of humor—rarely very funny. As is true of all authors, everything that Clemens wrote does contain clues to his professional and cultural evolution: the sketches give us, for example, indications of his developing skill in handling the vernacular and remind us of what we know, from other sources, about such things as his racist attitudes. Together with the apparatus, they enable the reader to understand the gradualness of Clemens's inclination towards newspaper work and to perceive the rapidity with which he advanced from tentative juvenilia to mastery of the short forms which characterized journals of the period. These loose forms—hoax, sketch, mock feud, anecdote, satire, to mention a few of the names given them—defy exact categorization; they use similar devices, similar tones, suffuse the whole with the personality of the implied author, and blur into one kaleidoscopic pattern of hyperbolic or underplayed Western comedy.

The first volume of Clemens's new, definitive *Letters* makes a kind of companion piece to the early sketches and informs us in much the same way that they do. Robert H. Hirst, the textual editor, presents them with a modified version of the Greg-Bowers principles fully in place and, so far as I can tell, rigorously executed. The diacritical marks offer few hindrances to an easy reading of what is called a "plain" text. A large number of the letters published here and of those which are to come later have been previously published, many of them very inexpertly edited, strewn in books or periodicals. A notable exception to the complaint of inadequate editing would be the Mark Twain-Howells letters (1960), edited by Henry Nash Smith and William M. Gibson. Although without benefit of Greg-Bowers principles, the editorial work was faithfully done and abundant information was supplied.

More than forty of the lettters in this first volume are published for the first time. Explanatory footnotes, invaluable for biographical detail, are, if anything, too full. In the back matter, preceding the elaborate textual commentaries, references, and index, are a genealogy of the Clemens family, a steamboat calendar showing Clemens's piloting assignments, maps of the Nevada Territory, photographs, and photographic reproductions of selected letters.

What we do not find in the letters possesses its own importance. Just as when the first three volumes of the *Notebooks and Journals* appeared, we do not, to use Keats's phrases, "see horrible clear" Clemens's "whole life, as if we were God's spies." Nor do we see the whole life as if we were Freud's spies. The letters that have been preserved—many have been lost or burned—are not openly, psychoanalytically revelatory. In general, they are too self-consciously literary for that. Adolescent and postadolescent storms and stresses appear, but no jeremiads, no outpourings of the soul. Though written by a young person who contemplated suicide on one or more occasions, the letters are relatively self-contained. They are not great letters: as a letter-writer, Clemens was no Keats, no Mary Wortley Montagu, no Tocqueville, and no Jefferson.

These early letters do hold, however, considerable interest because of the peculiarly American ideologies, virtues, and social pathologies that they exhibit. We find in them a combination of energy and lassitude, hope and despair, idealism and selfishness. The young Clemens is making his way, but with no sense of definite direction. He is culturally ambitious, within limits, eager for wealth, almost habitually restless, but inclined to drift. Because the letters represent beginnings, constitute a kind of disjointed *Bildungsroman,* they capture attention in some ways more than do the later, busier, more mannered, more self-consciously posed letters. There, curiously enough, Clemens's unguarded self may be most manifest in business communications—hurried, querulous, anxious, angry, demanding letters to his publishers and their underlings, or letters to his own employees.

A number of the letters were intended for publication in newspapers or were written with that possibility in mind. Others were just as much literary exercises, divertimenti intended apparently as much for the amusement of the writer as that of the recipient. Clemens was not so scheming and posing a letter-writer as was Mozart, but he regularly adjusted his style and content to his correspondents. Students of Clemens will note that he experimented from the beginning with what became favorite modes, manners, and voices, favorite comic voices being those of the *naïf* or of the *faux naïf*. At times a streak of Southwestern cruelty may be noted in the comedy. The impulse to bowdlerize also appears, as in his writing "Shighte" and "d——d." A certain amount of posturing and stylization are nearly constant. He often tried his hand at "fine" writing and once or twice burlesqued that style. Social letters, like newspaper squibs, were a minor art form; and Clemens rarely stopped his stylistic exercises.

During Clemens's first travels as a journeyman printer, he exhibited a keen sense of reportorial curiosity, prowled around each new place he visited, and was likely to practice descriptive writing in his next letter. He wrote home reasonably often, sent money home when he could, corresponded brightly, lightly, with several young ladies, was brash, eager, uncertain, and aspiring. He expressed nativist principles and was blatantly, ignorantly racist.

Clemens began speculating in commodities while a pilot on the Mississippi and joined eagerly in the frenzied Western buying and selling of mining stocks when he reached Nevada. It is clear that his infatuation with the idea of riches was fixed well before he considered returning to the East or ever heard of Olivia Langdon.

When Clemens did leave San Francisco for New York on 15 December 1866, he had established himself on the Pacific slope as its premier humorist, had been heard of in the East, and had given successful public lectures. Yet he was not sorry to move on. He spoke more than once of his restlessness, and a year before he sailed he wrote, "I am tired of being a beggar—tired of being chained to this accursed homeless desert,—I want to go back to a Christian land once more." Statements like this may not be taken altogether seriously, for there were periods when he luxuriated in "putting up" at San Francisco's best hotels and living, as he said, "in this Paradise . . . like a lord." Nevertheless, at the end of this volume of the letters, he was finished with Nevada and California except in retrospect: New York, Europe, the Holy Land, fame, and marriage lay in the future. The West, to be sure, was not through with him. To the American people he became less a Tenth Muse, lately sprung up, than the Representative American out of the West, the lovable hero of a myth of origins.

Huckleberry Finn, Twain's only established contribution to the canon of world fiction, is an unusual "classic" in that it is enormously popular, unlike such respected American works as Emerson's best known essays and poems. The novel has become an icon standing for the American experience in the nineteenth century. At latest report, it is first among all works recommended for study in our junior and senior high schools. It is a favorite, too, at the college level, where students may find it assigned in freshman, sophomore, and upper-division classes. The redundance may not be so bad as it sounds: the book has depths.

The new *Huckleberry Finn* in the Mark Twain Library series is advertised as "sure to become the standard edition for the next generation of readers and for students of Mark Twain." This at once invites the question whether this volume is really for the general reader, or have the editors turned themselves too much into pedagogues? The book is cheap enough in paperback (a hardcover version is planned), but it is not the September Morn volume promised for readers by the MLA authorities as they explained their program to Edmund Wilson.

The book contains a foreword (4 pages), maps (6), explanatory notes (151), glossary (7), references (35), and a note on the text (4). Total, 207 pages. The text of the novel, set in larger type than is the apparatus, runs to 362 pages. These numbers suggest the extent to which the apparatus may separate text from reader. This is not to say that the apparatus does not also connect the two, but is the reader over-informed? Does the volume become an "Approach to Reading and Teaching" for uncertain teachers and their still more uncertain students?

I have nothing but praise for the work of the Press and for the learning and industry displayed in all textual and technical matters insofar as I feel at all competent to judge them. The "plain" text, like that of the letters, is easily readable; and the note on the text impresses me as being superbly done. The explanatory notes are wonderfully well researched; some present epiphanic delights. Maps, glossary, and references are all that anyone could ask for. I have some doubts, however, about introductions for this and other volumes out of Berkeley.

Probably the most dangerous task facing editors of a book like this—a volume intended for the ages—is that of writing a general introduction. Editors lose their privileged positions, become less magisterial. Even in the case of a brief foreword, questions arise. My chief misgiving has to do with the hortatory and directive tone. But any doubts, in the light of the total achievement, are minor: "all readings are misreadings"; all biographies distort.

I revert to the idea of completeness, which has dominated the minds of MLA editors and, at least since the editorship of Frederick Anderson, the minds of the editors of Mark Twain. Is this idea an offshoot of Romanticism, of the concept of organicism in art? But Nature tolerates errancy. Toes are omitted, arms deleted; writers destroy their own work. Practical reasons for being selective when dealing with such a mass of papers as Berkeley holds—many of them of low literary quality or thoroughly unimportant—are so obvious that it is not necessary to draw up an inventory.

To question completeness is not a Wilsonian invention. A

Dutch correspondent of John Locke put the matter strongly: "What I cannot at all approve of . . . is the absurdity of editors whose way it is to collect with the greatest care everything that learned men have written and given to the world." Excellent bibliographers approve of full publication, but I have not seen anything resembling a convincing argument for carefully edited publication in handsomely bound books of everything that Mark Twain wrote. Teachers of American literature examine volumes from Berkeley as they appear, much as climbers scale the highest peaks—because they are there. Twainians value them for their own idiosyncratic reasons. Major libraries will buy them, and I shall welcome whatever future splendors the editors produce. But *all* of the notebooks? *All* of the autobiographical dictations? *Five* volumes of early tales and sketches? *Twenty* volumes of letters? Microfiches do exist.

Notes

1. Bowers took his chief cue from the famous essay by W. W. Greg, "The Rationale of Copy-Text," *Studies in Bibliography*, 3 (1950–51), 19–36. Bowers has written voluminously and has edited texts in several fields, but his chief ideas may be found in *Principles of Bibliographical Description* (Princeton: Princeton Univ. Press, 1949); and *Textual Criticism* (Oxford: Clarendon Press, 1964).

2. Most of the examples cited below are drawn from the following volumes. O M Brack, Jr., and Warner Barnes, eds., *Bibliography and Textual Criticism: 1700 to the Present* (Chicago: Univ. of Chicago Press, 1969); and G. Thomas Tanselle, *Textual Criticism since Greg: A Chronicle, 1950–1985* (Charlottesville: Univ. Press of Virginia, 1987).

3. Here—and often below in passages discussing the Greg-Bowers theory of the copy-text—I refer to Tanselle, *Textual Criticism since Greg*.

4. "Reflections upon the CEAA by a Departing Editor," *Resources for American Literary Study*, 4 (Autumn 1974), 131.

5. Editors of presses were on the whole very helpful when I attempted several years ago to gather representative information on the states of their several editions, and I am glad to express my thanks for their assistance.

6. See Eleanor Tilton, "Washington Irving—Edited," *Early American Literature*, 17 (Fall 1982), 166–79.

7. See John Freehafer, "*The Marble Faun:* and the Editing of Nineteenth-Century Texts," *Studies in the Novel*, 2 (Winter 1970), 487–503.

8. Thomas A. Gullason in *Southern Humanities Review*, 6 (Summer 1972), 295–99.

9. N. F. Blake, *Non-Standard Language in English Literature* (London: André Deutsch, 1981), p. 24.

10. Phalanxes of writers have exemplified and explained "structuralism" and "deconstruction." For my citations, I rely in considerable part on Jonathan Culler's excellent *On Deconstruction: Theory and Criticism after Structuralism* (Ithaca: Cornell Univ. Press, 1982). Culler supplies an extensive bibliography.

11. E. L. Epstein, *Language and Style* (London: Methuen and Co., Ltd., 1978).

Milton's Gaze

Mary Thomas Crane

Joseph Wittreich. *Feminist Milton*. Ithaca: Cornell University Press, 1987. xxiii, 173 pp.

The opening pages of Joseph Wittreich's *Feminist Milton* raise the expectation that this will be a timely and significant book. In the course of proving that from 1700 to 1830, "in Milton studies, women have a history and have had an influence of their own" (p. ix), Wittreich will, he informs us, engage a number of current and pressing critical issues: "historical readerships, especially women; the politics of reading, writing, and interpretation; the canonizing of Milton's poetry and the institutionalizing of certain interpretations of it, at what cost and at what loss; the complicated relation between literature and ideology and the collusion of criticism with ideology" (p. x). The book promises a contribution to the debate over Milton and women that is informed by sound historicism and scholarship as well as a sophisticated awareness of feminist and post-structuralist theory.

In some ways, *Feminist Milton* lives up to its promises. Wittreich raises a number of important questions about who reads (and has read) Milton how, and why. He provides a trenchant critique of the oversimplifications that undermine both sides of the debate about Milton's view of women, and rightly suggests that *Paradise Lost* and *Samson Agonistes* inscribe complex and contradictory attitudes toward patriarchal values. His account of the efforts of conservative male critics in the late seventeenth and early eighteenth centuries to co-opt Milton for political and theological orthodoxy is fascinating and might be fruitfully pursued at greater length.

Unfortunately *Feminist Milton* is, in other ways, disappointing. Its argument that, in the eighteenth century, "Milton was not just an ally of feminists but their early sponsor" (p. ix) is not convincing. And Wittreich's polemical application of that argument in his attack on recent feminist and new historicist critiques of Milton involves him in theoretical self-contradiction. Although he invokes feminist and post-structuralist theory in the preface, his readings of *Paradise Lost* and *Samson Agonistes* seem directed against many of the presuppositions of those critical schools.

At first, it seems that the case for an early and admiring feminist readership of Milton is simply rhetorically weak, undermined by the brief and elliptical nature of Wittreich's quotations from the women in question. Two of five chapters are devoted to establishing the existence of an early feminist tradition in Milton scholarship: chapter 2 describes the "Cross-Currents and Cross-Purposes" in eighteenth-century Milton criticism as conservative male readers attempted to assert Milton's theological and political orthodoxy while women allegedly recognized and embraced his radicalism on all issues. His account of the efforts of conservative men to contain Milton's radicalism is extremely interesting, but he does not successfully demonstrate the existence of an alternative feminist critical tradition. Chapter 3 is devoted solely to establishing the views of "Milton's Early Female Readership." Both chapters are loosely organized and although Wittreich several times lists Milton's early female readers, he does not provide a sustained account of the political views or writings of these women. Instead, they are represented by short, fragmentary quotations, with little or no description of their context. As a result, the reader must constantly flip back and forth between Wittreich's lists of names, his scattered quotations, and their original sources in an attempt to gain a clearer sense of who these women were and how they were reading Milton.

When the original sources have been checked, however, the problems appear to be more serious. In many instances, when Wittreich's quotations are returned to their context or when ellipses are restored, the passages in question admit of very different interpretation. Although space prohibits an exhaustive examination, I would like to focus on two central figures, Mary Wollstonecraft and Hannah More, in order to demonstrate the range of problems inherent in Wittreich's approach. I choose

Wollstonecraft and More because they have figured prominently in quite different accounts of Milton's early female readership, and because the problems encountered in Wittreich's use of these two authors are typical of those found throughout the book.[1]

Because Mary Wollstonecraft has been recognized (by Gilbert and Gubar, as well as Mary Poovey) as an example of an early female reader of Milton who saw him not as an enabling feminist but as an inhibiting patriarch, and because Wittreich explicitly sets out to refute Poovey's account (pp. 3, 76), feminists will examine his evidence with interest. Early in the book, Wittreich challenges the accepted view of Wollstonecraft's opinions by asserting that because Milton's comments on Eve's role are inconsistent, it is "very possible to infer from them, as did Wollstonecraft, that for Milton a woman is *not* 'a mere satellite'" (p. 13). A footnote identifies the cited phrase as "Mary Wollstonecraft's" and refers to page 56 of Ulrich Hardt's critical edition of *A Vindication of the Rights of Women*. The phrase does appear there, but in a context which suggests a quite different interpretation:

For if it be allowed that women were destined by Providence to acquire human virtues, and by the exercise of their understandings, that stability of character which is the firmest ground to rest our future hopes upon, they must be permitted to turn to the fountain of light, and not forced to shape their course by the twinkling of a mere satellite. Milton, I grant, was of a very different opinion; for he only bends to the indefeasible right of beauty...."[2]

Here, the "mere satellite" refers to men who come between women and God, and Milton's "different opinion" is that, in fact, women ought to look to the satellite and not directly to God.

At several other points, Wittreich places great weight on Wollstonecraft's recognition that *Paradise Lost* is not always consistent in its depiction of the role of women. He notes early in the book that Wollstonecraft was "faithful to a text torn by ideological contradictions that do not do irreparable damage and are evidence of Milton's subversion of stereotypical representations of Eve and of women generally" (p. 3), and later he argues that "Mary Wollstonecraft typifies a more alert, sensitive, and chiefly female response to Milton in her detection of calculated contradictions and conflicting signals in *Paradise Lost,* and in her directive that those contradictions and signals do not diminish women but work to their advantage" (p. 41). In neither case does he offer a page reference to support his assertion about Wollstonecraft's response to Milton; however, the only passage in the *Vindication* which seems relevant immediately follows the one cited above and deserves to be quoted in full:

Milton, I grant, was of a very different opinion; for he only bends to the indefeasible right of beauty, though it would be difficult to render two passages which I now mean to contrast, consistent. But into similar inconsistencies are great men often led by their senses:

    To whom thus Eve with *perfect beauty* adorn'd.
    My Author and Disposer, what thou bidst
    Unargued I obey; so God ordains;
    God is *thy law, thou mine:* to know no more
    Is Woman's *happiest* knowledge and her *praise.*
    [emphasis is Wollstonecraft's]

Yet in the following lines Milton seems to coincide with me; when he makes Adam thus expostulate with his Maker.

    Hast thou made me here thy substitute,
    And these inferior far beneath me set?
    Among *unequals* what society
    Can sort, what harmony or true delight?
    Which must be mutual, in proportion due
    Giv'n and receiv'd; but in *disparity*
    The one intense, the other still remiss
    Cannot well suit with either, but soon prove
    Tedious alike: of *fellowship* I speak
    Such as I seek, fit to participate
    All rational delight ——

In treating, therefore, of the manners of women, let us, disregarding sensual arguments, trace what we should endeavor to make them in order to co-operate, if the expression is not too bold, with the supreme Being.[3]

Wollstonecraft does note an inconsistency in the account given in *Paradise Lost* of the nature of relations between men and women; while Eve seems to accept a subordinate position, Adam asks God to furnish him an equal as his mate. Wollstonecraft does not, however, claim that this inconsistency works to the "advantage" of women, nor does she see it as a sign of Milton's calculated "subversion" of stereotypes. Instead, she attributes the inconsistency to the male sensuality which she believes is responsible in large part for the subjugation of women. Although she does intend to "disregard" the sensual argument, she does not attribute to Milton any directive that it ought to be disregarded.

The following sentence from Wittreich's second chapter contains three debatable citations of Wollstonecraft:

> On the other hand, Wollstonecraft can also speak of "Milton's pleasing picture of paradisiacal happiness" and even of a coincidence between her ideas concerning women and Milton's own, as when in *Paradise Lost* Milton subscribes to the view that "women, considered not only as moral, but rational creatures, ought to endeavour to acquire human virtues (or perfections) by the *same* means as men, instead of being educated like a fanciful kind of *half* being," or when, also in Milton, she finds "proofs of reason, as well as genius," against all those arguments contemptuous of "the female understanding." [p. 42]

The first reference to "Milton's pleasing picture" of paradise occurs in a footnote as Wollstonecraft discusses the domestic life of Rousseau's Sophia:

> Yet, has not the sight of moderate felicity excited more tenderness than respect? An emotion similar to what we feel when children are playing, or animals sporting.* (*Similar feelings has Milton's pleasing picture of paradisiacal happiness ever raised in my mind; yet, instead of enjoying the lovely pair, I have, with conscious dignity, or Satanic pride, turned to hell for sublimer objects.)[4]

Surely Wollstonecraft's description of Milton's paradise as "pleasing" conveys less than unqualified approval, especially when she associates it with a domesticity for which she lacks "respect," and which her dignity and pride lead her to reject.

The second reference attributes to Milton a statement of Wollstonecraft's ideas about the moral and rational equality of women, yet Wollstonecraft herself does not make that connection. While discussing the argument that study injures the health of women, she illustrates the point that even men have spent much time exercising the imagination without damaging mind or body by arguing that "Shakespeare never grasped the airy dagger with a nerveless hand, nor did Milton tremble when he led Satan far from the confines of his dreary prison— These were not the ravings of imbecility."[5] She then proceeds with her own argument, and concludes (in the quotation cited by Wittreich) that, despite man's physical superiority, women are capable of the same education. The reference to Milton is thus only tangentially related to her conclusion and is certainly not cited as evidence that Milton "subscribes" to the same conclusion.

The third reference is similarly qualified when contextualized. Wollstonecraft actually says: "the female understanding has often been spoken of with contempt, as arriving sooner at maturity than the male. I shall not answer this argument by alluding to the early proofs of reason, as well as genius, in Cowley, Milton, and Pope."[6] Here, Wollstonecraft does not say, as Wittreich seems to imply, that Milton argues for the equality of female reason and genius; instead, she uses Milton (and two other authors) to demonstrate that some men of genius have arrived at maturity early.

These and other instances of brief, out-of-context quotation damage Wittreich's contention that Wollstonecraft regarded *Paradise Lost* as "a text, rife with ideological contradictions, that could now be enlisted in [her] own cause" (p. 77). Upon close scrutiny, his evidence for this claim is either absent (as when he fails to provide page references, for example, for the idea that Wollstonecraft values Milton's "nonpatriarchal representation of Eve after the fall," p. 78), or, at best, open to very different interpretation when seen in context. The examples cited above represent all but one or two of Wittreich's references to Wollstonecraft's texts, and he appears to employ a similar methodology when citing other women.[7] It would be tedious to recapitulate all of the examples to be found in the book. It must suffice to say that restoration of full context and of deleted passages would similarly change the interpretation of passages by Owenson (p. xiii) and Bradburn (pp. 77–78) and would erode the assertion that they looked to Milton for support of feminist principles.

Wittreich's references to Hannah More illustrate a different set of problems in his argument that an early female readership looked to Milton as an ally against patriarchy. Quotations from More are longer and more faithful to their context; indeed, two lengthy selections from More's works are included among the appendices of the book. The problems here arise from uncertainty about the extent to which More is herself dominated by patriarchy and seem to be related to deeper ambiguities involved in the use of such key terms as "feminism," "patriarchy," and "misogyny."

At times, Wittreich seems to concur with Beth Kowaleski-Wallace's account of More as a "good" daughter who voluntarily submits to patriarchal values.[8] He acknowledges, for example, that the image of Milton as "a poet who would constrain women to the reigning ideologies of female inferiority and female virtue, of what women should and should not be and do—can be inferred from some of the writings of Hannah More" (p. 30). However, he lists her among the women who make up his early feminist readership (p. xvi) and by including two of her pieces in the appendix seems to offer her as a prominent example of it.

Wittreich argues that More "is a more complicated figure than she is often represented as being" (p. 33), but he does not adequately explain the nature of that complexity. He asserts that her ideas about education and some of her ideas about Milton would not seem "outmoded" to a more feminist generation and offers as evidence the passages cited in the appendices. These passages, however, reveal that More accepted a limited education as appropriate for women. She uses Milton's Abdiel and Belial, by analogy, as support for her criticism of "sentimental" women who "affect the most lofty disregard for useful qualities and domestic virtues" and who have contempt for "those minute delicacies and little decorums which, trifling as they may be thought, tend at once to dignify the character, and to restrain the levity of the younger part of the sex" (p. 159). "Domestic virtues," "delicacies," "decorum," and "restraint" will be recognized by most modern feminists as patriarchal rather than feminist ideas about the proper behavior of women. Similarly, More's defense of Milton's Eve includes the view that "household good" comprises "the most indispensible, the most appropriate branch of female knowledge" (p. 163). These passages seem rather to confirm than to disprove Kowaleski-Wallace's view that "More's defense of Milton includes her implicit concession to patriarchal hierarchies."[9]

Similarly, Wittreich often cites female readers' approval of this description of Eve as evidence that they were feminists who embraced Milton as an ally: "Grace was in all her steps, Heaven in her eyes: / In all her motions Dignity and Love" (p. 58). While these lines, like the lines cited by More, may provide evidence that Milton was not always a misogynist, they do not disprove his involvement in patriarchy. As a result, the approval of female readers indicates that their feminism (if, indeed, it ought to be called feminism) was itself closely bound up with patriarchal values. In the case of More and some others, and of Milton himself, Wittreich seems to assume that the attribution of any positive qualities to women, or the advocacy of any kind of education for women, makes the writer a feminist, while the absence of overt misogyny absolves the writer of submission to patriarchy.

The remaining chapters of *Feminist Milton* (1, 4, and 5) offer Wittreich's own readings of the roles of Eve in *Paradise Lost* and Dalila in *Samson Agonistes,* as well as his criticism of recent feminist, reader response, and new historicist interpretations of these works. Although the central argument of the book is that the "feminist" Milton recognized by early women readers should guide our interpretation today, his own readings of the poems are only very distantly derived from those he attributes to eighteenth-century women. Wittreich summarizes the familiar critical history of the debate over woman in *Paradise Lost,* and finds fault with both sides: Miltonists have relied on "the tired cliches of Christian humanism" while the feminists are blinded by the "patriarchal criticism" of Harold Bloom, Stanley Fish, and Lawrence Stone (p. 8).

Wittreich several times quite rightly asserts that Milton's treatment of women is more "complex" and fraught with "ideological contradiction" than either feminists or humanists have tended to acknowledge, at least in the earlier stages of this debate, and he seems to call on post-structuralist and Marxist theory in support of a new, more "complex" reading (pp. 8–10). He also correctly criticizes the tendency to confuse Milton's views with those of his characters, especially in the case of Samson and the Chorus in *Samson Agonistes*. But he would also accept as Milton's the views of selected characters (Raphael, the Son, Dalila), and his own readings ultimately place all contradictions and complexities firmly in Milton's control; he argues at one point that "deconstructionist discourse" is "by Milton aligned with Satan and fallen human consciousness" (p. 89). Wittreich's own perspective on *Paradise Lost* is ultimately too simple: he argues that patriarchy and misogyny are aligned with Satan and fallen man, while a feminist point of view is to be associated with God, Raphael, and the Son. In order to support such a reading, Wittreich must argue that the bard's descriptions of Adam and Eve in Book 4 represent Satan's point of view, that the narrator and pre-lapsarian Adam often adopt this Satanic perspective, and that the phrase "thy subjection" in key speeches by Raphael (VIII.570) and the Son (X.153) refers not, as usually read, to Adam's subjection *to* Eve, but, improbably, to his subjection *of* her.

Chapters 4 and 5 contain lengthy critiques of "new historicist" articles by Stanley Fish and Richard Halpern, and of the feminist and new historicist volume *Rewriting the Renaissance*. These critics are accused of "flattening simplification," (p. 143; "historical humanists" are accused of the same thing on p. 9), of "voiding" both history and ideology (pp. 146, 149), and, most tellingly, of failing to differentiate "what is culturally bound from what is eternally valid" (p. 148). Ultimately, Wittreich seems to object less to these critics' theories or methodologies than to their failure to uphold a Milton who is in control of the ideological contradictions located in his texts, and who uses those contradictions to subvert the narrow patriarchal views of his contemporaries, demonstrating his own "wide . . . view of humanity," and thus, his "greatness" (p. ix).

Near the end of the book Wittreich asks, as he often does, an incisive question: "Texts are inscribed within structures of new authority, but so are their interpreters, and this should cause us to ask what is at stake in the survival of both—how does each subserve authority, and who *is* the authority?" (p. 152). What seems to be at stake for Wittreich is the preservation of Milton as an unassailable political, cultural, and literary authority. The sexual politics of this project become clearer when Milton is twice offered to feminists as a "potent ally" (pp. 48, 138) in their cause, more helpful to them than new historicists who are "neutered and gutless" (p. 152). Milton's text, on the other hand, is made to seem fragile; Wittreich twice describes misreading as "damaging" the text (pp. 27, 152), or "twisting it out of shape" (p. 40), while *Paradise Lost* "begs to be released from its own historical limitations" (p. 97). Wittreich seems to be using a strategy identified by Abbe Blum in "Areopagitica," where, "by insisting on the helplessness of the text, Milton can create a correspondingly powerful, threatening enemy who in turn prompts the appearance of an even stronger author-defender able to rescue his predecessors."[10]

The enemies, for Wittreich, are the feminist and new historicist critics who see in Milton's texts ideological conflicts not completely under the author's control, and who see in Milton something other than an early champion of modern liberalism. The issue, then, comes down to the preservation of Milton in the canon as a powerful political and cultural authority, an authority even more unimpeachable than humanists have previously described, because of his impeccable liberal politics. Ironically, Milton's place in the critical canon today is probably safer than it has ever been precisely *because* his texts are so controversial, and so open to dismemberment and re-membering.

Feminist Milton advances Milton studies when it urges awareness of ideological contradiction and complexity in Milton's relation to patriarchy and authority. Readings by Mary Nyquist, Christopher Kendrick, Abbe Blum, and others included in a new collection entitled *Re-Membering Milton*, however, better accomplish this than the readings offered in *Feminist Milton*.[11] More disturbing is Wittreich's contention that he can "restore the female perspective on Milton's writings" better than contemporary feminists whom he accuses of co-option by patriarchy when they "mount their antipatriarchal interpretations upon the patriarchal criticism (theoretical, literary, and historical) of Harold Bloom, Stanley Fish, and Lawrence Stone" (p. 8). Problematic here is Wittreich's contention that there is a single true "female perspective" on Milton which only this book can restore.

Metaphors of perspective, point of view, and the "critical lens" recur throughout the book, and its conclusion is that contemporary feminists should follow the example of eighteenth-century women and learn to see Milton and read his texts "with proper emphasis" (p. 154). The jacket of the book, perhaps inadvertently, reveals something about the point of view involved. From an anonymous pamphlet entitled "Female Rights Vindicated; or, the Equality of the Sexes Proved," it depicts a female figure of Justice seated on top of the world. The woman, in accordance with iconographic tradition, is blindfolded; above her, overlooking her, is the eye of God. This scene is unfortunately all too appropriate as a depiction of Wittreich's feminism. Despite its good intentions and claims to sympathy with feminist goals, *Feminist Milton* would construct a blindly obedient female readership confined within the poet's all-seeing male gaze.

Notes

1. On Wollstonecraft, see Mary Poovey, *The Proper Lady and the Woman Writer: Ideology as Style in the Works of Mary Wollstonecraft, Mary Shelley, and Jane Austen* (Chicago: Univ. of Chicago Press, 1984); on More, see Beth Kowaleski-Wallace, "Milton's Daughters: The Education of Eighteenth-Century Women Writers," *Feminist Studies*, 12 (1986), 275–93.

2. Ulrich H. Hardt, *A Critical Edition of Mary Wollstonecraft's* A Vindication of the Rights of Women, With Strictures on Political and Moral Subjects (Troy, N.Y.: Whitston, 1982), p. 56.

3. Hardt, p. 57.
4. Hardt, p. 66.
5. Hardt, p. 92.
6. Hardt, p. 154.
7. Wittreich also mentions Wollstonecraft's inclusion of Milton in her *Female Reader* (p. 35) but fails to note that in this early work she accepts a traditional role for women.

8. Kowaleski-Wallace, p. 287.

9. Kowaleski-Wallace, p. 287.

10. Abbe Blum, "The Author's Authority: *Areopagitica* and the Labour of Licensing," in *Re-Membering Milton: Essays on the Texts and Traditions*, ed. Mary Nyquist and Margaret W. Ferguson (New York: Methuen, 1988), p. 85.

11. Christopher Kendrick, "Milton and Sexuality: A Symptomatic Reading of *Comus*," pp. 43–73; Abbe Blum, "The Author's Authority," pp. 74–96; Mary Nyquist, "The Genesis of Gendered Subjectivity in the Divorce Tracts and in *Paradise Lost*," pp. 99–127. Another excellent reading by Mary Nyquist is her article "Textual Overlapping and Dalilah's Harlot-Lap," in *Literary Theory/Renaissance Texts*, ed. Patricia Parker and David Quint (Baltimore: Johns Hopkins Univ. Press, 1986), pp. 341–72.

Revising Anglo-American Feminism

Linda M. Shires

Toril Moi. *Sexual/Textual Politics*. New York: Methuen Press, 1985. xv, 206 pp.

Deirdre David. *Intellectual Women and Victorian Patriarchy: Harriet Martineau, Elizabeth Barrett Browning, George Eliot*. Ithaca: Cornell University Press, 1987. xvi, 273 pp.

Patricia Yaeger. *Honey-Mad Women: Emancipatory Strategies in Women's Writing*. New York: Columbia University Press, 1988. x, 317 pp.

Leonore Davidoff and Catherine Hall. *Family Fortunes: Men and Women of the English Middle Class, 1780–1850*. Chicago: University of Chicago Press, 1987. 576 pp.

Feminism addresses itself to changing unequal power relations between women and men in culture. These power relations structure all areas of society from the family to welfare to leisure activities. They shape, however, not only real lived practices but also our representations of reality: the narratives by which we make our culture mean. All feminists assume the *patriarchal* structure of society and many would agree that patriarchal power depends on the social meanings awarded biological sexual difference.

Feminists differ, however, about where to focus analysis and how to effect change. Generally speaking, four approaches have emerged. French feminists analyze the politics of language in order to displace the binary mode of thinking which governs Western metaphysics and which figures woman as Other. Some aim to uncover what they call the repressed feminine while others point to the (pre-gendered) semiotic as that repressed by the male order of language. Anglo-American feminism studies women's texts in order to recover lost voices and to analyze their silencing. They read the patriarchy as single and monolithic. One of the most important issues has been the establishment of a female canon, as well as the practice of reading otherwise (for woman). Marxist feminists stress economic structures as the cause of oppression. They analyze woman's relationship to the capitalist mode of production. Materialist feminists revise Marxist feminism at the same time they provide a corrective to less sociological models. They do not agree with the notion of either power or patriarchy as transhistorical or monolithic. Nor do they emphasize merely production but also consumption and reproduction. They are committed to analyzing the historically changing nature of both social meanings and social structures with a particular attention to intersections of class, gender, and race. Thus they do not essentialize "woman" either but recognize that differences exist in the oppression of a black from that of a white woman.

These differences among feminists are not merely those of "approach." Rather, each method is located in a specific feminist politics which is often taken to be incompatible with the others. Presently, the impasse in feminism concerns what relationship these various schools of theory and criticism should have to each other, if any. Should they be considered as fruitfully divergent "feminisms" which, however, may then easily be recuperated as feminist pluralism? Should they/could they be brought together in some way? Which solution could return the revolutionary impulse to feminism? Two main issues remain unresolved: 1) If change is effected through analysis of language and representation and through analysis of material practices, how should these two sites of analysis be related? 2) Should feminists devote themselves to separatist studies and locate man as the agent of oppressive culture or should feminists include men in their analysis—as speakers, as writers, as equal subjects of culture—thus treating the patriarchal as a position in culture which all biological men may not take up to the same degree and which itself can be figured differently at different historical moments. The question here is whether or not biological men can be included because of their always (and already) privileged position in culture.

Toril Moi, with whom I agree, advocates a way out of the impasse which would unite a form of French feminism with materialist feminism. Her point of view is informed by Julia Kristeva's essay "Women's Time" in which Kristeva argues that the feminist struggle must be viewed historically and politically as having three tiers, some of whose characteristics might be succinctly described as follows: 1. Women demand equal access to the symbolic order. Liberal feminism. Equality. 2. Women reject the male symbolic order in the name of difference. Radical feminism. Femininity extolled. 3. Women reject the dichotomy between masculine and feminine as metaphysical. Deconstruction of the opposition between masculinity and femininity.[1]

As Moi argues, adherence to the third position should not nullify adherence to the second. It is still important for feminists to defend women as women. But stage two can fall too easily into sexism by merely taking over the metaphysical categories set up by patriarchy. Kristeva's third position does begin to alter the goals and possible achievements of the feminist struggle. In being connected largely to the realm of representation, however, it does not go far enough. Thus, feminists must also attend to conflicting material structures of culture and to lived practices. A carefully theorized conjunction of these two approaches may rescue feminism from charges of pluralism or one-sidedness.

The four books under review here call for a reappraisal of central feminist issues. They raise important questions: How can women resist patriarchal meanings and structures? How are women inevitably co-opted into an agreement with the hegemony at particular historical moments? If the social value accorded to sexual difference remains crucial for feminist politics, should feminists remain separatist either by studying only women's texts or by figuring all men, at all social sites, as the "patriarchal" enemy, or should they conceptualize a diffuse and relational theory of oppression and power? These are questions which are not new to feminism, but they are issues which remain unresolved and hence carry a political urgency.[2]

Toril Moi's polemical and already much quoted *Sexual/Textual Politics* aims, as do other books in the New Accents Series, to respond to vast intellectual and social changes which have altered the shapes of academic disciplines, specifically literary studies, by stretching the boundaries. In her introduction to feminist literary theory, Moi presents what she calls "the two main approaches" in the field, the Anglo-American and the French. Hers is not merely a description, however, but a sharp opposition of the sexual orientation of American feminism and the textual orientation of the French. More important, it is a political critique derived from the third major position, British materialist feminism. Unfortunately her position is recoverable here only in brief snatches and in an interesting but impure form, as a feminism which allies itself forcefully with the deconstructive strategies of French feminism, particularly Julia Kristeva's, as well as with post-Althusserian Marxism. These positions are usually taken to be incompatible because of Kristeva's eschewal of material reality in favor of politicizing sites in language which she calls the symbolic and semiotic. Or as Leslie Rabine puts it: "The blind spot in the discursive practices of symbolic feminism [Kristeva's, for instance] is that they tend to repress the social dimension of gender by collapsing the social into the symbolic."[3] The result, Rabine argues, is a re-established hierarchical position in which the specificity of the social and the real are repressed, becoming merely the secondary term of the symbolic. Deconstruction and a focus on textuality alone cannot produce a social revolution. Moi agrees. For, analyzing the politics of language, Kristeva's theory takes no account of the conflicting material structures which must be studied and altered for any successful social change. Yet because Moi proposes such a powerful solution to the present feminist impasse, incorporation of Kristeva's ideas about language within a feminist theory of ideology, one wishes that she had theorized this integration more fully.

Moi is still effective in her political critique (not bashing, as some might insist) of American feminism and in her explanation of the strengths and shortcomings of the French feminists (Hélène Cixous and Luce Irigaray as well as Kristeva) who have found their way most quickly (partly due to the relative speed and proliferation of translations) into the American classroom and into feminist debate. Moi objects to American feminism, and it is regrettable that she targets specific authors and texts without setting them in any fleshed-out intellectual or philosophical tradition. Tracing the history of Anglo-American feminism, she begins with two classics of the 1960s, Kate Millett's *Sexual Politics* and Mary Ellman's *Thinking About Women,* in order to demonstrate the feminist break with New Criticism (a break, however, never fully accomplished). She justly credits Ellman with isolating the stereotypes of femininity as presented by male writers and with the theory that Western culture at all levels is permeated by our ludicrous tendency to interpret all phenomena in terms of sexual difference. She is harsher with Millet, whom she applauds for the idea that sexual domination pervades cultural ideology but whom she rightly cites as suppressing Freud's ideas on unconscious desire. Rejecting some of Freud's key ideas forces Millet to view patriarchy as always conscious, monolithic and conspiratorial which, in turn, dictates her vision of woman as pure and therefore unable to internalize any sexist attitudes and desires. This is a position which Deirdre David clearly refutes in her study of Martineau, Browning, and Eliot, about which I will have more to say.

Without repeating Moi's individual objections to various American feminist theories, one can draw some general conclusions from her work. The notion of a male conspiracy has had both positive and unfortunate consequences for later American feminism, which has treated woman separately by emphasizing their canon while often leaving all aesthetic judgment behind and which has uncritically taken women's texts as realistic reflections of experience.[4] Too often the monolithic patriarchy has remained an indistinct and carelessly historicized bogey man for an equally monolithic, biological femaleness as in Sandra Gilbert and Susan Gubar's monumentally influential and otherwise sophisticated analysis of nineteenth-century women's writing, *The Madwoman in the Attic.* For Gilbert and Gubar, power, untheorized, is known by the effects of victimization while all rebellions come to have the same essentialized meaning.

While Moi does not detail her objections to this theory of power, oppression, and resistance, it is clearly not persuasive and can be attacked from various intellectual positions. First, power is not an obsession restricted to biological males. As Ellie Ragland-Sullivan has argued from a psychoanalytic perspective, "Any group evolves its own phallocratic structure because recognition and power needs inhere in the structure of the human subject itself."[5] But, in addition, power can be more usefully theorized in terms of particular kinds of intersubjective relations (of relative advantage and disadvantage) which exist at certain sites formed by webs of practices around specific policies.[6] Such a theory allows for the great differences in power relations and opens gaps for resistance. Though Moi is sometimes gratuitously harsh and unsympathetic in the first sections of her book, her rigorous criticisms of Anglo-American theory are on the mark.

Moi is fully engaged and fairer when she turns to French feminism, which she finds more intellectually compatible. She claims for Simone de Beauvoir the status of "greatest feminist theorist of our time" (p. 91). De Beauvoir's classic statement—"One is not born a woman, one becomes one"—captures for Moi a resistance to the essentialism of a theory of "woman's nature." In great contrast to American feminists, the French after de Beauvoir study women's relationship to the language of the symbolic order which figures her as Other. In this emphasis they are influenced strongly by the re-reading of Freud initiated by Jacques Lacan. In different ways and with various successes, the French feminists seek to replace our phallogocentric gender system based on a logic of binaries with one based on a logic of difference, displacing difference between man and woman to reveal multiple differences within each sex and each speaking subject.[7] In their view the hierarchy now privileging male subjectivity should yield place to subjects oscillating between masculine and feminine positions (a both/and instead of an either/or situation).

Moi is absolutely lucid in her explanation of Cixous and Irigaray, who argue for the repressed feminine as the site where the play of sexual difference can emerge. And she nicely articulates their differences from each other. Her book would have been stronger, however, had she taken into account a host of other French voices. As mentioned, she has found some of Kristeva's theories most useful for her own theory because they promise more than "the simplest and defeatist vision of male power pitted against female helplessness that underpins Irigaray's theoretical investigations" (p. 147). Because Kristeva argues that we all use the same language but that we have different interests, Moi can adapt Kristeva's theory to buttress her own that particular political and power-related interests intersect at the sign. Further, unlike Cixous, Kristeva theorizes repression of the feminine in terms of *positionality* rather than in terms of essence. In Moi's suggestion of a union between Kristevan French feminism and materialist feminism, she lays out a fruitful agenda whose details remain to be worked out.

I have spent a good deal of space on Moi's book because it so usefully sets out the main ideas and arguments which the other books under consideration either respond to or revise. In *Intellectual Women and Victorian Patriarchy: Harriet Martineau, Elizabeth Barrett Browning, and George Eliot*, Deirdre David is also critical of American feminism and she too works from a Marxist perspective. Unlike Moi, David is an American. Thus her criticism of her sisters in academe is a shade riskier and, perhaps as a result, far more muted. In a sense she lets Antonio Gramsci do the revising for her. David works from the sensible assumption that these intellectual women were not pure vessels uncontaminated by male cultural norms, but that in their attempt to gain cultural power they simultaneously subverted and affirmed Victorian patriarchy. She thus rightly argues against a notion of easy biological opposition and generally corrects misreadings of Martineau, Barrett, and George Eliot by feminists too eager to make them into standard-bearers and freedom-fighters. David fails, however, to deconstruct the patriarchy in any way and continues the American tradition of figuring it as a monolith. Likewise, she offers no full explanation of how a woman gains acceptance into what she maintains is a male-governed domain; in other words, she offers no theory of power but imposes a rigid Gramscian description of two types of intellectuals on these women writers.

In March 1837, Robert Southey advised Charlotte Brontë:

"Literature cannot be the business of a woman's life, and it ought not to be. The more she is engaged in her proper duties, the less leisure will she have for it, even as an accomplishment and a recreation" (p. vii). Regarding Martineau, Browning, and Eliot as three women who defied such a patriarchal injunction, David claims to have selected them because of their different spheres of intellectual inquiry—journalism, poetry, and the novel—and because they were revered in their own time as intelligent and industrious. They were very successful and yet, David contends, they never freed themselves from "a tension inherent in the Victorian subjugation of woman's mind by male cultural authority" (p. vii). David assesses what she calls their "cultural performances" not only through the lens of nineteenth-century views of woman's mind and education but also through contemporary views of Victorian intellectual activity. It remains unclear why she also draws upon Antonio Gramsci's writings about the social functions of intellectuals—unclear why he is chosen and, given the elementary way his ideas are used, unclear why he is used at all.

Studying the social "meaning" of intellectuals, Gramsci distinguished between two types: the "organic" and the "traditional." Since, according to Gramsci's definition, "organic" intellectuals accompany a social class in its rise to power by transmitting its ideas, David places all three of her women in this category. Although they hold differing political views, each contributes to the hegemony of the emerging middle class. David claims that the Victorian woman intellectual is "organic" because of a "daughterly intellectual affiliation" (p. 4) with the middle class. Alongside male contemporaries, women intellectuals were part of the larger social group which gave "'awareness' and 'homogeneity' to an increasingly powerful social class" and performed "functions of 'legitimation' and 'elaboration' for the influential ideologies of that class" (p. 6). At the same time, David states, they were "traditional" intellectuals. "Traditional" intellectuals, according to Gramsci, are usually opposed to the emergent class and put themselves forward as an autonomous group untouched by even the most radical of social changes. They cling to fantasies that eschew progress. Martineau, Barrett, and George Eliot,

David argues, are "traditional" by locating themselves and the intellectual women about whom they write in an ahistorical realm transcending the vicissitudes of history.

David discusses George Eliot in terms of a major conflict which appears in various guises in her writings: that between an ideology of free individualism (her "organicism") and the yearning for a mythic pre-industrial world (her "traditionalism"). David argues that female characters often become emblems for Eliot's nostalgic conservatism. While correct on the one hand, if we think of Mrs. Poyser's organic farm in *Adam Bede*, for instance, this assertion leaves out the nostalgia in male figures—an Adam Bede or a Silas Marner—just as it leaves out complicated notions of gender identity. Furthermore, David never locates nostalgic conservatism in textual unions such as those in *The Mill on the Floss:* Maggie and Philip; Maggie and Stephen; Maggie and Tom. Yet the moments described in the Red Deeps, the boat, and the flood are important precisely because they transcend time, and not merely for Maggie.

More important, if one agrees that women intellectuals simultaneously affirm and subvert patriarchal norms, which I do, David's argument still remains seriously flawed. Her general definition of "organic" intellectuals renders them male and female while her definition of "traditional" intellectuals renders them female. Here she departs from Gramsci who uses the example of the priest. One thus wonders about intellectuals such as Carlyle, Tennyson, and Arnold. Do they not share with an intellectual like Eliot a nostalgic conservatism (or its equivalent) which would allow them into the ranks of resistance? Or are they merely "organic" intellectuals? Finally, the argument falls apart because while David has claimed that a position like nostalgic conservatism is not free of ideology, she dubiously locates it *only* as resistance. She does not show how it could actually *further* the agenda of the rising middle class. In other words, at the local level of analysis, she does not convincingly show that nostalgia can have the same function as progressive views. She fails to see that the *same* viewpoint can be used ideologically to serve different ends at the same time. I believe that her notion of patriarchy and her fixing the agenda of the Victorian middle class too rigidly, in spite of her strong understanding of process, are responsible for this sort of slippage.

David's great strengths lie not in theory but in her mastery of literary and historical materials. She has read widely and deeply. Her book does not convey any of the political conviction and theoretical sophistication of Moi's and its argument could stand without Gramsci. David's book, though, does raise a crucial question: can a work, such as Browning's *Aurora Leigh*, which many feminist critics read as subversive of the patriarchy, be called truly "feminist" if such a text—or *Jane Eyre*, which it in so many ways imitates—conservatively reifies hegemonic norms while subverting them?

Patricia Yaeger attacks this same issue and the biases of contemporary American feminist criticism from a nearly opposite point of view. She claims not that women's writing has been viewed too charitably by feminists seeking models and texts, but that it has not been viewed as open enough. Less historically specific than David, Yaeger's argument has to be taken in part on faith. The reader of her book should be versed not only in feminist theory but also in narrative theory to be able fully to appreciate her imaginative manifesto. *Honey-Mad Women: Emancipatory Strategies in Women's Writing* seeks a new way to talk about the relationship of woman to writing. Kristeva's contention that women are visionaries, estranged from language, is not good enough for Yaeger. Critical of French feminism, she also would not support the solution for feminism which Moi has proposed. Hers is an ebullient, optimistic book which does what she insists women's writing can do—work, by winning assent through the sheer force of the emancipated and emancipating strategies employed. Her goal is to "define a countertradition within women's writing, a tradition that involves the reinvention and reclamation of a body of speech women have found exclusive and alienating" (p. 2). She sets out to prove that women have persistently found language empowering by taking pleasure in speech until they are fulfilled or "honey-mad." The dancing woman on the cover of the book acts as the figure for "honey-mad" fulfillment which serves Yaeger as a symbol for a new mythology of feminine speech. It is important that the woman is

Revising Anglo-American Feminism

dancing—performing an action—since Yaeger attempts to convince the reader that speech can be action.

Yaeger challenges the French feminist mythology of feminine speech on the grounds that women's lexicon has not been completely restricted by male culture, that language itself is not masculine, that women have more than one relation to language, and that women can write subversively without deliberately employing avant-garde practices. As I read her work, Yaeger does not find a counter-tradition, nor does she offer a persuasive counter-theory to French feminism, but she does provide important reflections on practices of reading women's texts, reflections which call into question earlier American criticism. She is right in her assumption that many feminists have read through the lens of classic realism. In short, they have not been able to read for multiple meanings, simultaneous meanings, textuality, but have been tied to coherence, plot, and closure. In contrast to David, who is interested in a woman writer's necessary containment of her own subversive strategies, Yaeger demonstrates how that writer lightens the load of tradition as she attempts to play with and revise her culture. For example, she argues that Mary Wollstonecraft uses dialogue as an emancipatory strategy by entering into conversation with male texts, specifically Rousseau's *Emile*. Wollstonecraft, Yaeger points out, does not merely reproduce male meanings but "makes Rousseau into a new kind of social circulating message ... both a speaking partner and a sign. Rousseau—formerly the generator and arbiter of signs—is turned into someone who circulates: a sign whose meaning and value is [*sic*] designated by a woman" (pp. 175–76). Wollstonecraft's power over the circulation of Rousseau makes her into a producer of culture.

Certain questions arise, however, in part because of Yaeger's eclectic method. How, for example, is a notion of women's seizing words and using them for their own purposes different from Irigaray's theory of mimicry? What does Yaeger really mean by a revision of culture—what are the kinds of work that a feminist writing/reading performs? Since she claims that male authors "invent abnormal discourses as well" (p. 41), exactly how is Charlotte Brontë's subversion of dominant modes different from

Wordsworth's? Why is Wordsworth dismissed as participating in a "local variety of protest or change" while Brontë is credited with inventing a discourse that "will put the hegemonic structure of the primary language entirely into question" (p. 41)? Is it because Wordsworth is culturally privileged in his gender position? If, as she further argues, Wordsworth and Keats feel anxiety when words are displaced, torn from their roots, while Brontë finds freedom in fragmented words, often foreign words, who tells us so? In other words, Yaeger has not fully theorized relations between author, text, and reader. She too often slips from one to another and she finds no problem in comparing a lyric ode with a novel; it is no wonder that she finds more monologism in Romantic poetry than in examples which she selects from the Victorian novel.

On the other hand, though she has not set up her argument precisely enough or taken full account of multi-vocality in the male Romantics, Yaeger's conclusions are invariably interesting. She maintains, for instance, that Brontë discovers a double-voiced way of consuming and reshaping the Romantic tradition by splitting and fragmenting its plots. And she is sensitive to the explosive use of laughter and play in the nineteenth-century novel generally, viewing the novel of that era itself as a form of freedom instead of as a "form of tight lacing" or as yielding a "firm perspective" (pp. 295–96, n. 7). Here Yaeger alludes to and implicitly repeats criticisms of other American feminists' studies of the novel. Mary Jacobus refers to "tight lacing" in her review of Gilbert and Gubar's *The Madwoman in the Attic,* while Toril Moi criticizes Elaine Showalter's use of the term "firm perspective" in *A Literature of Their Own.* Writing against such metaphors of closure, Yaeger does not support either the pluralism advocated by Annette Kolodny or the random play of the signifier which Roland Barthes and French feminism hold out, but a "more concrete valorization of playful moments in women's texts" (p. 297, n. 33). Unlike Moi, she seems less positive about the value of deconstruction for feminism. While both see binarism and the imposition of one phallocentric truth as oppressive, Yaeger cannot defend play if it is defined as consisting of endless oscillations. Her need for a notion of organized play accounts for her relatively conservative reliance on narrative strategies, themes, and figurative language.[8]

In spite of her strong critical voice, which is particularly bold and attractive in her notes, Yaeger's problematic relationship to her audience should not go unnoticed. Her endless lists and quotations from other scholars may demonstrate her deep immersion in the criticism and theory she has mastered, but it also irritates the reader who finds that the many critical voices displace Yaeger's own narrative without adding to the playfulness of her tone. Yaeger also speaks about a *we* never clearly established. Who are those who "ignore the woman writer's double orality" (p. 5)—all critics? If so, she makes a rather large claim. Finally, in a crucial move on which much of our faith depends, the replacement of a theory of woman's repression in language with Hannah Arendt's idea of the word as "natality," Yaeger loses her usually firm grip. How Arendt, and Yaeger, get from word to action, how the different saying of a word "can operate as a form of action" (p. 94), remains fuzzy and hence, however suggestive, little more than a provocative assertion. Still, Yaeger's book deserves to be viewed as an important and daring contribution. It should be read by feminists if for no other reason than the fact that it serves as a strong corrective to power-centered analyses which leave little room for pleasure or play. Although it fails to persuade fully, it takes risks theoretically and it engages thoughtfully with critics from Kolodny to Foucault.

Inattentive to the politics of feminine language, and thus far removed from both Yaeger and French feminism, Leonore Davidoff and Catherine Hall in *Family Fortunes: Men and Women of the English Middle Class, 1780–1850* illustrate the other half of the method which Moi would forge out of Kirstevan theory and Marxism. Davidoff and Hall perform the kind of cultural analysis that Moi advocates when they explore a specific historical context and its ideological structures. Examining the intersection of beliefs, practices and representations across an economic, religious, and political axis, they rightly claim that gender constructions at the site of the family worked to form a class consciousness. The creation of separate spheres became inevitable because of a highly articulated system of sexual difference—

evident in cultural practices from clothing styles to education—which altered the distribution of power between the sexes during the early years of the nineteenth century.

Davidoff and Hall document how the intersection of gender and class shaped production and consumption, the family, manners, subjectivity, public and private roles, and other aspects of culture. A growing middle-class prosperity further strengthened the sexual division of labor which had served its rise so well. Throughout their discussion of the creation and solidification of the middle class, Davidoff and Hall stress the primary influence of religion. The middle class man was not, they convincingly show, propelled by a need for power or status based on salary, but rather by the need to secure a safe income earned respectably to support female dependents.

The argument may sound familiar enough. All the same, *Family Fortunes* makes significant contributions. One of the most important is its documentation about kinds of family units. Also this book studies woman and man together at the location where their interests, roles, and influence both interpenetrate and diverge, the family. It takes up such central issues as the formation of masculine identity at the same time that it studies the growing split between public and private spheres. While carefully noting that the middle class cannot be perceived as a unified essence, since it is crisscrossed by differences and divisions of interest geographical, social, denominational, and professional, they do locate a strong bond in a persistent moral code. Middle class men, they argue, "even while seeking 'to be someone' in the community, to count as individuals because of their wealth, their power to command, or their capacity to influence people, were, in fact, embedded in networks of familial and female support which underpinned their public prominence" (p. 13). Indeed, in some cases such support enabled the man's public prominence. The authors aim to illustrate, then, that in spite of woman's weakening position, she did have considerable influence and even power both in the family and in the local public sphere. In other words, they posit female power during the very time the middle class was rigidifying the exclusion of woman from the public world. One can only lament that this fine book was unavailable to David before she embarked on her own, for it would have enriched her discussion. To defend their argument, Davidoff and Hall draw on a variety of historical tools, including census data, wills, family diaries and letters, architectural designs, and several literary texts.

This type of authoritative book could easily have become tedious, as fact after fact is added to buttress the argument, but the facts come alive through a judicious and sensitive use of specific families. The Cadburys of Birmingham, who started off as drapers and food manufacturers and made their reputation with a chocolate drink, are counterpointed to the Taylors of Essex, who made their money by producing lectures, sermons, engravings, and their ideas about middle-class morality. By the end of the text, one has read an interpretation of history with the engagement usually devoted to a novel. Davidoff and Hall center their attention on the city of Birmingham and two adjoining provincial counties, Essex and Suffolk. This narrowing of focus on economically different yet representative locations importantly grounds their theories.

This book, however, presents feminists with at least two related problems. It is no surprise to the Victorian scholar to find that "the 'oppositional' culture of the provincial middle class cannot be understood outside a religious context" (p. 21). Nor is it surprising to see documented the fears and anxieties attending a growing commitment to new commercial forms. Dangers such as bankruptcy, failure, the relations of masters and their men, and the moral imperative for fair dealing haunted the middle class. But this argument leads the feminist to see female oppression face-lifted as the moral need to provide for one's loved ones. Davidoff and Hall document but do not fully discuss the relationship between morality and oppression. It would seem that their goal to heal the split of public and private spheres drives Davidoff and Hall away from attending to some of the implications of the argument. It is clear why they need to attend most closely to women within the family, rather than to those outside, but they do not give attention to women who subverted from within the cultural roles awarded them. Power and influence are by no means solely male prerogatives in this study. Indeed, the kind of power women held from within the family included not just moral influence, but money that established or rescued a husband's business, labor power in the shop, and education of the next generation. More examples of power from within would have been welcome.

And, in the course of this study, we fail to meet enough women who achieved success in the public world. Consider the historically silenced female evangelical preachers of the late 1700s. Those preachers, whom Davidoff and Hall mention only to note how intensely they suffered the tensions between a public path and private duties, wielded enormous power. Historically informed feminist work has been done on the Victorian woman's direct relationship to religion and her appropriation of male codes and male speech. Davidoff and Hall emphasize too strongly the degree to which women merely supported the initiatives of men. One is, therefore, grateful to hear about women's spiritual writing, which seems to have replaced evangelical preaching by women. "Women's spiritual writing could become a space, along with clubs, societies, and auxiliaries of the church," they write, as "an avenue of real if narrowly defined power and recognition within the local community" (p. 147). *Family Fortunes*, though, mainly tells the story of the withdrawal of women from the public sphere. As the authors report, "Risks of losing status by being seen in many public places, particularly alone, was a serious disadvantage to a woman doing business" (p. 286). Women even grew to fear payment for legitimate public jobs.

Davidoff and Hall have not written a radical text, one that demonstrates vast, secret pockets of female influence other than the power of moral conscience. They do not read the evidence that way and they do not find much evidence to support such a reading. In this respect, *Family Fortunes* is less ground-breaking than it might have been. However, it stands as one of the very few major analyses of the family which accounts for why woman withdrew from the public sphere. I recommend it highly as the most substantial of the books here under review.

But each of these four books makes important contributions. Each teaches us something valuable for a stronger and enabling feminism. Moi is bold in her proposed solution. David accounts for the simultaneous support and subversion of governing ideas. Yaeger demonstrates forcefully the open, playful qualities that can be read into women's writing if we take perspectives that we have not taken before. Davidoff and Hall illustrate how consensus (and a form of patriarchy as well as a class) is achieved through many private and public negotiations at various levels of society. They begin to theorize a relational theory of power, showing how men depend on women to survive in their roles of influence and how women depend on men for the same. In so doing, Davidoff and Hall also attempt to collapse the traditional separation of the public and private spheres. They show, for instance, how the model of the family could be used in business. But they cannot convincingly collapse biology—they do not feature enough the men with duties in the home or the women who rise to positions of influence outside of the home.

The male must be theorized as a position in culture which all biological men do not occupy similarly at the same historical moment. The female must likewise be analyzed first as a position. Both must be theorized so as to allow difference—and even biological difference—within the categories. And both must be analyzed for the various and conflicting social values awarded to each position and to the positions as they relate to each other. It should not be forgotten, ever, that the female position in culture is traditionally and regrettably perceived as inferior. Thus, while deconstructing the masculine and the feminine, we must also critique all representations and practices which persistently write the female as Other. In this way we can bring about change.

Notes

1. Julia Kristeva, "Women's Time," trans. Alice Jardine and Harry Blake, *Signs* 7.1 (Autumn 1981), 13–35.

2. For one of the most important exchanges on this issue, see Myra Jehlen, "Archimedes and the Paradox of Feminist Criticism," *Signs* 6.4 (Summer 1981), 575–601, and Elaine Showalter, "Comment on Jehlen," *Signs* 8.1 (Autumn 1982), 160–64.

3. Leslie W. Rabine, "No Lost Paradise: Social Gender and Symbolic Gender in the Writings of Maxine Hong Kingston," *Signs* 12.3 (Spring 1987), 471–92.

4. See, for instance, Ellen Moers, *Literary Women: The Great Writers* (New York: Doubleday, 1976), Elaine Showalter, *A Literature of Their Own: British Women Novelists from Brontë to Lessing* (Princeton: Princeton Univ. Press, 1977), Jane Thompkins, *Sensational Designs: The Cultural Work of American Fiction, 1790–1860* (New York and London: Oxford Univ. Press, 1985), and the commonsense appropriation of the issue of canon formation in James Atlas, "The Battle of the Books," *The New York Times Magazine,* June 5, 1988, p. 26. On feminist art, art by women, and aesthetic judgment, see Michele Barrett, "Feminism and the Definition of Cultural Politics," *Feminism, Culture and Politics,* eds. Brunt and Rowan (London: Lawrence and Wishart, 1982), pp. 37–58.

5. Ellie Ragland-Sullivan, "Jacques Lacan: Feminism and the Problem of Gender Identity," *Sub-Stance* 36 (1982), pp. 18–19.

6. See Gary Wickham, "Power and Power Analysis: Beyond Foucault?" in *Towards a Critique of Foucault,* ed. Mike Gane (London and New York: Routledge and Kegan Paul, 1986), especially pp. 163–77.

7. See Barbara Johnson, *The Critical Difference: Essays in the Contemporary Rhetoric of Reading* (Baltimore: Johns Hopkins Univ. Press, 1978).

8. On pluralism, see Annette Kolodny, "Dancing through the Minefield: Some Observations on the Theory, Practice, and Politics of a Feminist Literary Criticism," *The New Feminist Criticism: Essays on Women, Literature, and Art,* ed. Elaine Showalter (New York: Pantheon, 1985). For a detailed analysis of the ambivalent relationship of feminism to deconstruction, see Alice Jardine, *Gynesis: Configurations of Women in Modernity* (Ithaca: Cornell Univ. Press, 1985); Gayatri Chakravorty Spivack, "Displacement and the Discourse of Women," *Displacement: Derrida and After,* ed. Mark Krupnick (Bloomington: Indiana Univ. Press, 1983), pp. 169–96; and Leslie W. Rabine, "A Feminist Politics of Non-Identity," *Feminist Studies,* 14.1 (Spring 1988), 11–31.

What Do We Do with F. O. Matthiessen?

David S. Reynolds

    William E. Cain. *F. O. Matthiessen and the Politics of Criticism.* Madison: University of Wisconsin Press, 1988. xiv, 238 pp.

Nearly four decades have passed since F. O. Matthiessen's suicide, but the memory of the enigmatic Harvard critic continues to haunt us. The continuing interest in Matthiessen is due mainly, of course, to the fact that he authored *American Renaissance,* the monumental study of pre-Civil War literature, as well as worthwhile books on Eliot, James, and Dreiser. These scholarly achievements become doubly intriguing when seen against the backdrop of his life. Matthiessen was a man of resonant contradictions: a committed socialist incongruously devoted to aesthetic formalism, a homosexual who minimized homoerotic themes in literature, a professed democrat who has recently become infamous for canonizing a select group of American authors.

    Such contradictions are ably illuminated in William E. Cain's *F. O. Matthiessen and the Politics of Criticism.* In Cain's rendering, Matthiessen is a case study in good political intentions and strong critical talents gone awry. Matthiessen's leftist leanings, Cain argues, might have led him to take an interest in noncanonical writers had it not been for the ambivalent critical atmosphere in which he found himself. Cain does a good job of exploring the development of Matthiessen's critical sensibility, which often seemed at odds with his political convictions. On the one hand, Matthiessen was partly indebted to the extrinsic approaches that had been pioneered by such historical critics as Van Wyck Brooks, Vernon Parrington, and Louis Mumford. On the other hand, he wrote his major books at a time when the New Criticism, with its aesthetic and formalist emphasis, was in the first flush of its predominance. As a result, Cain writes, Matthiessen's work was "fissured by contradiction, limited by the temperament of the man himself, the historical conditions within which he lived and wrote, and the double edged assumptions about literature, criticism, and politics he embraced" (p. 23). With his dual allegiances to culture and to the text, Matthiessen has been depreciated by critics of opposing camps. Cain notes that strict formalists attack him for "drifting into sociology and politics" while historical critics scold him for "sticking too much to literary and aesthetic issues" (p. 19).

It seems Matthiessen can't win, even with sympathetic observers like Cain. To be sure, Cain tries to rescue Matthiessen from the undeserved infamy into which he has fallen among some of today's canon-revising critics. He calls attention to the subtlety of several of Matthiessen's close textual readings, and he notes that in fact Matthiessen's criticism became more and more politicized in the course of his career. In the early phase of Matthiessen's career Cain sees a "highly troubling" inconsistency between his professed socialism and his new New Critical posture, an inconsistency that impels Cain to comment, "One wants the socialist Matthiessen to query the formalist Matthiessen's terms for examining Eliot and other writers" (p. 60). When Matthiessen turned his attention to Henry James, Cain argues, his devotion to formalism began to be modified by a healthy awareness of political themes, as evidenced by his disapproval of racist passages in James's fiction. By the time he wrote his book on Dreiser in the late 1940s, Cain claims, Matthiessen had gained a new flexibility that permitted him to rise above the typical distaste for Dreiser's ungainly style and make a case for his powerful social realism.

Finally, however, Cain cannot cloak his own disappointment with Matthiessen. *American Renaissance* (1941), written in mid-career, is for Cain the quintessential embodiment of Matthiessen's strengths and weaknesses. Cain recognizes *American Renaissance* as a critical monument without rival in American literary studies, the book that galvanized the study of Emerson, Thoreau, Hawthorne, Melville, and Whitman. Like several other current Americanists, however, Cain cannot tolerate what he sees as Matthiessen's antipolitical stance and high-culture bias. He approvingly quotes a long indictment of Matthiessen by another revisionist critic, who brands Matthiessen's canon "exclusive and class-bound in the extreme." Cain adds: "One might have hoped that, given his politics, he would have been able to perceive the class, gender, and race restrictions of his canon" (p. 164). Weren't writers like Harriet Beecher Stowe, William Lloyd Garrison, and Frederick Douglass also interested in exploring "the possibilities of democracy," which Matthiessen saw as the common concern of his canonical Big Five? And why does Matthiessen devote so little space to a work so obviously saturated with racial themes as Melville's "Benito Cereno"? The answer, for Cain, is that Matthiessen ultimately lacked the courage of his political convictions and retreated from politics into the aestheticism of his day. By way of contrast, Cain provides an interesting race-related reading of "Benito Cereno" and asks for closer study of American authors ignored by Matthiessen—all of them women or minority writers—who embody qualities Cain deems essential in literature: "dissent, struggle, vision, conflict" (p. 207).

Cain's argument has a familiar, sometimes predictable ring, not only because the leftist argument against Matthiessen has been made by others but because canon revision in general has become a comfortable bandwagon from which to hurl darts at formalists, who are particularly convenient targets when they aren't alive to defend themselves. To Cain's credit, he avoids the shrilly ideological tone of most anti-Matthiessen commentary, and, in a winning moment of ironic self-awareness, he even manages to get at the *real* politics of much contemporary criticism:

It is important to consider the elements of professional self-aggrandizement involved when white academics proceed industriously to explicate Afro-American and minority texts. . . . Scholars at work in opening up the canon are doing something essential and valuably democratizing, but there is an exploitativeness to such work that we should acknowledge. [p. 203]

But Cain himself remains blithely undaunted by possible charges of opportunism or self-aggrandizement. The antebellum authors he selects for reconsideration (e.g., Stowe, Warner, Douglass, Harriet Wilson) are by now conventional among canon-busters, as are some of his later favorites, including Zora Neale Hurston and W. E. B. DuBois.

Cain is right in saying that such authors were unfairly neglected by Matthiessen and merit analysis on their own. He is especially eloquent in his defense of DuBois. One wonders, however, just how deeply engaged with the depths and varieties of noncanonical literature Cain is. For instance, he mentions Harriet Wilson, but he doesn't provide a close reading of *Our Nig* to show just why Matthiessen should have featured it along with, say *Moby-Dick*. Cain takes the now fashionable line that since all criticism is inevitably political, one must define explicitly one's political vantage point, and he accordingly proclaims himself a champion of the standards of dissent, struggle, vision, conflict. But these categories are a bit loose and baggy. They fit familiar writers like Jefferson, Dickinson, Whitman, and Faulkner just as surely as they do Warner, Stowe, or William Wells Brown. Moreover, if Matthiessen's canon was partial and exclusive, so is Cain's, though in an opposite direction. While posing as an avant-garde rebel, Cain in fact proves himself a joiner of the firmly established Marginal Literature Club—that group of faddish academics who foreground once-marginal writers for political reasons. Such writers certainly deserve attention, but so do literally thousands of other American authors who were ignored not only by Matthiessen but by the Marginal Literature Club as well.

The fact is that Matthiessen, despite the limitations Cain points out, made a more compelling case for his canonical authors than most recent critics have made for their noncanonical ones. It was precisely Matthiessen's combined recognition of culture and aesthetics that enabled him to produce a monument like *American Renaissance*. His cultural awareness was narrow but methodologically important because of its interdisciplinary emphasis; for instance, never before him had artists like Horatio Greenough and Frank Lloyd Wright been paired with American authors. His sensitivity to the texture and resonances of literary texts was, as Cain concedes, often remarkable. At his best, Matthiessen was able to rise above hackneyed New Critical shibboleths—paradox, irony, organic unity—and attain a new kind of critical humanism. Since Matthiessen's day we have learned a lot about the literary marketplace, about unfamiliar writers, about the historical contexts of major authors. But in the process we have tended to lose sight of the unique richness and evocative power of literary texts. Matthiessen had a keen sense of these qualities, and we should be thankful that he didn't try to superimpose his rather pedestrian Christian socialism upon texts whose depths he was the first to plumb.

Contributors

GUY CARDWELL is Professor of English, Emeritus, at Washington University, St. Louis.

MARY THOMAS CRANE is Assistant Professor of English at Boston College.

THOMAS GARDNER is Associate Professor of English, Virginia Polytechnic Institute and State University.

THOMAS M. LEITCH is Associate Professor of English at the University of Delaware.

JOSEPH R. MCELRATH, JR., is Professor of English at The Florida State University.

JEAN F. PRESTON is Curator of Manuscripts at the Firestone Library, Princeton University.

DAVID S. REYNOLDS is Professor of English at Baruch College, CUNY.

BETTY RIZZO is Professor of English, City College of New York.

KINLEY E. ROBY is Professor of English at Northeastern University.

LINDA M. SHIRES is Associate Professor of English at Syracuse University.

DAVID LIONEL SMITH is Associate Professor of English at Wiliams College.

JOHN STASNY is Professor of English and Editor of *Victorian Poetry* at West Virginia University.

MARTIN STEVENS is Distinguished Professor of English, CUNY Graduate School and University Center.

JOHN SUTHERLAND is Professor of English, California Institute of Technology.

ELIZABETH B. TENENBAUM is Professor of English, The Graduate School, CUNY.

JAMES GRANTHAM TURNER is Professor of English, University of Michigan–Ann Arbor.

STANLEY WEINTRAUB is Evan Pugh Professor of Arts and Humanities at The Pennsylvania State University.